INSTRUCTOR'S MANUAL
AND TEST-ITEM FILE FOR

The Enjoyment
of Music

SIXTH EDITION
SHORTER

INSTRUCTOR'S MANUAL
AND TEST-ITEM FILE FOR

The Enjoyment
of Music

SIXTH EDITION
SHORTER

KRISTINE FORNEY

CONTRIBUTORS:
JOHN BARCELLONA, RICHARD BIRKEMEIER,
GREGORY DONOVETSKY, ROGER HICKMAN, PAULA SABIN

W. W. NORTON & COMPANY
NEW YORK   LONDON

Composition by Roberta Flechner Graphics.

ISBN 0-393-96123-0

W. W. Norton & Company, Inc., 500 Fifth Avenue, New York, N.Y. 10110
W. W. Norton & Company Ltd., 10 Coptic Street, London WC1A 1PU

1 2 3 4 5 6 7 8 9 0

CONTENTS

INSTRUCTOR'S MANUAL
AND TEST-ITEM FILE FOR

The Enjoyment
of Music

SIXTH EDITION
SHORTER

INTRODUCTION

This manual is designed to serve as a guide to the shorter version of *The Enjoyment of Music,* Sixth Edition. In it you will find descriptions of the ancillary materials that have been prepared in conjunction with this and other versions of the text, advice on how best to use them, and discussion of various approaches to teaching a music appreciation course. Following a general introduction, we proceed chapter by chapter through the chronologically ordered text, highlighting the principal topics, suggested goals, and selected readings for each.

The shorter version of this text is designed for those who find that the sixth edition is too long and detailed, either because of the length of term or the level of students they teach. This version has been streamlined from the sixth edition Chronological, maintaining its overall structure in Parts and Units while cutting its general length by more than a third. This has been done through the judicious choice of a core listening repertory, through abridged biographies, and more tabular summaries of information.

The music appreciation course is now a standard part of the general education offerings at most colleges and universities. It is often intended for non-musicians, constituting in many cases their only contact with the art. In some institutions, such a course may serve as a general introduction for freshman music majors, to be followed by more in-depth music history classes. Class sizes vary widely, from lecture courses of up to five hundred students to small discussion groups made up of a handful of students. Regardless of how the course is structured, we who teach it have the unique opportunity to introduce music to significant numbers of students.

I am indebted to my colleagues from California State University, Long Beach, who contributed the questions for the Test-Item File: John Barcellona, Assistant Professor (Flute; Woodwind Coordinator; Music Appreciation); Richard Birkemeier, Professor (Trumpet; Brass Coordinator; Music Appreciation); Gregory Donovetsky, Instructor (Oboe; Music Appreciation); Roger Hickman, Associate Professor (Musicology; Orchestra Director; Music Appreciaton); Paula Sabin, Instructor (Music Theory; Musicology; Music Appreciation). The Test-Item File would not have materialized, however, without the expert help of my sister Susan Forney Hughes, who served as an editorial assistant for the project; her many contributions included the final editing and inputting of all the questions into the CTIF (Computerized Test-Item File) format. My thanks go as well to Deborah Gerish of W. W. Norton, whose expertise guided us in the creation of the CTIF.

I wish to also thank Claire Brook and Juli Goldfein of W. W. Norton for their constant support and counsel throughout the preparation of this Instructor's Manual and all the other ancillaries for *The Enjoyment of Music,* sixth edition. Finally, my appreciation is extended to the many teachers and colleagues who have made helpful recommendations for this project, not the least of whom are my brother, James Forney, and my husband, William Prizer, whose practical advice and assistance have been invaluable.

GOALS AND OBJECTIVES

What then should be the primary goal of such a course? According to Joe Machlis, it should be to bring students as far as possible along the road to being music lovers. How is this best accomplished? Should it be through maximum listening exposure to all styles of music in the classroom, through frequent attendance at live concerts, through relating music to the socio-cultural environment in which it was created, through an investigation of the lives and ideas of its leading composers, or through a balanced combination of all these?

Music appreciation instructors often face some hostility from students who come to the first class session believing that they already appreciate music, albeit usually not the classics, and who are not always prepared for the amount of factual and technical information they will be asked to absorb. They may be further disappointed to learn that the focus of the class will not be on popular styles, but on the classical or art traditions in music. We are also faced today with an international range of students, to whom the study of Western art music seems limited.

This new edition of *The Enjoyment of Music* has been created to assist instructors with these difficult issues and decisions. The text and its organization is somewhat simpler than previous editions: the writing is more concise, and detailed information, such as lists of compositions and musical analyses, is presented graphically. This allows instructors some flexibility in selecting the amount of detail most appropriate for individual classes and for individual teaching styles.

Although many institutions' course offerings now include separate classes on popular and non-Western musical styles, there are frequent proposals to "internationalize" existing courses by expanding their singularly "Western" focus to include comparison with other cultures. In response to this impulse, we have included chapters on American popular styles, especially ragtime, blues, jazz, and musical theater, and on the influence of non-Western traditions on Western art music, especially in the twentieth century. This seemed a more satisfactory solution than token inclusion of vernacular and non-Western musical phenomena in isolation at the end of the book. The hope here is that students will be stimulated to take a second, more specialized course in jazz, rock, or non-Western music.

APPROACHES TO TEACHING

We suggested above that there are a number of different ways to cultivate a love of music in our students, recognizing that each teacher will approach this in a slightly different manner. Because we come to the classroom with unique personal interests and strengths in music—some of us are performers, some theorists, some music historians, some generalists—we will each develop a plan or formula that works for us. In deciding where the emphasis should be for each class, we should not underestimate the learning capabilities of our students. In other disciplines, such as history or psychology, students are expected to read a great deal and to gain command of a large body of factual as well as theoretical material. Some of us, especially music historians like myself, might catch ourselves teaching a mini-course in music history; others, reacting against all the terms and factual material in such a text, might opt to focus nearly exclusively on listening in the classroom.

Below you will find some ideas on how to balance the presentation of different features of the discipline:

Biography: "Great Composers":   The Machlis text is known for its informative, highly-readable biographies of the great masters. Although abridged in this version, these still include information that students may well retain long after the course is over. This feature of the text allows students an enjoyable introduction to each composer that they can read on their own. Instructors may wish to review a composer's biography in class, emphasizing selected events and works. Test questions on biographical issues can reflect those events highlighted in class. The text remains focused on the "greats" of Western art music, but we have now added important transitional figures from one style to another as well.

Listening: Perhaps the single most important teaching tool for music appreciation is listening, either from recordings or in live performances. Something can be said for each of these listening formats: recordings afford students and teachers the means to replay a particular section or to stop at any time to read about or discuss a piece whereas live concerts involve the listener more directly in the music-making experience. And we want, after all, to foster concert-going among the younger generations, to ensure the continued stability of our symphonies, ballets, and operas.

Students will undoubtedly need some guidance in listening, especially in longer, more complex forms. This can best be carried out in the classroom, where themes can be isolated easily on CDs or reproduced on the piano. All listening should not be centered in class, however, since students will need to practice this kind of analytical listening on their own in order to develop some independence in making their way through a piece. Regular out-of-class listening should be encouraged through the use of the cassettes purchased for the course or for the library listening lab.

Analysis: How much musical analysis can the beginning student handle? We must all grapple with this issue: on the one hand, we do not want to put off students by overwhelming them with so much technical detail that they are swimming in facts, not in enjoyment; on the other hand, we have a responsibility to present some concrete information about the musical process, and there is much to present. As there is no "correct" amount of detail, we have devised for this new edition a kind of layered approach to each composition. The text itself includes a succinct summary of the highlights of each work, including brief remarks about style and form. Many works are then elucidated in a listening guide that presents an analysis in outline form: at the top of each guide there is a summary of historical information, after which a step-by-step analysis appears, with concise descriptions (and sometimes timings) of each event on the left and musical themes on the right. For those students who do not read music, the themes can be ignored without any significant loss of understanding. These analyses provide students with something concrete to follow visually while listening. (Consider the fact that today's students enjoy their favorite popular music groups on videos rather than on mere sound recordings.)

Development of Styles: Determining precisely what makes one style different than another is complex. Thus emphasis on styles and their development may not be appropriate for everyone. Several features of the text facilitate the assimilation of varying styles: the new genre organization allows for student exposure to several examples of a genre within one era; tabular summaries assist with the comparison of two consecutive style periods; new transition chapters show the intermediate steps between one style period and another; and the interdisciplinary introduction to each era places music within the context of concurrent artistic and literary styles. Thus the reader can grasp something of the development of opera, for example, from its inception in the humanist era of the late Renaissance through Monteverdi, Purcell, Handel, Mozart, Verdi, Wagner, and into the twentieth century.

TEACHING MATERIALS AVAILABLE
FOR USE WITH SIXTH EDITION SHORTER

A. Textbook
   1. Shorter version
   2. Chronological version (and Standard) version

B. Recordings
   1. 3 cassettes (for Shorter)
   2. Basic (8 LPs, Cassettes, or CDs)
   3. Supplementary (4 LPs, Cassettes, or CDs)

C. Music Example Bank (3 CDs plus index)

D. Transparency Package (55 Listening Guides from Chronological version)

E. *The Norton Scores,* 2 volumes

F. Videocassettes (opera, ballet, and *The Young Person's Guide to the Orchestra*)

G. Instructor's Manual and Test-Item File for the Shorter version

    A.   This Shorter version of *The Enjoyment of Music* has been extracted from the Chronological version of the sixth edition to produce a succinct 350-page text with a core listening repertory of thirty-five carefully chosen examples. Instructors may wish to refer to the longer Chronological text, which presents more biographical and analytical details. The following chart compares the contents of the two text versions as a quick cross-reference for the instructor:

CHRONOLOGICAL	SHORTER

Part One

THE MATERIALS OF MUSIC

Unit 1   The Elements of Music
    1. Melody: Musical Line
    2. Rhythm: Musical Time
    3. Harmony: Musical Space
    4. Musical Texture
    5. Musical Form
    6. Tempo and Dynamics

CHRONOLOGICAL	SHORTER

Part Two

MEDIEVAL AND RENAISSANCE MUSIC

Part Three

MORE MATERIALS OF MUSIC

Part Four

THE BAROQUE ERA

Part Five

MORE MATERIALS OF FORM

CHRONOLOGICAL	SHORTER

CHRONOLOGICAL	SHORTER
52. Hector Berlioz	44. The Rise of Musical Nationalism
53. Richard Strauss	
54. The Rise of Musical Nationalism	

Unit 19   Absolute Forms

55. The Romantic Symphony	45. The Romantic Symphony
56. Two Romantic Symphonies	46. The Romantic Concerto
57. The Romantic Concerto	47. Robert Schumann and the Romantic Concerto
58. Two Romantic Concertos	

Unit 20   Choral and Dramatic Music in the Nineteenth Century

59. The Nature of Romantic Choral Music	48. The Nature of Romantic Choral Music
60. Two Romantic Choral Works	49. Brahms and Romantic Choral Music
61. Romantic Opera	50. Romantic Opera
62. Giuseppe Verdi	51. Verdi and Italian Opera
63. Richard Wagner	52. Wagner and the Music Drama
64. Two Other Romantic Operas	53. Tchaikovsky and the Ballet
65. Tchaikovsky and the Ballet	

Part Eight

THE TWENTIETH CENTURY

Tr. 5 The Post-Romantic Era	Tr. 5 The Post-Romantic Era

Unit 21 The Impressionist and Post-Impressionist Era	**Unit 21 Turn-of-the Century Trends**
66. Debussy and Impressionism	54. Debussy and Impressionism
67. Ravel and Post-Impressionism	

Unit 22 The Early Twentieth Century	
68. Main Currents in Early Twentieth-Century Music	55. Main Currents in Early Twentieth-Century Music
69. New Elements of Musical Style	56. New Elements of Musical Style
70. Igor Stravinsky	57. Stravinsky and the Revitalization of Rhythm
71. Arnold Schoenberg	
72. Alban Berg	58. Schoenberg and the Second Viennese School
73. Anton Webern and Olivier Messiaen	

Unit 23 The Nationalism of the Twentieth Century	
74. The European Scene	59. Bartók and the European Scene
75. The American Scene: Art Music	60. The American Scene: Art Music
76. The American Scene: Popular Styles	61. The American Scene: Popular Styles

Unit 24 The New Music	
77. New Directions	62. New Directions
78. Non-Western Music and the Contemporary Scene	63. Non-Western Music and the Contemporary Scene
79. New Sounds on Traditional Instruments	64. New Sounds
80. Electronic Music	65. Recent Trends
81. Recent Trends	

A checklist of the repertory presented in the Shorter version follows, with respective chapter and listening guide numbers:

LG#	CHAPTER	MUSICAL SELECTION
1	9	Britten: *Young Person's Guide to the Orchestra*
2	11	A Gregorian Melody: *Haec dies*
3	11	Machaut: *Hareu! hareu! le feu—Hélas—Haec dies*
4	13	Dufay: *Alma redemptoris mater*
5	13	Palestrina: *Pope Marcellus Mass*
6	13	Monteverdi: *Ohimè! se tanto amate*
7	18	Purcell: *Dido and Aeneas*
8	19	Bach: Cantata no. 80, *A Mighty Fortress Is Our God*
9	20	Handel: *Messiah*
10	21	Vivaldi: *The Four Seasons*
11	22	Bach: *Prelude and Fugue in C minor*
12	28	Mozart: *Eine kleine Nachtmusik*
13	30	Haydn: Symphony no. 104
14	31	Beethoven: Symphony no. 5
15	32	Mozart: Piano Concerto in C major
16	33	Beethoven: Piano Sonata in C minor, Op. 13, *Pathétique*
17	34	Mozart: *The Marriage of Figaro*
18	37	Schubert: *Erlkönig*
19	40	Chopin: *Polonaise in A flat*
20	41	Clara Schumann: *Quatre pièces fugitives*
21	43	Berlioz: *Symphonie fantastique*
22	44	Smetana: *The Moldau*
23	47	Robert Schumann: Piano Concerto in A minor
24	49	Brahms: *A German Requiem*
25	51	Verdi: *La traviata*
26	52	Wagner: *Die Walküre*
27	54	Debussy: *Prelude to "The Afternoon of a Faun"*
28	57	Stravinsky: *The Rite of Spring*
29	58	Schoenberg: *Pierrot lunaire*
30	59	Bartók: *Music for Strings, Percussion, and Celeste*
31	60	Copland: *Rodeo*
32	61	Armstrong: *West End Blues*
33	61	Bernstein: "Symphonic Dances" from *West Side Story*
34	64	Crumb: *Ancient Voices of Children*
35	65	Adams: *Short Ride in a Fast Machine*

New features of the text:

   a.   A new **genre organization** replaces the composer organization of earlier editions. This does not in any way interfere with the presentation of individual composers, but it does facilitate the teaching of concepts and forms. It also unifies the organization of the book throughout all eras, some of which do not lend themselves to a "great composer" approach (the Middle Ages and Renaissance, for example).

b.   This new organizational plan is achieved through a **three-tiered structure:** the largest division is the *part* (generally comprising an entire era), which is subdivided into *units* (each focused on one or several genres), each of which in turn is subdivided into *chapters* (on a single composer or style).

c.   The text appears in two lengths, as in earlier editions: the Shorter, of about 350 pages, based on the Chronological version, of about 560 pages. A longer Standard version is also available, which follows the established Machlis approach of beginning with music of the nineteenth century, then moving to the eighteenth century, followed by the earlier eras of the Middle Ages, Renaissance, and Baroque, and concluding with the twentieth century.

d.   Listening Guides or study outlines appear in the text for the thirty-five works included on the Shorter cassette package. These Listening Guides and twenty additional ones from the longer text versions are available on transparency for classroom study. Instructors may supplement listening through the use of the Basic and Supplementary recording packages prepared for the longer text versions.

e.   Increased focus is placed on **musical life** and the **role of music in society** in each era. This is new to early music discussions, where the structure of society is not familiar to students.

f.   The **role of women** in music is highlighted throughout the book within the discussions of music and society. A work by the nineteenth-century composer, Clara Schumann, is included and a chart on page 317 highlights women musicians in the twentieth century. Further on in this manual, you will find a resource guide on women composers, with suggested works for study (available in score and on recordings) by five prominent musicians: Hildegard of Bingen (12th-century nun), Barbara Strozzi (17th-century singer and composer), Fanny Mendelssohn (19th-century composer and pianist), Ruth Crawford Seeger (early 20th-century composer), and Ellen Taaffe Zwilich (contemporary composer and first woman to win the Pulitzer Prize in composition).

g.   The **internationalism of music** is emphasized throughout the text, particularly with regard to non-Western music and its influences on the Western art tradition. A chapter is devoted to twentieth-century cross-influences.

h.   An **interdisciplinary focus** in each era places music within the context of the graphic arts, literature, and philosophy. The socio-historical setting of each era is emphasized, as are major scientific developments.

i.   **Transition chapters** link one era to the next. Each provides an insight into the shifting stylistic currents and three contain charts comparing adjacent style periods (Renaissance and Baroque, Baroque and Classical, Classical and Romantic).

j.   **Tabular summaries** and **graphic presentation of concepts** are included throughout the text. In addition to the tables mentioned above, the elements of music are presented with visual summaries of the characteristics of melody, melodic phrasing, examples of meters, the building of harmony, textures and contrapuntal devices, binary and ternary form, motives and sequences, and the make-up of standard chamber ensembles—to mention but a few. Other graphic synopses include the plan of the sonata cycle, sonata-allegro form, the symphony, and the concerto.

k.   **American popular styles** are discussed, focusing on ragtime, blues, jazz, and the American musical theater. Further on in this manual there is a resource guide to extended study of American popular music.

l.   Each major composer is treated as follows:
1.   an informative and very readable biography in a concise style, accompanied by a small portrait of the composer;
2.   an outline of the composer's Principal Works with dates, set off from the text by highlighting;
3.   a short discussion of style or style periods, if appropriate;
4.   a brief analysis of a representative work;
5.   a Listening Guide in simple, easy-to follow outline format, with musical themes and timings.

B.   The recording package for the Shorter consists of three cassettes containing thirty-five musical examples. A new feature of this package is the announcement of each piece or movement, for ease in finding one's place. These cassettes have been carefully assembled from the Basic recording set to include a maximum number of selections. This specially created cassette package is available shrink-wrapped with the text at a spectacularly low price. Here's a checklist of the contents of the cassette package:

CASSETTE 1, Side A

1	GREGORIAN CHANT Gradual, *Haec dies*	2:20
	St. Meinrad Archabbey Schola Cantorum,	
	Rev. Columba Kelly, O.S.B., Dir.	
	©1976 Southern Illinois University Press	
2	MACHAUT *Hareu! hareu! le feu—Helas! ou sera pris confors—*	1:58
	Obediens usque ad mortem	
	The Early Music Consort of London (James Bowman, Charles Brett,	
	Countertenors; Alan Lumsden, Slide Trumpet); David Munrow, Dir.	
	©1973 EMI Records Ltd.	
3	DUFAY *Alma redemptoris mater*	4:24
	Pro Cantione Antiqua, London (James Bowman, Countertenor;	
	Ian Partridge, Tenor; James Griffett, Tenor; David Thomas, Bass;	
	Roderick Skeaping, Treble Rebec; Trevor Jones, Tenor Rebec);	
	Bruno Turner, Dir.	
	Deutsche Grammophon/©1975 Polydor Int. GmbH, Hamburg	

4	PALESTRINA *Missa Papae Marcelli*, Gloria	6:16
	The Tallis Scholars; Peter Phillips, Dir.	
	©1980 Gimmell Records Limited	
5	MONTEVERDI *Ohimè! se tanto amate*	2:42
	The Consort of Musicke; Anthony Rooley, Dir.	
	©1986 The Decca Record Company, Ltd.	
6	PURCELL *Dido and Aeneas,* Dido's Lament	5:04
	Janet Baker, Mezzo-soprano (Dido); St. Anthony Singers;	
	English Chamber Orch.; Thurston Dart, Harpsichord Continuo;	
	Anthony Lewis, Cond.	
	©1962 The Decca Record Company, Ltd. (MONO)	

BACH Cantata No. 80, *Ein feste Burg ist unser Gott*

7	Chorus, *Ein feste Burg ist unser Gott*	5:52
8	Duo, *Mit unsrer Macht ist nichts getan*	3:42
9	Chorale, *Das Wort, sie sollen lassen stehn*	1:27
	Edith Mathis, Soprano; Trudeliese Schmidt, Alto;	
	Peter Schreier, Tenor; Dietrich Fischer-Dieskau, Baritone;	
	Munich Bach Chorus; Munich Bach Orch.; Karl Richter, Cond.	
	Deutsche Grammophon/©1979 Polydor Int. GmbH, Hamburg	

HANDEL *Messiah*

10	No. 44: "Hallelujah"	3:49
11	No. 45: "I know that my Redeemer liveth"	6:13
	Heather Harper, Soprano; Ralph Downes, Organ; Leslie Pearson,	
	Harpsichord; William Lang, Trumpet; London Symphony Choir	
	(John Alldis, Chorus Master); London Symphony Orch.;	
	Sir Colin Davis, Cond.	
	©1967 Philips Classics Productions	

CASSETTE 1, Side B

1	VIVALDI *The Four Seasons,* "La Primavera"	
	I, Allegro	3:15
	Simon Standage, Violin; The English Concert (on period instr.);	
	Trevor Pinnock, Harpsichord and Dir.	
	Deutsche Grammophon/©1982 Polydor Int. GmbH, Hamburg	
2	J. S. BACH *The Well-Tempered Clavier,* Book I, Prelude and	
	Fugue in C minor	3:29
	Kenneth Gilbert, Harpsichord	
	Deutsche Grammophon/©1984 Polydor Int. GmbH, Hamburg	
3	HAYDN Symphony No. 104 in D major *(London)*	
	I, Adagio—Allegro	8:53

MOZART Piano Concerto in C major, K. 467

4	I, Allegro maestoso	14:06
5	II, Andante	6:09
6	III, Allegro vivace assai	7:23
	Malcolm Bilson, Fortepiano; The English Baroque Soloists	
	(on authentic instr.); John Eliot Gardiner, Dir.	
	(Cadenzas by Mr. Bilson)	
	Deutsche Grammophon/©1987 Polydor Int. GmbH, Hamburg	

CASSETTE 2, Side A

	MOZART *Eine kleine Nachtmusik,* K. 525	
1	I, Allegro	5:24
2	III, Menuetto: Allegretto	2:12

Orpheus Chamber Orch.

Deutsche Grammophon/©1986 Polydor Int. GmbH, Hamburg

	BEETHOVEN Symphony No. 5 in C minor, Op. 67	
3	I, Allegro con brio	7:28
4	II, Andante con moto	10:08
5	III, Allegro; IV, Allegro	14:18

Concertgebouw Orch. of Amsterdam; George Szell, Cond.

©1967 Philips Classics Productions

6	SCHUBERT *Erlkönig,* D. 328	4:10

Dietrich Fischer-Dieskau, Baritone; Gerald Moore, Piano

Deutsche Grammophonn/©1970 Polydor Int. GmbH, Hamburg

CASSETTE 2, Side B

1	BEETHOVEN Piano Sonata in C minor *(Pathétique)*	
	II, Adagio cantabile	5:13

Alfred Brendel, Piano

©1975 Philips Classics Productions

2	MOZART *Le Nozze di Figaro,* Scene from Act I	10:13

Lucia Popp, Soprano (Susanna); Frederica von Stade,
Mezzo-soprano (Cherubino); Robert Tear, Tenor (Don Basilio);
Thomas Allen, Baritone (Count Almaviva); London Philharmonic
Orch.; Jeffrey Tate, Continuo; Sir Georg Solti, Cond.

©1982 The Decca Record Company, Ltd.

3	CHOPIN Polonaise in A-flat major, Op. 53	6:17

Martha Argerich, Piano

Deutsche Grammophonn/©1967 Polydor Int. GmbH, Hamburg

4	BERLIOZ *Symphonie fantastique*	
	V, *Dream of a Witches' Sabbath:* Larghetto-Allegro	9:57

Amsterdam Concertgebouw Orch.; Sir Colin Davis, Cond.

©1974 Philips Classics Productions

5	SMETANA *Vltava (The Moldau)* from *Má Vlast*	11:59

Vienna Philharmonic Orch.; James Levine, Cond.

Deutsche Grammophonn/©1987 Polydor Int. GmbH, Hamburg

CASSETTE 3, Side A

1	C. SCHUMANN *Pièce fugitive* in D, Op. 15, No. 3	5:20

Hélène Boschi, Piano

©1987 Arpège

2	R. SCHUMANN Piano Concerto in A minor, Op. 54	
	I, Allegro affetuoso	14:02

Sviatoslav Richter, Piano; Warsaw National Philharmonic Orch.,
Witold Rowicki, Cond. (MONO)

Deutsche Grammophonn/©1959 Polydor Int. GmbH, Hamburg

3   BRAHMS *A German Requiem*
    IV, *Wie lieblich sind deine Wohnungen*   5:46
    Chicago Symphony Orch. and Chorus (Chorus Dir., Margaret Hillis);
    Sir Georg Solti, Cond.
    ©1979 The Decca Record Company, Ltd.

4   VERDI *La traviata,* Finale of Act II   10:15
    Joan Sutherland, Soprano (Violetta); Miti Truccato Pace,
    Contralto (Flora); Carlo Bergonzi, Tenor (Alfredo Germont);
    Piero de Palma, Tenor (Gastone); Robert Merrill, Baritone
    (Giorgio Germont); Paolo Pedani, Baritone (Baron Douphol);
    Giovanni Foiani, Bass (Doctor Grenvil);
    Silvio Maionica, Bass (Marquis d'Obigny); Chorus and Orch. of
    The Maggio Musicale Fiorentino; Sir John Pritchard, Cond.
    ©1963 The Decca Record Company, Ltd.

5   DEBUSSY *Prelude to "The Afternoon of a Faun"*   9:00
    London Symphony Orch.; Pierre Monteux, Cond.
    ©1962 The Decca Record Company, Ltd.

CASSETTE 3, Side B

1   WAGNER *Die Walküre*, Act III, Scene 3, *Magic Fire Music*   4:38
    James Morris, Bass (Wotan); Metropolitan Opera Orch.;
    James Levine, Cond.
    Deutsche Grammophonn/©1988 Polydor Int. GmbH, Hamburg

2   STRAVINSKY *The Rite of Spring,* Opening Scene   8:23
    Boston Symphony Orch.; Michael Tilson Thomas, Cond.
    Deutsche Grammophonn/©1972 Polydor Int. GmbH, Hamburg

    SCHOENBERG *Pierrot lunaire*
3   No. 18, "Der Mondfleck"   0:54
4   No. 21, "O alter Duft"   1:47
    Mary Thomas, Reciter; London Sinfonietta;
    David Atherton, Cond.
    ©1974 The Decca Record Company, Ltd.

5   BARTÓK *Music for Strings, Percussion, and Celesta*, IV   6:35
    London Symphony Orch.; Sir Georg Solti, Cond.
    ©1964 The Decca Record Company, Ltd.

6   COPLAND *Rodeo,* "Hoe-Down"   3:37
    Detroit Symphony Orch.; Antal Dorati, Cond.
    ©1982 The Decca Record Company, Ltd.

7   ARMSTRONG *West End Blues*   3:14
    Louis Armstrong and His Hot Five (Louis Armstrong,
    Trumpet and Vocal; Jimmy Strong, Clarinet and Tenor Saxophone;
    Earl Hines, Piano and Vocal; Mancy Cara, Banjo and Vocal;
    Zutty Singleton, Drums) (MONO)
    Under license from CBS Special Products, a division of
    CBS Records, Inc.

8   BERNSTEIN Symphonic Dances from *West Side Story,* "Cool" (Fugue)
    and "Rumble"   5:08
    Los Angeles Philharmonic Orch.; Leonard Bernstein, Cond.
    Deutsche Grammophonn/©1983 Polydor Int. GmbH, Hamburg

| 9 | CRUMB *Ancient Voices of Children,* No. 1, "El niño busca su voz" | 4:27 |

Jan DeGaetani, Mezzo-soprano; Michael Dash, Boy Soprano;
The Contemporary Chamber Ensemble; Arthur Weisberg, Cond.
Produced under license from Elektra Nonesuch

| 10 | ADAMS *Short Ride on a Fast Machine* | 4:13 |

San Francisco Symphony; Edo de Waart, Cond.
©1987 Elektra/Asylum/Nonesuch Records

CASSETTE 1, Side A, Track 1: Courtesy of Southern Illinois University Press. **CASSETTE 1, Side A, Track 2:** Courtesy of EMI Records Ltd. **CASSETTE 1, Side A, Track 4:** Courtesy of Gimmell Records Ltd. **CASSETTE 3, Side B, Track 7:** Used under license from Columbia Special Products, a division of CBS Records, Inc. **CASSETTE 3, Side B, Tracks 9, 10:** Produced under license from Elektra Nonesuch.

All other selections courtesy of PolyGram Special Products, a division of PolyGram Group Distribution, Inc.

Although CDs have not been prepared for this listening package, the works are all included on the Basic set of CDs for the sixth edition (and on the Basic LP and cassette sets as well). It is suggested that instructors use CDs in the classroom whenever possible for the best sound quality and for ease in accessing individual works, movements, themes, and sections, all of which have been tracked. Thus, for example, the Exposition and Recapitulation versions of the second theme of a sonata-allegro form can be easily compared by simply programming the appropriate track numbers on the CD player. The Listening Guides in the Shorter version of the text include the CD track numbers from the Basic set for classroom and listening lab use.

Throughout, careful attention has been given to choice of recording and performance. For the early music examples, historical authenticity was a principal consideration, along with musical vitality. The Baroque and Classical repertory draws upon performances with period instruments (e.g., Mozart's Piano Concerto in C major, K. 467) and those with modern ones (Mozart's *Eine kleine Nachtmusik*), reflecting the variety of current practice in the concert hall.

C. *Music Example Bank* by Richard Viano: This innovative teaching aid was created specifically for the sixth edition of *The Enjoyment of Music.* On three compact discs, it contains more than 200 short musical excerpts, selected to illustrate every major concept, element, genre, and style discussed in the text. Accompanying the CDs is a booklet in which the examples are indexed five ways:

1. in the sequence of the discs—that is, a table of contents giving, after each disc and track number, a complete citation of the music included;
2. alphabetically by composer and title, with disc and track number for each example by that composer;

3. alphabetically by concept, with disc and track number for each example illustrating that concept;

4. in the teaching sequence of the Chronological version of the book; for each concept or term the disc and track numbers of examples useful in illustrating that concept are given;

5. in the teaching sequence of the Standard version of the book; for each concept or term the disc and track numbers of examples useful in illustrating that concept are given.

For use with the Shorter version of the text, the instructor will find the alphabetical subject index (3) the most practical.

The *Music Example Bank* can be used throughout the course, but it will prove especially helpful in teaching the elements of music. Each concept can be illustrated with several excerpts, taken from different stylistic periods. At the same time, each example serves to illustrate several different aspects of music. While most versatile in its applications when there is a CD player in the classroom, the *Example Bank* will also greatly facilitate the process of making a lecture or classroom cassette in advance, or of preparing study tapes on particular topics for use in the listening lab. In addition, the contents of the *Example Bank* will prove useful in preparing listening tests of all kinds.

D. A package of transparencies is available containing all the Listening Guides from the sixth edition. These provide the instructor with the opportunity to project the Listening Guide of a work when studied in class, alleviating the necessity of having students bring their texts to class. The transparencies include additional movements not discussed in the Shorter version; thus, for example, one could teach the entire concerto "La Primavera" from Vivaldi's *The Four Seasons,* or simply use the transparency to emphasize the overall structure and to show how its program is distributed through the various movements. One could use an additional piece from the regular sixth edition in class, such as Schumann's "Ich grolle nicht," to further illustrate the Romantic Lied.

E. *The Norton Scores*, edited by Roger Kamien: *The Norton Scores,* fifth edition, is a two-volume anthology that contains ninety works discussed in the longer text version and included on the Basic and Supplementary recording sets. The repertory from the Shorter version is thus included in this resource. These scores are essential for the instructor, and can assist students at all levels with understanding the musical selections. The unique highlighting system used in the *Scores* helps the eye follow the score: the most prominent line at any time is highlighted in white. An arrow-like wedge directs you to the next system. *The Norton Scores* give composer dates, date of composition of each work, and pictographs keyed to all record formats. A handy glossary of terms and an index of genres are included in each volume.

F.   *Video Materials:*   Many video materials are available for use in the music classroom or in the media lab to assist in teaching the instruments of the orchestra and especially in introducing music for opera, ballet, or films in its original context. Good video recordings can bring dramatic works to life, providing a three-dimensional experience, much closer to actual performance than an audio-only recording (though that, of course, is also valuable when concentrating on the musical forms and structures of these genres). Audio recordings of the specific excerpts discussed in the text will be found in the Basic and Supplementary record packages.

An exceptionally fine film about musical instruments and the orchestra (not for sale) is available in videocassette form, free to adopters of *The Enjoyment of Music*, sixth edition: *The Orchestra and Its Instruments*, by Robin Lehman, is narrated by Andrew Davis, who conducts the Manhattan School of Music Orchestra in a performance of Benjamin Britten's *A Young Person's Guide to the Orchestra*. This 45-minute film also presents information about the history of instruments, how they are manufactured, and how they sound. Professional musicians talk about their instruments, and young musicians perform together in the orchestra.

Many of the dramatic works discussed in the text are available in complete video form. These video recordings may be used in several ways: for example, a video version of the specific excerpt discussed in the text may be played in class, or assigned for viewing in the media lab; alternatively, a whole act or even a whole opera may be assigned as supplementary viewing, or played in a special session.

The following videocassettes related to the shorter text version can be purchased directly from W. W. Norton at prevailing list prices:

1.   Mozart: *The Marriage of Figaro*; a Glyndebourne Festival production, with Kiri Te Kanawa, Ileana Cotrubas, Frederica von Stade, Benjamin Luxon, conducted by Sir John Pritchard. 2 cassettes, $59.95 (99174-1)

2.   Verdi: *La traviata*; a Glyndebourne Festival production, with Marie McLaughlin, Walter MacNeil, Brent Ellis, conducted by Bernard Haitink. 1 cassette, $39.95 (99175-X)

3.   Tchaikovsky: *The Nutcracker*; an American Ballet Theater production, with Mikhail Baryshnikov, Gelsey Kirkland, conducted by Kenneth Schermerhorn. 1 cassette, $19.95 (99178-4)

Other commercial video materials for the works mentioned above may be obtained from commercial video stores and mail-order dealers. Video laserdiscs, like audio CDs, include frequent internal tracking and are more versatile and flexible in the classroom than videocassettes, providing appropriate playback equipment is available.

Mozart: *The Marriage of Figaro*; a Salzburg Festival production with Kiri Te Kanawa, Mirella Freni, Maria Ewing, Hermann Prey, Dietrich Fischer-Dieskau, conducted by Karl Bohm. Laserdisc, $69.95

Verdi: *La traviata*; the film by Franco Zeffirelli, with Teresa Stratas, Placido Domingo, conducted by James Levine. Videocassette, $29.95

Wagner: *Die Walküre*; a Bayreuth Festival production (staged in a 19th-century milieu), with Gwyneth Jones, Jeannine Altmeyer, Peter Hofmann, Donald McIntyre, conducted by Pierre Boulez. Laserdisc, $89.95

As of this writing, no video recording is available of Purcell's *Dido and Aeneas*.

G. *The Instructor's Manual,* by Kristine Forney: This resource has been specially prepared to accompany the Shorter version of the text. The Teaching Guide, a detailed outline of the material in each chapter, focuses on only those points found in the Shorter version, making clear to the instructor what material has been omitted from the longer Chronological text. The Test-Item File (see below), included in book form in the Instructor's Manual, has been annotated with chapter and page numbers for those questions appropriate to use with this text version. When using the computerized versions, which contain the entire bank of questions, it will be necessary to refer to this book in order to select questions that apply to the Shorter sixth edition.

Test-Item File, edited by Kristine Forney: The Computerized Test-Item File (CTIF) is a new feature with the sixth edition of *The Enjoyment of Music.* The bank of some 1480 questions were written by experienced faculty members at California State University, Long Beach; the contributors come from diverse musical backgrounds (performance, music theory, music criticism, musicology), but all have taught music appreciation for some years. The Test-Item File comes in both disk and book form; the computerized form is available in three formats: IBM (both 5.25" and 3.5" disks), MacIntosh (3.5" disks), and Apple (5.25" disks).
This resource is provided as a convenience to the instructor, since it takes a good deal of time to write a fair examination. It further allows you to change your tests from class to class or semester to semester without much effort. You may even make two or three forms of the same exam and alternate them when handing them out. Specific directions for constructing an exam with the CTIF come with the disks. For those who do not wish to work on the computer, or who do not have the necessary equipment, the book form of the test bank found at the conclusion of this Instructor's Manual is a valuable resource for writing exams. You can xerox the pages on which the desired questions appear, then cut and paste together an exam; alternately, you can simply type your exam from the bank of questions.

The question bank is organized chronologically, keyed to the chapter numbers in both versions of the book. The questions are largely multiple choice and true/false in format. In the computerized version only, each is graded according to a level of difficulty: 1 is easy; 2 is medium; 3 is difficult. There are enough questions of each type to allow you to build any of the three following exam formats: all multiple choice, all true/false, or some combination of the two. The recommended exam format would include at least 75%-80% multiple choice questions, with the rest true/false.

In addition to the questions that follow the text chapter-by-chapter, there are over fifty listening questions, in both multiple choice and true/false form. Some of these are keyed to chapters, such as ones that concern a particular element (melodic character, meter, texture, dynamics). A number of the multiple-choice questions have no musical selections filled in, leaving the choice of examples you wish to play up to you. The blank questions test the following:

1. recognition of examples (*Identify the following excerpt.*);
2. forms (*Which best describes the form of this excerpt?*);
3. tempos (*Which is the most likely tempo marking for this excerpt?*);
4. dynamics (*Which is the most likely dynamic marking for this excerpt?*);
5. instrumental timbre (*Identify the solo instrument heard in this excerpt.*); and
6. musical style (*In which style period was this work most likely written?*).

Often you will find more than one blank question in each category. This facilitates the construction of an exam in which you would ask the same question (for example, listening identification) about more than one selection.

It is recommended that listening questions be used throughout the course, either in association with the basic repertory studied, or in relation to a new musical example.The latter is, of course, more challenging, for you are asking students to use their knowledge of music rather than simply remembering what they read or what was said in class. For these questions, a correct answer must be keyed in by the instructor, based on the listening example chosen.

The test bank also includes a file of some seventy essay questions. These are keyed to chapters in which information is centered, but no answers are provided. These questions can be used with all levels of classes, as long as the expectation for student response is appropriately set. The essay questions are particularly recommended for music major classes using this text as an introduction to musical styles.

THE COURSE PLAN

In the following chart, you will find suggestions for apportioning the available class hours in order to cover the material in the text. The columns refer to the following course lengths:

30 hours = quarter course (10 weeks) of 3 units
40 hours = quarter course (10 weeks) of 4 units
45 hours = semester course (15 weeks) of 3 units
60 hours = semester course (15 weeks) of 4 units
               or 2 quarter course (20 weeks) of 3 units
90 hours = 2 semester course (30 weeks) of 3 units

Shorter Version

Part		Total hours 30	40	45	60	90
1	Materials	3	4	5	7	9
2	Medieval/ Renaissance	2	3	4	5	8
3	More Materials of Music	1	1	1	1	2
4	Baroque	3	4	5	7	10
5	More Materials of Form	1	1	1	2	2
6	18th century	5	7	7	9	15
7	19th century	6	8	8	12	19
8	20th century	6	8	8	11	17
Exams/vacations		3	4	6	6	8

PLANNING AN EXAM SCHEDULE

PLAN A

(Possible Quiz)	Part One: The Materials of Music
Exam 1 (Midterm)	Part Two: Medieval and Renaissance Music Part Four: The Baroque Era Part Six: Eighteenth-Century Classicism
Exam 2 (Final)	Part Seven: The Nineteenth Century Part Eight: The Twentieth Century

Advantages to Plan A:
1. Takes small number of class periods to administer examinations
2. Fits traditional scheme of testing in many institutions
3. Works well with 3- or 4-unit quarter system courses
4. Allows for listening quizzes between exams
5. Grading and paperwork kept to a minimum, especially important for large-enrollment classes

Disadvantages to Plan A:
1. Vast amount of reading and listening material on each exam
2. Does not allow students many demonstrations of competence; increases pressure on students.

PLAN B

(Possible Quiz)	Part One: The Materials of Music
Exam 1	Part Two: Medieval and Renaissance Music Part Four: The Baroque Era
Exam 2	Part Six: Eighteenth-Century Classicism
Exam 3	Part Seven: The Nineteenth Century
Exam 4 (Final)	Part Eight: The Twentieth Century

Advantages to Plan B:
1. Frequent testing allows for manageable amount of material and listening for each examination

2. Provides students more demonstrations of competence
3. Possible to drop lowest test grade (or not give make-ups for a missed exam)
4. De-emphasizes testing on materials of music until put to use in individual eras
5. Takes pressure off student of having a comprehensive final exam and at midterm time
6. Works well with 3- or 4-unit semester system courses

Disadvantages to Plan B:
1. Takes considerable class time to administer four exams
2. Era focus does not allow for testing comparison of styles

OTHER ASSESSMENTS OF COMPETENCE

A. Quizzes on specialized topics
   1. Listening (use *Music Example Bank* to prepare)
      a. Elements of music: comprehension and application of terms
      b. Identification of instruments
      c. Identification of required repertory
      d. Identification or comparison of styles
   2. Objective (Use Test-Item File)
      a. Materials of music (elements, instruments, ensembles)
      b. Other sections of text (terms, forms, etc)
      c. Musical Notation: in Appendix I

Note: Quizzes can be conveniently written from the Test-Item File with musical examples taken from the *Music Example Bank*. They can be very short (10-15 questions), so they do not take up too much class time to administer. Depending on how many quizzes are given during the course, the lowest grade or missed quiz could be dropped.

B. Concert Reports (Required or Optional)
   1. Use outlines similar to those in the *Listening and Study Guide*
      a. Instrumental (Orchestra, Band, Chamber Music, Solo Recital)
      b. Choral/Vocal (Choir/Chorus, Chamber Choir/Madrigal Choir, Solo Vocal Recital)
      c. Dramatic music (Opera/Operetta, Musical/Play with incidental music)
      d. Popular music (Jazz combo/ensemble, rock group, solo singer)
      e. Non-Western music
   2. Use free essay format

THE COURSE SYLLABUS

A good syllabus should provide specific information about course requirements and course goals. Here are some suggestions for inclusion in your syllabus:

1. Course name, number, registration number, prerequisites
2. Instructor name, office location and telephone, office hours
3. Overview of course goals and scope
4. Required and optional textbooks and recordings
5. Type of course (lecture, discussion, combination)
6. Examinations and quizzes: how many, when, what percentage of grade does each count
7. Concert reports or other assignments: how many, what kind of music, format for reports, how to find concerts, how graded
8. Attendance policy
9. Make-up policy for exams and quizzes
10. Out-of-class study for students: reading text, listening (to purchased tapes or in listening lab)
11. Week-by-week plan, with reading assignments from text

TEACHING GUIDE

This section of the manual is intended to assist the instructor with the preparation of in-class lectures through detailed outlines of the material discussed in each chapter of the text. For each unit you will find a prose summary of the principal topics, and suggested teaching goals as well as a chapter-by-chapter overview. The highlights of each Listening Guide are given as well. Each unit closes with a bibliography of suggested readings. Composers are included where lives and works are discussed; these basic references are not repeated in later units where composers may reappear.

Prelude: Listening to Music Today

Overview: This introductory section is designed to make students think about how the technological society in which they live has affected how they listen to music. It justifies the need to establish a working vocabulary of terms and the goals achieved by applying these to all styles of music.

PART ONE: THE MATERIALS OF MUSIC

Unit I: The Elements of Music

Overview: The component parts that make up music—melody, rhythm, harmony, texture, form, tempo, and dynamics—are presented in an order that moves from the simplest and most familiar, melody, to the most complex, including issues of structure and musical expression. This unit introduces a working vocabulary of terms, each of which is defined and illustrated with a familiar musical example. (A survey was carried out at California State University, Long Beach to determine which songs were most widely known to students today.) The concepts presented in these six chapters are reinforced by graphic summaries and marginal sideheads assist with locating definitions of terms.

Unit goals for students:
1. To become familiar with the individual elements or components of music and the role of each
2. To develop a working vocabulary of terms
3. To perceive form as a conscious unifying feature in music
4. To become aware of the subtleties of expression possible in music

1. Melody: Musical Line

Principal points

Three basic characteristics of melody:
    a.   range, measured as narrow, medium, or wide
    b.   shape or direction in which it moves
    c.   the way it moves (conjunct or disjunct)
Phrase and cadence structure of melody

Discussion topics

The central role of melody in music
The diversity of melody
Melody as the horizontal element in music

2. Rhythm: Musical Time

Principal points

Meter and measure: organizing the beats
Simple and compound meters:
    duple, triple, quadruple, compound
Complexities of rhythm: syncopation

Discussion topics

The relationship between rhythm and physical movement
Means of organizing music in time

3. Harmony: Musical Space

Principal points

Intervals and chords: building triads
The tonic, scales, and tonality
Consonance vs. dissonance

Discussion topics

Harmony as the vertical element in music
Harmony as perspective in music
Tonality as an organizing structure in music
The role of dissonance in music

4. Musical Texture

Principal points

Three types of texture:
    monophonic
    polyphonic, involving counterpoint
    homophonic

Contrapuntal devices:
    imitation, canon, and round
    inversion, retrograde, and retrograde inversion
    augmentation and diminution

Discussion topics

Compare musical texture with that of various fabrics
How musical texture has changed in different eras
Texture in non-Western music
Levels of concentration necessary to hear different textures

5. Musical Form

Principal points

Three basic elements of form:
    repetition, contrast, and variation
Two common forms:
    binary (**A-B**) and ternary (**A-B-A**)
Building blocks of form:
    themes and motives
Types of construction:
    thematic development and sequence
Formal sections: movements

Discussion topics

Clarity and order in art
Conscious choices of the artist
Repetition and contrast in all things
Developing formal ideas

6. Tempo and Dynamics

Principal points

Rate of speed: Italian tempo terms
    allegro, andante, adagio
Loud vs. soft: Italian dynamic markings
    forte, piano, crescendo, decrescendo

Discussion topics

Increased expression markings in music over the ages

Selected Readings for Unit:

Bernstein, Leonard. *The Joy of Music*. New York: New American Library, 1967.

Clough, John, and Joyce Conley. *Scales, Intervals, Keys, Triads, Rhythm, and Meter*. New York: Norton, 1983.

Copland, Aaron. *What to Listen for in Music*. Rev. ed. New York: Mentor, 1964.

Kivy, Peter. *The Corded Shell: Reflections on Musical Expression*. Princeton: Princeton Univ. Press, 1980.

Manoff, Tom. *The Music Kit*. 2nd ed. New York: Norton, 1984.

Meyer, Leonard B. *Emotion and Meaning in Music*. Chicago: Univ. of Chicago Press, 1961.

Ratner, Leonard. *The Listener's Art*. 3rd ed. New York: McGraw-Hill, 1977.

Tovey, Donald. *The Forms of Music*. New York: Meridian, 1956.

Unit II: Musical Instruments and Ensembles

Overview: This unit builds familiarity with instrument families and their individual members, as well as with the various ranges of the human voice. It further provides basic information about the history and traditional role of individual instruments. Vocal and instrumental musical ensembles are discussed, with a focus on the make-up of standard chamber groups, the orchestra, the concert band, and the jazz band. The unit is summed up with a Listening Guide to Britten's *Young Person's Guide to the Orchestra*, for which a special video is available. This video reinforces visual as well as aural familiarity with orchestral instruments, presents detailed information about the construction of various instruments, and shows a professional conductor in action. Transition I introduces the concept and characteristics of musical style, and offers dates for the various periods.

Unit goals for students:
1. To become aware of the classification, means of sound production, and characteristic sound of each orchestral instrument
2. To understand the development of the orchestra
3. To know the basic make-up of other musical ensembles, such as choirs, bands, and jazz groups
4. To discern differences in artistic styles from one era to the next

7. Musical Instruments I

Principal points

Four properties of musical sound:
    a.   pitch or rate of vibration
    b.   duration or length

      c.   volume or amplitude
      d.   timbre or tone color
Instrument, register, and vocal ranges
    soprano, alto, tenor, bass
String instruments: violin, viola, cello, double bass, harp, guitar
String techniques: legato, pizzicato, glissando, tremelo, trill, double
    stopping, mute, harmonics
Woodwind instruments: flute, piccolo, oboe, English horn, clarinet,
    bass clarinet, bassoon, contrabassoon, saxophone

Discussion topics

The voice as the model for all instruments
The development of the string instrument family
Types of sound production among woodwind instruments

8. Musical Instruments II

Principal points

Brass instruments:
    trumpet, French horn, trombone, tuba
Two categories of percussion instruments:
    pitched and unpitched
Keyboard instruments: piano and organ

Discussion topics

Sound production on brass instruments
The variety of percussion instruments
The piano: a string or percussion instrument?

9. Musical Ensembles

Principal points

Choral a cappella singing
Chamber music and ensembles:
    duo sonata
    trios, string and piano
    quartets, string and piano
    quintets, string, piano, woodwind, brass
Make-up of the orchestra
Bands: concert, marching, jazz, rock

Basic Listening

Britten: *Young Person's Guide to the Orchestra* (LG 1)
    theme and variations and fugue form
    instrument families and their individual members (from high to
      low in range)

Discussion topics

The make-up of various choral and chamber groups
The development of the modern orchestra
The role of bands in American society
The role of the conductor in ensembles

Transition I: Hearing Musical Styles

Principal points

Overview of historical periods, with dates

Discussion topics

What constitutes differing styles?
Dates for style periods differ in various disciplines

Selected Readings for Unit:

Baines, Anthony, ed. *Musical Instruments Through the Ages.* New York: Walker, 1975.
Bekker, Paul. *The Orchestra.* New York: Norton, 1963.
Belt, Philip R., et al. *The Piano.* New York: Norton, 1988.
Boyden, David, et al. *Violin Family.* New York: Norton, 1989.
Marcuse, Sybil. *Musical Instruments: A Comprehensive Dictionary.* New York: Norton, 1975.
Remnant, Mary. *Musical Instruments of the West.* New York: St. Martin's, 1978.
Sachs, Curt. *The History of Musical Instruments.* New York: Norton, 1940.

PART TWO: MEDIEVAL AND RENAISSANCE MUSIC

Unit III: The Middle Ages

Overview: With the music of most ancient civilizations lost to the modern world, we begin our chronological survey of music with the Middle Ages, an era that lasted some one thousand years. The culture of the era was dominated by the Church. Monasteries and convents were, along with the earliest universities, important centers of learning and preservation of knowledge. The sacred forms of music, mass and motet, are first explored, beginning with Gregorian chant in the mass, then the early polyphonic forms of organum and the early motet. A survey of secular music includes troubadour and trouvère monophony, the Ars Nova motet, and early instruments and instrumental music.

Unit goals for students:
1. To view the Middle Ages as a time of ascendant Christianity rather than as the "Dark Ages"
2. To recognize the elevated status of women during the era
3. To understand the roles music played in society of earlier times
4. To grasp the importance of the development of polyphony in music

Chapter 10. The Culture of the Middle Ages

Principal points

Two centers of power in Medieval society:
  Church—center of learning
      a.   monasteries
      b.   convents
  State—centralized government, advocated by Charlemagne
National literary landmarks:
  France: *Chanson de Roland*
  Italy: Dante's *Divine Comedy*
  England: Chaucer's *Canterbury Tales*

Discussion topics

Structure of feudal society
Role of monasteries and convents in the preservation of knowledge
View of women in chivalric society

Chapter 11. Music of the Medieval World

Principal points

Gregorian chant:
      a.   style: single-line, non-metric, conjunct
      b.   notation: neumes, on four-line staff
Three styles of setting texts in chant:
  syllabic, melismatic, and neumatic
Organization of the Mass: Proper and Ordinary
Notre Dame School in Paris:
      a.   development of polyphony (organum)
      b.   development of musical notation
      c.   principal composers: Léonin and Pérotin
Growth of secular forms: the motet
Secular musicians:
      a.   Goliards (students) and jongleurs (wandering minstrels)
      b.   Courtly poet musicians: troubadours (southern France), trouvères (northern France)
French Ars Nova (New Art), focus on secular music

Overview of early instruments (strings, winds, keyboard, percussion)
and importance of improvisation

Basic Listening

Haec dies (LG 2)
Gregorian chant, from Proper (Gradual for Easter), melismatic
Machaut: *Hareu! Hareu! le feu/Helas!/Obediens* (LG 3)
polytextual, isorhythmic motet, secular

Discussion topics

Modal vs. tonal music
Role of music in the Mass
Importance of the rise of polyphony
Development of musical notation
Roles of secular music in society
Mixture of secular and sacred texts in motet
Early instruments as precursors of modern ones

Selected Readings for Unit:

Apel, Willi. *Gregorian Chant.* Bloomington, IN: Univ. of Indiana Press, 1973.
Hoppin, Richard. *Medieval Music.* New York: Norton, 1978.
Seay, Albert. *Music in the Medieval World.* 2nd ed. Englewood Cliffs, NJ: Prentice-Hall, 1975.
Yudkin, Jeremy. *Music in Medieval Europe.* Englewood Cliffs, NJ: Prentice-Hall, 1989.

Unit IV: The Renaissance

Overview: The Renaissance is best viewed as an era of intellectual awareness of past cultures and learning. Its secular focus is highlighted in a discussion of the philosophical, intellectual, and artistic developments of the era. The various roles musicians played in society are emphasized as well. Sacred music is discussed, with examples of the motet and the mass. The organization of the Mass is outlined, including the structure of the movements of the Ordinary. The effects of the Council of Trent on music for the Mass is presented. Secular music-making at court, in the city, and at home is highlighted through the fifteenth- and sixteenth-century chanson and the Italian and English madrigal. The Venetian polychoral style is discussed as a transitional style between the Renaissance and the Baroque eras.

Unit goals for students:
1. To understand that the era is not entirely one of rebirth but of a new awareness
2. To recognize the major institutions of society that fostered music and music making

3. To understand the era as having an increasingly secular focus
4. To perceive relationships between texts and music settings

Chapter 12. The Renaissance Spirit

Principal points

Philosophical developments: focus on human wisdom
Historical developments: printing, explorations
Artistic developments: focus on human form
Musicians in society: court, church, civic

Discussion topics

Secularisms of society
The force of humanism
Musicians in society; rise of musical literacy

Chapter 13. Renaissance Music

Principal points

Renaissance style: a capella, polyphonic, use of cantus firmus, word
   painting
Renaissance motet: sacred, Latin, often dedicated to Virgin
Structure of Ordinary of Mass:
   Kyrie and Agnus dei: tripartite
   Gloria and Credo: longest texts
Cantus firmus mass: use of chant, ostinato, popular song
Council of Trent and music:
   no secularisms or irreverance, focus on words
   Palestrina as model
Burgundian chanson, fixed forms: rondeau, ballade, virelai
16th-century chanson: freer texts and forms
Italian madrigal: short, lyric love poem, set with word painting
English madrigal: adopted from Italy, preferred lighter forms
Instrumental dance types: pavane, galliard, allemande, ronde

Basic Listening

Dufay: *Alma redemptoris mater* (LG 4)
   motet to Virgin, based on chant in top voice
Monteverdi: *Ohimè! se tanto amate* (LG 5)
   Italian madrigal, poem by Guarini, word painting

Discussion topics

Church rituals and calendar
Council of Trent, the Counter Reformation, and music
The rise of Protestant churches and their music

Rise of amateur music making and women in music
Relationship between texts and music
Courtly vs. popular texts

Transition II: From Renaissance to Baroque

Principal points

Dramatic style changes between the two eras
polychoral (antiphonal) style:
> developed in St. Mark's basilica, Venice
> principal exponent: Giovanni Gabrieli

Discussion topics

Simplification of musical style: polyphonic to homophonic

Selected Readings for Unit:

Arnold, Denis. *Giovanni Gabrieli and the Music of the Venetian High
> Renaissance.* Oxford and New York: Oxford Univ. Press, 1979.
> _____. *Monteverdi Madrigals.* Seattle: Univ. of Washington Press, 1967.
Brown, Howard M. *Music in the Renaissance.* Englewood Cliffs, NJ: Prentice-
> Hall, 1976.
Fallows, David. *Dufay.* New York: Vintage, 1982.
Lowinsky, Edward, ed. *Josquin Desprez.* London: Oxford Univ. Press, 1976.
Palestrina, Giovanni. *Pope Marcellus Mass.* Lewis Lockwood, ed. Norton
> Critical Scores. New York: Norton, 1975.
Reese, Gustave. *Music in the Renaissance.* Rev. ed. New York: Norton, 1959.
Reese, Gustave, *et al. The New Grove High Renaissance Masters.* New York:
> Norton, 1984.
Roche, Jerome. *The Madrigal.* New York: C. Scribner's Sons, 1972.

PART THREE: MORE MATERIALS OF MUSIC

Unit V: The Organization of Musical Sounds

Overview: This brief section introduces more advanced concepts of harmony
which are needed in order to understand music of later eras. The concept of
tonality is explained, as are the patterns from which major and minor scales
are built. Transposition, modulation, and active and rest chords are described
in order that tonality can be understood as an element of form in the ensuing
chapters.

Unit goals for students:
1. To understand tonality as a unifying feature in music
2. To observe the different patterns for major and minor scales
3. To view key as an element of form

Chapter 14. Tonality, Key, and Scale

Principal points

Tonality and key
Intervals: whole and half steps
Scales: major, minor, chromatic

Discussion topics

Perceiving tonality

Chapter 15. The Major-Minor System

Principal points

Using the major and minor system:
    transposition: choosing a key
    modulation: related keys
Active chords: dominant, subdominant
Rest chord: tonic

Discussion topics

Key as an element of form

PART FOUR: THE BAROQUE ERA

Unit VI: The Baroque and the Arts

Overview: The Baroque era is introduced as a turbulent time of change in politics, science, and in the arts. The new musical style of the Baroque is discussed in detail, first focusing on the origins of monody and its manifestations in the developing genre of opera; after this, the harmonic structures (leaning towards major and minor tonality) and rhythmic and melodic characteristics of the new style are discussed. The role of virtuosity and improvisation, especially in realizing a figured bass, is explored, along with the expressive element manifest in the doctrine of the affections.

Unit goals for students:
1.   To understand the state of culture, politics, science, and learning during the Baroque era
2.   To comprehend the goals of the Camerata in developing monody
3.   To appreciate the significance of the origins of opera and the resulting new style of music
4.   To perceive the beginnings of modern tonality system, modern forms, and melodic structures

5.   To understand the doctrine of affections as an expressive element in music, tied to the text

Chapter 16. The Baroque Spirit

Principal points

Term Baroque, from Portuguese, "irregular pearl"
Art (painting): dramatic, turbulent, movement
Politics: absolute monarchies
Science: New World and stars, new frontiers
Middle class culture: amateur music making
Religion: Protestant vs. Catholic
    focus of political struggles
Artist under patronage

Discussion topics

Expression of drama in Baroque arts
Music at court and at home

Chapter 17. Main Currents of Baroque Music

Principal points

Development of monody:
    a.   Florentine Camerata
    b.   birth of opera
Harmonic structures:
    a.   thorough bass—2 instruments
    b.   major-minor tonality
    c.   birth of equal temperament
Style characteristics:
    a.   driving rhythm, freer in vocal music
    b.   melody continuous, tied to text
    c.   terraced dynamics
Virtuosity and improvisation:
    a.   realizing figured bass
    b.   solo singer (castrato)
Doctrine of Affections: union of music and text
International culture of the Baroque

Discussion topics

Importance of text vs. music
Origins of modern tonality and forms
Relationship between Baroque and jazz improvisation

Selected Readings for Unit:

Blume, Friedrich. *Renaissance and Baroque Music.* New York: Norton, 1967.
Bukofzer, Manfred. *Music in the Baroque Era.* New York: Norton, 1947.
Donington, Robert. *Baroque Music Style and Performance.* New York: Norton, 1982.
Palisca, Claude. *Baroque Music.* Englewood Cliffs, NJ: Prentice-Hall, 1968.
Strunk, Oliver, ed. *Source Readings in Music History: The Baroque Era.* New York: Norton, 1965.

Unit VII: Vocal Music of the Baroque

Overview: This unit presents the three major vocal forms of the Baroque: opera, cantata, and oratorio. Because of the genre focus, the entire era is discussed in this unit, from early Baroque opera (Monteverdi and Purcell) through Handelian opera and oratorio. Bach is representative of the Lutheran tradition and its service music, the cantata. The biographies and works of both Bach and Handel appear in this unit.

Unit goals for students:
1. To perceive the origins and early development of opera as a manifestation of the desire to unite text and music
2. To understand the chorale as the basis for the cantata and its movements
3. To view the Baroque oratorio as an outgrowth of religious dramas and opera
4. To appreciate the opposition of solo song and choral polyphony

Chapter 18. Baroque Opera

Principal points

Components of opera:
  a. recitative: secco and accompagnato
  b. aria (often da capo aria, **A-B-A**)
  c. ensembles, choruses
  d. overture, sinfonia
  e. libretto: text of opera
Monteverdi: early Baroque Italian composer known for madrigals and operas (*Orfeo, The Coronation of Poppea*)
Purcell: mid-Baroque English composer of operas, instrumental music, odes
Handel: composer of Italian opera seria, in England

Basic Listening

Purcell: *Dido and Aeneas,* Lament and Chorus (LG 7)
  based on Virgil; ground bass aria

Discussion topics

Opera plots: mythology and history
Development of operatic style and forms (da capo aria)

Chapter 19. Bach and the Baroque Cantata

Principal points

Cantata—secular or sacred, vocal, narrative text
Lutheran cantata—sacred, based on chorale (hymn)
J.S. Bach—known as virtuoso organist
    principal positions:
        Weimar: court organist
        Cöthen: chamber musician at court
        Leipzig: cantor and organist, St. Thomas's
    orchestral music and concertos
    sacred vocal music (cantatas and masses)
    keyboard music (organ and harpsichord)

Basic Listening

Bach: Cantata No. 80: *A Mighty Fortress is Our God* (LG 8)
    based on chorale tune by Luther; used in 4 of 8 movements
    I: choral fugue
    II: duet with chorale in soprano
    VIII: 4-part chorale

Discussion topics

Music in the Lutheran service
Bach's positions and the music he wrote in each
Various musical settings of chorale tunes

Chapter 20. Handel and the Baroque Oratorio

Principal points

Oratorio: large-scale narrative with soloists, chorus, orchestra; no sets,
    costumes, acting
Handel: international composer
    German-born, trained in Italy, worked in England
    opera, oratorios, orchestral music and concertos

Basic Listening

Handel: *Messiah* (LG 9)
    3 parts: Christmas, Easter, Resurrection
    French overture; "Hallelujah Chorus";
    Aria: "I know that my Redeemer liveth"

Discussion topics:

Oratorio as sacred operas
Opera seria vs. ballad opera in London
Continued popularity of *Messiah*

Selected Readings for Unit:

Arnold, Denis, and Nigel Fortune, eds. *The New Monteverdi Companion.* London: Faber and Faber, 1985.

David, Hans T. and Arthur Mendel, eds. *The Bach Reader*, rev. ed. New York: Norton, 1966.

Dean, Winton. *Handel's Dramatic Oratorios and Masques.* Oxford and New York: Oxford Univ. Press, 1983.

Dean, Winton, and Anthony Hicks. *The New Grove Handel.* New York: Norton, 1983.

Felix, Werner. *Johann Sebastian Bach.* New York: Norton, 1985.

Geiringer, Karl. *Johann Sebastian Bach: The Culmination of an Era.* Oxford and New York: Oxford Univ. Press, 1966.

Hogwood, Christopher. *Handel.* London: Thames and Hudson, 1984.

Hutchings, Arthur. *Purcell.* Seattle: Univ. of Washington Press, 1982.

Lang, Paul Henry. *George Frideric Handel.* New York: Norton, 1966.

Purcell, Henry. *Dido and Aeneas, An Opera.* Curtis Price, ed. Norton Critical Scores. New York: Norton, 1986.

Robbins Landon, H. C. *Handel and His World.* Boston: Little, Brown and Co., 1984.

Westrup, J.A. *Bach Cantatas.* Seattle: Univ. of Washington, 1966.

Wolff, Christoph, et al. *The New Grove Bach Family.* New York: Norton, 1983.

Unit VIII: Instrumental Music of the Baroque

Overview: The Baroque witnessed the increased importance of instrumental music and the creation of independent instrumental forms. This unit covers the concerto forms of the high Baroque and describes a variety of other instrumental ensemble forms. Keyboard instruments, especially organ and harpsichord, are discussed, along with a variety of keyboard forms; the emphasis is on the prelude and fugue represented by Bach.

Unit goals for students:
1. To become aware of the difference between original and modern instruments
2. To view instrumental music as comparable in importance to vocal music
3. To understand formal structures as means of unification

Chapter 21. The Baroque Concerto

Principal points

Instrumental music and forms increase in popularity
Concerto types: solo and concerto grosso
 opposition of two dissimilar groups
Vivaldi: Italian composer, much orchestral music
Bach: concerti grossi, six for Margrave of Brandenburg
 solo = concertino
 tutti = ripieno

Basic Listening

Vivaldi: "Spring" from *The Four Seasons* (LG 10)
 programmatic violin concerto, based on sonnet; ritornello form

Discussion topics

Concerto form: focus on contrast
Programmatic instrumental music
Ritornello as unification procedure

Chapter 22. Other Baroque Instrumental Forms

Principal points

Sonata: chamber (da camera) and church (da chiesa)
 trio sonata—4 players
ground bass forms: chaconne and passacaglia
Overtures:
 French: two sections (slow, fast)
 Italian: three sections (fast, slow, fast)
Suite: series of dance types
 international character: allemande (German), courante (French),
  sarabande (Spanish), jig (English)
Keyboard instruments: organ, harpsichord, clavichord
Keyboard forms:
 free: prelude
 strict: fugue
Fugue and devices: subject, answer, countersubject, episode, stretto
fugato: fugue-like section

Basic Listening

Bach: Prelude and Fugue in C minor (LG 11)
 Well-Tempered Clavier, Book I, 3 voices

Discussion topics

Character of dance movements and national origin
Pairing of free and strict forms (prelude and fugue)

Transition III: To the Age of Enlightenment

Principal points

Pre-classical styles: Rococo and *Empfindsamkeit*
Reform opera and Gluck
Rise of opera buffa and "War of the Buffoons"
Comparison of Baroque and Classical styles

Discussion topics

Pre-classical styles: Rococo and *Empfindsamkeit*
The changes in opera: opera seria vs. opera buffa
Baroque vs. Classical styles

Selected Readings for Unit:

Boyd, Malcolm. *Domenico Scarlatti*. New York: Schirmer, 1987.
Einstein, Alfred. *Gluck*. New York: McGraw-Hill, 1972.
Grout, Donald J. and Hermine W. Williams. *A Short History of Opera.* 3rd ed.
    New York: Columbia Univ. Press, 1987.
Kirkpatrick, Ralph. *Domenico Scarlatti*. New York: Apollo, 1968.
Newman, William S. *A History of the Sonata Idea.* 3 vols., rev. ed. New York:
    Norton, 1983.
Veinus, Abraham. *The Concerto*. New York: Dover, 1964.

PART FIVE: MORE MATERIALS OF FORM

Unit IX: Focus on Form

Chapter 23. The Development of Musical Themes

Principal points

Themes and thematic development
Motives, fragmented from themes

Discussion topics

Building forms through thematic development

Chapter 24. The Sonata Cycle

Principal points

Absolute (pure) music vs. programmatic
Sonata, from *suonare*, to sound
Sonata cycle:
1.   sonata-allegro form
      most developed and complex
      Exposition—Development—Recapitulation—Coda
2.   Slow movement
      theme and variations typical
3.   minuet and trio form
      overall form is ternary (**A-B-A**)
      scherzo—19th century
4.   sonata-allegro or rondo form, fast

Discussion topics

Repetition and contrast in form
Use of sonata cycle

Selected Readings for Unit:

Cone, Edward T. *Musical Form and Musical Performance.* New York: Norton, 1968.
LaRue, Jan. *Guidelines for Style Analysis.* New York: Norton, 1970.
Newman, William S. *A History of the Sonata Idea.* 3 vols., rev. ed. New York: Norton, 1983.
Ratner, Leonard. *Classic Music: Expression, Form, and Style.* New York: Norton, 1980.
Rosen, Charles. *Sonata Forms.* New York: Norton, 1980.

PART SIX: EIGHTEENTH-CENTURY CLASSICISM

Unit X: The Classical Spirit

Overview: Romanticism and classicism are compared, first as general styles, then as specific periods. The eighteenth century is presented as a time of enlightened despotism, refinement, and order, against which the middle classes arose. Music and musicians thrived at court, sponsored by the system of aristocratic patronage. Women found increasing acceptance in the music world, notably as performers and teachers.

Unit goals for students:
1.   To contrast the ideals of classicism and romanticism
2.   To understand the dualism of the time: the refined aristocracy vs. the rising middle classes

3. To appreciate the importance of the patronage system to the arts

Chapter 25. Classicism in the Arts

Principal points

Classicist: seeks order, objectivity
    represented by Apollo, god of light
    idealized civilizations of Greece and Rome
Era of aristocrats: Frederick the Great of Prussia
    Catharine the Great of Russia
    Louis XV of France
Rise of the bourgeois: French Revolution
Augustan Age (after Roman emperor Augustus)
Age of Sensibility or Reason
Sturm und Drang (storm and stress)
Aristocratic patronage—new art needed at court
Women—rising careers as performers and teachers

Discussion topics

Nietsche's view of classicism vs. romanticism
Aristocracy vs. the rising middle classes

Chapter 26. Classicism in Music

Principal points

Viennese School: four Viennese composers
    Haydn, Mozart, Beethoven, Schubert
Style:
    melody—singable, symmetrical
    harmony—diatonic
    rhythm—regular
    texture—homophonic
    orchestra—small (30-40), strings as core
    folk elements

Discussion topics

Elements of classical style
Importance of symphony

Selected Readings for Unit:

Blume, Friedrich. *Classic and Romantic Music.* New York: Norton, 1970.
Pauly, Reinhard G. *Music in the Classic Period.* 2nd ed. Englewood Cliffs, NJ:
    Prentice-Hall, 1973.

Ratner, Leonard. *Classic Music: Expression, Form, and Style.* New York: Oxford Univ. Press, 1970.

Rosen, Charles. *The Classical Style.* New York: Norton, 1972.

Strunk, Oliver, ed. *Source Readings in Music History: The Classic Era.* New York: Norton, 1965.

Unit XI: Classical Chamber Music

Overview: An introductory chapter in which the chamber music style so popular in the eighteenth century is discussed, then the most prominent chamber form, the string quartet, is described. A Mozart Serenade exemplifies the style.

Unit Goals for Students:
1. To understand the Classical era as the golden age of chamber music
2. To appreciate the central position of the string quartet
3. To grasp the special challenge that chamber music presents to the listener

Chapter 27. Eighteenth-Century Chamber Music Style

Principal points

Chamber music: one on a part, up to ten players
18th century: Golden Age of chamber music
String quartet: central position, sonata cycle
> Haydn—contrapuntal, developmental, folk elements
> Mozart—lyrical, elegant
> Beethoven—motivic, introduced scherzo

Discussion topics

String quartet as a challenge to the listener

Chapter 28. Mozart and Classical Chamber Music

Principal points

Mozart: Austrian, child prodigy, free artist
> symphonies, concertos, chamber music,
> opera (buffa, seria, Singspiel)

Basic Listening

Mozart: *Eine kleine Nachtmusik,* K. 525 (LG 12)
> serenade, concise sonata cycle

Discussion topics

Mozart's failure under the patronage system
Lyricism in Mozart

Selected Readings for Unit:

Anderson, Emily, ed. *The Letters of Mozart and His Family.* New York: Norton, 1985.

Blom, Eric. *Mozart.* New York: Macmillan, 1966.

Deutsch, Otto E. *Mozart: A Documentary Biography,* 2nd ed. Stanford, CA: Stanford Univ., 1966.

Griffiths, Paul. *The String Quartet.* London: Thames and Hudson, 1983.

Hughes, Rosemary. *Haydn String Quartets.* Seattle: Univ. of Washington, 1966.

Hyatt King, A. *Mozart Chamber Music.* Seattle: Univ. of Washington, 1968.

Kerman, Joseph. *The Beethoven Quartets.* New York: Norton, 1979.

Lam, Basil. *Beethoven String Quartets.* Seattle: Univ. of Washington, 1975.

Lang, Paul Henry, ed. *The Creative World of Mozart.* New York: Norton, 1969.

Sadie, Stanley. *The New Grove Mozart.* New York: Norton, 1983.

Smith, Erik. *Mozart Serenades, Divertimenti, and Dances.* Seattle: Univ. of Washington, 1982.

Ulrich, Homer. *Chamber Music.* 2nd ed. New York: Columbia, 1966.

Unit XII: The Classical Symphony

Overview: This unit covers the symphonies of two great masters: Haydn and Beethoven. The origins of the form in the Italian opera overture are mentioned and the individual character of each movement is outlined. The life and works of Haydn and Beethoven are included in this unit as well.

Unit Goals for Students:
1. To understand the structure of the symphony within the sonata cycle
2. To appreciate the contributions of Haydn to the symphony genre
3. To view Beethoven's symphonies as masterworks

Chapter 29. The Nature of the Symphony

Principal points

Symphony: developed from 3 sections of Italian overture
Mannheim School (Germany):
    a.   rocket theme—quickly rising
    b.   addition of minuet and trio movement

Classical orchestra
 strings—heart
 30–40 players
Sonata cycle:
 1st movement: sonata-allegro form
   1st theme rhythmic; 2nd theme lyrical
   opposition of two keys, Haydn monothematic
 2nd movement: slow, **A-B-A**, theme and variations, modified
   sonata-allegro, lyrical
 3rd movement: minuet and trio (**A-B-A**), home key
 4th movement: quick, light, rondo or sonata-allegro

Discussion topics

Development of the symphony

Chapter 30. Haydn and the Classical Symphony

Principal points

Productive life spent at Esterházy, late commissions in London;
 symphonies, strings quartets, masses

Basic Listening

Symphony No. 104 (London), first movement (LG 13)
 monothematic, slow introduction

Discussion topics

Haydn's contributions to the symphony

Chapter 31. Beethoven and the Symphony in Transition

Principal points

German-born, individualistic, grew deaf and introverted
Three periods:
1. Classical elements from Haydn and Mozart, first three
  symphonies, Op. 18 quartets, early piano sonatas
2. Romantic tendencies, expanded forms
3. chromatic harmonies, late piano sonatas and symphonies

Basic Listening

Symphony no. 5 in C minor (LG 14)
 rhythmic idea as basis of cyclic form; motivic development;
  double theme and variations; scherzo; last movement recalls
  first

Discussion topics

Beethoven as Classicist and Romantic

Selected Readings for Unit:

Anderson, Emily, ed. *The Letters of Beethoven.* 3 vols. New York: Norton, 1985.

Beethoven, Ludwig van. *Symphony No. 5 in C minor,* Elliot Forbes, ed. Norton Critical Scores. New York: Norton, 1971.

Cuyler, Louise. *The Symphony.* New York: Harcourt Brace Jovanovich, 1973.

Forbes, Elliot, ed. *Thayer's Life of Beethoven,* 2nd ed. Princeton: Princeton Univ. Press, 1967.

Geiringer, Karl. *Haydn: The Creative Life in Music,* 2nd ed. Berkeley: Univ. of California, 1982.

Hopkins, Anthony. *The Nine Symphonies of Beethoven.* Seattle: Univ. of Washington, 1981.

Larsen, Jens Peter. *The New Grove Haydn.* New York: Norton, 1983.

Mozart, Wolfgang Amadeus. *Symphony in G minor,* K.550. Nathan Broder, ed. Norton Critical Scores. New York: Norton, 1967.

Robbins Landon, H.C., and David Wyn Jones. *Haydn: His Life and Music.* Bloomington, IN: Indiana Univ. Press, 1988.

Robbins Landon, H.C. *Haydn Symphonies.* Seattle: Univ. of Washington, 1966.

Simpson, Robert, ed. *The Symphony,* 2 vols. London: David and Charles, 1972.

Solomon, Maynard. *Beethoven.* New York: Norton, 1972.

Stedman, Preston. *The Symphony.* Englewood Cliffs, NJ: Prentice-Hall, 1979.

Tovey, Donald Francis. "Beethoven: Symphony in C minor, No. 5, Op. 67." In *Symphonies and Other Orchestral Works.* Oxford and New York: Oxford Univ. Press, 1989, pages 53-58. (originally printed in 1935-39)

_____. "Haydn: Symphony in D, No. 104." In *Symphonies and Other Orchestral Works,* pages 373-75.

_____. "Mozart: Symphony in G minor, No. 40, K. 550." In *Symphonies and Other Orchestral Works,* pages 439-42.

Tyson, Alan, and Joseph Kerman. *The New Grove Beethoven.* New York: Norton, 1983.

Unit XIII: The Eighteenth-Century Concerto and Sonata

Overview: The three movements of the Classical concerto and their characteristics are presented. The form is illustrated through a work by Mozart. The Classical sonata became an important genre for amateurs; the solo sonata for piano and the duo sonata for violin and piano were favored. A Beethoven piano sonata serves to illustrate the genre.

Unit Goals for Students:
1. To understand Classical concerto and double exposition form
2. To grasp Mozart's and Beethoven's contributions to the Classical concerto
3. To recognize the solo and duo sonata as important amateur genres
4. To view the two instruments of the duo sonata as equal partners
5. To appreciate the drama and intensity of Beethoven's piano sonatas

Chapter 32. The Classical Concerto

Principal points

Components of the concerto:
3 movements: fast—slow—fast
1st movement: double exposition form with cadenza

Basic Listening

Mozart: Piano Concerto in C major, K. 467 (LG 15)
opera buffa-like themes, brilliant piano writing, lyrical

Discussion topics

Virtuosity and the concerto

Chapter 33. The Classical Sonata

Principal points

Sonata cycle format: 3 or 4 movements

Basic Listening

Beethoven: *Pathétique Sonata* in C minor, Op. 13 (LG 16)
dramatic quality, sudden dynamic changes; hymnic adagio

Discussion topics

Romantic qualities in Beethoven

Selected Readings for Unit:

Fiske, Roger. *Beethoven Concertos and Overtures.* Seattle: Univ. of Washington, 1970.

Girdlestone, Cuthbert. *Mozart and His Piano Concertos.* New York: Dover, 1964.

Matthews, Denis. *Beethoven Piano Sonatas.* Seattle: Univ. of Washington, 1967.

Newman, William S. *A History of the Sonata Idea.* 3 vols., rev. ed. New York: Norton, 1983.

Rosen, Charles. *Sonata Forms.* 2nd ed. New York: Norton, 1988.

Tovey, Donald Francis. *A Companion to Beethoven's Pianoforte Sonatas.* London: Royal School of Music, 1931.

_____. "Beethoven: Pianoforte Concerto No. 5 in E flat, Op. 73." In *Concertos and Choral Works.* Oxford and New York: Oxford Univ. Press, 1989, pages 67-69 (originally printed in 1935-39).

Veinus, Abraham. *The Concerto.* New York: Dover, 1964.

Unit XIV: Vocal Forms of the Classical Era

Overview: This unit introduces the major choral forms of the era, the mass, the Requiem, and the oratorio. Classical opera, both seria and buffa forms, are examined; the new developments in comic opera, a social force of the time, are presented. Mozart's *The Marriage of Figaro* is discussed as an example of the new opera buffa.

Unit Goals for Students:

1. To appreciate the great choral forms of the Classical era and the tradition from which they grew
2. To view eighteenth-century opera as an important social force of the time
3. To understand the trend for simplicity and naturalness that led to reforms in opera
4. To appreciate the new forms of popular comic opera that developed in the Classical era

Chapter 34. Classical Choral Music and Opera

Principal points

Choral forms: mass, Requiem, oratorio
Haydn: wrote 2 oratorios and many masses
opera seria most prevalent
rise of opera buffa (opéra comique, Singspiel)
interest in simplicity, vernacular, real people

Basic Listening

Mozart: *The Marriage of Figaro,* Act I (LG 17)
    librettist Da Ponte, based on Beaumarchais
    farcical comedy; leads to terzetta (trio)

Discussion topics

The mass in church and in the concert hall
Opera as a social force
Real humans and emotions in *The Marriage of Figaro*

Transition IV: From Classicism to Romanticism

Principal points

Schubert and Beethoven as transitional figures
    Schubert symphonies and chamber music—Classical
    Schubert songs—Romantic
Comparison of Classical and Romantic styles (in chart form)

Discussion topics

Classical vs. Romantic characteristics

Selected Readings for Unit:

Brown, Maurice J.E., with Eric Sams. *The New Grove Schubert.* New York: Norton, 1983.

Gossett, Philip, et al. *The New Grove Masters of Italian Opera.* New York: Norton, 1983.

Grout, Donald J. and Hermine W. Williams, *A Short History of Opera.* 3rd ed. New York: Columbia, 1987.

Kerman, Joseph. *Opera as Drama.* New rev. ed. Berkeley: Univ. of California, 1988.

Lang, Paul Henry. *The Experience of Opera.* New York: Norton, 1973.

MacIntyre, Bruce. *The Viennese Concerted Mass of the Early Classic Period.* Ann Arbor, MI: UMI Press, 1985.

Mann, William S. *The Operas of Mozart.* New York: Oxford Univ. Press, 1977.

Sadie, Stanley, ed. *History of Opera.* New York: Norton, 1990.

Schubert, Franz. *Symphony in B Minor ("Unfinished").* Martin Chusid, ed. Norton Critical Scores. New York: Norton, 1971.

Tovey, Donald Francis. "Schubert: Unfinished Symphony in B Minor." In *Symphonies and Other Orchestral Works.* Oxford and New York: Oxford Univ. Press, 1989, pages 464-67 (originally printed in 1935-39).

PART SEVEN: THE NINETEENTH CENTURY

Unit XV: The Romantic Movement

Overview: This unit is focused on the social and political forces that shaped nineteenth-century history and the arts. The effects on music of the Industrial Revolution and the democratization of society are explored as are the impact of nationalism and exoticism. The principal musical traits of Romantic style are outlined and the role of the musician in nineteenth-century society is examined.

Unit Goals for Students:

1. To understand the social and political forces that shaped nineteenth-century views on the arts
2. To perceive the artistic qualities of Romanticism
3. To appreciate the rising force of nationalism in the arts
4. To grasp the effect of new democratic societies on the lives of composers and performers, men and women alike.

Chapter 35. The Spirit of Romanticism

Principal points

Effect of French Revolution: rise of middle class
Poets abandon conventional forms and subjects:
                Germany: Heinrich Heine
                France: Victor Hugo, Alphonse de Lamartine
                England: Burns, Wordsworth, Byron, Shelley, Coleridge, Keats
Emergence of artist as bohemian: pessimistic views
Exoticism in painting: Turner, Delacroix

Discussion topics

Social and political forces of 19th century
Values of 19th-century artists

Chapter 36. Romanticism in Music

Principal points

Results of Industrial Revolution:
     cheaper instruments
     technical advances on instruments
Expanded educational opportunities
Rise of public concert hall: larger orchestras
Increased expressiveness in music: new terms
Rise of nationalism: use of folklore
Interest in exoticism: fascination with East
Romantic musical style:
     lyrical melody
     expressive, chromatic harmony
     expanded forms
Rise of virtuoso soloist
Expansion of musical life: schools, ensembles, printed scores, music journals
Musicians as educators
Women musicians: performers, composers, patronesses
     Piano socially acceptable for women
     lyric opera—famous women soloists

Discussion topics

Effects of Industrial Revolution on music and instruments
Rise of middle class and its effect on music
Interest in nationalism and exoticism
Romantic style and expressiveness in music
Role of musician in 19th-century society, including women

Selected Readings for Unit:

Blume, Friedrich. *Classic and Romantic Music.* New York: Norton, 1970.
Brown, David, et al. *The New Grove Russian Masters 1.* New York: Norton, 1986.
Cooke, Deryck, et al. *The New Grove Late Romantic Masters.* New York: Norton, 1985.
Dahlhaus, Carl. *Nineteenth-Century Music,* tr. by J. F. Robinson. Berkeley: Univ. of California Press, 1989.
Einstein, Alfred. *Music in the Romantic Era.* New York: Norton, 1947.
Longyear, Rey M. *Nineteenth-Century Romanticism in Music.* 2nd ed. Englewood Cliffs, NJ: Prentice-Hall, 1973.
Plantinga, Leon. *Romantic Music.* New York: Norton, 1984.
Praz, Mario. *The Romantic Agony.* Oxford: Oxford Univ. Press, 1970.
Strunk, Oliver, ed. *Source Readings in Music History. The Romantic Era.* New York: Norton, 1965.
Temperley, Nicholas, Gerald Abraham, and Humphrey Searle. *The New Grove Early Romantic Masters 1.* New York: Norton, 1985.
Warrack, John, Hugh MacDonald, and Karl-Heinz Köhler. *The New Grove Early Romantic Masters 2.* New York: Norton, 1985.

Unit XVI: The Nineteeth-Century Art Song

Overview: In this unit, the art song, specifically the German Lied, is presented as a manifestation of Romantic lyricism. Standard song structures are discussed as is the poetry of the Lied. A Schubert Lied, based on a text by Goethe, illustrates the genre.

Unit Goals for Students:
1.   To become acquainted with standard song forms
2.   To understand the union of poetry and music in the Lied
3.   To recognize the significant role of the piano in the Lied

Chapter 37. The Romantic Song

Principal points

Song structures:
strophic form
through-composed form (*durchkomponiert*)

Lied: solo vocal song with accompaniment
Lieder composers: Schubert, Schumann, Brahms, Wolf
Song cycle: unified by text
Poets: Goethe, Heine

Discussion topics

Union of poetry and music in the Lied

Chapter 38. Schubert and the Romantic Lied

Principal points

Schubert: Viennese, gifted song writer, bohemian life, died young
    and impoverished
    Genres: Lieder, symphonies, chamber music

Basic listening

Schubert: *Erlkönig* (LG 18)
    dramatic ballad by Goethe
    through-composed form, varied ranges in dialogue

Discussion topics

Schubert as Romantic
The supernatural in *Erlkönig*

Selected Readings for Unit:

Brody, Elaine, and R. A. Fowkes. *The German Lied and Its Poetry.* New
    York: New York Univ. Press, 1971.
Brown, Maurice J. E., with Eric Sams. *The New Grove Schubert.* New York:
    Norton, 1983.
Brown, Maurice. *Schubert Songs.* Seattle: Univ. of Washington, 1967.
Desmond, Astra. *Schumann Songs.* Seattle: Univ. of Washington, 1972.
Deutsch, Otto Erich. *Schubert: Memoirs by His Friends.* New York:
    Humanities, 1958.
Dickinson, A. E. F. "Fine Points in 'The Erl King'," *Monthly Musical Record*
    88 (1958), 141ff.
Fischer Dieskau, Dietrich. *Schubert's Songs,* tr. by K. S. Whitton. New York:
    Limelight Editions, 1984.
Gál, Hans. *Franz Schubert and the Essence of Melody.* New York: Crescendo,
    1977.
_____. *Johannes Brahms: His Work and Personality.* Westport, CT:
    Greenwood, 1977.
Harrison, Max. *The Lieder of Brahms.* New York: Praeger, 1972.
Hilmar, Ernst. *Franz Schubert in His Time.* Portland, OR: Amadeus, 1989.
Ivey, Donald. *Song: Anatomy, Imagery, and Style.* New York: Free Press,
    1970.

Meister, Barbara. *An Introduction to the Art Song.* New York: Taplinger, 1980.

Sams, Eric. *Brahms Songs.* London: BBC, 1972.

_____. *The Songs of Robert Schumann,* 2nd ed. London: Methuen, 1975.

Stevens, Denis. *A History of Song.* London: Hutchinson, 1960.

Walsh, Stephen. *The Lieder of Schumann.* New York: Praeger, 1972.

Unit XVII: The Nineteenth-Century Piano Piece

Overview: The rise in popularity of the piano is emphasized, along with technical improvements in the instrument. The short lyric piano piece is presented as the instrumental form that parallels the art song. Representative of this genre are Chopin, Liszt, Clara Wieck Schumann, and Robert Schumann. Clara Schuman is featured as one of the most distinguished woman musicians of the Romantic era.

Unit Goals for Students:
1. To understand the importance of the piano in the musical life of the Romantic era
2. To appreciate the short, lyric piano piece as the equivalent instrumental form to the Lied
3. To recognize the originality and virtuosity of Chopin's and Liszt's artistry
4. To comprehend the difficulties that women faced as composers in the nineteenth century

Chapter 39. The Piano in the Romantic Era

Principal points

Piano popular for home use, among amateurs
Rise of the piano recital—virtuoso players—Chopin and Liszt
Technical developments—leads to modern piano
Short lyric piano piece:
    parallel to song
    new descriptive titles

Discussion topics

Influence of piano on developing musical tastes
Piano as the instrument of amateurs and of virtuosi

Chapter 40. Chopin and Nineteenth-Century Piano Music

Principal points

Chopin: "poet of the piano"
    Polish-born, worked in Paris

relationship with George Sand, died young
focus on piano music, developed modern piano style, rubato
Genres: piano with orchestra and solo piano works
sonatas, ballades, noctures, Polish dances

Basic listening

Chopin: Polonaise in A flat (LG 19)
   A-B-A' form, dramatic, dance theme, virtuosic, nationalistic

Discussion topics

Nationalism in Chopin
Chopin and the development of modern piano style

Chapter 41. Clara Schumann: A Nineteenth Century Woman Musician

Principal points

Clara Wieck Schumann—pianist, composer
   wife of Robert Schumann, friend of Brahms
   leading interpreter of R. Schumann, Brahms, Chopin
   Genres: piano music, piano concerto, songs, chamber music

Basic listening

Clara Schumann: *Quatre pièces fugitives*, Op. 15, No. 3 (LG 20)
   melancholy, lyrical, **A-B-A** form

Discussion topics

Woman composers and nineteenth-century society

Selected Readings for Unit:

Chissell, Joan. *Clara Schumann: A Dedicated Spirit.* New York: Taplinger, 1983.
Chopin, Frédéric. *Preludes, Op. 28.* Thomas Higgins, ed. Norton Critical Scores. New York: Norton, 1973.
Litzmann, Berthold, ed. *Letters of Clara Schumann and Johannes Brahms, 1853-1896.* New York: Longmans, Green, 1927; repr. 1974.
Perényi, Eleanor. *Liszt: The Artist as Romantic Hero.* New York: Little, Brown, 1974.
Reich, Nancy B. *Clara Schumann: The Artist and the Woman.* Ithaca: Cornell Univ. Press, 1985.
Searle, Humphrey. "Franz Liszt." In *The New Grove Early Romantic Masters 1.* New York: Norton, 1985.
_____. *The Music of Liszt.* 2nd ed. London: Williams & Norgate, 1966.
Temperley, Nicholas. "Fryderyk Chopin." In *The New Grove Early Romantic Masters I.* New York: Norton, 1985.

Tovey, Donald Francis. "Schumann: Carnaval," In *Illustrative Music.* London: Oxford Univ. Press, 1972, 109ff.

Walker, Alan. *The Chopin Companion: Profiles of the Man and the Musician.* New York: Norton, 1973.

_____. *Franz Liszt: The Virtuoso Years, 1811-47.* Ithaca: Cornell Univ. Press, 1987.

_____. *Franz Liszt: The Weimar Years, 1848-61.* New York: Knopf, 1989.

Unit XVIII: Romantic Program Music

Overview: Program music is presented as a nineteenth-century phenomenon, and four types are listed: concert overture, incidental music, program symphony, and symphonic poem. The latter two are illustrated with examples by Berlioz and Smetana respectively; biographies of these composers appear in this unit. Musical nationalism is tied to program music with examples of how it is expressed; a brief discussion of various national schools and their output follows.

Unit Goals for Students:
1. To understand the special importance of program music in the Romantic era
2. To grasp the difference between programmatic and absolute forms
3. To relate political conditions of the nineteenth century to the rise of musical nationalism

Chapter 42. The Nature of Program Music

Principal points

program music: instrumental, with literary/pictorial association, supplied by composer
important to Romantic era
4 types of program music:
    concert overture: one movement, literary basis
    incidental music: accompanied plays, tone painting
    program symphony: multi-movement (Liszt, Berlioz)
    symphonic poem: one movement, contrasting sections invented by Liszt (*Les Préludes*)

Discussion topics

Form in program music
Expression of nationalism in music

Chapter 43. Berlioz and the Program Symphony

Principal points

Berlioz: French, innovative, master orchestrator, critic
    Genres: orchestral music (overtures, program symphonies), choral
        music, opera

Basic listening

Berlioz: *Symphonie fantastique,* "Dream of the Witches' Sabbath"
    (LG 21), five-movement program symphony,
    idée fixe in all movements, autobiographical
    vulgarization of fixed melody, use of *Dies irae,*
    diabolical character, morbid, bizarre

Discussion topics

Symphonie fantastique as epitomy of Romanticism
Unification of multi-movement works

Chapter 44. The Rise of Musical Nationalism

Principal points

Political conditions encouraged nationalism
Musical nationalism expressed in various ways:
    native songs and dances, folklore or native life,
    national hero, scenes from homeland
Schools of musical nationalism

Basic listening

Smetana: *The Moldau* (LG 22)
    from cycle of six symphonic poems, *My Country*
    scenes along river in Bohemia, river theme;
    hunting, peasant dance, moonlight, rapids, castle

Discussion topics

Nationalism and music: subjects and how expressed

Selected Readings for Unit:

Berlioz, Hector. *Fantastic Symphony*, Edward T. Cone, ed. Norton Critical
    Scores. New York: Norton, 1971.
Holoman, Kern. *Berlioz.* Cambridge, MA: Harvard Univ. Press, 1989.
Kennedy, Michael. *Richard Strauss.* London: Dent, 1976.
Macdonald, Hugh. *Berlioz Orchestral Music.* Seattle: University of
    Washington, 1969.
Orrey, Leslie. *Programme Music.* London: Davis-Poynter, 1975.

Primmer, Brian. *The Berlioz Style.* New York: Oxford Univ. Press, 1973.
Temperley, Nicholas. "The *Symphonie Fantastique* and its Program." *Musical Quarterly* 57 (1971); 593ff.
Tovey, Donald Francis. "Berlioz: Symphonie Fantastique, Op. 14," In *Symphonies and Other Orchestral Works.* Oxford and New York: Oxford Univ. Press, 1989, pages 164-70 (originally printed in 1935-39).

Unit XIX: Absolute Forms

Overview: This unit surveys the symphony and the concerto in the Romantic era. Beginning with the model established by Classical masters, the nineteenth-century symphony is explored, illustrated with Mendelssohn's *Italian* Symphony. The nature of the nineteenth-century concerto is examined, illustrated with Schumann's Piano Concerto in A minor.

Unit Goals for Students:
1. To appreciate the proportions and freedom that appear in the Romantic symphony
2. To recognize the nineteeth-century treatment of concerto form, with its increased virtuosity and freedom

Chapter 45. The Romantic Symphony

Principal points

Symphony: new proportions, movements/tempos not standard
First movement: dramatic, basic sonata-allegro form, long Development, new keys
Second movement: slow, lyrical, more moods, ABA
Third movement: scherzo, humor, surprise, fast
Fourth movement: balances first, various forms
Mendelssohn's *Italian*: An Early Romantic Symphony

Discussion topics

Comparison of Classical and Romantic symphony
Mendelssohn and Symphony form

Discussion topic

Classical and Romantic traits in *Italian* Symphony

Chapter 46. The Romantic Concerto

Principal points

3-movement structure remains, expanded
First movement: double exposition—more free placement of cadenza

Second movement: lyrical, loose **A-B-A**
Third movement: dramatic, flashy cadenza
Rise of the concert virtuoso: Franz Liszt and Nicolo Paganini

Discussion topic

Comparison of Classical and Romantic concerto

Chapter 47. Robert Schumann and the Romantic Concerto

Principal points

Robert Schumann: German, pianist, composer, critic, conductor
    married Clara Wieck, suffered mental breakdown
Genres: Lieder, orchestral, chamber, and piano music

Basic listening

Schumann: Piano Concerto in A minor (LG 23)
    I. dramatic introduction, haunting first theme
    II. Intermezzo, **A-B-A**
    III. vigorous, sonata form

Discussion topics

Freedom in Romantic concerto form
Schumann and German Romanticism

Selected Readings for Unit:

Abraham, Gerald. "Robert Schumann." In *The New Grove Early Romantic Masters 1*. New York: Norton, 1985.
Horton, John. *Brahms Orchestral Music.* Seattle: Univ. of Washington, 1969.
Kohler, Karl-Heinz. "Felix Mendelssohn." In *The New Grove Early Romantic Masters 1*. New York: Norton, 1985.
Nieman, A. "The Concertos." In *Robert Schumann: The Man and His Music*, ed. A. Walker. Rev. ed. London: Barrie and Jenkins, 1976, 241-76.
Tovey, Donald Francis. "Brahms: Symphony in E minor No. 4, Op. 98." In *Symphonies and Other Orchestral Works.* Oxford and New York: Oxford Univ. Press, 1989. (originally printed 1935-39)
_____. "Mendelssohn: Italian Symphony in A major, Op. 90." *Ibid.*
_____. "Schumann: Pianoforte concerto in A minor, Op. 54." In *Concertos and Choral Works.*
Walker, Alan, ed. *Robert Schumann: The Man and His Music.* London: Barrie and Jenkins, 1976.
Werner, Eric. *Mendelssohn: A New Image of the Composer and His Age.* New York: Macmillan, 1963.

Unit XX: Choral and Dramatic Music
in the Nineteenth Century

Overview: The expansion of the musical public in the 19th century was reflected in the rise of amateur choral societies, especially in France and England. The German tradition is examined in this unit through works by Brahms. The various national styles of Romantic opera are reviewed, with emphasis on the Italian lyric style of Verdi, the German music dramas of Wagner, the new realism of French lyric opera, notably in Bizet, and Post-Romantic Italian opera by Puccini. An historical overview of ballet is presented, with particular attention to its role in the opera. Tchaikovsky is introduced as representative of the Russian school of ballet, a discussion of *The Nutcracker* concluding the unit.

Unit Goals for Students:
1. To appreciate the role of choral music in nineteenth-century society
2. To recognize the great choral heritage of the Romantic era
3. To become familiar with the different national styles of opera that developed during the nineteenth century
4. To identify the *bel canto* style of Italian opera and the contributions of Verdi to that genre
5. To understand the music drama as conceived by Wagner
6. To comprehend the realism of late Romantic opera, as epitomized by the works of Bizet and Puccini

Chapter 48. The Nature of Romantic Choral Music

Principal points

Rise of amateur choruses—outlet for the masses
Repertory by great Romantic masters
Choral forms: mass, Requiem, oratorio, partsongs
Texts in choral music: repeated text lines, mood established

Discussion topic

Social conditions and amateur singing groups

Chapter 49. Brahms and Romantic Choral Music

Principal points

Brahms: German, worked in Vienna
    traditionalist, preferred absolute forms
Genres: orchestral, piano, and chamber music, Lieder, choral music

Basic listening

Brahms: *A German Requiem*, no. 4 (LG 24)
> Protestant tradition, biblical texts
> 7 movements; no. 4 is center movement, rondo form (**A-B-A-C-A**)

Discussion topics

Brahms as a traditionalist
Brahms and nationalism

Chapter 50. Romantic Opera

Principal points

Components of opera:
> recitative—aria—ensembles—libretto

National opera styles:
> Grand opera and opéra comique—France
> merged in lyric opera
> Opera seria and opera buffa—Italy
> bel canto singing
> Singspiel—Germany

Discussion topics

Development of national styles
Rise of popular, lighter opera styles

Chapter 51. Verdi and Italian Opera

Principal points

Verdi: Italian nationalist opera composer, wrote 28 operas
> Early: *Rigoletto, Il trovatore, La traviata*
> Middle: *Un ballo in maschera, La Forza des destino, Don Carlos*
> Late: *Aïda, Otello, Falstaff*

Basic listening

Verdi: *La traviata*, Act II, finale (LG 25)
> play by Dumas, libretto by Piave, bel canto style
> Violetta is tragic heroine; spectacular ensemble closes act; each
>> character expresses own feelings

Discussion topic

Verdi the nationalist

Chapter 52. Wagner and the Music Drama

Principal points

Wagner: German-born composer, conductor, writer
    developed idea of music drama—inseparable components
    cycle of four music dramas—*The Ring of the Nibelung*
    festival playhouse at Bayreuth; opera with endless melody;
    leitmotifs as main themes; chromatic harmony

Basic listening

Wagner: *Die Walküre* (LG 26)
    3rd opera in *The Ring*
    about Siegfried's parents, Sigemund and Sieglinde
    Act III: Ride of Valkyries, Wotan strips Brünnhilde of
        godhood, places her in deep sleep with ring of fire, Magic
        Fire Music; leitmotifs for magic sleep, magic fire, Siegfried

Discussion topics

Integration of music and drama in Wagner
Expressive harmony and endless melody in Wagner

Chapter 53. Tchaikovsky and the Ballet

Principal points

Tchaikovsky: Russian composer of orchestral music and 3 ballets:
    Swan Lake, Sleeping Beauty, and *The Nutcracker*
The Nutcracker: based on Hoffmann, expanded by Dumas, scenario by
    Petipa

Discussion topic

Influence of Russians on development of ballet

Selected Readings for Unit:

Abraham, Gerald. *The Music of Tchaikovsky*. New York: Norton, 1974.

Becker, Heinz. "Johannes Brahms." In *The New Grove Late Romantic Masters 1*. New York: Norton, 1985.

Budden, Julian. *The Operas of Verdi*. 3 vols. New York: Oxford Univ. Press, 1981.

Curtiss, Mina. *Bizet and His World*. Westport, CT: Greenwood, 1977.

Deathridge, John, and Carl Dahlhaus. *The New Grove Wagner*. New York: Norton, 1983.

Dent, Edward J. *The Rise of Romantic Opera*, ed. by W. Dean. Cambridge: Cambridge Univ. Press, 1976.

Gál, Hans. *Johannes Brahms: His Work and Personality.* Westport, CT: Greenwood, 1977.

Garden, Edward. *Tchaikovsky.* London: J. M. Dent, 1973.

Geiringer, Karl. *Brahms: His Life and Works.* 3rd ed. New York: Da Capo, 1981. (repr. of 1948 ed.)

Gossett, Philip, et al. *The New Grove Masters of Italian Opera.* New York: Norton, 1983.

Grout, Donald J. and Hermine W. Williams. *A Short History of Opera.* 3rd ed. New York: Columbia Univ. Press, 1987.

Gutman, Robert. *Richard Wagner: The Man, His Mind, and His Music.* New York: Harcourt Brace Jovanovich, 1974.

Hutchison, Ernest. *A Musical Guide to the Richard Wagner Ring of the Nibelung.* New York: Simon and Schuster, 1940; repr. 1972.

Jacobson, Bernard. *The Music of Johannes Brahms.* London: Tantivy, 1977.

Kerman, Joseph. *Opera as Drama.* Rev. ed. Berkeley: University of California, 1988.

Kimball, David. *Verdi in the Age of Italian Romanticism.* Cambridge: Cambridge Univ. Press, 1981.

Millington, Barry. *Wagner.* New York: Vintage, 1987.

Newman, Ernst. *The Life of Richard Wagner.* 4 vols. New York: Cambridge Univ. Press, 1976.

_____. *The Wagner Operas.* New York: Knopf, 1972.

Robertson, Alec. *Requiem: Music of Mourning and Consolation.* London: Praeger, 1967.

Tovey, Donald Francis. "Brahms: Requiem, Op. 45," In *Concertos and Choral Works.* Oxford: Oxford Univ. Press, 1989, 294-307 (originally printed in 1935-39)

Walker, Frank. *The Man Verdi.* Chicago: Univ. of Chicago, 1982.

Wagner, Richard. *Wagner on Music and Drama: a Compendium of Richard Wagner's Prose Works*, ed. A. Goldman and E. Sprinchorn. New York: Dutton, 1964.

Weaver, William, and Martin Chusid. *The Verdi Companion.* New York: Norton, 1979.

Wiley, R. J. *Tchaikovsky's Ballets.* Oxford: Oxford Univ. Press, 1985.

PART EIGHT: THE TWENTIETH CENTURY

Transition V: The Post-Romantic Era

Principal points

Post-Romantic Italian opera
    verismo (realism)
Puccini: *La bohème, Tosca, Madama Butterfly, Turandot*
    Leoncavallo: *I pagliacci*
    Mascagni: *Cavalleria rusticana*

Mahler: German Post-Romantic; director of NY Philharmonic
> song cycles and symphonies; lyricism, expressive harmony

Strauss: German, transitional composer
> early works classical in form; symphonic poems Romantic
> twentieth-century operas

Discussion topics

Mahler and the Viennese symphonists
The paths of Post-Romanticism
Orchestration in Strauss
The new realism in late Romantic operas

Unit XXI: Turn-of-the-Century Trends

Overview: This unit surveys some of the late nineteenth-century trends that strongly affected the arts in the twentieth century. The Impressionist style is introduced in painting, followed by a discussion of the Symbolist literary movement. The traits of musical Impressionism are presented (parallel chords, ninth chords, unresolved dissonances), including those resulting from non-Western influences (new scales, rhythms, instrumental colors). Debussy is described as the most important French Impressionist composer whereas Ravel is presented as representative of Post-Impressionism.

Unit Goals for Students:

1. To appreciate the goals of Impressionist painters and the influence they had on music
2. To perceive the new sonorities of Impressionism
3. To understand the relationship between Symbolist poetry and musical Impressionism
4. To view Debussy as the epitomy of musical Impressionism

Chapter 54. Debussy and Impressionism

Principal points

Impressionism: term from Monet painting
Parisian style: Pissarro, Manet, Degas, Renoir
> pure color juxtaposed; luminous sheen;
> studies in light; everyday scenes

Symbolist poets: parallel movement
> Baudelaire, Mallarmé, Verlaine
> indirect language, suggestion, free verse

Musical style
> parallel chord movement; novel scales (whole tone)
> non-Western influences; unresolved dissonances;
> interest in instrumental color; ninth chords

Debussy: Parisian composer; short lyric forms; program music
   opera *Pelléas et Mélisande*, based on symbolist drama
   Genres: orchestral tone poems, piano music, vocal music
Ravel: French Post-Impressionist and Neo-Classicist
   association with intellectual group, Apaches; interest
   in jazz; style differs from Debussy; more dissonant
   Genres: orchestral music; piano music; ballets; operas

Basic listening

Debussy: *Prelude to "The Afternoon of a Faun"* (LG 27)
   based on Mallarmé pastoral poem, mythological faun;
   free **A-B-A** form, languid chromatic scales, moves from
   one instrument to another; more movement in B section

Discussion topics

Impressionism in painting and music
Debussy and the Symbolist poets
Post-Impressionism vs. Neo-Classicism in Ravel

Selected Readings for Unit:

Armstrong, Thomas. *Strauss's Tone Poems.* New York: Oxford Univ. Press,
   1931.
Ashbrook, William. *The Operas of Puccini.* Ithaca: Cornell Univ. Press, 1985.
Blaukopf, Kurt. *Mahler: A Documentary Study.* New York: Oxford Univ.
   Press, 1976.
Banks, Paul, and Donald Mitchell. "Gustav Mahler." In *The New Grove Turn-
   of-the-Century Masters.* New York: Norton, 1985.
Cooke, Deryck. *Gustav Mahler: An Introduction to His Music.* London: Faber
   and Faber, 1980.
Debussy, Claude. *Prelude to "The Afternoon of a Faun."* William W. Austin,
   ed. Norton Critical Scores. New York: Norton, 1970.
Del Mar, Norman. *Richard Strauss: A Critical Commentary on His Life and
   Work.* 3 vols. Philadelphia: Chilton, 1978.
Kennedy, Michael. "Richard Strauss." In *The New Grove Turn-of-the-Century
   Masters.* New York: Norton, 1985.
Lebrecht, Norman, ed. *Mahler Remembered.* New York: Norton, 1987.
Lesure, François, ed. *Debussy on Music.* Ithaca, NY: Cornell Univ. Press,
   1977.
Lockspieser, Edward. *Debussy.* Rev. 5th ed. London: Dent, 1980.
Mahler, Alma Schindler. *Gustav Mahler: Memories and Letters,* ed. by
   D. Mitchell. Rev. ed. Seattle: Univ. of Washington, 1971.
Mitchell, Donald. *Gustav Mahler: The Wunderhorn Years.* Berkeley: Univ. of
   California, 1980.

Nichols, Roger. "Claude Debussy." in *The New Grove Twentieth-Century Masters*. New York: Norton, 1986.

_____, ed. *Ravel Remembered.* New York: Norton, 1988.

Orenstein, Arbie. *Ravel: Man and Musician.* New York: Columbia Univ. Press, 1975.

Vallas, Leon. *Debussy: His Life and Works*. New York: Dover, 1973.

Unit XXII: The Early Twentieth Century

Overview: The early twentieth century is characterized by a reaction against Romanticism and an interest in non-Western music, especially in new rhythms. Other artistic trends that influenced music were Expressionism, the German answer to Impressionism, and the New Classicism. New elements of early twentieth-century musical style are outlined; these include more complex rhythms, a non-vocal melody, a highly-expanded harmonic language that eventually abandoned tonality, the emancipation of dissonance, a new textural conception of linear dissonance, a new orchestral sound, and an increased interest in form. The development of the serial system and its devices is reviewed as well. The first generation of early twentieth-century composers is represented by Stravinsky and Schoenberg, with *The Rite of Spring* featured as an example of primitivism and *Pierrot Lunaire* as an Expressionist work. Schoenberg's pupils, Alban Berg and Anton Webern, are discussed in brief.

Unit Goals for Students:
1. To view the currents of the early twentieth century as a reaction against Romanticism
2. To appreciate the non-Western influences exerted on early twentieth-century arts
3. To recognize the influence of Expressionism and New Classicism on musical style
4. To grasp the new elements of twentieth-century musical style, especially the innovative harmonic systems
5. To recognize Expressionist features in the works of Schoenberg and an interest in primivitism in early works of Stravinsky

Chapter 55. Main Currents in Early Twentieth-Century Music

Principal points

Reaction against Romanticism
Non-Western influences: uninhibited, spontaneous
    African influence; primitive, powerful rhythms
Expressionism: German response to Impressionism
    realm of subconscious; hallucinations; dreams
    artists—Kadinsky, Klee, Kokoschka

composers—Schoenberg, Berg
musical characteristics—expressive harmony
extreme ranges; very disjunct melodies
New Classicism: interest in Baroque/Classical eras
objective style; clear forms
absolute music rather than programmatic

Discussion topics

Non-Western influences on early 20th-century music
Expressionism and music
The New Classicism

Chapter 56. New Elements of Musical Style

Principal points

Rhythm: increasingly complex
polyrhythm—several simultaneous patterns
borrowings from popular styles (ragtime, jazz)
Melody: instrumental in concept, not vocal
wide leaps, dissonant intervals,
sometimes no melodic orientation
Harmony: polychords, "skyscraper" chords
creation of polyharmony
quartal harmony (built in fourths, not thirds)
expanded tonality; interest in modes and non-Western music
polytonality—two or more keys together (Stravinsky)
atonality—abandonment of tonality (Schoenberg)
12-tone method (serialism)—unifying procedure developed by
Schoenberg; all 12 tones treated equally
tone row—arrangement of all 12 chromatic tones
forms of row: transposed, inverted, retrograde, retrograde
inversion
treatment of dissonance—not resolved
Counterpoint: dissonant lines
Orchestration: smaller orchestras; linear colors
strings no longer core; use of dark instruments
Form: Neo-Classicists returned to absolute music
formal beauty over expressive beauty; formalism

Discussion topics

New freedoms and new constraints in 20th-century music
Abandonment of tonality
Increased interest in form

Chapter 57. Stravinsky and the Revitalization of Rhythm

Principal points

Stravinsky: Russian; 3 ballets with Diaghilev
    revolutionized rhythm, orchestration; nationalism
    primitivism; Neo-Classical period; 12-tone works

Basic listening

Stravinsky: *The Rite of Spring,* Part I (LG 28)
    Scenes of pagan Russia, ballet, primitivism
    polyrhythms and polytonality; Russian folk songs
    extreme dissonance and extreme registers in instruments

Discussion topics

Stravinsky and nationalism
Development of Stravinsky's style

Chapter 58. Schoenberg and the Second Viennese School

Principal points

Schoenberg: Second Viennese school
    1st period—post-Wagnerian Romantic
    2nd period—atonal Expressionism
    3rd period—12-tone period
    teacher of Berg and Webern, taught in US
Berg: Second Viennese school, pupil of Schoenberg
    Expressionist style and Neo-Classical forms
    2 operas: *Wozzeck* and *Lulu*
Webern: Second Viennese school, pupil of Schoenberg
    interest in brevity; unusual orchestration;
    extreme ranges; *Klangfarbenmelodie*; total serialism

Basic listening

Schoenberg: *Pierrot lunaire,* nos. 18, 21 (LG 29)
    Voice (*Sprechstimme*) and chamber orchestra;
    21 poems by Giraud; *Klangfarbenmelodie*;
    #18: *The Moonfleck*—contrapuntal devices
    #21: *O Scent of Fabled Yesteryear*—nostalgic

Discussion topics

Schoenberg and the abandonment of tonality
Symbolism and Expressionist poetry set by Schoenberg

Selected Readings for Unit:

Austin, William. *Music in the Twentieth Century*. New York: Norton, 1966.

Craft, Robert. *Stravinsky: Chronicle of a Friendship*. New York: Vintage, 1972.

Griffiths, Paul. "Anton Webern." In *The New Grove Second Viennese School*. New York: Norton, 1983.

Jarman, Douglas. *The Music of Alban Berg*. Berkeley: Univ. of California, 1978.

Kolneder, Walter. *Anton Webern: An Introduction to His Works*, tr. by Humphrey Searle. Berkeley: Univ. of California, 1968.

Machlis, Joseph. *Introduction to Contemporary Music*. 2nd ed. New York: Norton, 1979.

Morgan, Robert. *Twentieth-Century Music*. New York: Norton, 1990.

Neighbour, Oliver. "Arnold Schoenberg." In *The New Grove Second Viennese School*. New York: Norton, 1983.

Perle, George. "Alban Berg." In *The New Grove Second Viennese School*. New York: Norton, 1983.

Reich, Willi. *The Life and Works of Alban Berg*. New York: Da Capo, 1982.

Rosen, Charles. *Arnold Schoenberg*. New York: Viking, 1975.

Schoenberg, Arnold. *Style and Ideas: Selected Writing of Arnold Schoenberg*, ed. by Leonard Stein. New York: Faber and Faber, 1982.

Salzman, Eric. *Twentieth-Century Music: An Introduction*. 3rd ed. Englewood Cliffs, NJ: Prentice-Hall, 1988.

Simms, Bryan R. *Music of the Twentieth Century: Style and Structure*. New York: Schirmer, 1986.

Slominsky, Nicholas. *Music Since 1900*. 4th ed. New York: Scribner, 1971; suppl. 1986.

Watkins, Glenn. *Soundings: Music in the Twentieth Century*. New York: Schirmer, 1988.

White, Eric Walter. *Stravinsky, the Composer and His Works*, 2nd ed. Berkeley: Univ. of California, 1980.

_____. "Igor Stravinsky." In *The New Grove Modern Masters*. New York: Norton, 1984.

Unit XXIII: The Nationalism of the Twentieth Century

Overview: Twentieth-century nationalism in Europe and in the United States is surveyed in this unit, and its resulting product is contrasted with that of the nineteenth century. The various European national schools are mentioned, suggesting representative composers for each: the English school with Vaughan Williams; the Russian school by Prokofiev; and the Eastern European school by Bartók. All these composers made extensive use of folk idioms. The music of early America is presented as a pastiche of ingredients, drawing heavily on English styles. The developing concert life of nineteenth-century America is discussed, as are the beginnings of American nationalism.

Composers such as William Billings, Stephen Foster, and Louis Gottschalk are introduced, along with the debt each owed to other styles. Charles Ives is presented as one of the most extraordinary American spirits in music, one who was much ahead of his time. Aaron Copland represents the more modern generation of American composers. Both these men drew heavily on their native traditions and tunes. The American popular scene is explored, beginning with ragtime and its best-known proponent Scott Joplin. Jazz and blues are introduced as truly American forms of music, created principally by black Americans. The textual and musical forms of blues is presented, along with an example by Louis Armstrong. The big band era, represented by Duke Ellington, and third stream jazz, represented by John Lewis, are discussed. The American musical *West Side Story* is surveyed, Leonard Bernstein exemplifying the best of our theater music.

Unit Goals for Students:

1. To identify the goals of twentieth-century nationalism and recognize how they differ from those of earlier eras
2. To acknowledge that political events were an important inspiration for nationalistic works
3. To observe the differences in the music of the various European national schools
4. To view American music as highly eclectic, drawing from many European and African sources
5. To realize the genius and originality of Charles Ives
6. To understand ragtime, jazz, and blues as truly American styles created mainly by black Americans
7. To grasp the influence of jazz on classical styles
8. To recognize American musical theater as a unique contribution to world theater

Chapter 59. Bartók and the European Scene

Principal points

Béla Bartók: Hungarian; interest in native folklore
    Classical forms; new scales and rhythms
    Genres: string quartets, orchestal works, piano music
20th-century national schools
    French: Satie, Milhaud, Honegger, Poulenc
    Russian: Rachmaninoff, Prokofiev, Shostakovich
    English: Elgar, Delius, Vaughan Williams, Britten
    German: Hindemith, Orff
    Hungarian: Bartók, Kodály
    Czech: Janácek
    Nordic: Sibelius, Nielsen

Basic listening

Bartók: *Music for Strings, Percussion and Celesta* (LG 30)
    chamber group: two string groups and percussion; 4 movements;
        fourth is rondo, with Hungarian folk dance tunes (modal);
        contrapuntal devices

Discussion topics

Nineteenth- vs. twentieth-century nationalism
Use of folk song and dance in the twentieth century

Chapter 60. The American Scene: Art Music

Principal points

Early American music: oral tradition
    influenced by English styles
        Bay Psalm Book—Protestant
19th-century concert life: in English tradition
    German musicians; French and Italian opera
American music and composers
    William Billings: anthems, "fuguing tunes"
    Stephen Foster: popular songs
    Louis Gottschalk: use of native song and dance
Charles Ives: highly original composer
    ideas ahead of his time; businessman by day
    used images from childhood and from New England; patriotic
    realism in music; polytonality; polyrhythms
    Genres: orchestral music; songs; piano music
Aaron Copland: American composer; Neo-Classicist
    studied with Boulanger; used jazz idiom; classical forms
    Genres: ballets; orchestral music; film scores

Basic listening

Copland: "Hoe-Down" from *Rodeo* (LG 31)
    ballet; Agnes de Mille, choreographer; Western theme
    concert suite: 4 movements as dance episodes
    last is "Hoe-Down": sets 2 square dance tunes

Discussion topics

America: a musical "melting pot"
American patriotism and music
Original spirit of Charles Ives

Chapter 61. The American Scene: Popular Styles

Principal points

Ragtime: late 19th-century piano style
    "ragged" rhythm
Joplin: "King of Ragtime"; piano rags
    attempted merger of styles; Classical and ragtime
    operas unsuccessful in his lifetime
    awarded Pulitzer Prize posthumously for *Treemonisha*
jazz: Black American music, from African and popular styles
blues: American folk music; simple poetic/musical structure
    text=3 line stanzas, first two the same
    music=12 or 16 bar progression
New Orleans: birthplace of jazz
    fusion of various traditional styles; improvisation
Louis Armstrong: great improvisor; trumpet player
    swing=his melodic/rhythmic style; scat singing
    new features=stop-time choruses; double-time choruses
Duke Ellington: composed jazz; pianist and orchestrator
    big band; larger orchestral palette
bebop: new jazz style of 1940s—two-note phrases
third stream: merger of Classical and jazz
    term coined by Gunther Schuller
John Lewis: founder of Modern Jazz Quartet; third stream
    piano, vibraphone, drums, string bass
influence of jazz on Classical composers:
    Stravinsky, Krenek, Ravel, Milhaud, Weill
American Musical Theater
    developed from European operetta
    romantic plots, lyrical melodies, choruses
    Cole Porter, Lerner and Loewe, Rodgers and Hammerstein,
    Stephen Sondheim, and Andrew Lloyd Webber
Leonard Bernstein: conductor of NY Philharmonic
    crossed over between popular and Classical music
    theater and film music as well as orchestral music
    Broadway musicals; great orchestrator and melodist, jazz
        influence

Basic listening

Armstrong: *West End Blues* (LG 32)
    12-bar blues; recorded in 1922; Savoy Ballroom Five
    Armstrong on trumpet and vocal; also trumbone, clarinet, banjo,
        drums, piano
    introduction and 5 choruses; "blue" notes
Bernstein: Symphonic Dances from *West Side Story* (LG 33)
    collaborated with Sondheim; Romeo and Juliet story updated

dance sequences from musical in orchestral work
"Cool," Fugue—rhythmic motives, tritone
syncopated, jazz-inspired rhythms
fugue, dotted rhythms, jazz feel; builds to climax

Discussion topics

Influence of African-American music on American popular styles
Jazz as art music
Influence of jazz on contemporary composers
Musical theater: an American invention

Selected Readings for Unit:

Austin, William W. "Aaron Copland." In *The New Grove Twentieth-Century American Masters*. New York: Norton, 1988.

Chase, Gilbert. *America's Music, from the Pilgrims to the Present*, 2nd rev. ed. Westport, CT: Greenwood, 1981.

Collier, James L. *The Making of Jazz*. New York: Houghton, Mifflin, 1978.

Copland, Aaron. *Copland on Music*. New York: Norton, 1963.

_____, and Vivian Perlis. *Copland: 1900 through 1942*. New York: St. Martin's, 1984.

_____. *Copland: Since 1943*. New York: St. Martin's, 1989.

Cowell, Henry. *American Composers on American Music*. New York: Ungar, 1962.

Hamm, Charles. *Yesterdays: Popular Song in America*. New York: Norton, 1979.

Kingman, Daniel. *American Music: A Panorama*. 2nd ed. New York: Schirmer, 1990.

Kirkpatrick, John. "Charles Ives." In *The New Grove Twentieth-Century American Masters*. New York: Norton, 1988.

_____, ed. *Charles E. Ives Memos*. New York: Norton, 1972.

Lampert, Vera and László Somfai. "Béla Bartók." In *The New Grove Modern Masters*. New York: Norton, 1984.

McAllister, Rita. "Sergey Prokofiev." In *The New Grove Russian Masters 2*. New York: Norton, 1986.

Megill, Donald D., and Richard S. Demory. *Introduction to Jazz History*. Englewood Cliffs, NJ: Prentice-Hall, 1984.

Oliver, Paul, et al. *The New Grove Gospel, Blues and Jazz*. New York: Norton, 1986.

Ottaway, Hugh. "Ralph Vaughan Williams." In *The New Grove Twentieth-Century English Masters*. New York: Norton, 1986.

Perlis, Vivian. *Charles Ives Remembered: An Oral History*. New York: Norton, 1976.

Rockwell, John. *All American Music: Composition in the Late Twentieth Century*. New York: Knopf, 1983.

Rossiter, Frank. *Charles Ives and His America*. New York: Liveright, 1975.

Schuller, Gunther. *Early Jazz*. New York: Oxford Univ. Press, 1968.

_____. *The Swing Era: The Development of Jazz, 1930-1945*. Oxford and New York: Oxford Univ. Press, 1989.

Southern, Eileen. *The Music of Black Americans*. 2nd ed. New York: Norton, 1983.

_____. *Readings in Black American Music*. 2nd ed. New York: Norton, 1982.

Stevens, Halsey. *The Life and Music of Béla Bartók*. Rev. ed. Oxford and New York: Oxford Univ. Press, 1967.

Thomson, Virgil. *American Music Since 1910*. New York: Holt, Rinehart & Winston, 1971.

Tirro, Frank. *Jazz: A History*. New York: Norton, 1977.

Tischler, Barbara. *An American Music: The Search for an American Musical Identity*. Oxford and New York: Oxford Univ. Press, 1986.

Unit XXIV: The New Music

Overview: In this unit we are introduced to modern trends in the arts, including Dadaism, Surrealism, Cubism, and Abstract Expressionism, and the effect of each on musical styles is discussed. Moves toward greater organization in music through extension of serial principles as well as movements away from organization, including aleatory or indeterminate music, are covered. Many significant international composers, including a number of women, are mentioned. The effects of non-Western music on contemporary composers is surveyed, with particular emphasis on the music of John Cage. The role of music in society and the various harmonic/melodic/rhythmic languages of music are discussed. The scientific classification system for instruments is also presented. The use of unusual techniques and highly virtuosic demands on traditional instruments is given particular attention. The development of electronic music is surveyed, from musique concrète of the 1940s to computer-generated music of today. Two recent trends are discussed: one of which, minimalism, is illustrated with a piece by John Adams.

Unit Goals for Students:
1. To recognize recent trends in the arts and their impact on musical composition
2. To appreciate the recent movements towards both greater and lesser organization in music
3. To view the contemporary musical scene as an international one
4. To realize the prominent role played in contemporary music by women, both as performers and composers
5. To understand the universal roles that music plays in all societies
6. To grasp the diversity of musical instruments and musical languages that exist world-wide

7. To appreciate the cross-cultural exchanges that have occurred in music and in other arts
8. To recognize the virtuosity and extreme technical demands required of modern performers
9. To understand how traditional instruments and the voice have been used in non-traditional ways
10. To accept the importance of electronic music, synthesizers, and computer-generated music
11. To view the New Romanticism as an attempt to close the gap between composer and audience
12. To view minimalism as a return to simplicity

Chapter 62. New Directions

Principal points

New trends in the arts:
    Dadaism: rejection of art, return to simplicity (Satie)
    Surrealism: exploited world of dreams (Dali)
    Cubism: world in geometric terms (Picasso)
    Abstract Expressionism: independence from reality (Moore, Motherwell)
    Pop art: themes from modern life (Warhol, Dine)
    Theater of the Absurd: disillusionment (Ionesco, Beckett)
    New Wave cinema: Fellini
Greater organization
    extension of serialism—total serialism (Boulez)
Greater freedom
    aleatory music—details left to choice or chance (Cage)
    improvisation (Foss)
Internationalism of new music
    Boulez: French avant-garde composer
    Berio: Italian avant-garde composer
    Xenakis: Greek avant-garde composer
    Penderecki: Polish avant-garde composer
New concepts of form: not predetermined
Microtones: quarter tones, non-Western influence
New concepts of rhythm: irregular, assymetrical
Contemporary women musicians:
    Nadia Boulanger: great French teacher
    Ruth Crawford: early 20th century; total organization in String Quartet (1931)
    Ellen Taaffe Zwilich: 1st woman to win Pulitzer Prize for composition

Discussion topics

Contemporary trends in the arts
Freedom of form in new music
Role of women in contemporary music

Chapter 63. Non-Western Music and the Contemporary Scene

Principal points

Cross-over between West and East, both directions
Roles of music in society: universal
    ceremony, religious, civic, during work, entertainment, singing,
        dancing
Oral tradition: most music passed this way
Musical languages
    different scales: pentatonic, tritonic, heptatonic
    different rhythm/meter concepts (tala in India)
    use of drone: sustained tone or tones
    call and response (responsorial singing)
Musical instruments classification system
    aerophone: use air to vibrate
    chordophone: vibrating string
    idiophone: sound from instrument itself (blown, struck)
    membranophone: stretched membranes
Exoticism: 19th-century movement
Primitivism: early 20th-century; influence from Africa
Composers greatly influenced by non-Western music
    Henry Cowell: koto concertos, pentatonic scales, tone clusters
    Harry Partch: microtonal music; built microtonal
        instruments
    John Cage: developed prepared piano; simulates gamelan
        orchestra; interest in aleatory music; indeterminacy

Discussion topics

Influence of Western music on other cultures
New scale types and microtones
Diversity of musical instruments
Universal roles of music in society

Chapter 64. New Sounds

Principal points

New Virtuosity: new technical demands of avant-garde music
        vocal and instrumental: microtones, noises
Carter: Abstract Expressionist
        metrical modulation; speed of pulse subtly modified

Ligeti: traditional instruments sounding like electronic
    micropolyphony; many instruments woven into complex
        polyphonic fabric, barely perceptible changes
Lutosławski: Polish, interest in aleatoric music
Crumb: American professor; sets poetry of Federico García Lorca;
    emotional music
Early instruments: ondes Martenot, electronic generator
musique concrète: natural sounds, recorded and manipulated
invention of synthesizer: sound generators and modifiers
    1955, RCA Electronic Music Synthesizer, huge
    composer had control of all elements
    synthesizers now small and less expensive
computer-generated music, digital to analog conversion
novel aspects of electronic music:
    creation of new sounds
    composer needs no performer
    important pioneers: Stockhausen, Ussachevsky
Davidovsky: series for live performer (various) and tape
Varèse: original spirit
    experiments in musique concrète
    interest in percussion; sound masses; realism in music
Babbitt: intellectualization of music
    total serialism of melody, rhythm, dynamics, timbre
    electronic music with live performers

Basic listening

Crumb: *Ancient Voices of Children* (LG 34)
    based on poems by Federico García Lorca
    for mezzo-soprano, boy soprano, unusual instruments
    (various percussion, including non-Western; toy piano)
    1. El niño busca su voz—free, virtuosic vocal part

Discussion topics

Unusual instruments in contemporary music
New virtuosic demands
The future of electronic music
The popular music scene and electronic music

Chapter 65. Recent Trends

Principal points

New Romanticism: attempt to close gap between audiences and
    composers; emotional appeal; Romantic harmonies; sweeping
    melodies; rich orchestration

New Romantic composers: Samuel Barber, Ned Rorem, David Del
    Tredici; John Corigliano
Thea Musgrave: Scottish woman composer; New Romantic
    nationalistic; operas and ballets
Minimalism: simplification of musical language
    repetition of melodic, rhythmic, harmonic patterns
    changes slowly; "trance music"
    Terry Riley, Steve Reich, Philip Glass
John Adams: second generation of minimalists

Basic listening

Adams: *Short Ride in a Fast Machine* (LG 35)
    for large orchestra and 2 synthesizers
    ostinato rhythm; energetic and hypnotic

Discussion topics

New Romanticism vs. minimalism: the wave of the future

Selected Readings for Unit:

Cage, John. *Silence: Lectures and Writings.* Middletown, CT: Wesleyan Univ.
    Press, 1961.
Carter, Elliott Cook. *The Writings of Elliott Carter*, ed. by Else and Kurt
    Stone. Bloomington: Indiana Univ. Press, 1977.
Cope, David. *New Directions in Music.* 3rd ed. Dubuque, Iowa: W. C. Brown,
    1981.
Griffiths, Paul. *A Guide to Electronic Music.* London: Thames and Hudson,
    1979.
      . *Modern Music: The Avant-Garde Since 1945.* London: Dent, 1981.
Hamm, Charles. "John Cage." In *The New Grove Twentieth-Century American
    Masters.* New York: Norton, 1988.
Hamm, Charles, Bruno Nettl, and Ronald Byrnside. *Contemporary Music and
    Music Cultures.* Englewood Cliffs, NJ: Prentice-Hall, 1975.
Manning, Peter. *Electronic and Computer Music.* Oxford: Clarendon Press,
    1985.
Nyman, M. *Experimental Music: Cage and Beyond.* New York: Schirmer,
    1981.
Schrader, Barry. *Introduction to Electro-Acoustic Music.* Englewood Cliffs,
    NJ: Prentice-Hall, 1982.
Vinton, John, ed. *Dictionary of Contemporary Music.* London: Thames and
    Hudson, 1974.

RESOURCE MATERIALS

American Popular Styles

AMERICAN MUSICAL THEATER

For those who wish to incorporate this genre into their course, this resource guide offers a selection of typical examples from the musical theater literature. Proceeding chronologically through the various decades and styles of the Broadway musical, the trends and most important shows and writers for each are named. Suggested listening and reading is provided for each category, and a general bibliography and discography may be found at the end of the section.

A. Early American musical theater: 1890-1930: American musical stage works derived from European operetta; several immigrant composers, such as Victor Herbert and Sigmund Romberg, were particularly important to early success of the genre; American composer and showman George M. Cohan began in vaudeville and achieved considerable stage success, writing snappy up-tempo songs such as "Yankee Doodle Boy" and "Give My Regards to Broadway," both from *Little Johnny Jones* (1904), patriotic songs such as "You're a Grand Old Flag" from *George Washington, Jr.* (1906), and "Over There," the most popular song of the World War I era.

Suggested listening:

> Herbert: *Babes In Toyland*
> > *The Early Victor Herbert.* Reissues. Smithsonian R-017.
> > *The Operetta World of V. Herbert.* JIA Records 1980-5.
> Cohan: *Little Johnny Jones*
> > George M. Cohan: *Yankee Doodle Dandy.* Olympic 7111.
> > *George M. Cohan Songs Sung by George M. Cohan, Jr.* Camden 167.

Selected reading:

> Cohan, George M. *Twenty Years on Broadway.* New York: Harper & Brothers, 1924.
> Waters, Edward N. *Victor Herbert: a Life in Music.* New York: Macmillan, 1955.

B. Broadway in the 1930s: the early period of great achievements on the Broadway stage; the collaboration of Jerome Kern and Oscar Hammerstein II produced *Showboat* in 1927; landmark musical clearly derived from operetta, with real characters and drama from book by Edna Ferber; favorite songs include "Ol' Man River," "Can't Help Lovin' Dat Man," and "Bill"; George Gershwin, pianist and song writer, followed in this tradition; known for his jazz-inspired songs ("I Got Rhythm," "Fascinating Rhythm"); best known for his folk-opera *Porgy and Bess* (1935), based on novel by DuBose Heyward; developed his own popular idiom instead of using folk songs; wrote real arias, recitatives, choruses, orchestral, and ensemble numbers; the work reflects his affinity for black music and musicians; has had many successful revivals; favorite songs from *Porgy and Bess* include "I Got Plenty o' Nothin," "Bess, You Is My Woman Now," "It Ain't Necessarily So," and "Summertime"; other important song and musical theater composers include Irving Berlin ("White Christmas") and Cole Porter (*Anything Goes*).

Suggested listening:

Kern: *Showboat*
Helen Morgan, Paul Robeson (1932 cast). RCS AVM1-1741.
John Raitt, Barbara Cook, William Warfield (1962 cast)
   Columbia CK-02220; cassette JST-02220.
Frederica Von Stada, Teresa Stratas, Jerry Hadley (1988 Studio
   cast) Angel LP A13-19108; CD A23-94108; cassette
   A43-49108.

Gershwin: *Porgy and Bess*
Dale, Abert, Smith, Houston Grand Opera. 3-RCA ARL3- 2109;
   CD RCD3-2109; cassette ARK3-2109.
Haymon, Blackwell, Clarey, White, Baker, Evans. London
   Philharmonic and Glyndebourne Opera Chorus. 3-Angel
   CD CDCC-49568; cassette 4D3S-49568.
Mitchell, White, Boatwright, Quivar, Cleveland Orchestra and
   Chorus. 3-London CD 414559-2 LH3.

Selected reading:

Bordman, Gerald. *Jerome Kern: His Life and Music.* New York:
   Oxford University Press, 1980.
Ewen, David. *The World of Jerome Kern: A Biography.* New York:
   Holt, 1960.
Jablonski, Edward, and Lawrence Stewart. *The Gershwin Years.*
   Garden City: Doubleday, 1973.
Kimball, Robert, and Alfred Simon. *The Gershwins.* New York:
   Atheneum, 1973.
Schwartz, Charles. *Gershwin: His Life and Music.* New York: Bobbs-
   Merrill, 1973.

C. Stage works of the 1940s: collaboration of composer Richard Rodgers and lyricist Oscar Hammerstein II produced some of the best loved musicals of all times, including *Oklahoma* (1943), based on book by Lynn Riggs; represented a return to folk setting in a sophisticated musical idiom; double love triangle characterizes plot; favorite songs include "Oh, What a Beautiful Mornin'," "People Will Say We're In Love," and "The Surrey With the Fringe On Top"; other significant composers of the era include Kurt Weill (*Three-Penny Opera*) Burton Lane (*Finian's Rainbow*); Irving Berlin's *Annie Get Your Gun* a big success; first collaborations of Frederick Loewe and Alan Jay Lerner prove even more fruitful in the 1950s.

Suggested listening:

> Rodgers and Hammerstein: *Oklahoma*
>> Alfred Drake, Joan Roberts (Original cast). MCA cassette MCAC-1630E.
>> John Raitt, Florence Henderson (1964 cast). CSP AOS-2610; cassette BT-2610.
>> Guittard, Andreas (1979 revival). RCA CBL1-3571; CD RCD1-3572; cassette CBK1-3572.

Selected reading:

> Rodgers, Richard. *Musical Stages: an Autobiography*. New York: Random House, 1975.

D. Musical theater in the 1950s: height of the popularity of American musicals; reached a high point in Bernstein's *West Side Story* (1957), especially in songs such as "Maria," "There's a Place For Us," and the elaborate dance episodes; partnership of composer Loewe and lyricist Lerner produced a number of favorite shows, culminating with *My Fair Lady* (1956) and *Camelot* (1960); other popular musicals include Rodgers and Hammerstein's *The King and I*, Meredith Willson's *The Music Man*, and Jule Styne's *Gypsy*, which was recently revived on Broadway with great success.

Suggested listening:

> Bernstein: *West Side Story*
>> Carol Lawrence, Chita Rivera, Larry Kert (1957 Original cast). Columbia JS-32603; CD CK-32603; cassette JST 32603.
>> Te Kanawa, Carreras, Troyanos, Ollmann (Studio cast). 2-DG 415253-1 GH2; CD 415253-2 GH2; cassette 415253-4 GH2.
> Lerner and Loewe: *My Fair Lady*
>> Rex Harrison, Julie Andrews (Original cast). Columbia CD CK-5090; cassette JST-5090.
>> Rex Harrison, Julie Andrews (1959 London cast). Columbia JS-2015; CD CK-2015; cassette JST-2015.
>> Kiri Te Kanawa, Jeremy Irons, John Gielgud (1987 Studio cast). London 421200-1 LH; CD 421200-2 LH; cassette 421200-4 LH.

Selected Reading:

> Lerner, Alan J. *The Musical Theatre: A Celebration*. New York:
> McGraw-Hill, 1986.
> _____. *The Street Where I Live*. New York: Norton, 1980.

E. The 1960s and Beyond: musicals saw the influence of rock (especially
Charles Strouse's *Bye, Bye, Birdie* and Galt McDermot's *Hair*); appeal to
young audiences; shows built on striking female personalities (Jerry
Herman's *Hello, Dolly* and *Mame*); shows with ethnic focus, such as Jerry
Bock's *Fiddler On The Roof*; recent shows characterized by elaborate sets and
stage effects (Andrew Lloyd Webber's *Cats* and *The Phantom of the Opera*);
Sondheim began new trend by unifying music and drama for a through-
composed musical in which tuneful melodies are not prominant (exception is
"Send in the Clowns" from *A Little Night Music*).

Suggested listening:

> Sondheim: *A Little Night Music*
> > Glynis Johns, Len Cariou, Hermione Gingold (Original cast).
> > > Columbia JS-32265; CD CK-32265; cassette JST 32265.
> > Jean Simmons, Hermione Gingold (1975 London Original cast).
> > > RCA LRL1-5090; CD RDC1-5090; cassette LRK1-5090.
> Webber: *Cats*
> > (London Original cast). 2-Geffen 2GHS-2017; cassette 2G5-2017.
> > (1982 Broadway cast). 2-Geffen 2GHS-2031; cassette 2G5-2031.

Selected List of American musicals:

> George M. Cohan:
> > *Little Johnny Jones* (1904)
> > *Forty-Five Minutes from Broadway* (1906)
> > *George Washington, Jr.* (1906)
> Victor Herbert:
> > *The Wizard of the Nile* (1895)
> > *The Fortune Teller* (1898)
> > *Babes in Toyland* (1903)
> > *Mlle. Modiste* (1905)
> > *The Red Mill* (1906)
> > *Naughty Marietta* (1910)
> > *Sweethearts* (1913)
> Sigmund Romberg:
> > *Maytime* (1917)
> > *The Student Prince* (1924)
> > *The Desert Song* (1926)
> > *The New Moon* (1928)
> > *May Wine* (1935)

Jerome Kern:
  Showboat (1927)
  Roberta (1933)
George Gershwin:
  Funny Face (1927)
  Strike Up the Band (1930)
  Of Thee I Sing (1931)
  Porgy and Bess (1935)
Irving Berlin:
  Face the Music (1932)
  As Thousands Cheer (1933)
  Annie Get Your Gun (1946)
Cole Porter:
  Anything Goes (1934)
  Leave It to Me (1938)
  Can-Can (1953)
  Silk Stockings (1955)
Richard Rodgers: (with Lorenz Hart)
  The Girl Friend (1926)
  A Connecticut Yankee (1927)
  On Your Toes (1936)
  I Married An Angel (1938)
  The Boys From Syracuse (1938)
  Pal Joey (1940)
Richard Rodgers: (with O. Hammerstein)
  Oklahoma (1943)
  Carousel (1945)
  Allegro (1947)
  South Pacific (1949)
  The King and I (1951)
  My Fair Lady (1956)
  The Sound of Music (1959)
Kurt Weill:
  Lady in the Dark (1941)
  Street Scene (1947)
  Three-Penny Opera (1954)
Harold Arlen:
  Bloomer Girl (1944)
  St. Louis Woman (1946)
  House of Flowers (1954)
Burton Lane:
  Finian's Rainbow (1947)
  On a Clear Day You Can See Forever (1965)
Frederick Loewe: (with A. J. Lerner)
  Brigadoon (1947)
  Paint Your Wagon (1951)

My Fair Lady (1956)
Camelot (1960)
Harold Rome:
Fanny (1954)
Leonard Bernstein:
Wonderful Town (1953)
On the Town (1954)
Candide (1956)
West Side Story (1957)
Meredith Willson:
The Music Man (1957)
The Unsinkable Molly Brown (1960)
Frank Loesser:
Guys and Dolls (1950)
The Most Happy Fella (1956)
How to Succeed in Business Without Really Trying (1961)
Jule Styne:
Gypsy (1959)
Peter Pan (1954)
Funny Girl (1964)
Harvey Schmidt:
The Fantasticks (1960)
Charles Strouse:
Bye, Bye, Birdie (1960)
Annie (1977)
Jerry Bock:
Fiddler On the Roof (1964)
Jerry Herman:
Hello Dolly! (1964)
Mame (1966)
La Cage aux Folles (1983)
Mitch Leigh:
Man of La Mancha (1965)
Cy Coleman:
Sweet Charity (1966)
John Kander:
Cabaret (1966)
Galt MacDermot:
Hair (1968)
Sherman Edwards:
1776 (1969)
Stephen Sondheim:
Company (1970)
A Little Night Music (1973)
Sweeney Todd (1979)

Sunday in the Park with George (1983)
Into the Woods (1988)
Stephen Schwartz:
    Godspell (1971)
Andrew Lloyd Webber:
    Jesus Christ Superstar (1971)
    Evita (1978)
    Cats (1981)
    The Phantom of the Opera (1986)
Marvin Hamlisch:
    A Chorus Line (1975)
Arthur Malvin:
    Sugar Babies (1979)
Henry Krieger:
    Dreamgirls (1981)
Roger Miller:
    Big River (1985)

Selected Readings:

Bloom, Ken, ed. *American Song: The Complete Musical Theatre Companion.* New York: Facts-On-File, 1985.

Bordman, Gerald. *American Musical Theatre: A Chronicle.* New York: Oxford Univ. Press, 1978.

_____. *American Operetta: From H.M.S. Pinafore to Sweeney Todd.* New York: Oxford Univ. Press, 1981.

_____. *American Musical Comedy: From Adonis to Dreamgirls.* New York: Oxford Univ. Press, 1982.

_____. *American Musical Revue: From The Passing Show to Sugar Babies.* New York: Oxford Univ. Press, 1985.

_____. *Oxford Companion to American Musical Theatre.* New York: Oxford Univ. Press, 1984.

Green, Stanley. *Broadway Musicals Show By Show.* Milwaukee, WI: Hal Leonard, 1985.

_____. *Encyclopedia of the Musical Theatre.* New York: Dodd, Mead, 1976; repr, 1980.

_____. *The World of Musical Comedy.* 4th ed. New York: A.S. Barnes, 1980.

Mates, Julian. *America's Musical Stage: Two Hundred Years of Musical Theatre.* Westport, CT: Greenwood, 1985.

Mordden, Ethan. *Better Foot Forward: The History of the American Musical Theater.* New York: Grossman, 1976.

_____. *The Hollywood Musical.* New York: St. Martin's 1971.

Wildbibler, Hubert, and Sonja Völklein. *The Musical: An International Annotated Bibliography.* Munich: Saur, 1986.

Selected Discographies:

> American Society of Composers, Authors, and Publishers. *40 Years of Show Tunes: the Big Broadway Hits from 1917-57.* New York: ASCAP, 1958.
> Hodgins, Gordon W. *The Broadway Musical: A Complete LP Discography.* Metuchen, NJ: Scarecrow, 1980.
> Raymond, Jack. *Show Music on Record from the 1890s to the 1980s.* New York: Frederick Munger, 1982.

BLUES AND JAZZ

This resource is designed to help integrate the instruction of various blues and jazz styles into the music appreciation curriculum. It is organized chronologically through three blues styles (Rural, City, and Urban) and eight jazz styles (New Orleans and Chicago; Big Band and Swing; Bebop; Cool; Hard Bop and Funk; Free; Third Stream; and Fusion). For each, a brief overview is provided, along with a list of suggested listening and readings. The suggested listening examples for jazz are all well-known works, for which a number of recordings exist. For convenience, most of them may be found in *The Smithsonian Collection of Classic Jazz,* a five-cassette package with an informative booklet by Martin Williams. A general bibliography and list of discographies concludes each section.

Blues

A. Rural Blues: originated in Mississippi Delta and east Texas; characteristically performed by male singer with acoustic guitar; 12-bar form with individual singing styles; prevalent use of bending notes; spread with first recordings by Blind Lemon Jefferson in 1926; other important early rural blues singers include Charley Patton and Robert Johnson.

Suggested Recordings:

> *Afro-American Blues and Games Songs.* AAFS L-4.
> *Anthology of American Folk Music,* vol. 3. Folkways 2953.
> *The Blues,* vol. 2 of *The History of Jazz.* Folkways 2802.
> *Blues Roots: Mississippi.* Folkways RF-14.
> *Negro Blues and Hollers.* AAFS L-5.
> *Roots of the Blues.* New World NW-252.
> *The Rural Blues: A Story of Vocal and Instrumental Resources.* Folkways RF-202.
> *The Story of the Blues.* 2 LPS. Columbia CG 30008.

B. City Blues: "classic" period begins with recordings (c. 1920); dominated by women singers with large, "throaty," alto voices; earthy, sexual themes; outstanding were Gertrude "Ma" Rainey, who remained close to the folk tradition, and Bessie Smith, perhaps the greatest early blues singer whose style was more jazz-inspired; recorded with leading jazz musicians.

Suggested recordings:

Ma Rainey:
Blame It On the Blues. Milestone 2008.
Blues the World Forgot. Biograph 12001.
Ma Rainey. 2 LPs Milestone 47021.
Ma Rainey's Black Bottom. 7 LPs. Yazoo 1071.
Oh My Babe Blues. Biograph BLP 12011.
Queen of the Blues. Biograph BLP 12032.
Bessie Smith:
Any Woman's Blues. Columbia CGT-30126.
The Empress. Columbia CGT 30818.
Empty Bed Blues. Columbia CGT 30450.
Nobody's Blues But Mine. Columbia CGT 31093.
The Collection (1922-23). Columbia Jazz Masterpieces CJ 44441; CD CK 44441; cassette CJT 44441.

C. Urban Blues: developed post-World War II; employs amplification with a solo male singer and instrumental group; characterized by saxophones and brass with sustained chords and riffs; most important performers were T-Bone Walker and B. B. King.

Suggested recordings:

Anthology of Rhythm and Blues. Columbia CS 9802.
The Best of B. B. King, 2 vols. Ace 198-99.
Super Black Blues. Bluestime BT 29003.

General Bibliography:

Baraka, Amiri (Leroy Jones). *Blues People.* New York: Morrow, 1963.
Bogaert, Karel. *Blues Lexikon: Blues, Cajun, Boogie Woogie, Gospel.* Antwerp: Standaard, 1972.
Cook, Bruce. *Listen to the Blues.* New York: Scribner's 1973.
Ferris, William. *Blues from the Delta.* New York: Da Capo, 1984.
Gillett, Charlie. *The Sound of the City.* New York: Dell, 1970.
Harris, Shelton. *Blues Who's Who: A Biographical Dictionary of Blues Singers.* New York: Da Capo, c. 1979.
Keil, Charles. *Urban Blues.* Chicago: Univ. of Chicago Press, 1966.
Oliver, Paul. *Bessie Smith.* New York: Barnes, 1961.
_____. *The Meaning of the Blues.* New York: Macmillan, 1960.
_____. *The Story of the Blues.* New York: Chilton, 1969.
Shaw, Arnold. *Black Popular Music in America.* New York: Schirmer, 1986.

_____. *Honkers and Shouters: The Golden Years of Rhythm & Blues.* New York: Macmillan, 1978.

_____. *The World of Soul: Black America's Contribution to the Pop Music Scene.* New York: Cowles, 1970.

Stambler, Irwin. *Encyclopedia of Pop, Rock, and Soul.* New York: St. Martin's, 1977.

Taft, Michael. *Blues Lyric Poetry: An Anthology.* New York: Garland, 1983.

Titon, Keff Todd. *Early Downhome Blues: A Musical and Cultural Analysis.* Urbana: Univ. of Illinois, 1977.

Discography:

Godrich, J. and R. Dixon. *Blues and Gospel Records, 1902-1942.* 2nd ed. London: Storyville, 1969.

Leadbitter, Mike, and Neil Slaven. *Blues Records, January 1943 to December 1966.* London: Hanover, 1968.

Marsh, Dave, and John Swenson. *The Rolling Stone Record Guide.* New York: Random House, 1979.

Jazz

A. Early Jazz (New Orleans and Chicago): evolved parallel to ragtime, around 1900; New Orleans jazz was polyphonic, with melody in cornet, clarinet countermelody, simpler trombone melody and rhythm section; telegraphed chord changes; some solos; influential figures include cornetist Joseph "King" Oliver, pianist Ferdinand "Jelly Roll" Morton, and trumpeter Louis "Satchmo" Armstrong; action moved to Chicago where recordings were made; derivative New Orleans style lacking some of its spontaneity; Armstrong's melodic-rhythmic style called "swing"; he was first great improvising soloist; scat singing introduced by Armstrong.

Suggested listening:

King Oliver:
    Dippermouth Blues (Smithsonian 1/5).
Jelly Roll Morton:
    Black Bottom Stomp (Smithsonian 1/6).
    Dead Man's Blues (Smithsonian 1/7).
    Grandpa's Spells (Smithsonian 1/8).
Louis Armstrong:
    Big Butter and Egg Man From the West (Smithsonian 1/13).
    Potato Head Blues (Smithsonian 2/1).
    Struttin' With Some Barbecue (Smithsonian 2/6).
    Hotter Than That (Smithsonian 2/7).

Selected reading:

> Armstrong, Louis. *Satchmo: My Life in New Orleans.* New York: Prentice-Hall, 1954.
>
> Charters, Samuel B. *Jazz: New Orleans.* Rev. ed. New York: Oak, 1963.
>
> Schuller, Gunther. *Early Jazz: Its Roots and Musical Development.* New York: Oxford Univ. Press, 1968.
>
> Williams, Martin. *Jazz Masters of New Orleans.* Rev. ed. New York: Macmillan, 1979.

B. Big Band and Swing: beginning of big bands with Fletcher Henderson's group which reached height of popularity in mid-1930s; Henderson ensemble of 3 trumpets, 2 trombones, 4 saxophones (doubling on clarinets), and 4 rhythm instruments; sections played antiphonally; use of riffs and written-out variations; Benny Goodman brought style of swing to a pinnacle; Count Basie began as pianist in Bennie Motin band; important vocal improvisations including those by Billie Holliday and Ella Fitzgerald.

Suggested listening:

> Fletcher Henderson:
> > *The Stampede* (Smithsonian 3/7).
> > *Wrappin' It Up* (Smithsonian 3/8).
>
> Bennie Motin:
> > *Motin Swing* (Smithsonian 4/1).
>
> Billie Holiday:
> > *He's Funny That Way* (Smithsonian 4/7).
> > *These Foolish Things* (Smithsonian 4/8).
>
> Ella Fitzgerald:
> > *You'd Be So Nice to Come Home To* (Smithsonian 5/1).
>
> Count Basie:
> > *Doggin' Around* (Smithsonian 5/9).
> > *Taxi War Dance* (Smithsonian 6/1).
> > *Lester Leaps In* (Smithsonian 6/2).
>
> Benny Goodman:
> > *I Found a New Baby* (Smithsonian 6/3).
> > *Breakfast Feud* (Smithsonian 6/4).
>
> Duke Ellington:
> > *East St. Louis Toodle-Oo* (Smithsonian 6/5-6).
> > *Concerto for Cootie* (Smithsonian 7/1).
> > *Cotton Tail* (Smithsonian 7/2).

Selected reading:

> Dance, Stanley. *The World of Count Basie.* New York: Scribner's, 1980.
>
> _____. *The World of Duke Ellington.* New York: Scribner's, 1970.
>
> _____. *The World of Swing.* New York: Scribner's, 1974.

Ellington, Duke. *Music is My Mistress*. Garden City, NY: Doubleday, 1973.

Schuller, Gunther. *The Swing Era: The Development of Jazz, 1930-45*. New York: Oxford Univ. Press, 1989.

C. Bebop or bop: a jazz style of the 1940s and 50s based on melodic improvisation; the two syllables of word bebop suggest a two-note phrase which was trademark of the style; first outstanding proponents of style were saxophonist Charlie Parker, trumpeter Dizzy Gillespie, pianist Thelonius Monk, and drummer Kenny Clarke; small ensembles of virtuoso performers; fast tempos with light rhythm accompaniment; harmonically complex; music for listening rather than dancing.

Suggested listening:

Dizzy Gillespie:
I Can't Get Started (Smithsonian 7/6).
Shaw 'Nuff (Smithsonian 7/7).
Charlie Parker:
Ko-Ko (Smithsonian 7/8).
Lady Be Good (Smithsonian 8/1).
Embraceable You (Smithsonian 8/2-3).
Klactoveedsedstene (Smithsonian 8/42).
Crazeology (Smithsonian 8/5-6).
Parker's Mood (Smithsonian 8/7).

Selected reading:

Gillespie, D., and A. Fraser. *To Be, or Not . . . to Bop: Memoirs*. Garden City, 1979.

Russell, R. "Bebop." In *The Art of Jazz: Essays on the Nature and Development of Jazz*, ed. by M. Williams. New York, 1979.

Spellman, A. B. *Black Music: Four Lives in the Bebop Business*. New York: Schocken, 1970.

D. Cool jazz: a 1950s jazz adapted from bebop in a more detached, objective style; characterized by moderate tempos and volume levels, middle registers, mellow timbres, and smoothly-delivered phrases; gave rise to West Coast jazz; representatives include Miles Davis, Dave Brubeck, Stan Getz, Lennie Tristano, Thelonius Monk, and the Modern Jazz Quartet.

Suggested listening:

Miles Davis:
Boplicity (Smithsonian 9/3).
Lenny Tristano:
Subconscious Lee (Smithsonian 9/4).

Gene Norman's "Just Jazz," featuring Red Norvo and Stan Getz:
> *Body and Soul* (Smithsonian 9/5).

Thelonius Monk:
> *Criss-Cross* (Smithsonian 10/3).

Modern Jazz Quartet:
> *Django* (Smithsonian 11/3).

Selected reading:

> Gridley, Mark C. *Jazz Styles.* 2nd ed. Englewood Cliffs, NJ: Prentice Hall, 1984.
>
> Williams, Martin. "Bebop and After." In *Jazz: New Perspectives on the History of Jazz.* Rev. ed., ed. by N. Hentoff and A. J. McCarthy. New York, Da Capo, 1974.

E. Hard bop and funk: evolved from bop as a reaction to cool jazz; interest in black gospel roots of jazz; characteristics much like those of bop with more relaxed tempos; funky jazz featured complex syncopation or Latin beats played with darker timbres, especially the tenor saxophone; leader of style was drummer Art Blakey.

Suggested listening:

> Horace Silver Quintet:
> > *Moon Rays* (Smithsonian 10/6).

Selected reading:

> Bruynincx, Walter. *Jazz: Modern Jazz, Be-Bop, Hard Bop, West Coast.* Mechelen: 60 Years of Recorded Jazz Team, 1985.

F. Free jazz: developed in late 1950s as a reaction against conventions of bop; explores simultaneous improvisations, thematic variation, motivic development, open forms, new timbral effects, extreme registers of instruments, and free meter; free chord progressions and approach to tonality; representative artists are saxophonists Ornette Coleman and John Coltrane.

Suggested listening:

> Ornette Coleman:
> > *Lonely Woman* (Smithsonian 13/4).
> > *Congeniality* (Smithsonian 14/1).
> > *Free Jazz*, excerpt (Smithsonian 14/2).
>
> John Coltrane:
> > *Alabama* (Smithsonian 13/3).
>
> World Saxophone Quartet:
> > *Steppin'* (Smithsonian 14/3).

Selected reading:

Carles, P., and J.-L. Comolli. *Free Jazz, Black Power.* Paris, 1971.
Jost, Ekkehard. *Free Jazz.* Graz: Universal, 1974.
Litweiler, J. *The Freedom Principle: Jazz After 1958.* New York, 1984.
Rabin, E. *A Discography of Free Jazz.* Copenhagen, 1969.

G. Third Stream: merger of classical and jazz elements; term coined by Gunther Schuller; incorporates instruments and procedures from classical traditions; adopted by several big bands, including those of Woody Herman and Duke Ellington, and by small combos, especially of West Coast School (Dave Brubeck, Paul Desmond, Gerry Mulligan); John Lewis and the Modern Jazz Quartet were important to the movement.

Suggested listening:

Duke Ellington:
> *Black, Brown and Beige.* 1943; rerecorded by A. Cohen, Argo
> ZDA 159, 1972.

Dave Brubeck:
> *Time Out.* Columbia CS 8192, 1960.

Gunther Schuller:
> *Variations on a Theme of John Lewis.* Atlantic 1365, 1960.
> *Abstraction and Variations on a Theme by Thelonius Monk.*
> Atlantic 1365, 1960.

Selected reading:

Schuller, G. "Third Stream Revisited." In *Musings: The Musical Worlds
of Gunther Schuller.* New York: Oxford Univ. Press, 1986.
Williams, M. "Third Stream Problems." In *Jazz Heritage.* New York:
Oxford Univ. Press, 1985.

H. Fusion: style of the 1970s that combines jazz and rock; characterized by long, improvised melodies on electronic instruments, strong Latin or rock rhythms, and ostinato harmonies and rhythms; exemplified by Miles Davis's band of the 1960s and work of pianists Chick Corea and Herbie Hancock.

Suggested listening:

Miles Davis:
> *Bitches' Brew.* Columia 2-Gp26, 1969.

Chick Corea:
> *Return to Forever.* ECM ST 2011, 1972.

Herbie Hancock:
> *Sextant.* Columbia KC 32212, 1973.

Selected Reading:

> Chambers, J. *Milestones II: Miles Davis Since 1960*. Toronto, 1985.
> Feather, Leonard G., and Ira Gitler. *The Encyclopedia of Jazz in the Seventies*. New York: Horizon, 1976.

General Bibliography

> Carl Gregor, Duke of Mecklenburg. *International Jazz Bibliography: Jazz Books from 1919-1968*. Strasbourg: Heitz, 1969.
> Chilton, John. *Who's Who of Jazz*. Philadelphia: Chilton, 1972.
> Collier, Paul. *The Making of Jazz: A Comprehensive History*. New York, 1978.
> Feather, Leonard. *The Encyclopedia of Jazz*. New York: Da Capo, 1984.
> Gitler, Ira. *Jazz Masters of the Forties*. New York: Macmillan, 1966.
> _____. *Swing to Bop*. New York: Oxford Univ. Press, 1986.
> Goldberg, Joe. *Jazz Masters of the Fifties*. New York: Macmillan, 1966.
> Gridley, Mark C. *Jazz Styles*. 2nd ed. Englewood Cliffs, NJ: Prentice Hall, 1989.
> Hadlock, Richard. *Jazz Masters of the Twenties*. New York: Macmillan, 1965.
> Hefele, Bernhard. *Jazz-bibliography*. New York: Saur, 1981.
> Hentoff, Nat, and Albert McCarthy, eds. *Jazz: New Perspectives on the History of Jazz*. New York: Da Capo, 1974.
> Kinkle, Roger D. *The Complete Encyclopedia of Popular Music and Jazz, 1900-1950*. New Rochelle: Arlington, 1974.
> Meadows, Eddie S. *Jazz Reference and Research Materials: A Bibliography*. New York: Garland, 1981.
> Sales, G. *Jazz: America's Classical Music*. Englewood Cliffs: Prentice-Hall, 1984.

General Discography

> Allen, Walter C. *Studies in Jazz Discography*. Rutgers, NJ: Institute of Jazz Studies, 1971.
> Harrison, M., C. Fox, and E. Thacker. *The Essential Jazz Records I: Ragtime to Swing*. London, 1984.
> Harrison, M., et al. *Modern Jazz: the Essential Records (1945-70)*. London, 1975.
> Jepson, Jorgen Grunnet. *Jazz Records: A Discography, 1942-[1969]*. Holte, Denmark: Knudsen, 1963-70.
> McCarthy, A., et al. *Jazz on Record: a Critical Guide to the First Fifty Years: 1917-67*. London, 1968.

ROCK AND COUNTRY MUSIC

This guide is designed to assist those who wish to include some American popular music in their music appreciation curriculum. Although there are many different styles, rock and country/western have been chosen as two that have had a great impact on society. (Note that there are separate resource guides for blues, jazz, and musical theater as well.) Rock has become the dominant form of popular music since its emergence only a quarter of a century ago. It is the product and expression of our urban society. Similarly, country music is the product of contemporary rural life and its values. In this resource we survey some of the dominant trends of these two musical styles, suggesting representative performers, recordings, and readings.

Rock Music

A. Early Rock: white popular music style that grew out of black rhythm and blues; first rock and roll hit was Bill Haley's *Rock Around the Clock* (1955); black rhythm and blues influence strong, along with white country music influences in work of Elvis Presley; black artists, such as Chuck Berry, easily adapted the rhythm and blues style to white tastes; electric guitar became standard to rock group.

Suggested listening:

> Bill Haley:
>> *Rock Around the Clock*. Golden Hits, Bill Haley and the Comets. MCA 2-4010.
>
> Elvis Presley:
>> *Heartbreak Hotel*. World Wide 50 Gold Award Hits. RCA 6401.
>
> Chuck Berry:
>> *Johnny B. Goode*. Chuck Berry's Golden Decade, vol. 1, Chess 1514; vol. 2, Chess 60023

B. Rock of the 1960s: regional styles developed (California surfing songs, Beach Boys) and spread in popularity among teens; British popular music invaded the American scene, especially the Beatles, who were much imitated; the British and American rock music styles became interwoven, characterized by eclecticism.

Suggested listening:

> Beatles:
>> *And I Love Her* (early period)
>>> A Hard Day's Night. United Artists 6366.
>>> Something New. Capitol ST 2108
>
> Beatles:
>> *Lucy In the Sky With Diamonds* (late period)
>>> Sgt. Pepper's Lonely Hearts Club Band. Capitol SMAL 2835

Rolling Stones:
> *Satisfaction*. Out of Our Heads. London PS 429

C. Folk-rock: a fusion of folk music with the amplification of rock; grew out of the urban folk tradition of the 50s and 60s (Kingston Trio, Peter, Paul, and Mary, and Joan Baez); best-known proponent is Bob Dylan, who switched to rock-style accompaniment in 1965; lyrics reflect social and political issues, often presented with satirical tone; other folk-rock performers include Paul Simon, Judy Collins, and Joni Mitchell.

Suggested listening:

Bob Dylan:
> *Mr. Tambourine Man*. Bringing It All Back Home. Columbia PC
> 9128

Simon and Garfunkel:
> *Sounds of Silence*. Greatest Hits. Columbia PC 9529

Selected reading:

> Stanley, Lana. *Folk Rock: A Bibliography on Music of the Sixties*. San
> Jose, CA: San Jose State College, 1979.

D. Jazz-rock: fusion of rock and jazz in the late 1960s, especially by Blood, Sweat, and Tears, and Chicago; rock band with added instruments (saxophones, brass); combines insistent rock beat with freedom of jazz improvisation, producing lengthy pieces.

Suggested listening:

> Blood, Sweat, and Tears: *Spinning Wheel*. Greatest Hits. Columbia PC
> 31170

> Chicago: *Does Anybody Really Know What Time It Is?* Greatest Hits.
> Columbia JC 33900

E. Some Recent Trends

1. Art rock (or progressive rock): a style developed in the 1970s characterized by use of large forms and complex harmonies; one of earliest examples is adaptation made by Emerson, Lake, and Palmer of Mussorgsky's *Pictures at an Exhibition*; representative performers include Yes and Kansas.

2. Punk and New Wave: underground rock movements characterized by spontaneity and anti-art attitude; punk evolved as a social protest among working class youth in the mid-1970s; movement began in New York City, then spread to London (the Sex Pistols); devotees intended to shock society in their dress and violent or base behavior; new wave was an outgrowth of punk rock with intent to simplify; well-known performers include Elvis Costello, Patti Smith, the Talking Heads, and Brian Eno.

Selected reading:

> Coon, Caroline. *1988: The New Wave Punk Rock Explosion*. New York: Hawthorn, 1988.

3. Reggae: an ethnic style that originated in Jamaica in the 1960s; characterized by strongly syncopated rhythms, accenting weak beats of quadruple meter; reggae represents a synthesis of various styles, including rhythm and blues and African and Jamaican folk music, especially ska; lyrics of reggae relate to Rastafarianism, a black religious movement that venerates the late Haile Selassie, emperor of Ethopia; best-known reggae musicians in the United States are Bob Marley and the Wailers, Toots and the Maytails, Peter Tosh, and Black Uhuru.

Selected Reading:

> Bennetzen, Jorgen. "Reggae." *Fontis artis musicae* 29 (1982): 182-86.

4. Rap: an ethnic style that originated in the black culture of New York's South Bronx; characterized by rapid talking rather than singing over a rock accompaniment; lyrics are often political or social in content; style originated with black disk jockeys, and earlier, with black preaching and the "talking blues." Representative performers include Run D.M.C., Tonloc, and Bobby Brown.

5. Heavy Metal: a rock style characterized by high amplification, a languid beat, and blues-type forms; style originally flourished in the late 1960s and 70s; Jimi Hendrix was an early heavy metal performer; has undergone a revival in the 1980s; representative performers include Ozzy Osborne, Iron Maiden, and Metallica.

6. New Age: a recent style characterized by a return to simplicity; often uses folk-like melodies and folk instruments; also combines acoustic instruments with extensive use of synthesizer; draws on minimalism through use of ostinati and short repeated progressions; effect is hypnotic, meditative; important performers include Mannheim Steamroller, George Winston, and Kitaro.

General Bibliography

> Bane, Michael. *Who's Who in Rock*. New York: Everest House, 1982.
> Belz, Carl. *The Story of Rock*. New York: Oxford University Press, 1972.
> Bianco, David. *Who's New Wave in Music: An Illustrated Encyclopedia, 1976-1982*. Ann Arbor, Mich.: Pierian Press, 1985.
> Brown, Charles. *The Art of Rock and Roll*. Englewood Cliffs, NJ: Prentice-Hall, 1983.

Clifford, Mike. *The Harmony Illustrated Encyclopedia of Rock.* 5th ed. New York: Harmony, 1986.

Gillett, Charlie. *The Sound of the City.* Rev. ed. New York: Pantheon, 1984.

Grossman, L. *A Social History of Rock.* New York, 1976.

Hamm, Charles. *Yesterdays: Popular Song in America.* New York: Norton, 1979.

Herbst, Peter, ed. *The Rolling Stone Interviews: Talking with the Legends of Rock and Roll.* New York: St. Martin's, 1981.

Helander, Bruce. *The Rock Who's Who: a Biographical Dictionary and Critical Discography.* New York: Schirmer, 1982.

Hendler, Herb. *Year by Year in the Rock Era: Events and Conditions Shaping the Rock Generations that Reshaped America.* Westport, CT: Greenwood, 1983.

Hoffmann, Frank. *The Literature of Rock, 1954-1978.* Metuchen: Scarecrow Press, 1981.

Jaspar, Tony, and Derek Oliver. *The International Encyclopedia of Hard Rock & Heavy Metal.* Rev. ed. London: Sidgwick & Jackson, 1986.

Middletown, Richard, and David Horn, eds. *Popular Music.* Cambridge: Cambridge Univ. Press, 1981.

Miller, Jim, ed. *The Rolling Stone Illustrated History of Rock & Roll.* New York: Rolling Stone, c. 1980.

Pareles, John, and Patricia Romanowski. *The Rolling Stone Encyclopedia of Rock & Roll.* New York: Rolling Stone, 1983.

Rockwell, John. *All American Music.* New York: Knopf, 1983.

Roxon, Lillian. *Rock Encyclopedia.* Rev. ed. New York: The University Library, 1978.

Shaw, Arnold, ed. *Dictionary of American Pop/Rock.* New York: Schirmer, 1982.

York, William. *Who's Who in Rock Music.* Rev. ed. New York: Scribner, 1982.

General Discography

Gargan, William, and Sue Sharma. *Find That Tune: An Index to Rock, Folk-Rock, Disco, and Soul in Collections.* New York: Neal-Shumann, 1984.

Helander, Bruce. *The Rock Who's Who: a Biographical Dictionary and Critical Discography.* New York: Schirmer, 1982.

Helander, Brock. *Rock 'n Roll: A Discography.* Sacramento: Helander, 1978.

Marsh, Dave, and John Swenson. *The New Rolling Stone Record Guide.* New York: Random House, 1983.

Rohde, H. Kandy, ed. *The Gold of Rock & Roll, 1955-1967.* New York: Arbor House, 1970.

Tudor, Dean. *Popular Music: An Annotated Guide to Recordings.* Littleton, CO: Libraries Unlimited, 1983.

Country Music

This music spread in popularity from rural South in the 1930s and 40s, aided by radio broadcasting; mainly played on string instruments (fiddle, guitar, dulcimer, banjo, mandolin, steel guitar, string bass); vocal tone characterized by nasal, high, tense sound; folk-like melodies with simple harmonic accompaniments; sentimental subjects; commercialization began with Jimmie Rodgers; more recent stars include Hank Williams, a masterful songwriter who sang his own earthy material nearly exclusively, viewed as a sex symbol; style derived from black blues singers; Johnny Cash, who excelled in up-tempo country ballads, especially prison songs; and Loretta Lynn, viewed as "Queen of Country Music"; sang her own songs in lyrical style; early figure in women's liberation front; influence of blues produced bluegrass music, a virtuoso style of playing with driving speed, intricate string instrumentation, and traditional lyrics; Bill Monroe and the Blue Grass Boys gave style its name.

Suggested listening:

Hank Williams:
> *Your Cheatin' Heart.* In the Beginning. BM 705 (Canadian issue)

Johnny Cash:
> *I Walk the Line.* Greatest Hits. 3 vols. Columbia PC 9478,
> PC 30887; KC 35637

Bill Monroe:
> *Muleskinner Blues.* The Classic Bluegrass Recordings. 2 vols.
> County CCS 104-5

General Bibliography

Dellar, Fred, Roy Thompson, and Douglas Green. *The Illustrated Encyclopedia of Country Music.* New York: Harmony, 1977.

Gentry, Linnell, ed. *A History and Encyclopedia of Country, Western, and Gospel Music.* 2nd ed. Nashville: Clairmont, 1969.

Green, Douglas B. *Country Roots: The Origins of Country Music.* New York: Hawkins, 1976.

Grissim, John. *Country Music: White Man's Blues.* New York: Paperback Library, 1970.

Kahn, Kathy. *Hillbilly Women.* Garden City: Doubleday, 1973.

Malone, Bill C. *Country Music, U.S.A.: A Fifty-Year History*, rev. ed. Austin: Univ. of Texas Press, 1985.

_____. *Southern Music— American Music.* Lexington: Univ. of Kentucky, 1979.

Rooney, James. *Bossmen: Bill Monroe and Muddy Waters.* New York: Dial, 1971.

Rosenberg, Neil. *Bluegrass: A History.* Urbana: Univ. of Illinois Press, 1985.

Shestack, Melvin. *The Country Music Encyclopedia.* New York: Crowell, 1974.

Stambler, Irwin, and Grelun Landon. *The Encyclopedia of Folk, Country & Western Music.* 2nd ed. New York: St. Martin's, 1983.

Selected Recordings:

Country Music in the Modern Era: 1940s-1970s. New Works NW-207.
Country Music South and West. New World NW-287.
Hills and Home: Thirty Years of Bluegrass. New World NW-225.
The Smithsonian Collection of Classic Country Music, ed. by B. Malone. 8 LPs.

Discography:

Rosenberg, Neil. *Bill Monroe and His Bluegrass Boys: An Illustrated Discography.* Nashville: Country Music Foundation, 1974.

Tudor, Dean, and Nancy Tudor. *Grass Roots Music.* Littleton, CO: Libraries Unlimited, 1979.

Tudor, Dean. *Popular Music: An Annotated Guide to Recordings.* Littleton, CO: Libraries Unlimited, 1983.

Whitburn, Joel. *Top Country and Western Records, 1949-1971.* Menemonee Falls, WI: Record Research, 1972.

Music of Black Americans

The following are suggestions for teaching a unit on black American music, exclusive of blues and jazz which are covered in a separate resource guide in this handbook. The topics covered here include: spirituals and minstrelsy; ragtime, represented by Scott Joplin; African-American elements incorporated into a nationalist idiom, as represented by William Grant Still; third stream composition, represented by David Baker; and Neo-Classicism, represented by Julia Perry. We have provided a list of the best-known works with recordings and a short bibliography of readings on each topic. This is followed by a more extensive general bibliography.

A. Spirituals and minstrelsy: spirituals were religious songs of blacks with texts formed from bits of prayers, Biblical verses, psalms, and pledges, with melodies that were improvised or borrowed from existing tunes. They were generally sung after regular church services, along with a type of religious dancing known as "shouts"; both reflect enduring African traditions among black Christians. After the emancipation, black plantation songs persisted as an important part of minstrel shows, often sung by black musicians in updated arrangements. Several blacks were celebrated minstrel song writers, whose newly-composed works made direct reference to slave songs in music and text; among them was Gussie Lord Davis, who was the first black composer to succeed in Tin Pan Alley.

Selected recordings:

> *Afro-American Spirituals, Work Songs, and Ballads.* Library of
> Congress AAFS-L3.
> *An Introduction to American Negro Folk Music.* Folkways FA 2691.
> *Music from the South.* Folkways FP 650-58.
> *Southern Folk Heritage Series,* ed. by A. Lomax. Atlantic 1346-52.
> *The Rural Blues*, ed. S. Charters. RFB Records RF 202.

Selected Readings:

> Brooks, R. *America's Black Musical Heritage.* Englewood Cliffs, NJ:
> Prentice-Hall, 1984.
> Epstein, D. *Sinful Tunes and Spirituals: Black Folk Music to the Civil
> War.* Urbana, IL, 1977.
> Floyd, S. A. and M. J. Reisser. *Black Music in the United States: an
> Annotated Bibliography of Selected References and Research
> Materials.* Millwood, NY: Kraus International, 1983.
> Jackson, George Pullen. *White and Negro Spirituals.* New York:
> Augustin, 1943.
> Nettl, Bruno. *Folk and Traditional Music of the Western Continents.*
> 2nd ed. Englewood Cliffs, NJ: Prentice Hall, 1973.
> Roberts, John Storm. *Black Music of Two Worlds.* New York: Praeger,
> 1972.
> Southern, Eileen. *The Music of Black Americans.* 2nd ed. New York:
> Norton, 1983.
> _____. *Readings in Black American Music.* 2nd. New York: Norton,
> 1983.

B. Scott Joplin (1868-1917), the "King of Ragtime," one of the important precursors to jazz; published many rags, the most famous of which is *The Maple Leag Rag* (1899); 2 operas and a ballet; opera *Treemonisha* awarded a Pulitzer Prize in 1972.

Best-known works include:
> *Maple-Leaf Rag* (1899) and *The Entertainer* (1902)
> > Recorded by Joshua Rifkin. Nonesuch H-71248; and by Joplin
> > himself, reproduced by piano rolls on Biograph BCD-101
> *Treemonisha* (1911)
> > Recorded by Houston Grand Opera; Balthrop, Allen, White,
> > Schuller. 2-DG 423308-1 GH2

Selected Readings

Berlin, E. *Ragtime: a Musical and Cultural History.* Berkeley, CA: Univ. of California Press, 1980; repr. 1984.

Blesh, Rudi and Harriet Janis. *They All Played Ragtime.* 4th ed. New York: Oak, 1971.

Gammond, P. *Scott Joplin and the Ragtime Era.* New York, 1978.

Haskins J., and K. Benson. *Scott Joplin: the Man who made Ragtime.* New York, 1978.

Jasen, D. and T. Tichenor. *Rags and Ragtime: a Musical History.* New York: Seabury Press, 1978.

Lawrence, V. B. *The Complete Works of Scott Joplin,* 2 vols. New York: 1981.

Reed, Addison. "Scott Joplin." In *The New Grove Dictionary of Music and Musicians*, ed. by S. Sadie. London: Macmillan, 1980, 9:708-09.

C. William Grant Still (1895-1978), studied at Oberlin Conservatory and with Edgard Varèse and George Chadwick; best known for his Romantic, tonal style in nationalist works, many of which use black folk idioms; he was the first black composer to have a work played by a major orchestra (*Afro-American Symphony*, 1930) and to have an opera performed by a leading opera company (*Troubled Island*, 1949); output includes 5 symphonies, other orchestral works, choral works, piano music, and songs.

Best-known works include:

Afro-American Symphony (1930)

Recorded by Orchestra of the Vienna Opera; Karl Krueger, conductor. NRLP 205 New Records; and London Symphony Orchestra; Paul Freeman, conductor. Columbia M 32782 (1974). Musical Score: rev. 1969. London: Novello, 1970.

Festive Overture (1944)

Recorded by Royal Philharmonic Orchestra; Lipkin, conductor. CRI C-259.

Selected Readings:

"A Birthday Offering to William Grant Still." *Black Perspective in Music* 3 (1975), 129ff.

Haas, R., ed. *William Grant Still and the Fusion of Cultures in American Music.* Los Angeles: 1972.

Southern, Eileen. *The Music of Black Americans: A History.* 2nd ed. New York: W. W. Norton, 1983, 422-27.

_____. "William Grant Still." In *The New Grove Dictionary of American Music*, ed. by H. W. Hitchcock and S. Sadie. London: Macmillan, 1986, 4:311-12.

Still, William Grant. "The Structure of Music." In *Readings in Black American Music*, ed. by E. Southern. New York: Norton, 1983, 314-17.

D. David Baker (b. 1931), studied at Indiana University and with Gunther Schuller; made his reputation as a jazz cellist and arranger; currently head of jazz program at Indiana University; output includes many works for jazz chamber orchestra or ensemble in third stream style, traditional chamber works, solo piano and vocal works, some based on texts by black poets, and works for chorus and jazz ensemble; wrote several books on jazz improvisation.

Best-known works include:
> *Black Cantata* (1968), dedicated to Martin Luther King.
> *Contrasts*, for piano trio recorded by Western Arts Trio. Laurel 106.

Selected Readings:

> Baker, David N., Lida M. Belt, and Herman C. Hudson, eds. *The Black Composer Speaks*. Metuchen, NJ: Scarecrow Press, 1978.
> Moore, Carmen. "David Baker." In *The New Grove Dictionary of American Music*, ed. by H. W. Hitchcock and S. Sadie. London: Macmillan, 1986, 1: 114.

E. Julia Perry (1924-79), studied at Westminster Choir School and the Juilliard School, and later was awarded two Guggenheim Fellowships to study with Nadia Boulanger and Luigi Dallapiccola; her works follow Neo-Classical traditions; output includes 11 symphonies, concertos, opera-ballet, and chamber works for voice and instruments.

Best-known works include:
> *Stabat mater* (1951), solo voice and orchestra
> > Recorded by Japan Philharmonic; William Strickland, conductor. CRI SD-133.
> *Short Piece* for Orchestra (1952)
> > Recorded by Tokyo Imperial Philharmonic; William Strickland; conductor. CRI SD-145.
> *Homunculus C.F.* (1960), for 10 percussionists
> > Recorded by Tokyo Imperial Philharmonic; William Strickland, conductor. CRI S-252.

Selected Readings:

> Green, Mildred Denby. *Black Women Composers: A Genesis*. Boston: Twayne, 1983, 71-98.
> Machlis, Joseph. *An Introduction to Contemporary Music*. 2nd ed. New York: Norton, 1979, 576-77.

Southern, Eileen. "Julia Perry." In *The New Grove Dictionary of American Music*, eds. H. W. Hitchcock and S. Sadie. London: Macmillan, 1986, 3:539.

_____. *The Music of Black Americans: A History*. 2nd ed. New York: W. W. Norton, 1983, 381.

General Bibliography

Baker, David, Dominique-René de Lerma, and Austin B. Caswell. *Black Music Now: A Source Book on 20th-Century Black-American Music*. Kent State Univ. Press, forthcoming.

Baker, David N., Lida M. Belt, and Herman C. Hudson, eds. *The Black Composer Speaks*. Metuchen, NJ: Scarecrow Press, 1978.

Baker, David N. et al. *Humanities through the Black Experience*. Ed. by Phyllis R. Klotman. Dubuque, IA: Kendall/Hunt, 1977.

Black Music Research Journal (1980-)

Black Perspective in Music (1973-)

Courlander, Harold. *A Treasury of Afro-American Folklore*. New York, 1976.

De Lerma, Dominique-René. *Bibliography of Black Music*. 4 vols. The Greenwood Encyclopedia of Black Music. Westport, CT: Greenwood Press, 1981-84.

Floyd, S. A. and M. J. Reisser. *Black Music in the United States: an Annotated Bibliography of Selected Reference and Research Materials*. Millwood, NY: Kraus International, 1983.

Green, Mildred Denby. *Black Women Composers: A Genesis*. Boston: Twayne, 1983.

Jackson, I.V., ed. *More than Dancing: Essays on Afro-American Music and Musicians*. Westport, CT: Greenwood Press, 1985.

Lovell, Jr., John. *Black Song: The Forge and the Flame*. New York: Macmillan, 1972.

Maultsby Portia K. "Selective bibliography: U.S. Black music." *Ethnomusicology* 19 (1975), 421-49.

Nettl, Bruno. *Folk and Traditional Music of the Western Continents*. 2nd ed. Englewood Cliffs, NJ: Prentice Hall, 1973.

Roach, Hildred. *Black American Music*. Malabar, FL, 1985

Skowronski, J. *Black Music in America: a Bibliography*. Metuchen, NJ: Scarecrow Press, 1981.

Southern, Eileen. *The Music of Black Americans, A History*. 2nd ed. New York: W. W. Norton, 1983.

_____, ed. *Readings in Black American Music*. 2nd ed. New York: W. W. Norton, 1983.

Tischler, A. *Fifteen Black American Composers: a Bibliography of their Works*. Detroit, 1981.

Selected Recordings, Discographies, and Scores:

> *Art Songs by Black American Composers.* Ann Arbor, MI, University of Michigan Records, 1981.
>
> *Songs from Anthology of Art Songs by Black American Composers*, ed. by W. Patterson. New York: E.B. Marks, 1977.
> Includes Coleridge-Taylor Perkinson, Noel DaCosta, William Grant Still, Charles Brown, Maurice McCall, Cecil Cohen, George Walker, Wendell Logan, David N. Baker, Howard Swanson, Leslie Adams, John Work, Jr., Florence Price, Margaret Bonds, Robert Owens, Olly Wilson, Hale Smith, Thomas Kerr, Jr., Adolphus Hailstork
>
> Tudor, Dean, and Nancy Tudor. *Black Music.* Littleton, CO: Libraries Unlimited, 1979. [discography]

Women Composers

The following resource guide focuses on five significant women composers and provides an overview of their compositional output as well as a list of available scores and recordings. If you wish to emphasize women's accomplishments in a more specific manner than the text does, you may add discussion and study of each or any of these women within the context of their time. A bibliography of specific readings is included for each and a general bibliography on women in music follows.

A. Hildegard of Bingen: twelfth-century abbess at Benedictine abbey in Germany; composer, poet, teacher, mystic whose musical works are preserved in a collection entitled *Symphonia harmoniae caelestium revelatiunum* (Symphony of the Harmony of Heavenly Revelations), containing seventy-seven songs and dating from 1150-60; author of an early morality play entitled *Ordo Virtutum* (The Play of Virtues).

Musical Scores:

> Briscoe, James, ed. *Historical Anthology of Music by Women.* Bloomington: Indiana Univ. Press, 1987. Facsimile scores for sequence "O virga," antiphon "O rubor sanguinis," and a "Kyrie."
>
> Hildegard von Bingen. *Lieder*, ed. by P. Barth, I Ritscher, and J. Schmidt-Görg. Salzburg: Otto Müller Verlag, 1969. Music for all extant pieces.

Suggested Reading:

> Dent, Jan. "Hildegard of Bingen." *The New Grove Dictionary of Music and Musicians*, ed. by Stanley Sadie. London: Macmillan, 1980.

"Hildegard of Bingen: Abbess and Composer." In *Women in Music*, ed. by Carol Neuls-Bates.

Jezic, Diane Peacock. *Women Composers, The Lost Tradition Found.* New York: Feminist Press at CUNY, 1988, 11-16.

Yardley, Anne G. "Ful weel she soong the service dyvyne: The Cloistered Musician in the Middle Ages." In *Women Making Music*, ed. by Jane Bowers and Judith Tick. Urbana: Univ. of Illinois Press, 1986, 15-38.

Recordings:

A feather on the breath of God: Sequences and hymns by Abbess Hildegard of Bingen. Gothic Voices, directed by Christopher Page. Hyperion LP A66039.

Ordo virtutum (The Play of Virtues). Sequentia, Ensemble for Medieval Music, directed by Barbara Thornton and Magriet Tindemans. 2 compact discs. Angel CDCB-49249

Symphoniae (Spiritual Songs). Sequentia, Ensemble for Medieval Music, directed by Barbara Thornton and Magriet Tindemans. Compact disc. Angel CDC-49251.

Music for the Mass by Nun Composers. University of Arkansas Schola Cantorum, Leonarda 115.

B. Barbara Strozzi (1619-64), seventeenth-century Italian singer and composer of madrigals, arias and cantatas.

Musical Scores:

MacClintock, Carol, ed. *The Solo Song.* New York: Norton, 1973. Includes "Lagrime mie" (Op. 7)

Raney, Carolyn, ed. *Nine Centuries of Music by Women.* New York: Broude Brothers, 1977. Includes "Con le belle non ci vuol fretta" and "Consiglio amoroso" (Op. 1)

Suggested Reading:

Bowers, Jane. "Women Composers in Italy, 1566-1700." In *Women Making Music*, 116-67.

Raney, Carolyn. "Strozzi, Barbara." In *The New Grove Dictionary of Music and Musicians*.

Rosand, Ellen. "The Voice of Barbara Strozzi." In *Women Making Music*, 168-90.

Recordings:

Barbara Strozzi virtuosissima cantatrice: Cantate, with Judith Nelson. Harmonia Mundi HM 1114.

Arias. Carol Plantamura, soprano. Leonarda 123.

C. Fanny Mendelssohn Hensel (1805-47), nineteenth-century concert pianist and composer, sister of composer Felix Mendelssohn-Bartholdy; wrote piano music, songs, and chamber music, including a piano trio, Op. 11.

Suggested Reading:

> Citron, Marcia. "Women and the Lied, 1775-1850." In *Women Making Music*, 224-48.
> _____. *The Letters of Fanny Hensel to Felix Mendelssohn.* New York: Pendragon Press, 1986.
> Jezic, Diane Peacock. "Fanny Mendelssohn Hensel." In *Women Composers*, 73-82.
> Koehler, Karl-Heinz. "Hensel, Fanny Mendelssohn." In *The New Grove Dictionary of Music and Musicians.*
> Neuls-Bates, Carol. "Fanny Mendelssohn Hensel." In *Women in Music*, 143-52.

Recordings:

> Songs. Leonarda 107, also 112.
> Trio in D minor for Violin, Cello and Piano, Op. 11. With various Songs and Romance Without Words for Piano. 2-LP set: Calliope 1213/14. Cassette: Calliope 4213/14.

D. Ruth Crawford Seeger (1901-53), early twentieth-century composer and first woman to hold a Guggenheim Fellowship to study composition abroad; married to musicologist Charles Seeger and stepmother of folksinger Pete Seeger; wrote much chamber music, including String Quartet (1931).

Musical Scores:

> String Quartet. Bryn Mawr: Marion Music Inc., 1941.

Suggested Readings:

> Gaume, Matilda. "Ruth Crawford Seeger." In *Women Making Music*, 370-88.
> _____. *Ruth Crawford Seeger: Her Life and Works.* Ann Arbor, MI: University Microfilms, 1973.

Recordings:

> Quartet (1931). Composer Quartet. Elektra/Nonesuch LP H-71280; Fine Arts Quartet. Gasparo 205.

E. Ellen Taaffe Zwilich (b. 1939), contemporary American composer in New Romantic style; first woman to win the Pulitzer Prize in composition, awarded for her Symphony No. 1 (1983).

Musical Score:

> Symphony No. 1, in Briscoe, *Historical Anthology of Music By Women*, 375-401.

Suggested Readings:

> Jezic, Diane Peacock. "Ellen Taaffe Zwilich." In *Women Composers*, 173-182.
> Roy, James G., Jr."Zwilich, Ellen Taaffe." In *The New Grove Dictionary of American Music.*

Recordings:

> Symphony No. 1 (Three Movements for Orchestra, 1982), John Nelson and Indianapolis Symphony, with *Celebration* (1984) and *Prologue and Variations* (1984). New World LP NW 336. New World cassette NW-336-2.

Selected Bibliography

General Readings on Women

> Anderson, Bonnie S. and Judith P. Zinsser. *A History of their Own: Women in Europe.* 2 vols. New York: Harper & Row, 1988.
> Labarge, Margaret Wade. *A Small Sound of the Trumpet: Women in Medieval Life.* Boston: Beacon Press, 1986.
> O'Faolain, Julia and Lauro Martines, eds. *Not in God's Image: Women in History from the Greeks to the Victorians.* New York: Harper & Row, 1973.

Women and Music, General

> Bowers, Jane and Judith Tick, eds. *Women Making Music: The Western Art Tradition, 1150-1950.* Urbana and Chicago: Univ. of Illinois Press, 1986.
> Cohen, Aaron. *International Encyclopedia of Women Composers.* 2nd rev.ed., 2 vols. New York: Books and Music, 1987.
> Hixon, Donald and Donald Hennessee, comps. *Women in Music: A Bibliography.* Metuchen, NJ: Scarecrow Press, 1975.
> Neuls-Bates, Carol, ed. *Women in Music: An Anthology of Source Readings from the Middle Ages to the Present.* New York: Harper & Row, 1982.
> Sadie, Stanley, ed. *The New Grove Dictionary of Music and Musicians,* 6th ed. 20 vols. London, Macmillan, 1980. Individual composer articles.
> Zaimont, Judith and Karen Famera, eds. *Contemporary Concert Music by Women: A Directory of the Composers and Their Works.* Westport, CT: Greenwood Press, 1981.

American Women Composers

Ammer, Christine. *Unsung: A History of Women in American Music.* Westport, CT: Greenwood Press, 1980.

Block, Adrienne Fried, and Carol Neuls-Bates. *Women in American Music: Bibliography of Music and Literature.* Westport, CT: Greenwood Press, 1979.

Green, Mildred Denby. *Black Women Composers: A Genesis.* Boston, Twayne, 1983.

Hitchcock, H. Wiley and Stanley Sadie, eds. *The New Grove Dictionary of American Music.* London: Macmillan, 1986. Individual composer articles.

Skowronski, JoAnn. *Women in American Music: A Bibliography.* Metuchen, NJ: Scarecrow Press, 1978.

Tick, Judith. *American Women Composers Before 1879.* Ann Arbor, MI: UMI Research Press, 1983.

Music Anthologies

Briscoe, James, ed. *Historical Anthology of Music by Women.* Bloomington: Indiana Univ. Press, 1987.

Drucker, Ruth and Helen Strine, eds. *A Collection of Art Songs by Women Composers.* Fulton, MD: HERS Publishing, 1988.

Raney, Carolyn, ed. *Nine Centuries of Music by Women.* New York: Broude Brothers, 1977.

Wind Band Music In America

In this section we offer suggestions for incorporating wind music into the curriculum of your music appreciation course. A brief overview of bands in America is followed by some specific sources for teaching early band music, marches of Sousa, and music by Gustav Holst as well as works by Stravinsky, Hindemith, Schuman, and Husa. The resource guide also includes a selected list of other contemporary band works by well-known composers and a general bibliography of readings.

Overview: The concert band of today descended from the historical "haut" or loud instrumental ensemble of the Middle Ages and Renaissance. The seventeenth-century American colonists adopted some earlier European customs, such as the use of fife-and-drum ensembles for military purposes. The French military band, which originated in the army of Louis XIV, also influenced the development of the American band. The Revolutionary period and early nineteenth century saw the rise of American military ensembles with increasingly diversified instrumentation. Interest in the Turkish Janissary music brought about a much enlarged and varied percussion section. In the Federal period there was further development of the band's instrumentation through the addition of still more instruments, notably the piccolo, bass clarinets, trombones, and the serpent. A tradition of civilian bands sprang up across the country in addition to the military ensembles; both were essentially brass groups. Recent research has unearthed much of the repertory of nineteenth-century bands from manuscript sources. Patrick Gilmore has been viewed as the "father of the modern symphonic band," while John Philip Sousa, director of the U.S. Marine Band, is perhaps the most significant figure in American band history. Professional as well as civic bands continued to thrive across America through the First World War, at which time they were absorbed by the academic world, where they have been nurtured in public schools, colleges, and universities. Among the composers who have contributed to the repertory of the concert band are Gustav Holst, Ralph Vaughan Williams, Igor Stravinsky, Arnold Schoenberg, Paul Hindemith, Darius Milhaud, Vincent Persichetti, Karel Husa, and Joseph Schwantner.

A. Revolutionary and Civil War Bands: bands were active during the Revolutionary War and after for military, civic, or festive display; woodwind instruments were replaced by brass ones in the nineteenth century; U.S. Army bands were small, numbering from ten to sixteen players; during the Civil War, the Union Army included some 500 bands totaling 9000 players; Confederate bands flourished as well.

Selected readings:

> Camus, Raoul F. *The Military Music of the American Revolution.* Chapel Hill, 1976.
> Newsom, Jon. "The American Brass Band Movement," *Quarterly Journal of the Library of Congress* 15 (1979), 114ff.

Suggested listening:

> *Battle Cry of Freedom: Military Music of Union Army Bands.* Heritage Americana, 1982.
> *The Yankee Brass Band: Music from Mid-Nineteenth-Century America.* New World NW-312.

B. French Military Bands: Revolutionary groups were popular at public ceremonies of the new republic; influential in the rise of brass and military bands in the United States; the most important composer was François-Joseph Gossec (1734-1839), a noted symphonist who, during the Revolution, directed the band of the Guarde Nationale and wrote many pieces for large wind and vocal forces. His works include *Marche lugubre* (1773) and *Classic Overture* (1794-95).

Selected readings:

> Whitwell, David. *Band Music of the French Revolution.* Tutzing: Schneider, 1979; Alta Music, Bd. 5.

Suggested listening:

> Gossec, Classic Overture in C, Goldman Band, Decca DL 78633;
> University of Southern Mississippi Band, Crest CBD-69-4A; The
> American Band of Providence, Redwood ES-30.
>
> Gossec, *Marche lugubre*, Musique des guardiens de la Paix; Les
> éditions constallat; available also on *Recordings to accompany A
> History of Western Music, 4th ed.* and *Norton Anthology of Western
> Music, 2nd ed.* Album 2, side 2, No. 3; Cassette 1B, No. 3

C. John Philip Sousa: American bandmaster, known as the "March King";
formed the Sousa band, popular from 1892 until 1931; composer of marches,
including *The Washington Post* (1889) and *The Stars and Stripes Forever*
(1897); fine showman and musician who helped shaped American taste.

Selected readings:

> Berger, K. W. *The March King and His Band: The Story of John Philip
> Sousa.* New York: Exposition Press, 1957.
>
> Bierley, Paul E. *John Philip Sousa: American Phenomenon.* New York:
> Appleton-Century-Crofts, 1973.
>
> Mitziga, Walter. *The Sound of Sousa: John Philip Sousa Compositions
> Recorded.* Chicago: South Shore Printers, 1986.
>
> Smart, James R. *The Sousa Band, A Discography.* Washington, DC:
> Library of Congress, 1970.

Suggested listening:

> *The Pride of America: The Golden Age of the American March.*
> Goldman Band. New World NW-266.
>
> *Sousa Marches.* Eastman Wind Ensemble. 2-Mercury SRI-77010.
>
> *Sousa On Review.* Eastman Wind Ensemble. Mercury 420970-4 EH.
>
> *The Sousa and Pryor Bands*: Original recordings, 1901-26. New World
> NW-282.
>
> *The United States Marine Band Presents the Heritage of John Philip
> Sousa*, U.S. Marine Band. 18 LPs. 1975-78.

D. Gustav Holst: English composer; wrote several of the earliest classics in
the repertory; two suites for band: Suite no. 1 in E-flat (1909) and Suite no. 2
in F (1911); also *Hammersmith: Prelude and Scherzo.*

Selected reading:

> Holst, Imogen. *The Music of Gustav Holst; and Holst's music
> Reconsidered.* New York: Oxford Univ. Press, 1985.
>
> Rubbra, Edmund, and Stephen Lloyd, eds. *Gustav Holst.* London:
> Triad, 1974.

Suggested listening:

> Holst: Suites Nos. 1 and 2 for Band. Cleveland Winds. Telarc DG-10038; CD-80038.
> Holst Suites. RAF Central Band. Angel 4AE-34477.
> The Regimental Band of the Coldstream Guards. Bandleader BNA 5002.

D. Igor Stravinsky: Russian composer who shaped the main currents of twentieth-century music; his Neo-Classical period is characterized by an interest in clarity of timbre and attack typical of wind bands; wind works include *Symphonies for Wind Instruments* (1920), dedicated to the memory of Debussy, the wind Octet (1922-23), and Concerto for Piano and Winds (1923-24), a work featuring counterpoint harkening back to Bach; also the *Circus Polka* (1942), a dance for young elephants written for the Barnum and Bailey Circus.

Selected reading:

> Bowles, R. W. "Stravinsky's *Symphonies of Wind Instruments* for 23 Winds: an Analysis," *Journal of Band Research* 15 (1972), 355ff.
> Tyra, T. "An Analysis of Stravinsky's *Symphonies of Wind Instruments,*" *Journal of Band Research* 8 (1972), 6ff.

Suggested listening:

> *Symphonies of Wind Instruments*
> > Munich Wind Soloists Academy. Orfeo S-004821 A.
> > Nash Ensemble. Chandos 1048.
> > Eastman Wind Ensemble. Mercury MG 50143/SR90143; reissued as Mercury SRI 75057.
> Concerto for Piano and Winds
> > Cornell Wind Ensemble. Cornell U. 13.
> > Peabody Wind Ensemble. Golden Crest CBD 69-3.
> > Budapest Symphony Orchestra. Hungaroton SLPX 12021.
> > Royal Philharmonic. Hyperion A66167.
> *Circus Polka*
> > Cornell University Wind Ensemble. Cornell U 29.
> > University of Wisconsin-Milwaukee Symphony Band. Golden Crest CBDNA 78-4.
> > University of Illinois Concert Band. ERRL BP-127.
> > Tokyo Kosei Wind Orchestra. Kosei KOR-7905.

E. Paul Hindemith: German composer; also wrote much chamber music; wrote in nearly every genre, including sonatas for most standard instruments; composed music for new instruments and for student players; author of a theoretical treatise ranking intervals and harmonies from most consonant to most dissonant (*Craft of Musical Composition*, 1937-39); works for band include *Konzertmusik*, Op. 41 (1926), written originally for a small German band with saxhorns, and the Symphony in B-flat (1951), composed for the United States Army Band; the latter quickly established itself in the central repertory for winds as a masterwork of counterpoint and orchestration.

Suggested listening:

> Symphony in B-flat
>> Eastman Wind Ensemble. Mercury MG 50143/SR90143; reissued as Mercury SRI 75057.
>> University of Michigan Symphony Band. Golden Crest CRS 4214.
>> University of Northern Colorado Wind Ensemble. Soundmark R 990 BSCR.
>> Cornell Wind Ensemble. Cornell U. 12.

F. William Schuman: American composer who was president of the Julliard School of Music and later of Lincoln Center in New York; wrote a nationalistic work for orchestra entitled *New England Triptych: Three Pieces for Orchestra after William Billings*, each based on a hymn by the early American composer; two movements were later arranged by the composer for band: *Chester* (1957), based on the most popular song of the American Revolution, and *When Jesus Wept* (1958), based on a Billings round of the same name; also wrote *George Washington Bridge* (1951).

Recordings:

> *George Washington Bridge*
>> University of Michigan Symphony Band. ERRL BP-117.
>> Eastman Symphonic Wind Ensemble. Mercury MG50079; reissued as Mercury SRI 75086.
>> El Camino College Symphonic Band. Golden Crest CBDNA 75-1.
> *Chester Overture*
>> Cornell University Symphonic Band.   Cornell U. 10.
>> Goldman Band. Decca DL 78633
>> University of Michigan Symphony Band. Vanguard VSD 2124.
>> Arizona State University Band. Golden Crest ABA 76-2.
> *When Jesus Wept*
>> Cornell University Wind Ensemble. Cornell U. 9
>> University of Michigan Symphony Band. Golden Crest CRS-42028.
>> Louisiana State University Symphonic Band. Golden Crest ABA 75-1.
>> Brigham Young Symphonic Wind Ensemble. Golden Crest CBDNA 75-3.

G. Karel Husa: American composer of Czech origin; studied in Prague and Paris; teaches at Cornell University; he was the first to employ aleatory procedures in works for band, such as *Music for Prague 1968*, symbolic of the struggles of the Czech people through the use of an ancient Hussite song, "Ye Warriors of God and His Law," and *Apotheosis of this Earth* (1970), which musically depicts the destruction of the earth through war, famine, and environmental abuse.

Suggested listening:

> *Music for Prague 1968*
> > Eastman Wind Ensemble. CD CBS MK-44916; cassette CBS MT-44916.
> > University of Michigan Symphony Band. Golden Crest CRS 4214.
> > University of Michigan Band. Golden Crest CRS 4134.
> > University of Texas Symphony Band. ERRL BP-136.
>
> *Apotheosis of this Earth*
> > University of Michigan Symphonic Band. Golden Crest CRS 4134.
> > University of Northern Colorado Wind Ensemble. Soundmark R972 BSCR.

Selected Wind Works By Other Composers:

> Wagner: *Trauermusik* (1844)
> Dvorak: Serenade, Op. 55 (1879)
> R. Strauss: Serenade, Op. 7 in E-flat (1881)
> Schoenberg: Theme and Variations, Op. 43a (1943)
> Ives: *At the Beach* (1949); *A Solemn Music* (1949)
> Vaughan Williams: *English Folk Song Suite* (1923)
> Varèse: *Octandre* (1923)
> > *Déserts* (1954)
>
> Barber: *Commando March* (1943)
> Copland: *Fanfare for a Common Man* (1942)
> > *Emblems* (1964)
> > *Inaugural Fanfare* (1969)
>
> Milhaud: *Suite française* (1947)
> Schuller: Symphony (1949)
> Hanson: *Chorale and Alleluia* (1955)
> > *Laude* (1976)
>
> Persichetti: Divertimento for Band (1950)
> > Symphony for Band (1956)
>
> Messiaen: *Couleurs de la cité céleste* (1963)
> > *Et expecto resurrectionem mortuorum* (1964)
>
> Dahl: *Sinfonietta* (1969)
> Krenek: *Dream Sequence*, Op. 224 (1977)
> Kraft: *Dialogues and Entertainment* (1980)

Selected Bibliography, Wind Music

Berger, Kenneth, ed. *The Band Encyclopedia*. Evansville, IN: Band Associates, 1960.

_____. *The Band in the United States*. Evansville, IN: Band Associates, 1961.

_____. *The College and University Band: An Anthology of Papers*. Reston, VA: MENC, 1977.

Band Music Guide; alphabetical listing of titles and composers of all band music. 8th ed. Evanston: Instrumentalist Co., 1982.

Bryant, C. *And the Band Played On*. Washington, D.C., 1975.

Camus, Raoul. "Bands." *The New Grove Dictionary of American Music*. Ed. by H. Wiley Hitchcock and Stanley Sadie. London: Macmillan, 1986.

Goldman, Richard Franko. *The Concert Band*. New York: Rinehart, 1946.

_____. *The Wind Band*. Boston: Allyn & Bacon, 1961.

Helm, Sanford. *Catalog of chamber music for wind instruments*. Rev. ed. New York: Da Capo, 1969.

The Instrumentalist (1946-)

The Journal of Band Research (1964-)

Schwartz, H. W. *Bands of America*. Garden City, NY, 1957.

Whitwell, David. *A Concise History of the Wind Band*. Northridge, CA: Winds, 1985.

_____. *The History and Literature of the Wind Band and Wind Ensemble*. 9 vols. Northridge, CA: Winds, 1982-84.
   v. 1. The Wind Band and Wind Ensemble before 1500.
   v. 2. The Renaissance Wind Band and Wind Ensemble.
   v. 3. The Baroque Wind Band and Wind Ensemble.
   v. 4. The Wind Band and Wind Ensemble of the Classic Period, 1750-1800.
   v. 5. The Nineteenth-Century Wind Band and Wind Ensemble in Western Europe.
   v. 6. A Catalog of Multi-Part Instrumental Music for Winds or for Undesignated Instrumentation before 1600.
   v. 7. A Catalog of Baroque Multi-Part Instrumental Music for Wind Instruments or for Undesignated Instrumentation.
   v. 8. Wind Band and Ensemble Literature of the Classic Period.
   v. 9. Wind Band and Ensemble Literature of the Nineteenth Century.

_____. *A New History of Wind Music*. Evanston, IL: Instrumentalist Co., 1972.

Wallace, David and Eugene Corporon. *Wind ensemble/band repertoire*. University of Northern Colorado School of Music, 1984.

Wright, A. G. and S. Newcomb. *Bands of the World*. Evanston, IL, 1970.

Selected Discography, Wind Band

Berger, Kenneth, ed. *Band Discography.* 4th ed. Evansville, IN: Band Associates, 1956.

Band Record Guide: Alphabetical Listening of Band Records. Evanston, IL: Instrumentalist Co., 1969.

Rasmussen, Richard M. *Recorded Concert Band Music, 1950-1987: A Selected, Annotated Listing.* Jefferson, NC: McFarland, 1988.

World Music

This resource is designed to aid in the instruction of some non-Western styles, including music of Africa, American Indians, European folk traditions, India, and Northeastern Asia. These five were selected as representative of the wide diversity of world music. This subject could easily be incorporated into the teaching plan of Chapter 78, Non-Western Music and the Contemporary Scene. It could be taught earlier, however, if comparisons with Western styles were emphasized. A non-technical presentation could be made immediately after the elements of music in Part I. Selected readings and recordings are suggested for each of the five styles covered, and a general bibliography and discography are included.

A. Music of Africa: considers only black sub-Saharan Africa; most music is functional in African society; a wide diversity of idiophones and membranophones used to accompany singing and in ensembles; complex rhythm patterns and polyrhythms lead to polyphony, as in Yoruba drumming of Nigeria; music taught through oral tradition rather than written down; relationship between language and music is close in most African cultures; melodies are usually short, built from motives that are varied, featuring small intervals; group performance with leader typical; much use of improvisation; *kete* music of Asante people of Ghana representative of complexity of African drumming; basic rhythm or "timeline" around which instruments play increasingly complex patterns; master drummer plays the most complicated, varied of all rhythmic patterns; percussion ensembles also used, with drums, rattles, and bells, each with own rhythmic pattern producing polyphony and rhythmic "chords"; used to accompany social songs in Ghana.

Suggested styles:

Yoruba drumming of Nigeria
Ritual music of Ghana

Suggested listening:

Africa: Drum, Chant and Instrumental Music. Nonesuch Explorer H-72073.

Africa East and West. UCLA Institute of Ethnomusicology IE Records
IER-6751.
Africa South of the Sahara. Folkways FE-4503.
Drums of the Yoruba of Nigeria. Folkways P-441.
Drums of West Africa: Ritual Music of Ghana. Lyrichord LLST-7303.
Folk Music of the Western Congo. Folkways P-427.
Music of Equatorial Africa. Folkways P-402.
Songs of the Watusi. Folkways P-428.
Voice of the Congo. Riverside RLP-4002.

Selected books and scores

Beybey, Francis. *African Music, A People's Art.* Westport, CT:
Lawrence Hill, 1975.
Brandel, Rose. *The Music of Central Africa.* The Hague: Nijhoff, 1962.
Chernoff, John M. *African Rhythm and African Sensibility.* Chicago:
Univ. of Chicago, 1981.
Jones, A. M. *Studies in African Music.* 2 vols. London: Oxford Univ.
Press, 1959.
Kwabena Nketia, J. H. *African Music in Ghana.* Evanston, IL:
Northwestern Univ. Press, 1963.
_____. *The Music of Africa.* New York: Norton, 1974.
Merriam, Alan P. *African Music on LP: An Annotated Discography.*
Evanson, IL: Northwestern University Press, 1970.
Thieme, Darius. *African Music, a Briefly Annotated Bibliography.*
Washington: Library of Congress, 1964.
Varley, Douglas H. *African Native Music: an Annotated Bibliography.*
Folkestone: Dawsons, 1970.
Wachsmann, Klaus, ed. *Essays on Music and History in Africa.*
Evanston: Northwestern Univ., 1971.

B. Music of Native Americans: these people originally came from Asia, of
Mongoloid race; settled throughout North and South America, producing
wide variety of musical styles and instruments; six main cultural areas
identified in North America: Northwest Coast-Eskimo; California-Yuman;
Great Basin; Athabascan (Navaho and Apache); Plains-Pueblo (Blackfoot,
Crow, Comanche, Dakota, Hopi, Zuni), and eastern U.S./Southern Canada
(Iroquois); South America not so easily classified; the music of two Indian
cultures chosen as representative: Navaho and Iroquois.

1. Navaho: has wide-ranging melodies that move in large intervals,
often sung in falsetto; one type includes *Yeibichai* songs, a category of dance
songs about the grandfathers of the gods and their supernatural powers; from
Nightway ceremony.

2. Iroquois: makes use of responsorial singing; short ideas tossed back
and forth between leader and chorus; elaborate forms with recurring phrases.

Suggested Recordings, North America

> *Songs of the Red Man.* Library of Congress issue.
> *Indian Music of the Canadian Plains.* Folkways P-464.
> *American Indians of the Southwest.* Folkways FW-8850.
> *Music of the Sioux and Navaho.* Folkways FE-4401.
> *Sioux Favorites.* Canyon Records ARP-6059.

Suggested Recordings, Latin America

> *Indian Music of Mexico.* Folkways P-413.
> *Music from the Mato Grosso.* Folkways P-446.
> *Instruments and Music of Bolivia.* Folkways FM-4012.
> *Mountain Music of Peru.* Folkways FE-4539.

Selected Books and Scores:

> Collier, John. *Indians of the Americas.* New York: Norton, 1947.
> Densmore, Frances. *The American Indians and Their Music.* New
>   York: Womans Press, 1926.
> Driver, Harold. *Indians of North America.* Chicago: Univ. of Chicago,
>   1970.
> Gill, Sam. *Sacred Words, A Study of Navajo Religion and Prayer.*
>   Westport, CT: Greenwood, 1981.
> McAllester, David. *Peyote Music.* New York: Viking, 1949.
> Merriam, Alan. *Ethnomusicology of the Flathead Indians.* Chicago:
>   Aldine Press, 1967.
> Nettl, Bruno. *North American Indian Musical Styles.* Philadelphia:
>   American Folklore Society, 1954.
> Roberts, Helen H. *Musical Areas in Aboriginal North America.* New
>   Haven: Yale Univ. Press, 1936.
> Rhodes, Willard, ed. *Navajo: Folk Music of the United States.*
>   Washington, D. C.: Library of Congress, n.d.
> Stevenson, Robert. *Music in Aztec and Inca Territory.* Berkeley: Univ.
>   of California Press, 1968.
> Underhill, Ruth M. *Red Man's America.* Chicago: Chicago Univ. Press,
>   1953.

C. European Folk Music: various scale types used, diatonic and modal; metric patterns employed; strophic form prevalent; songs are ballads, love songs, ceremonial songs, work songs, and dance music; folk instruments important (flutes, bagpipes, fiddles, percussion); regions include Germanic Europe (British Isles, Germany, Netherlands, Scandanavia); Eastern Europe (Hungary, Czechoslovakia, Balkan states, Yugoslavia, Russia, Rumania, Poland, Finland); and southwestern Europe (Italy, France, Spain, and Portugal).

1. English ballads: most characteristic type of English folk song; many codified by Francis James Child; usual subjects include love, the sea, and tragic events; refrains common; broadside ballads were printed on large single sheets, often with only the title of the tune; much use of iambic meter; prevalent modes are Dorian, Mixolydian, Aeolian, and Ionian; pentatonic scales heard; favorite ballads include "Lord Randall," "The Golden Vanity," and "The Foggy Dew."

2. Rumanian songs: rhythmically complex with changing meters; large body of Christmas carols; ritual songs (for example, for weddings, for rain) important; polyphony used, especially in church music.

3. Spanish songs: much Arabic influence; scales with augmented and minor seconds; much vocal ornamentation; terse, nasal singing style; triple meter prevalent; *copla* is one type of short lyrical song of one stanza; many Spanish dance types; *flamenco* typical of southern Spain (Andalusia).

Suggested listening

Germanic Europe:
   English and Scottish Ballads. Washington Records 715-723.
   Songs and Pipes of the Hebrides. Folkways P-430.
   Songs and Dances of Holland. Folkways 3576.
   Songs and Dances of Norway. Folkways FE-4008.

Eastern Europe:
   Czech, Slovak and Moravian Folksongs, Monitor MF-389.
   Czech Songs and Dances, Apon 2473.
   Folk Music of Greece. Folkways FE-4454.
   Folk Music from Hungary. Folkways P-1000.
   Folk Music of Rumania. Folkways 419.
   Folk Music of Yugoslavia. Folkways 4434.
   Polish Folk Songs and Dances. Folkways FP-848.
   Russian Folk Songs. Vanguard VRS-9023.

Southwestern Europe:
   Folk Music from France. Folkways P-414.
   Folk Music from Italy. Folkways F-4220.
   Flamenco Music of Andalusia. Folkways 4437.
   Music of Portugal. Folkways 4538.
   Songs and Dances of Spain. Westminster WF 12001-5.

Selected readings:

Abrahams, Roger D. and George Foss. *Anglo-American Folksong Style.* Englewood Cliffs, NJ: Prentice-Hall, 1968.
Bartók, Béla, and Albert Lord. *Serbo-Croatian Folk Songs.* New York: Columbia Univ. Press, 1951.

Bronson, Bertrand H. *The Ballad as Song.* Berkeley: Univ. of
California, 1969.
_____. *The Traditional Tunes of the Child Ballads.* Princeton:
Princeton Univ. Press, 1958.
Deutsch, Leonhard. *A Treasury of the World's Finest Folk Song.* New
York: Howell, Siskin, 1942.
Gurvin, Olaf. *Norwegian Folk Music.* Oslo: Oslo Univ. Press, 1958.
Karpeles, Maud. *Folk Song of Europe.* London: Novello, 1956.
Kodály, Zoltán. *Folk Music of Hungary.* London: Barrie and Rockliff,
1960.
O'Sullivan, Donal. *Songs of the Irish.* New York: Crown, 1960.
Rubin, Rose, and Michael Stillman. *A Russian Song Book.* New York:
Random House, 1962.
Schindler, Kurt. *Folk Music and Poetry of Spain and Portugal.* New
York: Hispanic Institute, 1941.
Vetterl, Karel. *A Select Bibliography of European Folk Music.* Prague:
Czechoslovak Academy of Sciences, 1966.
Wells, Evelyn. *The Ballad Tree.* New York: Ronald, 1950.

D. Music of India: divides into two classical styles: Hindustani in Northern
India and Karnatic music in Southern India; sixteenth-century writer
Purandara Dasa is viewed as "father of Karnatic Music"; typical instruments
used in Karnatic music include the *veena*, a 7-stringed plucked lute-like
instrument, the *tambura*, a 4-string plucked lute used for drones, the
mridangam, a barrel-shaped double-headed drum; drone is central idea to
Indian folk and classical music; each melody built from *raga*, a scale with
expressive features (associated with an emotion, color, time of day or
season); rhythmic structure built on a *tala* or time cycle (uneven groupings of
beats); two types of classical music: written and improvised; all Karnatic
music is songs with words; various types of improvisations (*alpana* = exposition and exploration of raga; *tanam* = more lively rhythmic working of raga;
niravel = variation on one melody or phrase; *Svara kalpana* = more improvised, not on text).

Suggested recordings:

The Anthology of Indian Music. World Pacific WDS-26200. Lecture by
Ravi Shankar.
Classical Indian Music. London CM 9282. Lecture by Y. Menuhin.
Folk Music of India (Orissa). Lyrichord LLST-7183.
Folk Music of India (Uttar Pradesh). Lyrichord LLSG-7271.
Folk Songs and Dances of Northern India. Olympic 6108.
Music from South Kerala. Folkways FE-4365.
Religious Music of India. Folkways FE-4431.
Raga. Folkways FE-3530.

General Bibliography:

Brown, Robert E. "India's Music," In *Readings in Ethnomusicology*, ed. David McAllester. New York: Johnson Reprint, 1971, 293-329.

Popler, Herbert. *The Music of India*. Boston: Crescendo, 1971.

Wade, Bonnie. *Music in India: The Classical Tradition*. Englewood Cliffs, NJ: Prentice-Hall, 1979.

Discography:

Barnett, Elise. *A Discography of the Art Music of India*. Society for Ethnomusicology. 1975.

E. Northeast Asia (Japan, Korea): Japanese folk music characterized by parlando style with rubato; high, tense, melismatic style; folk instruments include flutes, drums, and *shamisen* lute with three strings; art music has long-standing tradition; court music has two basic scales: *ryo* (pentatonic) and *ritsu*; have particular character, range, and formulas, as do Indian ragas; court music called *gagaku*, of which there are several types; use of double reed instrument (*hichiriki*) and various flutes with percussion; *koto*, of the zither family, used in concert presentation of court music; major theatrical genre is *noh*; combines music, costume, dance, poetry; music has ensemble of flute and 3 drums; poetry structured into five or seven syllable lines; elastic rhythm necessitates calling from drummers; *kabuki* is drama and dancing; uses flute and drums of *noh* with various types of music; Korean music influenced by Chinese; various types of court music; use of melody instruments of double reed or flute family with zither-like instrument (*kayakeum*), bowed lute (*haekeum*), and percussion; free, slow rhythms; triple meter; pentatonic-based scales; virtuosic vocal effects used.

Suggested listening:

Japanese Music (UNESCO series). Musicaphon BM 30 L 2011-16.

Korean Court Music. Lyrichord LLST-7206.

Music of Korea. East West EWM-1001.

Traditional Music of Japan. Japan Victor JL-52-54.

Selected readings:

Adriaansz, Willem. *The Danmono of Japanese Koto Music*. Berkeley: Univ. of California, 1973.

Harich-Schneider, Eta. *A History of Japanese Music*. New York: Oxford Univ. Press, 1972.

Malm, William. *Japanese Music and Musical Instruments*. Tokyo: Tuttle, 1963.

Piggott, Francis T. *The Music and Musical Instruments of Japan*. 1909; repr. 1971.

Song, Bang-Song. *Korean Music*. Providence: Asian Music, 1971.

General Bibliography:

Malm, William. *Music Cultures of the Pacific, the Near East and Asia.* 2nd ed. Englewood Cliffs, NJ: Prentice-Hall, 1977.

Nettl, Bruno. *Reference Materials in Ethnomusicology.* Detroit: Information Service, 1961.

Nettl, Bruno, Gerard Behague, and Valerie Goertlen. *Folk and Traditional Music of the Western Continents.* 3rd ed. Englewood Cliffs, NJ: Prentice Hall, 1990.

Sachs, Curt. *The History of Musical Instruments.* New York: Norton, 1940.

_____. *The Wellsprings of Music.* The Hague: Nijhoff, 1962.

_____. *A World History of the Dance.* New York: Norton, 1937.

Titon, Jeff Todd, ed. *Worlds of Music: An Introduction to the Music of the World's People.* New York: Schirmer, 1984.

General Discography:

Columbia World Library of Folk and Primitive Music, ed. by Alan Lomax.

Man's Early Musical Instruments. Folkways P-525.

Music of the World's Peoples, ed. by Henry Cowell. Folkways FE-4504-4507.

Primitive Music of the World, ed. by Henry Cowell. Folkways FE-4581.

TEST-ITEM FILE

THE MATERIALS OF MUSIC

The Test-Item File printed here is in eight sections: The Materials of Music, Medieval and Renaissance Music, The Baroque Era, Eighteenth-Century Classicism, The Nineteenth Century, The Twentieth Century, Essay Questions, and Listening Questions. Within each category (except Essay), there are multiple choice and true/false questions for each chapter.

Note: For those using the Computerized Test-Item File, it is recommended that you annotate this printed version with the question numbers you find on your disk. Each of the computer programs has a slightly different numbering system.

MULTIPLE CHOICE QUESTIONS

Answer: b
Chronological Edition: Ch. 1, p. 7
Standard Edition: Ch. 1, p. 7
*Shorter Edition: Ch. 1, p. 7
Date used:

1. According to your text, the musical element that makes the widest and most direct appeal is:
   a. rhythm.
   b. melody.
   c. timbre.
   d. texture.

Answer: b
Chronological Edition: Ch. 1, p. 7
Standard Edition: Ch. 1, p. 7
*Shorter Edition: Ch. 1, p. 7
Date used:

2. A succession of single tones or pitches perceived as a unity is called:
   a. an interval.
   b. a melody.
   c. a harmony.
   d. a chord.

Answer: d
Chronological Edition: Ch. 1, p. 7
Standard Edition: Ch. 1, p. 7
*Shorter Edition: Ch. 1, p. 7
Date used:

3. A melody can be characterized by:
   a. its range.
   b. its shape.
   c. the way it moves.
   d. all of the above.

Answer: b
Chronological Edition: Ch. 1, p. 7
Standard Edition: Ch. 1, p. 7
*Shorter Edition: Ch. 1, p. 7
Date used:

4. The distance between the highest and lowest note of a melody is called:
   a. the tempo.
   b. the range.
   c. the phrase.
   d. the tonic.

Answer: d
Chronological Edition: Ch. 1, p. 8
Standard Edition: Ch. 1, p. 8
*Shorter Edition: Ch. 1, p. 8
Date used:

5. Which term describes a melody that moves with many leaps?
   a. consonant
   b. conjunct
   c. dissonant
   d. disjunct

Answer: b
Chronological Edition: Ch. 1, p. 8
Standard Edition: Ch. 1, p. 8
*Shorter Edition: Ch. 1, p. 8
Date used:

6. Which characteristic does NOT correctly describe the melody of *America*?
   a. wavelike shape
   b. wide range
   c. conjunct motion
   d. uses symmetrical phrases

Answer: a
Chronological Edition: Ch. 1, p. 9
Standard Edition: Ch. 1, p. 9

Date used:

7. A unit of meaning within a larger structure of a melody is called:
   a. a phrase.
   b. a stanza.
   c. a cadence.
   d. a climax.

Answer: c
Chronological Edition: Ch. 1, p. 9
Standard Edition: Ch. 1, p. 9
*Shorter Edition: Ch. 1, p. 9
Date used:

8. The resting place at the end of a phrase is called:
   a. a pause.
   b. a period.
   c. a cadence.
   d. a comma.

Answer: a
Chronological Edition: Ch. 1, p. 9
Standard Edition: Ch. 1, p. 9
*Shorter Edition: Ch. 1, p. 9
Date used:

9. Musical punctuation, similar to a comma or period in a sentence, is called:
   a. a cadence.
   b. a syncopation.
   c. a chord.
   d. a scale.

Answer: b
Chronological Edition: Ch. 2, p. 10
Standard Edition: Ch. 2, p. 10
*Shorter Edition: Ch. 2, p. 10
Date used:

10. The controlled movement of music in time is called:
    a. harmony.
    b. rhythm.
    c. texture.
    d. timbre.

Answer: c
Chronological Edition: Ch. 2, p. 11
Standard Edition: Ch. 2, p. 11
Date used:

11. A unit of length that represents the regular pulsation of the music is called:
    a. the meter.
    b. the syncopation.
    c. the beat.
    d. the accent.

Answer: b
Chronological Edition: Ch. 2, p. 12
Standard Edition: Ch. 2, p. 12
*Shorter Edition: Ch. 2, p. 11
Date used:

12. _____ denotes fixed time patterns within which musical events occur.
    a. Tempo
    b. Meter
    c. Range
    d. Syncopation

Answer: b
Chronological Edition: Ch. 2, p. 12
Standard Edition: Ch. 2, p. 12
*Shorter Edition: Ch. 2, p. 11
Date used:

13. The metric pattern in which a strong beat alternates with a weak one is called:
    a. triple meter.
    b. duple meter.
    c. quadruple meter.
    d. compound meter.

Answer: c
Chronological Edition: Ch. 2, p. 12
Standard Edition: Ch. 2, p. 12
*Shorter Edition: Ch. 2, p. 11
Date used:

Answer: a
Chronological Edition: Ch. 2, p. 12
Standard Edition: Ch. 2, p. 12
*Shorter Edition: Ch. 2, p. 11
Date used:

Answer: c
Chronological Edition: Ch. 2, p. 12
Standard Edition: Ch. 2, p. 12
*Shorter Edition: Ch. 2, p. 11
Date used:

Answer: a
Chronological Edition: Ch. 2, p. 12f
Standard Edition: Ch. 2, p. 12f
*Shorter Edition: Ch. 2, p. 11f
Date used:

Answer: b
Chronological Edition: Ch. 2, p. 12f
Standard Edition: Ch. 2, p. 12f
*Shorter Edition: Ch. 2, p. 11f
Date used:

Answer: b
Chronological Edition: Ch. 2, p. 13
Standard Edition: Ch. 2, p. 13
*Shorter Edition: Ch. 2, p. 12
Date used:

Answer: b
Chronological Edition: Ch. 2, p. 13
Standard Edition: Ch. 2, p. 13
*Shorter Edition: Ch. 2, p. 12
Date used:

14. What meter is known as common time?
    a. compound
    b. triple
    c. quadruple
    d. sextuple

15. Which meter would most likely be associated with a march?
    a. duple
    b. triple
    c. quadruple
    d. compound

16. Meters in which each beat is subdivided into three rather than two are known as:
    a. simple meters.
    b. complex meters.
    c. compound meters.
    d. unequal meters.

17. In triple meter, the strongest pulse occurs on:
    a. the first beat.
    b. the second beat.
    c. the third beat.
    d. all beats equally.

18. A repeated rhythmic pattern in which an accented beat is followed by two unaccented beats is:
    a. duple meter.
    b. triple meter.
    c. quadruple meter.
    d. compound meter.

19. Which of the following songs exemplifies compound meter?
    a. *Twinkle, Twinkle Little Star*
    b. *Rock-a-bye Baby*
    c. *America, the Beautiful*
    d. *America*

20. The patriotic song *America* ("My Country 'Tis of Thee") is an example of:
    a. duple meter.
    b. triple meter.
    c. quadruple meter.
    d. compound meter.

Answer: c
Chronological Edition: Ch. 2, p. 14
Standard Edition: Ch. 2, p. 14
*Shorter Edition: Ch. 2, p. 13
Date used:

Answer: c
Chronological Edition: Ch. 3, p. 14
Standard Edition: Ch. 3, p. 14
*Shorter Edition: Ch. 3, p. 13f
Date used:

Answer: d
Chronological Edition: Ch. 3, p. 14ff
Standard Edition: Ch. 3, p. 14ff
*Shorter Edition: Ch. 3, p. 13
Date used:

Answer: b
Chronological Edition: Ch. 3, p. 15
Standard Edition: Ch. 3, p. 15
*Shorter Edition: Ch. 3, p. 14
Date used:

Answer: a
Chronological Edition: Ch. 3, p. 15
Standard Edition: Ch. 3, p. 15
*Shorter Edition: Ch. 3, p. 14
Date used:

Answer: d
Chronological Edition: Ch. 3, p. 15
Standard Edition: Ch. 3, p. 15
*Shorter Edition: Ch. 3, p. 14
Date used:

Answer: d
Chronological Edition: Ch. 3, p. 15
Standard Edition: Ch. 3, p. 15
*Shorter Edition: Ch. 3, p. 14
Date used:

21. The deliberate shifting of the accent to a weak beat or an offbeat is called:
    a. rhythm.
    b. meter.
    c. syncopation.
    d. compound meter.

22. Harmony is to music what _____ is to painting.
    a. the frame
    b. color
    c. perspective
    d. the brush

23. The vertical dimension of music is called:
    a. rhythm.
    b. texture.
    c. melody.
    d. harmony.

24. The movement and relationship of intervals and chords is called:
    a. tonic.
    b. harmony.
    c. dissonance.
    d. melody.

25. The distance and relationship between two tones is referred to as:
    a. an interval.
    b. a scale.
    c. an octave.
    d. a chord.

26. The interval from one "do" to the next, having the same note name, is called:
    a. a chord.
    b. a fifth.
    c. a triad.
    d. an octave.

27. A combination of tones, normally three, that constitutes a single block of harmony is called:
    a. an interval.
    b. a scale.
    c. an octave.
    d. a chord.

Answer: d
Chronological Edition: Ch. 3, p. 15f
Standard Edition: Ch. 3, p. 15f
*Shorter Edition: Ch. 3, p. 14
Date used:

Answer: d
Chronological Edition: Ch. 3, p. 16
Standard Edition: Ch. 3, p. 16
*Shorter Edition: Ch. 3, p. 15
Date used:

Answer: b
Chronological Edition: Ch. 3, p. 16
Standard Edition: Ch. 3, p. 16
*Shorter Edition: Ch. 3, p. 15
Date used:

Answer: b
Chronological Edition: Ch. 3, p. 17
Standard Edition: Ch. 3, p. 17
*Shorter Edition: Ch. 3, p. 16
Date used:

Answer: a
Chronological Edition: Ch. 3, p. 17
Standard Edition: Ch. 3, p. 17
*Shorter Edition: Ch. 3, p. 16
Date used:

Answer: a
Chronological Edition: Ch. 3, p. 17
Standard Edition: Ch. 3, p. 17
*Shorter Edition: Ch. 3, p. 16
Date used:

Answer: b
Chronological Edition: Ch. 3, p. 17
Standard Edition: Ch. 3, p. 17
*Shorter Edition: Ch. 3, p. 16
Date used:

28. A triad is:
   a. the most common chord type found in Western music.
   b. a three-note chord.
   c. built on alternate scale steps.
   d. all of the above.

29. The first note of the scale:
   a. assumes greater importance than the rest of the notes.
   b. is called the tonic, or keynote.
   c. serves as the home base around which others revolve.
   d. all of the above.

30. The principle of organization around a central tone is called:
   a. chromaticism.
   b. tonality.
   c. consonance.
   d. centralization.

31. Which tonality would most likely be chosen for a triumphal march?
   a. minor
   b. major
   c. chromatic
   d. modal

32. The term diatonic describes melodies or harmonies that are:
   a. built from the notes of the major or minor scale.
   b. derived from all of the notes of the octave.
   c. triadic.
   d. all of the above.

33. Which of the following terms describes the full range of notes in the octave?
   a. chromatic
   b. diatonic
   c. major
   d. minor

34. Which of the following terms describes a concordant or agreeable combination of tones?
   a. conjunct
   b. consonant
   c. disjunct
   d. dissonant

Answer: c
Chronological Edition: Ch. 3, p. 17
Standard Edition: Ch. 3, p. 17
*Shorter Edition: Ch. 3, p. 16
Date used:

Answer: c
Chronological Edition: Ch. 4, p. 18
Standard Edition: Ch. 4, p. 18
*Shorter Edition: Ch. 4, p. 17
Date used:

Answer: a
Chronological Edition: Ch. 4, p. 18
Standard Edition: Ch. 4, p. 18
*Shorter Edition: Ch. 4, p. 17
Date used:

Answer: d
Chronological Edition: Ch. 4, p. 18
Standard Edition: Ch. 4, p. 18
*Shorter Edition: Ch. 4, p. 17
Date used:

Answer: a
Chronological Edition: Ch. 4, p. 18
Standard Edition: Ch. 4, p. 18
*Shorter Edition: Ch. 4, p. 17
Date used:

Answer: c
Chronological Edition: Ch. 4, p. 18
Standard Edition: Ch. 4, p. 18
*Shorter Edition: Ch. 4, p. 17
Date used:

Answer: a
Chronological Edition: Ch. 4, p. 18f
Standard Edition: Ch. 4, p. 18f
*Shorter Edition: Ch. 4, p. 17f
Date used:

35. A combination of tones that sounds discordant, unstable, or in need of resolution is called:
    a. a cadence.
    b. a consonance.
    c. a dissonance.
    d. a tonality.

36. The element that describes the musical fabric or the relationship of musical lines within a work is called its:
    a. harmony.
    b. meter.
    c. texture.
    d. timbre.

37. A texture featuring a single, unaccompanied line is called:
    a. monophonic.
    b. homophonic.
    c. polyphonic.
    d. contrapuntal.

38. The music of the Oriental world is largely:
    a. homophonic.
    b. contrapuntal.
    c. polyphonic.
    d. monophonic.

39. When two or more melodic lines are combined, the resulting texture is called:
    a. polyphonic.
    b. monophonic.
    c. homophonic.
    d. none of the above.

40. The predominant texture used in music up to about one thousand years ago was:
    a. polyphonic.
    b. homophonic.
    c. monophonic.
    d. all of the above.

41. A texture in which a single voice takes over the melodic interest while the accompanying voices are subordinate is called:
    a. homophonic.
    b. contrapuntal.
    c. polyphonic.
    d. monophonic.

Answer: c
Chronological Edition: Ch. 4, p. 19f
Standard Edition: Ch. 4, p. 19f
*Shorter Edition: Ch. 4, p. 18f
Date used:

Answer: a
Chronological Edition: Ch. 4, p. 19
Standard Edition: Ch. 4, p. 19
*Shorter Edition: Ch. 4, p. 18
Date used:

Answer: c
Chronological Edition: Ch. 4, p. 19
Standard Edition: Ch. 4, p. 19
*Shorter Edition: Ch. 4, p. 18
Date used:

Answer: d
Chronological Edition: Ch. 4, p. 19f
Standard Edition: Ch. 4, p. 19f
*Shorter Edition: Ch. 4, p. 18
Date used:

Answer: d
Chronological Edition: Ch. 4, p. 19f
Standard Edition: Ch. 4, p. 19f
*Shorter Edition: Ch. 4, p. 18
Date used:

Answer: c
Chronological Edition: Ch. 4, p. 19f
Standard Edition: Ch. 4, p. 19f
*Shorter Edition: Ch. 4, p. 18
Date used:

Answer: c
Chronological Edition: Ch. 4, p. 19f
Standard Edition: Ch. 4, p. 19f
*Shorter Edition: Ch. 4, p. 18
Date used:

42. Which of the following is NOT a contrapuntal device used by composers?
   a. inversion
   b. retrograde
   c. homophony
   d. augmentation

43. When the length of the imitation lasts for an entire work, this strict composition is called:
   a. a canon.
   b. a retrograde.
   c. an augmentation.
   d. a sequence.

44. A musical canon is closely related to:
   a. a theme.
   b. a motive.
   c. a round.
   d. a scale.

45. The procedure in which a subject or motive is presented in one voice and then restated in another is called:
   a. inversion.
   b. diminution.
   c. retrograde.
   d. imitation.

46. The technique that turns a melody upside down is called:
   a. retrograde.
   b. diminution.
   c. augmentation.
   d. inversion.

47. The term that describes a melody played backwards is:
   a. canon.
   b. inversion.
   c. retrograde.
   d. diminution.

48. Retrograde inversion is a device whereby a melody is:
   a. presented upside down.
   b. presented backwards.
   c. presented upside down and backwards.
   d. presented in shorter time values.

Answer: a
Chronological Edition: Ch. 4, p. 19f
Standard Edition: Ch. 4, p. 19f
*Shorter Edition: Ch. 4, p. 18
Date used:

49. A melodic device whereby a theme is presented in longer time values than its original form is called:
   a. augmentation.
   b. diminution.
   c. retrograde.
   d. inversion.

Answer: a
Chronological Edition: Ch. 4, p. 20
Standard Edition: Ch. 4, p. 20
*Shorter Edition: Ch. 4, p. 19
Date used:

50. Which musical texture is likely to demand the greatest concentration on the part of the listener?
   a. polyphonic
   b. homophonic
   c. monophonic
   d. stereophonic

Answer: c
Chronological Edition: Ch. 5, p. 22
Standard Edition: Ch. 5, p. 22
*Shorter Edition: Ch. 5, p. 21
Date used:

51. The quality of a work of art that represents clarity and order refers to its:
   a. themes.
   b. melody.
   c. form.
   d. harmony.

Answer: a
Chronological Edition: Ch. 5, p. 22
Standard Edition: Ch. 5, p. 22
*Shorter Edition: Ch. 5, p. 21
Date used:

52. The term _____ describes the technique whereby some aspects of the music are changed yet the whole remains recognizable.
   a. variation
   b. contrast
   c. form
   d. repetition

Answer: b
Chronological Edition: Ch. 5, p. 23f
Standard Edition: Ch. 5, p. 23f
*Shorter Edition: Ch. 5, p. 22
Date used:

53. The form based on a statement and a departure, without a return to the opening statement is called:
   a. ternary.
   b. binary.
   c. variation.
   d. repetition.

Answer: b
Chronological Edition: Ch. 5, p. 23f
Standard Edition: Ch. 5, p. 23f
*Shorter Edition: Ch. 5, p. 22
Date used:

54. Binary form is best outlined as:
   a. A–B–A
   b. A–B
   c. A–A
   d. B–B

Answer: a
Chronological Edition: Ch. 5, p. 24
Standard Edition: Ch. 5, p. 24
*Shorter Edition: Ch. 5, p. 22f
Date used:

55. A distinctive melody that serves as a building block in the structure of a musical work is called:
   a. a theme.
   b. a motive.
   c. a movement.
   d. a sequence.

Answer: a
Chronological Edition: Ch. 5, p. 25
Standard Edition: Ch. 5, p. 25
*Shorter Edition: Ch. 5, p. 23
Date used:

Answer: b
Chronological Edition: Ch. 5, p. 24f
Standard Edition: Ch. 5, p. 24f
*Shorter Edition: Ch. 5, p. 23
Date used:

Answer: c
Chronological Edition: Ch. 5, p. 24f
Standard Edition: Ch. 5, p. 24f
*Shorter Edition: Ch. 5, p. 23
Date used:

Answer: c
Chronological Edition: Ch. 5, p. 26
Standard Edition: Ch. 5, p. 26
*Shorter Edition: Ch. 5, p. 24
Date used:

Answer: d
Chronological Edition: Ch. 5, p. 26
Standard Edition: Ch. 5, p. 26
*Shorter Edition: Ch. 5, p. 24
Date used:

Answer: b
Chronological Edition: Ch. 6, p. 26
Standard Edition: Ch. 6, p. 26
*Shorter Edition: Ch. 6, p. 24
Date used:

Answer: a
Chronological Edition: Ch. 6, p. 26
Standard Edition: Ch. 6, p. 26
*Shorter Edition: Ch. 6, p. 24
Date used:

56. The smallest fragment of a theme that forms a melodic-rhythmic unit is called:
   a. a motive.
   b. a sequence.
   c. variation.
   d. thematic development.

57. A basic technique in thematic development is the fragmentation of themes into:
   a. melodies.
   b. motives.
   c. rhythms.
   d. notes.

58. The compositional technique whereby a composer searches out a theme's capacity for growth and expansion is known as:
   a. augmentation.
   b. diminution.
   c. thematic transformation.
   d. ternary form.

59. The separate sections of a large musical work are called:
   a. songs.
   b. symphonies.
   c. movements.
   d. chapters.

60. The integration of a multitude of details, both large and small, into a spacious structure known as a musical artwork can be compared to the unity we perceive in:
   a. novels.
   b. paintings.
   c. architecture.
   d. all of the above.

61. The rate of speed at which a piece of music is played is its:
   a. meter.
   b. tempo.
   c. movement.
   d. mood.

62. In what language are tempo markings generally given?
   a. Italian
   b. French
   c. German
   d. Dutch

Answer: b
Chronological Edition: Ch. 6, p. 26
Standard Edition: Ch. 6, p. 26
*Shorter Edition: Ch. 6, p. 24
Date used:

Answer: c
Chronological Edition: Ch. 6, p. 26
Standard Edition: Ch. 6, p. 26
*Shorter Edition: Ch. 6, p. 24f
Date used:

Answer: a
Chronological Edition: Ch. 6, p. 26
Standard Edition: Ch. 6, p. 26
*Shorter Edition: Ch. 6, p. 25
Date used:

Answer: c
Chronological Edition: Ch. 6, p. 27
Standard Edition: Ch. 6, p. 27
*Shorter Edition: Ch. 6, p. 25
Date used:

Answer: b
Chronological Edition: Ch. 6, p. 27
Standard Edition: Ch. 6, p. 27
*Shorter Edition: Ch. 6, p. 25
Date used:

Answer: d
Chronological Edition: Ch. 6, p. 27
Standard Edition: Ch. 6, p. 27
*Shorter Edition: Ch. 6, p. 25
Date used:

Answer: a
Chronological Edition: Ch. 6, p. 27
Standard Edition: Ch. 6, p. 27
*Shorter Edition: Ch. 6, p. 25
Date used:

63. Which marking is appropriate for a slow, solemn tempo?
    a. Andante
    b. Adagio
    c. Piano
    d. Allegro

64. Which of the following tempo markings does NOT indicate a slow tempo?
    a. Grave
    b. Largo
    c. Presto
    d. Adagio

65. Which of the following tempo markings is the fastest?
    a. Presto
    b. Vivace
    c. Moderato
    d. Allegro

66. Accelerando is a term indicating that the tempo is:
    a. getting slower.
    b. staying the same.
    c. getting faster.
    d. returning to the original tempo.

67. Which of the following modifiers should be added to an Allegro marking to indicate a very fast tempo?
    a. meno
    b. molto
    c. non troppo
    d. a tempo

68. The degree of loudness or softness at which music is played is called:
    a. texture.
    b. tempo.
    c. timbre.
    d. dynamics.

69. Which of the following dynamic markings is the softest?
    a. pianissimo (pp)
    b. piano (p)
    c. mezzo piano (mp)
    d. mezzo forte (mf)

Answer: b
Chronological Edition: Ch. 6, p. 27
Standard Edition: Ch. 6, p. 27
*Shorter Edition: Ch. 6, p. 26
Date used:

70. Which of the following symbols indicates growing louder?
   a. >
   b. <
   c. mp
   d. mf

Answer: d
Chronological Edition: Ch. 6, p. 27
Standard Edition: Ch. 6, p. 27
*Shorter Edition: Ch. 6, p. 26
Date used:

71. The gradual swelling and diminishing of the volume of music is called:
   a. forte–piano.
   b. allegro–adagio.
   c. accelerando–ritardando.
   d. crescendo–decrescendo.

Answer: a
Chronological Edition: Ch. 6, p. 28
Standard Edition: Ch. 6, p. 28
*Shorter Edition: Ch. 6, p. 26
Date used:

72. The markings for tempo and dynamics contribute most directly to:
   a. the expressive content of a piece of music.
   b. the form of a piece of music.
   c. the thematic development of a piece of music.
   d. the tonality of a piece of music.

Answer: c
Chronological Edition: Ch. 7, p. 30
Standard Edition: Ch. 7, p. 30
*Shorter Edition: Ch. 7, p. 28
Date used:

73. The term timbre refers to:
   a. the length of a tone.
   b. the pitch of a tone.
   c. the color of a tone.
   d. the falling of a tree.

Answer: b
Chronological Edition: Ch. 7, p. 30
Standard Edition: Ch. 7, p. 30
*Shorter Edition: Ch. 7, p. 28
Date used:

74. Which is NOT a property of a musical sound?
   a. pitch
   b. texture
   c. volume
   d. timbre

Answer: d
Chronological Edition: Ch. 7, p. 31
Standard Edition: Ch. 7, p. 31
Date used:

75. A mechanism that generates musical vibrations and launches them into the air is called:
   a. a mute.
   b. a podium.
   c. a baton.
   d. an instrument.

Answer: c
Chronological Edition: Ch. 7, p. 31
Standard Edition: Ch. 7, p. 31
*Shorter Edition: Ch. 7, p. 29
Date used:

76. The human voice:
   a. is an unnatural musical instrument.
   b. is limited in character and range.
   c. possesses lyric beauty and expressiveness that has served as a model for instrument builders and players.
   d. can be made to sound like any instrument.

Answer: a
Chronological Edition: Ch. 7, p. 31
Standard Edition: Ch. 7, p. 31
*Shorter Edition: Ch. 7, p. 29
Date used:

Answer: b
Chronological Edition: Ch. 7, p. 31
Standard Edition: Ch. 7, p. 31
*Shorter Edition: Ch. 7, p. 29
Date used:

Answer: b
Chronological Edition: Ch. 7, p. 33
Standard Edition: Ch. 7, p. 33
*Shorter Edition: Ch. 7, p. 29
Date used:

Answer: a
Chronological Edition: Ch. 7, p. 33
Standard Edition: Ch. 7, p. 33
*Shorter Edition: Ch. 7, p. 29f
Date used:

Answer: c
Chronological Edition: Ch. 7, p. 33
Standard Edition: Ch. 7, p. 33
*Shorter Edition: Ch. 7, p. 31
Date used:

Answer: b
Chronological Edition: Ch. 7, p. 33
Standard Edition: Ch. 7, p. 33
*Shorter Edition: Ch. 7, p. 31
Date used:

Answer: d
Chronological Edition: Ch. 7, p. 33
Standard Edition: Ch. 7, p. 33
*Shorter Edition: Ch. 7, p. 31
Date used:

77. The standard ranges of the human voice from top to bottom are as follows:
    a. soprano, alto, tenor, bass.
    b. bass, tenor, soprano, alto.
    c. tenor, soprano, alto, bass.
    d. soprano, tenor, alto, bass.

78. Which of the following voices has the lowest range?
    a. baritone
    b. bass
    c. tenor
    d. alto

79. Antonio Stradivari was the greatest master builder of:
    a. pianos.
    b. violins.
    c. harpsichords.
    d. flutes.

80. Which is the correct order of bowed string instruments from highest to lowest in range?
    a. violin, viola, cello, double bass
    b. violin, cello, viola, double bass
    c. viola, violin, cello, double bass
    d. double bass, cello, viola, violin

81. The special effect produced on a string instrument by plucking the string with the finger is called:
    a. vibrato.
    b. glissando.
    c. pizzicato.
    d. tremolo.

82. A rapid alternation between a tone and the one above it is called:
    a. a glissando.
    b. a trill.
    c. a double stop.
    d. a pizzicato.

83. The device placed on the bridge of string instruments to muffle the sound is called:
    a. a reed.
    b. a double reed.
    c. a bow.
    d. a mute.

Answer: b
Chronological Edition: Ch. 7, p. 33
Standard Edition: Ch. 7, p. 33
*Shorter Edition: Ch. 7, p. 31
Date used:

84. Harmonics on a string instrument are produced by:
     a. playing two strings simultaneously.
     b. lightly touching the string at certain points while the bow is being drawn.
     c. rapidly alternating two tones.
     d. sliding the hand from one note to the next.

Answer: c
Chronological Edition: Ch. 7, p. 34
Standard Edition: Ch. 7, p. 34
*Shorter Edition: Ch. 7, p. 31
Date used:

85. Chords whose notes are played in succession, as on the harp, are called:
     a. scales.
     b. glissandos.
     c. arpeggios.
     d. double stops.

Answer: a
Chronological Edition: Ch. 7, p. 34
Standard Edition: Ch. 7, p. 34
*Shorter Edition: Ch. 7, p. 31
Date used:

86. Which of the following instruments is NOT a member of the bowed string family?
     a. guitar
     b. violoncello
     c. viola
     d. violin

Answer: d
Chronological Edition: Ch. 7, p. 34
Standard Edition: Ch. 7, p. 34
*Shorter Edition: Ch. 7, p. 32
Date used:

87. Woodwind instruments are so called because:
     a. they are all made of wood.
     b. they are all played with a wooden reed.
     c. they all have a "woody" tone quality.
     d. none of the above.

Answer: d
Chronological Edition: Ch. 7, p. 34
Standard Edition: Ch. 7, p. 34
*Shorter Edition: Ch. 7, p. 32
Date used:

88. The highest sounding member of the woodwind family is:
     a. the flute.
     b. the oboe.
     c. the clarinet.
     d. the piccolo.

Answer: b
Chronological Edition: Ch. 7, p. 34ff
Standard Edition: Ch. 7, p. 34ff
*Shorter Edition: Ch. 7, p. 32ff
Date used:

89. Which of the following is NOT a woodwind instrument sounded by a reed?
     a. the bass clarinet
     b. the French horn
     c. the bassoon
     d. the contrabassoon

Answer: b
Chronological Edition: Ch. 7, p. 36
Standard Edition: Ch. 7, p. 36
*Shorter Edition: Ch. 7, p. 32ff
Date used:

90. Which of the following is a double reed instrument?
     a. the flute
     b. the oboe
     c. the clarinet
     d. the saxophone

Answer: d
Chronological Edition: Ch. 7, p. 36
Standard Edition: Ch. 7, p. 36
*Shorter Edition: Ch. 7, p. 32
Date used:

Answer: b
Chronological Edition: Ch. 7, p. 36
Standard Edition: Ch. 7, p. 36
*Shorter Edition: Ch. 7, p. 32
Date used:

Answer: d
Chronological Edition: Ch. 8, p. 36f
Standard Edition: Ch. 8, p. 36f
*Shorter Edition: Ch. 8, p. 34
Date used:

Answer: b
Chronological Edition: Ch. 8, p. 37
Standard Edition: Ch. 8, p. 37
*Shorter Edition: Ch. 8, p. 36
Date used:

Answer: c
Chronological Edition: Ch. 8, p. 37
Standard Edition: Ch. 8, p. 37
*Shorter Edition: Ch. 8, p. 36
Date used:

Answer: c
Chronological Edition: Ch. 8, p. 36ff
Standard Edition: Ch. 8, p. 36ff
*Shorter Edition: Ch. 8, p. 34ff
Date used:

Answer: d
Chronological Edition: Ch. 8, p. 39
Standard Edition: Ch. 8, p. 39
*Shorter Edition: Ch. 8, p. 36
Date used:

91. The instrument normally chosen to sound the tuning note in the orchestra is:
   a. the violin.
   b. the flute.
   c. the trumpet.
   d. the oboe.

92. To which instrument family does the English horn belong?
   a. brass
   b. woodwind
   c. string
   d. percussion

93. Which of the following is true of all brass instruments?
   a. They are made of metal.
   b. They are blown with a metal mouthpiece.
   c. The sound is created by the vibration of the lips.
   d. All of the above.

94. Which of the following brass instruments is sometimes played with the performer's hand plugging the bell?
   a. trumpet
   b. French horn
   c. trombone
   d. tuba

95. Which brass instrument uses a large, movable u-shaped slide to change notes?
   a. trumpet
   b. French horn
   c. trombone
   d. tuba

96. Which of the following is NOT a member of the brass family?
   a. trumpet
   b. French horn
   c. English horn
   d. tuba

97. The percussion family is comprised of a variety of instruments that are made to sound by:
   a. strumming.
   b. blowing air.
   c. plucking.
   d. striking or shaking.

Answer: a
Chronological Edition: Ch. 8, p. 39
Standard Edition: Ch. 8, p. 39
*Shorter Edition: Ch. 8, p. 36
Date used:

Answer: b
Chronological Edition: Ch. 8, p. 39f
Standard Edition: Ch. 8, p. 39f
*Shorter Edition: Ch. 8, p. 36ff
Date used:

Answer: a
Chronological Edition: Ch. 8, p. 39ff
Standard Edition: Ch. 8, p. 39ff
*Shorter Edition: Ch. 8, p. 38
Date used:

Answer: c
Chronological Edition: Ch. 8, p. 41
Standard Edition: Ch. 8, p. 41
*Shorter Edition: Ch. 8, p. 38
Date used:

Answer: c
Chronological Edition: Ch. 9, p. 43
Standard Edition: Ch. 9, p. 43
*Shorter Edition: Ch. 9, p. 40
Date used:

Answer: d
Chronological Edition: Ch. 9, p. 43
Standard Edition: Ch. 9, p. 43
*Shorter Edition: Ch. 9, p. 40
Date used:

Answer: b
Chronological Edition: Ch. 9, p. 44
Standard Edition: Ch. 9, p. 44
*Shorter Edition: Ch. 9, p. 40
Date used:

98. The alternate term for the kettledrum is:
    a. timpani.
    b. glockenspiel.
    c. side drum.
    d. marimba.

99. Which of the following is NOT a percussion instrument?
    a. timpani
    b. harp
    c. xylophone
    d. celesta

100. Which of the following would be classified as an unpitched percussion instrument?
    a. bass drum
    b. timpani
    c. glockenspiel
    d. xylophone

101. The piano got its name, originally pianoforte, from:
    a. the name of the inventor.
    b. the fact that it could not sustain tones.
    c. its wide dynamic range.
    d. the way it was played late at night.

102. A fairly large body of singers who perform together is called:
    a. an orchestra.
    b. a chamber ensemble.
    c. a chorus.
    d. a band.

103. The term a cappella refers to choral music performed:
    a. with organ accompaniment.
    b. with orchestral accompaniment.
    c. with piano accompaniment.
    d. without any accompaniment.

104. What distinguishes chamber music from orchestral music?
    a. the forms of the movements
    b. the number of players to each part
    c. the room in which the music is being performed
    d. the number of movements in a work

Answer: b
Chronological Edition: Ch. 9, p. 44ff
Standard Edition: Ch. 9, p. 44ff
*Shorter Edition: Ch. 9, p. 42ff
Date used:

Answer: a
Chronological Edition: Ch. 9, p. 46
Standard Edition: Ch. 9, p. 46
*Shorter Edition: Ch. 9, p. 43
Date used:

Answer: d
Chronological Edition: Ch. 9, p. 47
Standard Edition: Ch. 9, p. 47
*Shorter Edition: Ch. 9, p. 43
Date used:

Answer: d
Chronological Edition: Ch. 9, p. 48
Standard Edition: Ch. 9, p. 48
*Shorter Edition: Ch. 9, p. 43
Date used:

Answer: b
Chronological Edition: Ch. 9, p. 48
Standard Edition: Ch. 9, p. 48
Date used:

Answer: c
Chronological Edition: Ch. 9, p. 49ff
Standard Edition: Ch. 9, p. 49ff
*Shorter Edition: Ch. 9, p. 44f
Date used:

Answer: a
Chronological Edition: Ch. 9, p. 52
Standard Edition: Ch. 9, p. 52
*Shorter Edition: Ch. 9, p. 46
Date used:

105. Approximately two-thirds of a symphony orchestra consists of:
a. woodwinds.
b. strings.
c. brass.
d. percussion.

106. Which instruments are traditionally seated in the front of the orchestra?
a. strings
b. woodwinds
c. brass
d. percussion

107. John Philip Sousa was famous as a composer of:
a. symphonies.
b. string quartets.
c. jazz.
d. marches.

108. A jazz band is normally comprised of:
a. woodwind instruments.
b. brass instruments.
c. percussion instruments.
d. all of the above.

109. Which meter would be conducted in a pattern of down–right–up?
a. duple
b. triple
c. quadruple
d. sextuple

110. Britten's *Young Person's Guide to the Orchestra* exemplifies the forms of:
a. concerto and sonata.
b. prelude and fugue.
c. variations and fugue.
d. variations and madrigal.

111. Musical style is best defined as:
a. the characteristic manner of presentation of the work.
b. the succession of dynamics from beginning to end of the work.
c. the shape of the melody line in the work.
d. the harmonics of the work.

Answer: d
Chronological Edition: Ch. 9, p. 52
Standard Edition: Ch. 9, p. 52
*Shorter Edition: Ch. 9, p. 46
Date used:

Answer: b
Chronological Edition: Ch. 9, p. 53
Standard Edition: Ch. 9, p. 53
*Shorter Edition: Ch. 9, p. 47
Date used:

Answer: c
Chronological Edition: Ch. 9, p. 53
Standard Edition: Ch. 9, p. 53
*Shorter Edition: Ch. 9, p. 47
Date used:

112. The concept of style can be identified with:
    a. individual artworks.
    b. a creator's personal manner of expression.
    c. music of an entire culture.
    d. all of the above.

113. The approximate dates for the Renaissance era are:
    a. 1150–1450.
    b. 1450–1600.
    c. 1600–1750.
    d. 1725–1775.

114. The Classical period:
    a. followed Antiquity and preceded the Middle Ages.
    b. followed the Renaissance and preceded the Baroque.
    c. followed the Baroque and preceded the Romantic era.
    d. followed the Romantic era and preceded the Twentieth century.

TRUE\FALSE QUESTIONS

Answer: T
Chronological Edition: Ch. 1, p. 7
Standard Edition: Ch. 1, p. 7
*Shorter Edition: Ch. 1, p. 7
Date used:

Answer: T
Chronological Edition: Ch. 1, p. 8
Standard Edition: Ch. 1, p. 8
*Shorter Edition: Ch. 1, p. 8
Date used:

Answer: T
Chronological Edition: Ch. 1, p. 8
Standard Edition: Ch. 1, p. 8
*Shorter Edition: Ch. 1, p. 8
Date used:

Answer: F
Chronological Edition: Ch. 1, p. 8
Standard Edition: Ch. 1, p. 8
*Shorter Edition: Ch. 1, p. 8
Date used:

115. The upward or downward direction of a melody determines its shape.

116. Melodies that move principally in stepwise motion are conjunct.

117. Disjunct motion describes melodies that move principally by skip.

118. The melody of *The Star-Spangled Banner* is best described as conjunct.

Answer: T
Chronological Edition: Ch. 1, p. 9
Standard Edition: Ch. 1, p. 9
*Shorter Edition: Ch. 1, p. 9
Date used:

119. A component unit of a melody is a phrase.

Answer: F
Chronological Edition: Ch. 1, p. 9
Standard Edition: Ch. 1, p. 9
*Shorter Edition: Ch. 1, p. 9
Date used:

120. The phrases in the American tune *Amazing Grace* are of unequal length.

Answer: F
Chronological Edition: Ch. 2, p. 10
Standard Edition: Ch. 2, p. 10
*Shorter Edition: Ch. 2, p. 10
Date used:

121. The controlled movement of music in time is called harmony.

Answer: T
Chronological Edition: Ch. 2, p. 10
Standard Edition: Ch. 2, p. 10
Date used:

122. Rhythm is the element of music most closely associated with physical movement.

Answer: T
Chronological Edition: Ch. 2, p. 10
Standard Edition: Ch. 2, p. 10
Date used:

123. Meter is an organizing principle shared by music and poetry.

Answer: T
Chronological Edition: Ch. 2, p. 11
Standard Edition: Ch. 2, p. 11
*Shorter Edition: Ch. 2, p. 11
Date used:

124. Meter is the measurement of musical time.

Answer: T
Chronological Edition: Ch. 2, p. 11
Standard Edition: Ch. 2, p. 11
*Shorter Edition: Ch. 2, p. 11
Date used:

125. The measure marks off a grouping of beats, each with a fixed number that coincides with the meter.

Answer: T
Chronological Edition: Ch. 2, p. 14
Standard Edition: Ch. 2, p. 14
*Shorter Edition: Ch. 2, p. 13
Date used:

126. Syncopation is a rhythmic characteristic of American jazz.

Answer: F
Chronological Edition: Ch. 3, p. 14ff
Standard Edition: Ch. 3, p. 14ff
*Shorter Edition: Ch. 3, p. 13ff
Date used:

127. Melody and harmony function independently of one another.

Answer: T
Chronological Edition: Ch. 3, p. 15
Standard Edition: Ch. 3, p. 15
*Shorter Edition: Ch. 3, p. 14
Date used:

128. An interval may be defined as the distance between two notes.

Answer: T
Chronological Edition: Ch. 3, p. 15
Standard Edition: Ch. 3, p. 15
*Shorter Edition: Ch. 3, p. 14
Date used:

129. A triad is a chord made up of three tones.

Answer: T
Chronological Edition: Ch. 3, p. 15f
Standard Edition: Ch. 3, p. 15f
*Shorter Edition: Ch. 3, p. 14f
Date used:

130. Three alternate notes of a scale, sounded simultaneously, form a triad.

Answer: T
Chronological Edition: Ch. 3, p. 16
Standard Edition: Ch. 3, p. 16
*Shorter Edition: Ch. 3, p. 15
Date used:

131. The principle of organization around a central tone is called tonality.

Answer: T
Chronological Edition: Ch. 3, p. 16f
Standard Edition: Ch. 3, p. 16f
*Shorter Edition: Ch. 3, p. 15f
Date used:

132. The two scale types commonly found in Western music from about 1650 to 1900 are major and minor.

Answer: T
Chronological Edition: Ch. 3, p. 17
Standard Edition: Ch. 3, p. 17
*Shorter Edition: Ch. 3, p. 16
Date used:

133. Harmonic movement is generated by motion toward a goal or resolution.

Answer: F
Chronological Edition: Ch. 3, p. 17
Standard Edition: Ch. 3, p. 17
*Shorter Edition: Ch. 3, p. 16
Date used:

134. A combination of tones that is discordant and unstable produces a consonance.

Answer: F
Chronological Edition: Ch. 3, p. 17
Standard Edition: Ch. 3, p. 17
Date used:

135.   Generally speaking, music has grown more consonant through the ages.

Answer: T
Chronological Edition: Ch. 4, p. 18
Standard Edition: Ch. 4, p. 18
*Shorter Edition: Ch. 4, p. 17
Date used:

136.   A single-voiced texture is called monophonic.

Answer: T
Chronological Edition: Ch. 4, p. 18
Standard Edition: Ch. 4, p. 18
*Shorter Edition: Ch. 4, p. 17
Date used:

137.   The art of combining two or more simultaneous melodic lines is called counterpoint.

Answer: F
Chronological Edition: Ch. 4, p. 18
Standard Edition: Ch. 4, p. 18
*Shorter Edition: Ch. 4, p. 17
Date used:

138.   The art of counterpoint is most closely associated with monophonic texture.

Answer: F
Chronological Edition: Ch. 4, p. 18f
Standard Edition: Ch. 4, p. 18f
*Shorter Edition: Ch. 4, p. 17f
Date used:

139.   Homophonic describes a single-voiced texture without accompaniment.

Answer: F
Chronological Edition: Ch. 4, p. 19
Standard Edition: Ch. 4, p. 19
*Shorter Edition: Ch. 4, p. 18
Date used:

140.   Most compositions use one type of texture exclusively.

Answer: T
Chronological Edition: Ch. 4, p. 18f
Standard Edition: Ch. 4, p. 18f
*Shorter Edition: Ch. 4, p. 18
Date used:

141.   Imitation is a technique most often employed in polyphonic music.

Answer: T
Chronological Edition: Ch. 4, p. 19
Standard Edition: Ch. 4, p. 19
*Shorter Edition: Ch. 4, p. 18
Date used:

142.   *Row, Row, Row Your Boat* can be sung as a musical canon.

Answer: F
Chronological Edition: Ch. 4, p. 19f
Standard Edition: Ch. 4, p. 19f
*Shorter Edition: Ch. 4, p. 18
Date used:

143. The technique that turns the melody upside down is called retrograde.

Answer: T
Chronological Edition: Ch. 4, p. 19f
Standard Edition: Ch. 4, p. 19f
*Shorter Edition: Ch. 4, p. 18
Date used:

144. The terms augmentation and diminution refer to the time values of the melodic movement.

Answer: T
Chronological Edition: Ch. 5, p. 22
Standard Edition: Ch. 5, p. 22
*Shorter Edition: Ch. 5, p. 21
Date used:

145. Musical structure generally features a dualism between repetition and contrast.

Answer: F
Chronological Edition: Ch. 5, p. 22f
Standard Edition: Ch. 5, p. 22f
*Shorter Edition: Ch. 5, p. 21
Date used:

146. Forms are fixed molds into which composers force their material.

Answer: F
Chronological Edition: Ch. 5, p. 23f
Standard Edition: Ch. 5, p. 23f
*Shorter Edition: Ch. 5, p. 22
Date used:

147. A musical form based on statement, departure, and a restatement of the first idea is called binary form.

Answer: T
Chronological Edition: Ch. 5, p. 23f
Standard Edition: Ch. 5, p. 23f
*Shorter Edition: Ch. 5, p. 22
Date used:

148. Ternary form is best outlined as A-B-A.

Answer: T
Chronological Edition: Ch. 5, p. 23f
Standard Edition: Ch. 5, p. 23f
*Shorter Edition: Ch. 5, p. 22
Date used:

149. Ternary form extends the idea of statement and departure by bringing back the first statement.

Answer: T
Chronological Edition: Ch. 5, p. 25
Standard Edition: Ch. 5, p. 25
*Shorter Edition: Ch. 5, p. 23
Date used:

150. The restatement of a theme or motive at a higher or lower pitch level is known as a sequence.

Answer: T
Chronological Edition: Ch. 5, p. 25
Standard Edition: Ch. 5, p. 25
*Shorter Edition: Ch. 5, p. 23
Date used:

151. A motive is the smallest fragment of a theme that forms a melodic-rhythmic unit.

Answer: T
Chronological Edition: Ch. 6, p. 26
Standard Edition: Ch. 6, p. 26
*Shorter Edition: Ch. 6, p. 24
Date used:

152. The tempo is the rate of speed of the music.

Answer: T
Chronological Edition: Ch. 6, p. 26
Standard Edition: Ch. 6, p. 26
*Shorter Edition: Ch. 6, p. 24
Date used:

153. The tempo of a piece affects its mood and character.

Answer: T
Chronological Edition: Ch. 6, p. 26
Standard Edition: Ch. 6, p. 26
*Shorter Edition: Ch. 6, p. 25
Date used:

154. Allegro is an Italian term for a fast, cheerful tempo.

Answer: T
Chronological Edition: Ch. 6, p. 27
Standard Edition: Ch. 6, p. 27
*Shorter Edition: Ch. 6, p. 25
Date used:

155. The degree of loudness and softness in music is called dynamics.

Answer: F
Chronological Edition: Ch. 7, p. 30
Standard Edition: Ch. 7, p. 30
*Shorter Edition: Ch. 7, p. 28
Date used:

156. Other conditions being equal, the shorter a string or column of air, the lower the pitch will be on a musical instrument.

Answer: T
Chronological Edition: Ch. 7, p. 31
Standard Edition: Ch. 7, p. 31
*Shorter Edition: Ch. 7, p. 29
Date used:

157. The composer has available two basic mediums—human voices and musical instruments.

Answer: T
Chronological Edition: Ch. 7, p. 31
Standard Edition: Ch. 7, p. 31
*Shorter Edition: Ch. 7, p. 29
Date used:

158. Throughout history, the voice has served as a model to instrumentalists and to instrument builders.

Answer: F
Chronological Edition: Ch. 7, p. 31
Standard Edition: Ch. 7, p. 31
Date used:

159. Throughout history, women's voices have held a central role in the performance of church music.

Answer: T
Chronological Edition: Ch. 7, p. 33
Standard Edition: Ch. 7, p. 33
*Shorter Edition: Ch. 7, p. 29
Date used:

160. The violin was highly developed by Italian instrument makers between about 1600 and 1750.

Answer: F
Chronological Edition: Ch. 7, p. 33
Standard Edition: Ch. 7, p. 33
*Shorter Edition: Ch. 7, p. 31
Date used:

161. The viola is somewhat smaller and higher pitched than a violin.

Answer: F
Chronological Edition: Ch. 7, p. 33
Standard Edition: Ch. 7, p. 33
*Shorter Edition: Ch. 7, p. 31
Date used:

162. The term pizzicato means to play in a throbbing manner.

Answer: T
Chronological Edition: Ch. 7, p. 36
Standard Edition: Ch. 7, p. 36
*Shorter Edition: Ch. 7, p. 34
Date used:

163. The most recently invented member of the woodwind family is the saxophone.

Answer: T
Chronological Edition: Ch. 8, p. 37
Standard Edition: Ch. 8, p. 37
*Shorter Edition: Ch. 8, p. 34
Date used:

164. A player's embouchure refers to the position of the lips, jaws and facial muscles.

Answer: F
Chronological Edition: Ch. 8, p. 37
Standard Edition: Ch. 8, p. 37
*Shorter Edition: Ch. 8, p. 34
Date used:

165. The trumpet is the lowest in pitch of the brass family.

Answer: T
Chronological Edition: Ch. 8, p. 39
Standard Edition: Ch. 8, p. 39
*Shorter Edition: Ch. 8, p. 36
Date used:

166. The two categories of percussion instruments are pitched and unpitched.

Answer: F
Chronological Edition: Ch. 8, p. 41
Standard Edition: Ch. 8, p. 41
*Shorter Edition: Ch. 8, p. 38
Date used:

167. The piano is limited by a narrow range of pitches and dynamics.

Answer: T
Chronological Edition: Ch. 8, p. 41
Standard Edition: Ch. 8, p. 41
*Shorter Edition: Ch. 8, p. 38f
Date used:

168. The organ is a wind instrument, sounded by air.

Answer: T
Chronological Edition: Ch. 9, p. 44
Standard Edition: Ch. 9, p. 44
*Shorter Edition: Ch. 9, p. 40
Date used:

169. Chamber music is intended for a small group of performers, with one player to a part.

Answer: F
Chronological Edition: Ch. 9, p. 44
Standard Edition: Ch. 9, p. 44
*Shorter Edition: Ch. 9, p. 42
Date used:

170. The modern orchestra is typically made up of thirty to forty players.

Answer: T
Chronological Edition: Ch. 9, p. 44
Standard Edition: Ch. 9, p. 44
*Shorter Edition: Ch. 9, p. 41
Date used:

171. The standard instrumentation of a string quartet is 2 violins, viola, and cello.

Answer: F
Chronological Edition: Ch. 9, p. 45
Standard Edition: Ch. 9, p. 45
*Shorter Edition: Ch. 9, p. 41
Date used:

172. A piano trio is an ensemble of three pianos.

Answer: T
Chronological Edition: Ch. 9, p. 47
Standard Edition: Ch. 9, p. 47
*Shorter Edition: Ch. 9, p. 43
Date used:

173. The concert band had its origins in medieval wind groups.

Answer: T
Chronological Edition: Ch. 9, p. 48
Standard Edition: Ch. 9, p. 48
Date used:

174. Most large musical ensembles use a conductor in order to perform together.

Answer: F
Chronological Edition: Ch. 9, p. 48
Standard Edition: Ch. 9, p. 48
Date used:

Answer: F
Chronological Edition: Ch. 9, p. 49
Standard Edition: Ch. 9, p. 49
*Shorter Edition: Ch. 9, p. 44
Date used:

Answer: F
Chronological Edition: Ch. 9, p. 53
Standard Edition: Ch. 9, p. 53
*Shorter Edition: Ch. 9, p. 47
Date used:

175. The upbeat is the strongest in any meter.

176. The *Young Person's Guide to the Orchestra* by Benjamin Britten is based on a dance tune by Beethoven.

177. The dates given for the beginning and end of eras are precise ones.

MEDIEVAL AND RENAISSANCE MUSIC

MULTIPLE CHOICE QUESTIONS

Answer: a
Chronological Edition: Ch. 10, p. 58
Standard Edition: Ch. 52, p. 268
*Shorter Edition: Ch. 10, p. 51f
Date used:

1. The Frankish emperor who encouraged education and the concept of a centralized government was:
   a. Charlemagne.
   b. Pope Gregory.
   c. Hildegard von Bingen.
   d. Chaucer.

Answer: c
Chronological Edition: Ch. 10, p. 58
Standard Edition: Ch. 52, p. 268
*Shorter Edition: Ch. 10, p. 52
Date used:

2. Hildegard von Bingen is known as:
   a. a patroness of the troubadours.
   b. a legendary woman minnesinger.
   c. a nun and church composer.
   d. the mother of Richard the Lion-Hearted.

Answer: d
Chronological Edition: Ch. 10, p. 59
Standard Edition: Ch. 52, p. 269
*Shorter Edition: Ch. 10, p. 52
Date used:

3. The High Middle Ages witnessed:
   a. the building of great cathedrals.
   b. the founding of universities.
   c. the rise of the bourgeoisie.
   d. all of the above.

Answer: c
Chronological Edition: Ch. 11, p. 60
Standard Edition: Ch. 53, p. 270
*Shorter Edition: Ch. 11, p. 53
Date used:

4. _____ is traditionally associated with collecting and codifying the chants of the Church.
   a. Charlemagne
   b. Léonin
   c. Pope Gregory
   d. Machaut

Answer: d
Chronological Edition: Ch. 11, p. 60
Standard Edition: Ch. 53, p. 270
*Shorter Edition: Ch. 11, p. 53
Date used:

5. The single-line melodies of the music of the early Christian Church are known as:
   a. Gregorian chant.
   b. plainchant.
   c. plainsong.
   d. all of the above.

Answer: b
Chronological Edition: Ch. 11, p. 60
Standard Edition: Ch. 53, p. 270
*Shorter Edition: Ch. 11, p. 53
Date used:

6. Which is NOT true of Gregorian chant?
   a. It is monophonic in texture.
   b. It is accompanied by triadic harmony.
   c. It is generally in free-verse rhythm.
   d. It is generally conjunct in movement.

Answer: b
Chronological Edition: Ch. 11, p. 60
Standard Edition: Ch. 53, p. 270
*Shorter Edition: Ch. 11, p. 54
Date used:

Answer: a
Chronological Edition: Ch. 11, p. 60
Standard Edition: Ch. 53, p. 270
*Shorter Edition: Ch. 11, p. 54
Date used:

Answer: b
Chronological Edition: Ch. 11, p. 60
Standard Edition: Ch. 53, p. 270
*Shorter Edition: Ch. 11, p. 54
Date used:

Answer: b
Chronological Edition: Ch. 11, p. 62
Standard Edition: Ch. 53, p. 272
*Shorter Edition: Ch. 11, p. 54
Date used:

Answer: a
Chronological Edition: Ch. 11, p. 62
Standard Edition: Ch. 53, p. 272
*Shorter Edition: Ch. 11, p. 54
Date used:

Answer: d
Chronological Edition: Ch. 11, p. 62
Standard Edition: Ch. 53, p. 272
*Shorter Edition: Ch. 11, p. 54f
Date used:

Answer: b
Chronological Edition: Ch. 11, p. 63
Standard Edition: Ch. 53, p. 273
*Shorter Edition: Ch. 11, p. 56
Date used:

7. Early notation employed small ascending and descending signs written above the words to suggest the melodic contours of chants. These signs were called:
    a. melismas.
    b. neumes.
    c. motets.
    d. modes.

8. A setting of Gregorian chant with one note per syllable is called:
    a. syllabic.
    b. neumatic.
    c. melismatic.
    d. modal.

9. A setting of plainsong with two to four notes per syllable is called:
    a. syllabic.
    b. neumatic.
    c. melismatic.
    d. modal.

10. The portion of the Mass that remains the same in every celebration of the service is called:
    a. the Proper.
    b. the Ordinary.
    c. the Gradual.
    d. none of these.

11. The portion of the Mass that changes from day to day, dependent upon the feast celebrated, is called:
    a. the Proper.
    b. the Ordinary.
    c. the Liturgy.
    d. none of these.

12. Which is NOT true of the Gregorian chant, *Haec dies*?
    a. It is for the Mass on Easter Day.
    b. It is musically elaborate in melismatic style.
    c. It is a responsorial chant, performed with soloist and choir.
    d. It is from the Ordinary of the Mass.

13. The development in music, from about 1000 A.D., that paralleled the development of perspective in art was:
    a. monophony.
    b. polyphony.
    c. homophony.
    d. none of these.

Answer: b
Chronological Edition: Ch. 11, p. 64
Standard Edition: Ch. 53, p. 273
*Shorter Edition: Ch. 11, p. 56
Date used:

Answer: a
Chronological Edition: Ch. 11, p. 64
Standard Edition: Ch. 53, p. 273
*Shorter Edition: Ch. 11, p. 56
Date used:

Answer: b
Chronological Edition: Ch. 11, p. 64
Standard Edition: Ch. 53, p. 273
Date used:

Answer: b
Chronological Edition: Ch. 11, p. 65
Standard Edition: Ch. 53, p. 275
*Shorter Edition: Ch. 11, p. 56
Date used:

Answer: c
Chronological Edition: Ch. 11, p. 65
Standard Edition: Ch. 53, p. 275
Date used:

Answer: d
Chronological Edition: Ch. 11, p. 65
Standard Edition: Ch. 53, p. 275
Date used:

Answer: b
Chronological Edition: Ch. 11, p. 65f
Standard Edition: Ch. 53, p. 275f
*Shorter Edition: Ch. 11, p. 56f
Date used:

14. The earliest type of polyphony was:
    a. plainsong.
    b. organum.
    c. motet.
    d. none of these.

15. The Notre Dame style of polyphony in which the tenor line was based on a pre-existing chant melody in long note values and the upper voice moved freely (and more rapidly) was called:
    a. organal style.
    b. discant style.
    c. ostinato style.
    d. none of these.

16. The Notre Dame style of polyphony in which the tenor line moved faster, paralleling the movement of the upper voice was called:
    a. organal style.
    b. discant style.
    c. ostinato style.
    d. none of these.

17. The early polyphonic form that resulted from the addition of texts to all voices was called:
    a. organum.
    b. motet.
    c. duplum.
    d. triplum.

18. Medieval composers based their motets on a Gregorian chant fragment known as:
    a. a hocket.
    b. a triplum.
    c. a cantus firmus.
    d. a mot.

19. The part of a motet that contained the structural cantus firmus was:
    a. the duplum.
    b. the triplum.
    c. the clausulae.
    d. the tenor.

20. Which is NOT true of the early Medieval motet?
    a. Its name comes from the French word "mot".
    b. It always has texts in French.
    c. It is often polytextual, with several different texts.
    d. Instruments may have been used to perform it.

Answer: b
Chronological Edition: Ch. 11, p. 65f
Standard Edition: Ch. 53, p. 275f
Date used:

21. Which best describes the motet *O mitissima—Virgo—Haec dies*?
    a. a two-voice work, in duple meter, on Latin secular texts
    b. a two-voice work, in triple meter, with Latin text praising the Virgin Mary
    c. a three-voice work, in duple meter, with a single Latin text for Easter Sunday
    d. a three-voice work, in triple meter, with French texts of courtly love

Answer: a
Chronological Edition: Ch. 12, p. 69
Standard Edition: Ch. 54, p. 279
*Shorter Edition: Ch. 11, p. 57
Date used:

22. Versatile Medieval entertainers who played instruments, sang and danced, juggled, and performed tricks were known as:
    a. jongleurs.
    b. troubadours.
    c. Goliards.
    d. trouvères.

Answer: a
Chronological Edition: Ch. 12, p. 69
Standard Edition: Ch. 54, p. 279
*Shorter Edition: Ch. 11, p. 57
Date used:

23. Which of the following were the Medieval poet-musicians of southern France?
    a. troubadours
    b. trouvères
    c. jongleurs
    d. minnesingers

Answer: c
Chronological Edition: Ch. 12, p. 69
Standard Edition: Ch. 54, p. 279
*Shorter Edition: Ch. 11, p. 58
Date used:

24. Which was NOT a function of secular music in Medieval court life?
    a. accompaniment for dancing and banquets
    b. ceremonial occasions and tournaments
    c. devotional services
    d. military music, to support campaigns and troops

Answer: d
Chronological Edition: Ch. 12, p. 70
Standard Edition: Ch. 54, p. 280
*Shorter Edition: Ch. 11, p. 58
Date used:

25. Which was NOT a subject reflected in the poems of the troubadours and trouvères?
    a. politics and current events
    b. moralizing and devotional themes
    c. love and unrequited passion
    d. the rebirth of Classical learning

Answer: a
Chronological Edition: Ch. 12, p. 71
Standard Edition: Ch. 54, p. 281
Date used:

26. A melody which repeats with each stanza of a poem is called:
    a. strophic.
    b. isorhythmic.
    c. neumatic.
    d. syllabic.

Answer: d
Chronological Edition: Ch. 12, p. 71
Standard Edition: Ch. 54, p. 281
Date used:

Answer: c
Chronological Edition: Ch. 12, p. 73
Standard Edition: Ch. 54, p. 283
*Shorter Edition: Ch. 11, p. 59
Date used:

Answer: b
Chronological Edition: Ch. 12, p. 73f
Standard Edition: Ch. 54, p. 283f
Date used:

Answer: a
Chronological Edition: Ch. 12, p. 73
Standard Edition: Ch. 54, p. 283
*Shorter Edition: Ch. 11, p. 59
Date used:

Answer: b
Chronological Edition: Ch. 12, p. 75
Standard Edition: Ch. 54, p. 285
*Shorter Edition: Ch. 11, p. 59
Date used:

Answer: b
Chronological Edition: Ch. 12, p. 76
Standard Edition: Ch. 54, p. 286
Date used:

Answer: b
Chronological Edition: Ch. 12, p. 76
Standard Edition: Ch. 54, p. 286
Date used:

27. Which of the following was a Medieval string instrument?
    a. the psaltery
    b. the dulcimer
    c. the vielle
    d. all of the above

28. The fourteenth-century secular genre that flowered in the hands of Machaut was:
    a. the Mass.
    b. the clausulae.
    c. the motet.
    d. the trouvère song.

29. Machaut's motet *Hareu! hareu!—Helas!—Obediens* features:
    a. strophic form.
    b. an ostinato or cantus firmus.
    c. sacred Latin texts.
    d. free, non-metric rhythm.

30. The outstanding composer-poet of the French Ars Nova was:
    a. Machaut.
    b. Boccaccio.
    c. Chaucer.
    d. Petrarch.

31. Music of the fourteenth century underwent a change of style that encompassed developments in rhythm, meter, counterpoint, and harmony. This new style became known as:
    a. the Ars Antiqua.
    b. the Ars Nova.
    c. the Renaissance.
    d. the Notre Dame school.

32. The carol is a Medieval strophic song with a refrain known as:
    a. a clausulae.
    b. a burden.
    c. an ostinato.
    d. a cantus firmus.

33. The carol *Deo gratias, Anglia* celebrated:
    a. the victory of Charlemagne over the Turks.
    b. the victory of the English in the Battle of Agincourt.
    c. the marriage of Henry VIII to Anne Boleyn.
    d. the crowning of Elizabeth I of England.

Answer: c
Chronological Edition: Ch. 12, p. 78
Standard Edition: Ch. 54, p. 288
*Shorter Edition: Ch. 11, p. 62
Date used:

Answer: b
Chronological Edition: Ch. 12, p. 79
Standard Edition: Ch. 54, p. 289
Date used:

Answer: a
Chronological Edition: Ch. 12, p. 79
Standard Edition: Ch. 54, p. 289
Date used:

Answer: a
Chronological Edition: Ch. 12, p. 79f
Standard Edition: Ch. 54, p. 289f
*Shorter Edition: Ch. 11, p. 62
Date used:

Answer: d
Chronological Edition: Ch. 12, p. 80
Standard Edition: Ch. 54, p. 290
*Shorter Edition: Ch. 11, p. 62
Date used:

Answer: a
Chronological Edition: Ch. 12, p. 80
Standard Edition: Ch. 54, p. 290
*Shorter Edition: Ch. 11, p. 62
Date used:

Answer: d
Chronological Edition: Ch. 12, p. 80
Standard Edition: Ch. 54, p. 290
Date used:

34. The fretted string instrument of the guitar family with a pear-shaped back is:
   a. the rebec.
   b. the psaltery.
   c. the lute.
   d. the shawm.

35. An end-blown flute with a whistle mouthpiece is called:
   a. a crumhorn.
   b. a recorder.
   c. a shawm.
   d. a psaltery.

36. A Medieval "brass" instrument usually made from wood with fingerholes is called:
   a. the cornetto.
   b. the shawm.
   c. the sackbut.
   d. the vielle.

37. The Medieval ancestor of the modern trombone is:
   a. the sackbut.
   b. the cornetto.
   c. the shawm.
   d. the nakers.

38. To what family of instruments do the portative, positive, and regal belong?
   a. strings
   b. woodwinds
   c. brass
   d. keyboards

39. To what family of instruments do the nakers and tabor belong?
   a. percussion
   b. woodwinds
   c. strings
   d. brass

40. The principal instrument heard in the Medieval *Saltarello* is:
   a. the cornetto.
   b. the lute.
   c. the recorder.
   d. the shawm.

Answer: b
Chronological Edition: Ch. 12, p. 81
Standard Edition: Ch. 54, p. 291
Date used:

41. The Medieval *Saltarello* features an accompaniment of percussion and a sustained single note called:
a. an embellishment.
b. a drone.
c. a regal.
d. an isorhythm.

Answer: a
Chronological Edition: Ch. 13, p. 82
Standard Edition: Ch. 55, p. 293
*Shorter Edition: Ch. 12, p. 64
Date used:

42. All of the following represent the thinking of the Renaissance EXCEPT:
a. an exclusively religious orientation.
b. an interest in scientific inquiry.
c. a questioning of blind faith.
d. a focus on humanity and life.

Answer: b
Chronological Edition: Ch. 13, p. 84
Standard Edition: Ch. 55, p. 294
*Shorter Edition: Ch. 12, p. 67
Date used:

43. All of the following were Renaissance artists EXCEPT:
a. Michelangelo.
b. Goya.
c. Leonardo da Vinci.
d. Donatello.

Answer: c
Chronological Edition: Ch. 13, p. 84
Standard Edition: Ch. 55, p. 294
*Shorter Edition: Ch. 12, p. 66
Date used:

44. Which historical event did NOT take place in the Renaissance?
a. the discovery of the New World.
b. the introduction of printing in the West.
c. the writing of the Magna Carta.
d. the Protestant Reformation.

Answer: d
Chronological Edition: Ch. 13, p. 85
Standard Edition: Ch. 55, p. 295
*Shorter Edition: Ch. 12, p. 67
Date used:

45. Which was the chief institution that supported music in Renaissance society?
a. the Church
b. the city and state
c. the aristocratic courts
d. all of the above

Answer: d
Chronological Edition: Ch. 13, p. 85
Standard Edition: Ch. 55, p. 295
*Shorter Edition: Ch. 12, p. 67
Date used:

46. Renaissance musicians could make their living in all of the following ways EXCEPT:
a. as choirmasters, singers, and organists.
b. as instrument builders or players.
c. as music printers and publishers.
d. as professional orchestral conductors.

Answer: b
Chronological Edition: Ch. 13, p. 86
Standard Edition: Ch. 55, p. 296
*Shorter Edition: Ch. 13, p. 68
Date used:

47. In Renaissance polyphony, motives wander from voice line to voice line, imitating each other. This style is known as:
a. a cappella style.
b. continuous imitation.
c. chorale style.
d. responsorial style.

Answer: a
Chronological Edition: Ch. 13, p. 86
Standard Edition: Ch. 55, p. 296
*Shorter Edition: Ch. 13, p. 68
Date used:

48. A vocal work without instrumental accompaniment is said to be performed:
     a. a cappella.
     b. responsorially.
     c. antiphonally.
     d. improvisationally.

Answer: a
Chronological Edition: Ch. 13, p. 86f
Standard Edition: Ch. 55, p. 297
*Shorter Edition: Ch. 13, p. 68
Date used:

49. The expressive device used by Renaissance composers to musically pictorialize words from the text is called:
     a. word painting.
     b. a cappella.
     c. continuous imitation.
     d. isorhythm.

Answer: c
Chronological Edition: Ch. 13, p. 87
Standard Edition: Ch. 55, p. 297
*Shorter Edition: Ch. 13, p. 68
Date used:

50. The fixed melody used as a basis for elaborate polyphonic writing in the Renaissance was called:
     a. word painting.
     b. a cappella.
     c. a cantus firmus.
     d. a saltarello.

Answer: d
Chronological Edition: Ch. 14, p. 87
Standard Edition: Ch. 56, p. 297
Date used:

51. Which genre of vocal music was NOT used in Renaissance church services?
     a. Gregorian chant
     b. motets
     c. Magnificats
     d. chansons

Answer: b
Chronological Edition: Ch. 14, p. 88
Standard Edition: Ch. 56, p. 298
*Shorter Edition: Ch. 13, p. 69
Date used:

52. Who was the early Renaissance composer who wrote the Latin motet *Alma redemptoris mater*?
     a. Guillaume Machaut
     b. Guillaume Dufay
     c. Josquin Desprez
     d. Giovanni Pierluigi da Palestrina

Answer: a
Chronological Edition: Ch. 14, p. 88
Standard Edition: Ch. 56, p. 298
*Shorter Edition: Ch. 13, p. 69
Date used:

53. The text of *Alma redemptoris mater* is:
     a. in praise of the Virgin Mary.
     b. in praise of the English victory at Agincourt.
     c. in praise of chivalric love.
     d. in praise of the Archangel Michael.

Answer: b
Chronological Edition: Ch. 14, p. 88
Standard Edition: Ch. 56, p. 298
*Shorter Edition: Ch. 13, p. 69f
Date used:

54. Which of the following describes the musical basis on which the motet *Alma redemptoris mater* was built?
     a. a five-note figure (A–G–F–D–E)
     b. a Gregorian chant in the top voice
     c. an isorhythm in the two lower voices
     d. freely composed

Answer: b
Chronological Edition: Ch. 14, p. 88f
Standard Edition: Ch. 56, p. 298f
Date used:

Answer: c
Chronological Edition: Ch. 14, p. 89f
Standard Edition: Ch. 56, p. 299f
Date used:

Answer: c
Chronological Edition: Ch. 14, p. 90
Standard Edition: Ch. 56, p. 300
*Shorter Edition: Ch. 13, p. 71f
Date used:

Answer: d
Chronological Edition: Ch. 14, p. 90
Standard Edition: Ch. 56, p. 300
*Shorter Edition: Ch. 13, p. 71
Date used:

Answer: a
Chronological Edition: Ch. 14, p. 90
Standard Edition: Ch. 56, p. 300
*Shorter Edition: Ch. 13, p. 71
Date used:

Answer: c
Chronological Edition: Ch. 14, p. 91
Standard Edition: Ch. 56, p. 301
Date used:

Answer: d
Chronological Edition: Ch. 14, p. 92
Standard Edition: Ch. 56, p. 302
*Shorter Edition: Ch. 13, p. 72
Date used:

55. Which is true of Dufay, Josquin and Palestrina?
   a. They were all of French birth.
   b. They all worked in Italy.
   c. They were all early Renaissance composers.
   d. They all wrote Protestant church music.

56. Which Renaissance work is for the most number of voice parts?
   a. Dufay's *Alma redemptoris mater*
   b. Josquin's *La sol fa re mi* Mass
   c. Palestrina's *Pope Marcellus Mass*
   d. They are all for the same number of voices.

57. Which of the following make up the movements of the Ordinary of the Mass?
   a. Introit, Gradual, Ite missa est, Agnus Dei
   b. Kyrie, Collect, Epistle, Gradual
   c. Kyrie, Gloria, Credo, Sanctus, Agnus Dei
   d. Agnus Dei, Magnificat, Dies irae, Kyrie

58. The first section of the Ordinary of the Mass, a plea for mercy in A–B–A form, is called:
   a. the Sanctus.
   b. the Credo.
   c. the Gloria.
   d. the Kyrie.

59. Which section of the Ordinary of the Mass is a confession of faith?
   a. the Credo
   b. the Gloria
   c. the Kyrie
   d. the Sanctus

60. The special Mass sung at funerals and memorials in the Roman Catholic Church is:
   a. the Magnificat.
   b. the Haec dies.
   c. the Requiem.
   d. the Litany.

61. What is the musical basis of Josquin's *La sol fa re mi* Mass?
   a. freely composed
   b. a Gregorian chant in the top voice
   c. an isorhythm in the two bottom voices
   d. a five-note figure (A–G–F–D–E)

Answer: b
Chronological Edition: Ch. 14, p. 94
Standard Edition: Ch. 56, p. 304
*Shorter Edition: Ch. 13, p. 73
Date used:

62. Which of the following was a leader in the Protestant Reformation?
    a. Giovanni Pierluigi da Palestrina
    b. Martin Luther
    c. St. Ignatius Loyola
    d. Ascanio Sforza

Answer: d
Chronological Edition: Ch. 14, p. 94
Standard Edition: Ch. 56, p. 304
*Shorter Edition: Ch. 13, p. 73
Date used:

63. Which was NOT a recommendation of the Council of Trent?
    a. to remove all secularism from Church music
    b. to make the words more understandable
    c. to discipline the irreverent attitudes of church musicians
    d. to use more instruments to embellish church music

Answer: a
Chronological Edition: Ch. 14, p. 94
Standard Edition: Ch. 56, p. 304
*Shorter Edition: Ch. 13, p. 73
Date used:

64. Which composer responded to the reforms of the Council of Trent in an exemplary fashion?
    a. Palestrina
    b. Josquin
    c. Dufay
    d. Tomkins

Answer: c
Chronological Edition: Ch. 14, p. 94
Standard Edition: Ch. 56, p. 304
*Shorter Edition: Ch. 13, p. 73
Date used:

65. Who is the composer of the *Pope Marcellus Mass*?
    a. Dufay
    b. Josquin
    c. Palestrina
    d. Tomkins

Answer: a
Chronological Edition: Ch. 14, p. 97
Standard Edition: Ch. 56, p. 307
Date used:

66. The Church of England broke away from the Catholic Church during the reign of:
    a. Henry VIII.
    b. Elizabeth I.
    c. Oliver Cromwell.
    d. James I.

Answer: b
Chronological Edition: Ch. 14, p. 97
Standard Edition: Ch. 56, p. 307
Date used:

67. The service and the anthem are the musical genres for the _____ Church.
    a. Lutheran
    b. Anglican
    c. Catholic
    d. all of the above

Answer: b
Chronological Edition: Ch. 14, p. 97
Standard Edition: Ch. 56, p. 307
Date used:

68. An Anglican church work for solo voices with a choral refrain is likely to be:
    a. a mass.
    b. a verse anthem.
    c. a full anthem.
    d. a motet.

Answer: c
Chronological Edition: Ch. 14, p. 97
Standard Edition: Ch. 56, p. 307
Date used:

Answer: d
Chronological Edition: Ch. 14, p. 97
Standard Edition: Ch. 56, p. 307
Date used:

Answer: b
Chronological Edition: Ch. 15, p. 98
Standard Edition: Ch. 57, p. 308
*Shorter Edition: Ch. 13, p. 76
Date used:

Answer: a
Chronological Edition: Ch. 15, p. 99
Standard Edition: Ch. 57, p. 309
*Shorter Edition: Ch. 13, p. 76
Date used:

Answer: c
Chronological Edition: Ch. 15, p. 99
Standard Edition: Ch. 57, p. 309
Date used:

Answer: d
Chronological Edition: Ch. 15, p. 101
Standard Edition: Ch. 57, p. 311
*Shorter Edition: Ch. 13, p. 77
Date used:

Answer: a
Chronological Edition: Ch. 15, p. 103
Standard Edition: Ch. 57, p. 313
Date used:

69. Which genre best describes *When David Heard That Absalom Was Slain* by Tomkins?
   a. motet
   b. verse anthem
   c. full anthem
   d. mass

70. Which piece makes an emotional impact through its tragic Biblical text, repeated key words, and frequent use of half-steps?
   a. *Alma redemptoris mater*
   b. *La sol fa re mi* Mass
   c. *Pope Marcellus Mass*
   d. *When David Heard That Absalom Was Slain*

71. The rondeau, ballade, and virelai were fixed poetic forms frequently set to music as:
   a. madrigals.
   b. chansons.
   c. motets.
   d. anthems.

72. Ockeghem's chanson, *L'autre d'antan*, set a text in _____ form.
   a. rondeau
   b. virelai
   c. ballade
   d. ternary

73. Which best describes Ockeghem's *L'autre d'antan*?
   a. a madrigal set to a Petrarch poem
   b. a secular motet celebrating a battle
   c. a chanson set to a fixed text form with a refrain
   d. a dance based on a popular chanson

74. The chanson *Bon jour mon coeur* is set to a poem by:
   a. Petrarch.
   b. Marot.
   c. Luther.
   d. Ronsard.

75. The opening of *Bon jour mon coeur* is best described as:
   a. homophonic.
   b. monophonic.
   c. polyphonic.
   d. isorhythmic.

Answer: d
Chronological Edition: Ch. 15, p. 104
Standard Edition: Ch. 57, p. 314
Date used:

Answer: c
Chronological Edition: Ch. 15, p. 104
Standard Edition: Ch. 57, p. 314
Date used:

Answer: b
Chronological Edition: Ch. 15, p. 104
Standard Edition: Ch. 57, p. 314
*Shorter Edition: Ch. 13, p. 81
Date used:

Answer: a
Chronological Edition: Ch. 15, p. 104
Standard Edition: Ch. 57, p. 314
*Shorter Edition: Ch. 13, p. 81
Date used:

Answer: d
Chronological Edition: Ch. 15, p. 104
Standard Edition: Ch. 57, p. 314
Date used:

Answer: b
Chronological Edition: Ch. 15, p. 104
Standard Edition: Ch. 57, p. 314
Date used:

Answer: c
Chronological Edition: Ch. 15, p. 105
Standard Edition: Ch. 57, p. 315
*Shorter Edition: Ch. 13, p. 77
Date used:

76. Tielman Susato was known as:
   a. a music printer.
   b. a composer and arranger.
   c. a professional instrumentalist.
   d. all of the above.

77. Susato's pavane *Mille regrets* is based on:
   a. a motet by Dufay.
   b. a madrigal by Monteverdi.
   c. a chanson by Josquin.
   d. a Gregorian chant.

78. Which of the following was a lively circle or line dance, often performed outdoors?
   a. pavane
   b. ronde
   c. allemande
   d. galliard

79. A stately court dance that often served as the first number of a set was:
   a. the pavane.
   b. the galliard.
   c. the saltarello.
   d. the ronde.

80. Which of the following would be considered an appropriate outdoor instrument?
   a. the flute
   b. the recorder
   c. the vielle
   d. the shawm

81. Instruments used for outdoor performances, such as the shawm and sackbut, are categorized as:
   a. soft.
   b. loud.
   c. small.
   d. large.

82. Which of the following was the chief form of Italian secular music in the Renaissance?
   a. the galliard
   b. the chanson
   c. the madrigal
   d. the ronde

Answer: a
Chronological Edition: Ch. 15, p. 105
Standard Edition: Ch. 57, p. 315
*Shorter Edition: Ch. 13, p. 77
Date used:

83. A short, lyric poem, in Italian, of a reflective nature would be best suited set to:
   a. a madrigal.
   b. a chanson.
   c. a saltarello.
   d. a motet.

Answer: c
Chronological Edition: Ch. 15, p. 105
Standard Edition: Ch. 57, p. 315
*Shorter Edition: Ch. 13, p. 78
Date used:

84. Which master of the late madrigal saw the transition from the Renaissance to the Baroque era?
   a. Josquin
   b. Ockeghem
   c. Monteverdi
   d. Susato

Answer: d
Chronological Edition: Ch. 15, p. 105f
Standard Edition: Ch. 57, p. 316f
*Shorter Edition: Ch. 13, p. 78
Date used:

85. Which best describes the early madrigal?
   a. virtuosic display
   b. vivid word painting
   c. rich chromatic harmony
   d. simplicity suited to amateur performance

Answer: c
Chronological Edition: Ch. 15, p. 107
Standard Edition: Ch. 57, p. 318
*Shorter Edition: Ch. 13, p. 78f
Date used:

86. *Ohimè! se tanto amate* is a setting of a poem by:
   a. Petrarch.
   b. Ronsard.
   c. Guarini.
   d. Marot.

Answer: c
Chronological Edition: Ch. 15, p. 107f
Standard Edition: Ch. 57, p. 318
Date used:

87. Which work best illustrates the technique of word painting?
   a. Ockeghem: *L'autre d'antan*
   b. Lassus: *Bonjour mon coeur*
   c. Monteverdi: *Ohimè! se tanto amate*
   d. Gabrieli: *Plaudite, psallite*

Answer: a
Chronological Edition: Ch. 15, p. 108
Standard Edition: Ch. 57, p. 318
*Shorter Edition: Ch. 13, p. 77f
Date used:

88. The vivid depiction of the text through music, known as word painting, is a hallmark of:
   a. the madrigal.
   b. the chanson.
   c. the motet.
   d. the anthem.

Answer: b
Chronological Edition: Ch. 15, p. 109
Standard Edition: Ch. 57, p. 320
*Shorter Edition: Ch. 13, p. 77
Date used:

89. Where was the madrigal first developed?
   a. England
   b. Italy
   c. France
   d. Germany

Answer: b
Chronological Edition: Ch. 15, p. 110
Standard Edition: Ch. 57, p. 320
*Shorter Edition: Ch. 13, p. 81
Date used:

90. *Musica transalpina* was:
    a. a collection of Monteverdi madrigals.
    b. a collection of Italian madrigals published in England.
    c. a collection of French chansons.
    d. a collection of English madrigals by English court composers.

Answer: c
Chronological Edition: Ch. 15, p. 110
Standard Edition: Ch. 57, p. 320
Date used:

91. Which best describes the character of Farmer's *Fair Phyllis*?
    a. devotional and moralizing
    b. courtly and idealized
    c. pastoral and light
    d. bombastic and heavy

Answer: c
Chronological Edition: Ch. 15, p. 113
Standard Edition: Ch. 57, p. 323
*Shorter Edition: Ch. 13, p. 83
Date used:

92. During the late sixteenth century, the principal center for polychoral singing was:
    a. St. Peter's of Rome.
    b. Notre Dame of Paris.
    c. St. Mark's of Venice.
    d. Westminster Abbey of London.

Answer: b
Chronological Edition: Ch. 15, p. 113
Standard Edition: Ch. 57, p. 323
*Shorter Edition: Ch. 13, p. 83
Date used:

93. The singing style used at St. Mark's in Venice which featured groups singing in alternation and then together was called:
    a. responsorial.
    b. antiphonal.
    c. a cappella.
    d. melismatic.

Answer: c
Chronological Edition: Ch. 15, p. 114
Standard Edition: Ch. 57, p. 324
Date used:

94. The first composer to indicate dynamics and specific instrumentation in music was:
    a. Monteverdi.
    b. Palestrina.
    c. Gabrieli.
    d. Josquin.

Answer: d
Chronological Edition: Ch. 15, p. 114
Standard Edition: Ch. 57, p. 324
Date used:

95. Gabrieli's *Plaudite, psallite* is an example of:
    a. a Burgundian chanson.
    b. an Italian madrigal.
    c. an English anthem.
    d. a Latin motet.

TRUE/FALSE QUESTIONS

Answer: F
Chronological Edition: Ch. 10, p. 58
Standard Edition: Ch. 52, p. 268
*Shorter Edition: Ch. 10, p. 51
Date used:

96. The two centers of power in the Middle Ages were the feudal lord and the state.

Answer: T
Chronological Edition: Ch. 10, p. 58
Standard Edition: Ch. 52, p. 268
*Shorter Edition: Ch. 10, p. 52
Date used:

97. The knowledge of early civilizations and the culture of the Middle Ages was preserved largely in monasteries.

Answer: T
Chronological Edition: Ch. 10, p. 59
Standard Edition: Ch. 52, p. 269
*Shorter Edition: Ch. 10, p. 53
Date used:

98. Although feudal society was male-dominated, the status of women was raised by prevailing attitudes of chivalry and devotion to the cult of the Virgin Mary.

Answer: T
Chronological Edition: Ch. 11, p. 60
Standard Edition: Ch. 53, p. 270
*Shorter Edition: Ch. 11, p. 53
Date used:

99. Hebrew influences can be found in the early music of the Christian Church.

Answer: T
Chronological Edition: Ch. 11, p. 60
Standard Edition: Ch. 53, p. 270
*Shorter Edition: Ch. 11, p. 53
Date used:

100. The melodic lines of plainchant generally follow the inflections of the text.

Answer: T
Chronological Edition: Ch. 11, p. 60
Standard Edition: Ch. 53, p. 270
*Shorter Edition: Ch. 11, p. 54
Date used:

101. Melismatic text setting descended from the improvisational style of the Orient.

Answer: F
Chronological Edition: Ch. 11, p. 60
Standard Edition: Ch. 53, p. 270
*Shorter Edition: Ch. 11, p. 54
Date used:

102. A setting of plainchant with many notes per syllable is called syllabic.

Answer: T
Chronological Edition: Ch. 11, p. 61
Standard Edition: Ch. 53, p. 271
*Shorter Edition: Ch. 11, p. 54
Date used:

103. During the Middle Ages, Western music used a variety of scale patterns called modes.

Answer: F
Chronological Edition: Ch. 11, p. 61
Standard Edition: Ch. 53, p. 271
*Shorter Edition: Ch. 11, p. 54
Date used:

104. The modes served as the basis for European art music for less than 100 years.

Answer: T
Chronological Edition: Ch. 11, p. 61
Standard Edition: Ch. 53, p. 271
*Shorter Edition: Ch. 11, p. 54
Date used:

105. The most solemn ritual of the Catholic Church is the Mass.

Answer: T
Chronological Edition: Ch. 11, p. 62
Standard Edition: Ch. 53, p. 272
*Shorter Edition: Ch. 11, p. 54f
Date used:

106. A chant performed as a series of exchanges between a soloist and a choir is said to be responsorial.

Answer: F
Chronological Edition: Ch. 11, p. 62
Standard Edition: Ch. 53, p. 272
*Shorter Edition: Ch. 11, p. 54
Date used:

107. *Haec dies* is a chant from the Ordinary of the Mass.

Answer: T
Chronological Edition: Ch. 11, p. 64
Standard Edition: Ch. 53, p. 273
*Shorter Edition: Ch. 11, p. 56
Date used:

108. Léonin was a leader of the Notre Dame school of early polyphony.

Answer: T
Chronological Edition: Ch. 11, p. 64
Standard Edition: Ch. 53, p. 273
*Shorter Edition: Ch. 11, p. 56
Date used:

109. An early center for the development of polyphony was the Cathedral of Notre Dame in Paris.

Answer: F
Chronological Edition: Ch. 11, p. 64
Standard Edition: Ch. 53, p. 273
*Shorter Edition: Ch. 11, p. 56
Date used:

110. Organum was freely composed, with no pre-existent basis.

Answer: F
Chronological Edition: Ch. 11, p. 64
Standard Edition: Ch. 53, p. 274
Date used:

111. The upper voices in organum were generally sung by women.

Answer: T
Chronological Edition: Ch. 11, p. 65
Standard Edition: Ch. 53, p. 275
*Shorter Edition: Ch. 11, p. 56
Date used:

112. Pérotin was noted for writing polyphony in three and four voices.

Answer: T
Chronological Edition: Ch. 11, p. 65
Standard Edition: Ch. 53, p. 275
Date used:

Answer: F
Chronological Edition: Ch. 11, p. 66
Standard Edition: Ch. 53, p. 276
Date used:

Answer: T
Chronological Edition: Ch. 12, p. 69
Standard Edition: Ch. 54, p. 279
Date used:

Answer: T
Chronological Edition: Ch. 12, p. 69
Standard Edition: Ch. 54, p. 279
*Shorter Edition: Ch. 11, p. 58
Date used:

Answer: T
Chronological Edition: Ch. 12, p. 70
Standard Edition: Ch. 54, p. 280
*Shorter Edition: Ch. 11, p. 58
Date used:

Answer: T
Chronological Edition: Ch. 12, p. 70
Standard Edition: Ch. 54, p. 280
*Shorter Edition: Ch. 11, p. 58
Date used:

Answer: F
Chronological Edition: Ch. 12, p. 73
Standard Edition: Ch. 54, p. 283
*Shorter Edition: Ch. 11, p. 59
Date used:

Answer: F
Chronological Edition: Ch. 12, p. 73
Standard Edition: Ch. 54, p. 283
*Shorter Edition: Ch. 11, p. 59
Date used:

113. The second, third, and fourth voices of a motet were known respectively as duplum, triplum, and quadruplum.

114. A repetition of a musical pattern—melodic, rhythmic, or harmonic—is known as organum.

115. Troubadours, trouvères and minnesingers were Medieval poet-musicians.

116. Secular music was integral to Medieval court life, supplying entertainment, ceremonial, and dance music.

117. The poems of the troubadours and trouvères reflected some of the ideals of the age of chivalry—honor, valor, and unrequited love.

118. Moniot d'Arras was one of the last of the trouvères.

119. The fourteenth century witnessed a decreased focus on secular music.

120. Since Machaut was a cleric in the Church, he wrote only sacred music.

Answer: T
Chronological Edition: Ch. 12, p. 73
Standard Edition: Ch. 54, p. 283
*Shorter Edition: Ch. 11, p. 59
Date used:

121. An isorhythmic motet is based on an ostinato rhythm.

Answer: T
Chronological Edition: Ch. 12, p. 76
Standard Edition: Ch. 54, p. 286
Date used:

122. The Medieval English carol was often a Christmas song.

Answer: F
Chronological Edition: Ch. 12, p. 76
Standard Edition: Ch. 54, p. 286
Date used:

123. The text of the carol *Deo gratias, Anglia* is in old English with a French refrain or burden.

Answer: T
Chronological Edition: Ch. 12, p. 77
Standard Edition: Ch. 54, p. 287
*Shorter Edition: Ch. 11, p. 62
Date used:

124. Although the "learned" vocal music of Medieval church and court was routinely written down, much instrumental music was improvised.

Answer: F
Chronological Edition: Ch. 12, p. 77
Standard Edition: Ch. 54, p. 287
*Shorter Edition: Ch. 11, p. 62
Date used:

125. Modern instruments are more limited in range and volume than their Medieval counterparts.

Answer: F
Chronological Edition: Ch. 12, p. 77
Standard Edition: Ch. 54, p. 287
*Shorter Edition: Ch. 11, p. 62
Date used:

126. Surviving Medieval music contains very specific instrumental indications.

Answer: T
Chronological Edition: Ch. 13, p. 82
Standard Edition: Ch. 55, p. 293
*Shorter Edition: Ch. 12, p. 64
Date used:

127. Rather than a sudden rebirth in learning, the Renaissance saw a much increased awareness of the cultures of learned civilizations.

Answer: T
Chronological Edition: Ch. 13, p. 84
Standard Edition: Ch. 55, p. 294
*Shorter Edition: Ch. 12, p. 66
Date used:

128. The invention of printing in the West was a Renaissance development.

Answer: T
Chronological Edition: Ch. 13, p. 86
Standard Edition: Ch. 55, p. 296
*Shorter Edition: Ch. 12, p. 67f
Date used:

129. The Renaissance saw the rise of amateur musicians and home music-making.

Answer: T
Chronological Edition: Ch. 13, p. 86
Standard Edition: Ch. 55, p. 297
*Shorter Edition: Ch. 13, p. 68
Date used:

130. Renaissance composers leaned toward fuller sounding chords with more euphonious thirds and sixths.

Answer: T
Chronological Edition: Ch. 13, p. 86
Standard Edition: Ch. 55, p. 296
*Shorter Edition: Ch. 13, p. 68
Date used:

131. The sixteenth century has been regarded as the golden age of a cappella music.

Answer: T
Chronological Edition: Ch. 13, p. 86
Standard Edition: Ch. 55, p. 296
*Shorter Edition: Ch. 13, p. 68
Date used:

132. The Renaissance saw the growth of solo instrumental music, especially for lute and keyboard instruments.

Answer: T
Chronological Edition: Ch. 13, p. 87
Standard Edition: Ch. 55, p. 297
*Shorter Edition: Ch. 13, p. 68
Date used:

133. Renaissance composers showed a greater preference for duple meter than did Medieval composers.

Answer: T
Chronological Edition: Ch. 14, p. 87
Standard Edition: Ch. 56, p. 297
*Shorter Edition: Ch. 13, p. 68
Date used:

134. The Renaissance motet became a sacred form with a single Latin text.

Answer: F
Chronological Edition: Ch. 14, p. 88
Standard Edition: Ch. 56, p. 298
*Shorter Edition: Ch. 13, p. 69f
Date used:

135. Dufay's motet *Alma redemptoris mater* is based on a Gregorian chant that permeates all its voices.

Answer: T
Chronological Edition: Ch. 14, p. 91
Standard Edition: Ch. 56, p. 301
*Shorter Edition: Ch. 13, p. 72
Date used:

136. Like the Renaissance motet, the polyphonic setting of the mass was often based on a cantus firmus.

Answer: F
Chronological Edition: Ch. 14, p. 91
Standard Edition: Ch. 56, p. 301
Date used:

137.   The Roman Catholic Mass for the Dead is the Magnificat.

Answer: T
Chronological Edition: Ch. 14, p. 92
Standard Edition: Ch. 56, p. 302
Date used:

138.   The overall form of the Agnus Dei to Josquin's *La sol fa re mi* Mass is ternary, or A–B–A.

Answer: T
Chronological Edition: Ch. 14, p. 94
Standard Edition: Ch. 56, p. 304
*Shorter Edition: Ch. 13, p. 73
Date used:

139.   The reform movement in the Catholic Church brought about by the Protestant Reformation was the Counter-Reformation.

Answer: T
Chronological Edition: Ch. 14, p. 95
Standard Edition: Ch. 56, p. 305
*Shorter Edition: Ch. 13, p. 73
Date used:

140.   The upper voice parts of the *Pope Marcellus Mass* were sung by boy sopranos or adult males with high voices.

Answer: F
Chronological Edition: Ch. 14, p. 97
Standard Edition: Ch. 56, p. 30
Date used:

141.   The accepted language of the early Anglican church service was Latin.

Answer: F
Chronological Edition: Ch. 15, p. 98
Standard Edition: Ch. 57, p. 308
*Shorter Edition: Ch. 13, p. 75
Date used:

142.   During the Renaissance, the study of a musical instrument was considered highly improper for ladies.

Answer: T
Chronological Edition: Ch. 15, p. 98
Standard Edition: Ch. 57, p. 308
*Shorter Edition: Ch. 13, p. 76
Date used:

143.   The two most important forms of Renaissance secular music were the chanson and the madrigal.

Answer: T
Chronological Edition: Ch. 15, p. 99
Standard Edition: Ch. 57, p. 309
*Shorter Edition: Ch. 13, p. 76
Date used:

144.   Ockeghem's *L'autre d'antan* is a love song with a more popular text than many courtly chansons.

Answer: F
Chronological Edition: Ch. 15, p. 101
Standard Edition: Ch. 57, p. 311
*Shorter Edition: Ch. 13, p. 76
Date used:

Answer: T
Chronological Edition: Ch. 15, p. 103
Standard Edition: Ch. 57, p. 313
*Shorter Edition: Ch. 13, p. 81
Date used:

Answer: T
Chronological Edition: Ch. 15, p. 104
Standard Edition: Ch. 57, p. 314
Date used:

Answer: T
Chronological Edition: Ch. 15, p. 105
Standard Edition: Ch. 57, p. 315
*Shorter Edition: Ch. 13, p. 77
Date used:

Answer: F
Chronological Edition: Ch. 15, p. 105
Standard Edition: Ch. 57, p. 315
*Shorter Edition: Ch. 13, p. 77
Date used:

Answer: T
Chronological Edition: Ch. 15, p. 106
Standard Edition: Ch. 57, p. 316
*Shorter Edition: Ch. 13, p. 78
Date used:

Answer: T
Chronological Edition: Ch. 15, p. 106f
Standard Edition: Ch. 57, p. 317
*Shorter Edition: Ch. 13, p. 78
Date used:

Answer: T
Chronological Edition: Ch. 15, p. 109
Standard Edition: Ch. 57, p. 320
*Shorter Edition: Ch. 13, p. 80
Date used:

145. Roland de Lassus was a Flemish composer who is viewed as one of the masters of the English madrigal.

146. The sixteenth century saw a blossoming of instrumental dance music.

147. Stately indoor occasions most often called for soft instruments such as recorders and strings.

148. Italian madrigalists set words such as weeping, trembling, and dying with great expression.

149. The text of a madrigal is best described as one of three fixed forms: virelai, ballade, or rondeau.

150. Instruments participated in the performance of madrigals, either by doubling or substituting for a vocal line.

151. The late Renaissance madrigal was highly expressive through such devices as virtuosic display and chromatic harmony.

152. England adopted the Italian madrigal and developed it into a native form.

Answer: T
Chronological Edition: Ch. 15, p. 110
Standard Edition: Ch. 57, p. 320
Date used:

Answer: T
Chronological Edition: Tr. II, p. 113
Standard Edition: Tr. III, p. 323
Date used:

Answer: F
Chronological Edition: Tr. II, p. 114
Standard Edition: Tr. III, p. 324
Date used:

153. *Fair Phyllis* illustrates some examples of word painting.

154. The predominant texture of polychoral music is homophony.

155. Terraced dynamics refer to outdoor or "terrace" performances.

THE BAROQUE ERA

MULTIPLE CHOICE QUESTIONS

Answer: a
Chronological Edition: Ch. 18, p. 127
Standard Edition: Ch. 58, p. 327
*Shorter Edition: Ch. 16, p. 95
Date used:

1. The approximate dates of the Baroque period are:
   a. 1600–1750.
   b. 1700–1800.
   c. 1550–1600.
   d. 1800–1900.

Answer: b
Chronological Edition: Ch. 18, p. 127
Standard Edition: Ch. 58, p. 327
*Shorter Edition: Ch. 16, p. 95
Date used:

2. The term "baroque" probably derives from:
   a. a French word meaning broken.
   b. a Portuguese word meaning irregular in shape.
   c. a German word meaning barren.
   d. an Italian word meaning a type of wine.

Answer: b
Chronological Edition: Ch. 18, p. 127f
Standard Edition: Ch. 58, p. 327f
*Shorter Edition: Ch. 16, p. 95f
Date used:

3. Which of the following does NOT characterize the Baroque era?
   a. an age of reason
   b. an age of freedom and democracy
   c. an era of absolute monarchy
   d. an era of change, adventure and exploration

Answer: d
Chronological Edition: Ch. 18, p. 128
Standard Edition: Ch. 58, p. 328
*Shorter Edition: Ch. 16, p. 95
Date used:

4. All of the following artists exhibit the bold, dramatic style of the early Baroque EXCEPT:
   a. Michelangelo.
   b. Titian.
   c. Tintoretto.
   d. da Vinci.

Answer: c
Chronological Edition: Ch. 18, p. 128f
Standard Edition: Ch. 58, p. 328f
*Shorter Edition: Ch. 16, p. 96
Date used:

5. All of the following were important scientists of the Baroque era EXCEPT:
   a. Newton.
   b. Galileo.
   c. Curie.
   d. Kepler.

Answer: d
Chronological Edition: Ch. 18, p. 131
Standard Edition: Ch. 58, p. 331
*Shorter Edition: Ch. 16, p. 98
Date used:

6. Which best describes how Baroque musicians made a living?
   a. as servants to royalty or nobility
   b. as members of the church
   c. as employees of a free city
   d. all of the above

Answer: b
Chronological Edition: Ch. 19, p. 132f
Standard Edition: Ch. 59, p. 332f
*Shorter Edition: Ch. 17, p. 99
Date used:

7. The group of early Baroque writers, artists, and musicians whose aim was to resurrect the musical-drama of ancient Greece was known as:
   a. the Italian madrigalists.
   b. the Florentine Camerata.
   c. the Freemasons.
   d. the Notre Dame school.

Answer: c
Chronological Edition: Ch. 19, p. 132
Standard Edition: Ch. 59, p. 332
*Shorter Edition: Ch. 17, p. 99
Date used:

8. The Baroque period witnessed a new style of music which featured a single vocal melody with accompaniment. This was known as:
   a. monophony.
   b. melisma.
   c. monody.
   d. stile concitato.

Answer: a
Chronological Edition: Ch. 19, p. 133
Standard Edition: Ch. 59, p. 333
*Shorter Edition: Ch. 17, p. 99
Date used:

9. The Baroque technique of putting numerals, indicating the harmony required, above or below the bass notes is called:
   a. a figured or thorough-bass.
   b. an ostinato or ground bass.
   c. equal temperament.
   d. the doctrine of the affections.

Answer: c
Chronological Edition: Ch. 19, p. 133
Standard Edition: Ch. 59, p. 333
*Shorter Edition: Ch. 17, p. 99
Date used:

10. Which two instruments would most likely have played the basso continuo or thorough-bass in the Baroque era?
    a. bassoon and piano
    b. violin and cello
    c. cello and harpsichord
    d. bassoon and violin

Answer: b
Chronological Edition: Ch. 19, p. 133
Standard Edition: Ch. 59, p. 333
*Shorter Edition: Ch. 17, p. 99
Date used:

11. The number of players needed to perform a Baroque basso continuo or thorough-bass is:
    a. one.
    b. two.
    c. three.
    d. four.

Answer: c
Chronological Edition: Ch. 19, p. 133
Standard Edition: Ch. 59, p. 333
*Shorter Edition: Ch. 17, p. 99
Date used:

12. The primary tonality used during the Baroque was:
    a. modal.
    b. atonal.
    c. major-minor.
    d. chromatic.

Answer: a
Chronological Edition: Ch. 19, p. 133
Standard Edition: Ch. 59, p. 333
*Shorter Edition: Ch. 17, p. 99
Date used:

13. The ideas and music of the Florentine Camerata led the way directly toward:
    a. the development of opera.
    b. the development of the mass.
    c. the development of the symphony.
    d. the development of the concerto.

Answer: d
Chronological Edition: Ch. 19, p. 133f
Standard Edition: Ch. 59, p. 333f
*Shorter Edition: Ch. 17, p. 101f
Date used:

Answer: b
Chronological Edition: Ch. 19, p. 134
Standard Edition: Ch. 59, p. 334
*Shorter Edition: Ch. 17, p. 101
Date used:

Answer: b
Chronological Edition: Ch. 19, p. 136
Standard Edition: Ch. 59, p. 336
*Shorter Edition: Ch. 17, p. 101
Date used:

Answer: a
Chronological Edition: Ch. 19, p. 137
Standard Edition: Ch. 59, p. 337
*Shorter Edition: Ch. 17, p. 102
Date used:

Answer: c
Chronological Edition: Ch. 19, p. 138
Standard Edition: Ch. 59, p. 338
*Shorter Edition: Ch. 17, p. 102
Date used:

Answer: c
Chronological Edition: Ch. 19, p. 138
Standard Edition: Ch. 59, p. 338
*Shorter Edition: Ch. 17, p. 102f
Date used:

Answer: d
Chronological Edition: Ch. 20, p. 140
Standard Edition: Ch. 60, p. 339
*Shorter Edition: Ch. 18, p. 105
Date used:

14. All of the following characterize Baroque musical style EXCEPT:
   a. a driving, energetic rhythm.
   b. a continuously expanding melody.
   c. shifts of dynamic from one level to another.
   d. harmonies built on the early church modes.

15. A system of slightly adjusting the tuning of intervals within the octave, thus making it possible to play in every major and minor key without unpleasant results, was called:
   a. thorough-bass.
   b. equal temperament.
   c. terraced dynamics.
   d. the doctrine of the affections.

16. A shift from one level of dynamics to another in Baroque music is called:
   a. changing affections.
   b. terraced dynamics.
   c. monodic style.
   d. tone painting.

17. The artificially-created male soprano or alto who dominated opera was known as:
   a. the castrato.
   b. the contralto.
   c. the camerata.
   d. the continuo.

18. The compositional technique in which the music vividly mirrored the text is called:
   a. equal temperament.
   b. thorough-bass.
   c. word painting.
   d. terraced dynamics.

19. The belief that words and music were closely linked is reflected in:
   a. equal temperament.
   b. terraced dynamics.
   c. the doctrine of the affections.
   d. all of the above.

20. It was through the musical innovations of the _____ that opera was born.
   a. Medici family
   b. Notre Dame school
   c. Roman forum
   d. Florentine Camerata

Answer: a
Chronological Edition: Ch. 20, p. 140
Standard Edition: Ch. 60, p. 339
*Shorter Edition: Ch. 18, p. 105
Date used:

Answer: b
Chronological Edition: Ch. 20, p. 140
Standard Edition: Ch. 60, p. 339
Date used:

Answer: a
Chronological Edition: Ch. 20, p. 141
Standard Edition: Ch. 60, p. 340
*Shorter Edition: Ch. 18, p. 105
Date used:

Answer: b
Chronological Edition: Ch. 20, p. 141
Standard Edition: Ch. 60, p. 340
*Shorter Edition: Ch. 18, p. 105
Date used:

Answer: b
Chronological Edition: Ch. 20, p. 142
Standard Edition: Ch. 60, p. 341
*Shorter Edition: Ch. 18, p. 105
Date used:

Answer: d
Chronological Edition: Ch. 20, p. 142
Standard Edition: Ch. 60, p. 341
Date used:

Answer: a
Chronological Edition: Ch. 20, p. 142
Standard Edition: Ch. 60, p. 341
*Shorter Edition: Ch. 18, p. 107
Date used:

21. Who is best viewed as the first master of opera?
    a. Monteverdi
    b. Purcell
    c. Handel
    d. Puccini

22. The compositional style used by Monteverdi in which sound effects such as tremolo and pizzicato were used to express the hidden tremors of the soul is known as:
    a. stile reprensentativo.
    b. stile concitato.
    c. stile moderno.
    d. stile antico.

23. The earliest operas took their plots from:
    a. Greek mythology.
    b. historical events.
    c. real life situations.
    d. current events.

24. Monteverdi's opera *The Coronation of Poppea* was written and first performed in:
    a. Mantua.
    b. Venice.
    c. Florence.
    d. London.

25. Monteverdi's opera based on an episode from the court of the Roman emperor Nero is:
    a. *Orfeo.*
    b. *The Coronation of Poppea.*
    c. *Arianna.*
    d. *Dido and Aeneas.*

26. An instrumental passage that returns again and again, as a refrain in an aria, is called:
    a. a recapitulation.
    b. a coda.
    c. a sinfonia.
    d. a ritornello.

27. A short phrase repeated over and over in the bass is called:
    a. a ground bass.
    b. a figured bass.
    c. a contra bass.
    d. a ritornello.

Answer: b
Chronological Edition: Ch. 20, p. 142
Standard Edition: Ch. 60, p. 341
Date used:

Answer: d
Chronological Edition: Ch. 20, p. 142
Standard Edition: Ch. 60, p. 341
Date used:

Answer: b
Chronological Edition: Ch. 20, p. 144
Standard Edition: Ch. 60, p. 343
*Shorter Edition: Ch. 18, p. 106
Date used:

Answer: c
Chronological Edition: Ch. 20, p. 145
Standard Edition: Ch. 60, p. 344
*Shorter Edition: Ch. 18, p. 106
Date used:

Answer: b
Chronological Edition: Ch. 20, p. 146
Standard Edition: Ch. 60, p. 345
*Shorter Edition: Ch. 18, p. 107
Date used:

Answer: d
Chronological Edition: Ch. 20, p. 146
Standard Edition: Ch. 60, p. 345
*Shorter Edition: Ch. 18, p. 107
Date used:

Answer: c
Chronological Edition: Ch. 20, p. 146
Standard Edition: Ch. 60, p. 345
*Shorter Edition: Ch. 18, p. 107
Date used:

28. Which best describes the form of the final love duet in *The Coronation of Poppea*?
    a. A–B–A or da capo aria
    b. A–B–B–A with a ground bass
    c. A–A–A with intervening sinfonias
    d. none of the above

29. At the close of Monteverdi's opera *The Coronation of Poppea*:
    a. Nero is put to death.
    b. Seneca marries Poppea.
    c. Ottavia and Nero live happily ever after.
    d. Poppea is crowned Empress of Rome.

30. The English composer who paved the way for Purcell's operas was:
    a. Claudio Monteverdi.
    b. John Blow.
    c. George F. Handel.
    d. Oliver Cromwell.

31. The greatest native English composer of the Baroque was:
    a. George Handel.
    b. Thomas Morley.
    c. Henry Purcell.
    d. Oliver Cromwell.

32. Who was the librettist of Purcell's *Dido and Aeneas*?
    a. Josias Priest
    b. Nahum Tate
    c. John Milton
    d. John Dunne

33. Purcell's opera *Dido and Aeneas* was based on the epic poem:
    a. Milton's *Paradise Lost*.
    b. Homer's *Odyssey*.
    c. Homer's *Iliad*.
    d. Virgil's *Aeneid*.

34. Dido sings her famous lament in Purcell's opera *Dido and Aeneas* just prior to:
    a. marrying Aeneas.
    b. killing Aeneas.
    c. killing herself.
    d. leaving with Aeneas.

Answer: a
Chronological Edition: Ch. 20, p. 148
Standard Edition: Ch. 60, p. 347
*Shorter Edition: Ch. 18, p. 109
Date used:

Answer: b
Chronological Edition: Ch. 20, p. 148
Standard Edition: Ch. 60, p. 347
*Shorter Edition: Ch. 18, p. 109
Date used:

Answer: b
Chronological Edition: Ch. 20, p. 149
Standard Edition: Ch. 60, p. 348
*Shorter Edition: Ch. 18, p. 109
Date used:

Answer: c
Chronological Edition: Ch. 21, p. 150
Standard Edition: Ch. 61, p. 349
*Shorter Edition: Ch. 19, p. 109
Date used:

Answer: b
Chronological Edition: Ch. 21, p. 150
Standard Edition: Ch. 61, p. 349
*Shorter Edition: Ch. 19, p. 110
Date used:

Answer: d
Chronological Edition: Ch. 21, p. 150
Standard Edition: Ch. 61, p. 349
*Shorter Edition: Ch. 19, p. 110
Date used:

Answer: a
Chronological Edition: Ch. 21, p. 150
Standard Edition: Ch. 61, p. 349
*Shorter Edition: Ch. 19, p. 110
Date used:

35. Which composer was a master of late Baroque opera?
    a. Handel
    b. Mozart
    c. Monteverdi
    d. Blow

36. Handel's opera *Julius Caesar* is an example of:
    a. opera buffa.
    b. opera seria.
    c. opéra comique.
    d. masque.

37. The form of a da capo aria is:
    a. A–B.
    b. A–B–A.
    c. A–B–B–A.
    d. A–A–A.

38. Which genre is best described as a multi-movement work for vocalists, chorus and instrumentalists, based on a poetic narrative of a lyric or dramatic nature, with either a sacred or secular theme?
    a. the magnificat
    b. the oratorio
    c. the cantata
    d. the chorale

39. The chorale is a type of hymn tune created by:
    a. Johann Sebastian Bach.
    b. Martin Luther.
    c. George Frideric Handel.
    d. Claudio Monteverdi.

40. Chorale tunes were adapted from:
    a. Gregorian chant.
    b. popular songs.
    c. secular art music.
    d. all of the above.

41. In a simple four-part harmonization, the chorale tune was most likely put in:
    a. the soprano part.
    b. the alto part.
    c. the tenor part.
    d. the bass part.

Answer: d
Chronological Edition: Ch. 21, p. 151f
Standard Edition: Ch. 61, p. 350f
*Shorter Edition: Ch. 19, p. 110f
Date used:

Answer: b
Chronological Edition: Ch. 21, p. 151
Standard Edition: Ch. 61, p. 350
*Shorter Edition: Ch. 19, p. 111
Date used:

Answer: b
Chronological Edition: Ch. 21, p. 152
Standard Edition: Ch. 61, p. 351
*Shorter Edition: Ch. 19, p. 111
Date used:

Answer: c
Chronological Edition: Ch. 21, p. 154
Standard Edition: Ch. 61, p. 353
*Shorter Edition: Ch. 19, p. 112
Date used:

Answer: c
Chronological Edition: Ch. 21, p. 154
Standard Edition: Ch. 61, p. 353
Date used:

Answer: d
Chronological Edition: Ch. 21, p. 155
Standard Edition: Ch. 61, p. 354
Date used:

Answer: c
Chronological Edition: Ch. 21, p. 156
Standard Edition: Ch. 61, p. 357
*Shorter Edition: Ch. 19, p. 113
Date used:

42. During his lifetime, Bach held the position of:
    a. Cantor of St. Thomas's Church in Leipzig.
    b. court organist and chamber musician to the Duke of Weimar.
    c. court musician to the Prince of Anhalt-Cöthen.
    d. all of the above.

43. Bach was famous in his day as a performer on:
    a. the harpsichord.
    b. the organ.
    c. the piano.
    d. the clavichord.

44. Bach composed the majority of his secular instrumental works while working at:
    a. Weimar.
    b. Cöthen.
    c. Leipzig.
    d. London.

45. In the field of keyboard music, Bach's most important collection was:
    a. the *Brandenburg Concertos*.
    b. *The Art of the Fugue*.
    c. *The Well-Tempered Clavier*.
    d. *The Musical Offering*.

46. Which of the following is a set of forty-eight preludes and fugues by Bach?
    a. the *Brandenburg Concertos*
    b. *The Musical Offering*
    c. *The Well-Tempered Clavier*
    d. *The Art of the Fugue*

47. Which of the following is NOT a now obsolete woodwind instrument used in Bach's orchestra?
    a. oboe d'amore
    b. oboe da caccia
    c. taille
    d. contrabassoon

48. Which of the following was Bach's favorite librettist?
    a. Martin Luther
    b. St. Thomas
    c. Salamo Franck
    d. John Calvin

Answer: d
Chronological Edition: Ch. 21, p. 156
Standard Edition: Ch. 61, p. 355
Date used:

Answer: b
Chronological Edition: Ch. 21, p. 156
Standard Edition: Ch. 61, p. 355
*Shorter Edition: Ch. 19, p. 112f
Date used:

Answer: a
Chronological Edition: Ch. 21, p. 156f
Standard Edition: Ch. 61, p. 355f
*Shorter Edition: Ch. 19, p. 114
Date used:

Answer: a
Chronological Edition: Ch. 21, p. 156
Standard Edition: Ch. 61, p. 355
*Shorter Edition: Ch. 19, p. 113
Date used:

Answer: d
Chronological Edition: Ch. 21, p. 156f
Standard Edition: Ch. 61, p. 355f
*Shorter Edition: Ch. 19, p. 114f
Date used:

Answer: a
Chronological Edition: Ch. 22, p. 162
Standard Edition: Ch. 62, p. 361
*Shorter Edition: Ch. 20, p. 116
Date used:

Answer: a
Chronological Edition: Ch. 22, p. 162
Standard Edition: Ch. 62, p. 361
*Shorter Edition: Ch. 20, p. 116
Date used:

49.   Bach wrote his cantatas for use in:
    a.   the Anglican Church.
    b.   the Catholic Church.
    c.   the Calvinist Church.
    d.   the Lutheran Church.

50.   The chorale tune *A Mighty Fortress Is Our God* was:
    a.   a Gregorian chant.
    b.   written by Martin Luther.
    c.   written by Salamo Franck.
    d.   a popular German secular song.

51.   Bach's Cantata No. 80, *A Mighty Fortress Is Our God*, has _____ movements.
    a.   eight
    b.   seven
    c.   six
    d.   five

52.   The opening movement of Bach's cantata, *A Mighty Fortress Is Our God*, is best described as:
    a.   a choral fugue.
    b.   a duet for soprano and bass.
    c.   a soprano aria.
    d.   a four-part chorale.

53.   The chorale tune, *A Mighty Fortress Is Our God*, is heard in a simple, homophonic four-part setting in:
    a.   the first movement.
    b.   the second movement.
    c.   the fifth movement.
    d.   the last movement.

54.   Which does NOT characterize an oratorio?
    a.   elaborate scenery
    b.   recitative
    c.   arias
    d.   choruses

55.   George Frideric Handel was considered a master of:
    a.   the oratorio.
    b.   the symphony.
    c.   the cantata.
    d.   the chorale.

Answer: b
Chronological Edition: Ch. 22, p. 162f
Standard Edition: Ch. 62, p. 361f
*Shorter Edition: Ch. 20, p. 117f
Date used:

Answer: c
Chronological Edition: Ch. 22, p. 164
Standard Edition: Ch. 62, p. 363
*Shorter Edition: Ch. 20, p. 117
Date used:

Answer: d
Chronological Edition: Ch. 22, p. 165
Standard Edition: Ch. 62, p. 364
*Shorter Edition: Ch. 20, p. 117
Date used:

Answer: b
Chronological Edition: Ch. 22, p. 166
Standard Edition: Ch. 62, p. 365
Date used:

Answer: d
Chronological Edition: Ch. 22, p. 166f
Standard Edition: Ch. 62, p. 366f
*Shorter Edition: Ch. 20, p. 118f
Date used:

Answer: c
Chronological Edition: Ch. 22, p. 167f
Standard Edition: Ch. 62, p. 366f
*Shorter Edition: Ch. 20, p. 118f
Date used:

Answer: a
Chronological Edition: Ch. 22, p. 167
Standard Edition: Ch. 62, p. 366
Date used:

56. _____ was born in Germany, studied in Italy, but spent much of his creative life in England.
   a. Bach
   b. Handel
   c. Vivaldi
   d. Scarlatti

57. The introduction of _____ brought about a decrease in the popularity of Handel's operas.
   a. the cantata
   b. opera seria
   c. ballad opera
   d. the anthem

58. Late in life, Handel turned his efforts from the opera to:
   a. the cantata.
   b. the symphony.
   c. the mass.
   d. the oratorio.

59. Which of the following was NOT an oratorio by Handel?
   a. *Saul*
   b. *Julius Caesar*
   c. *Israel in Egypt*
   d. *Messiah*

60. Which of the following is Handel's most famous oratorio, frequently performed today?
   a. *Julius Caesar*
   b. *Israel in Egypt*
   c. *Samson*
   d. *Messiah*

61. Handel's *Messiah* is:
   a. an opera.
   b. a cantata.
   c. an oratorio.
   d. a masque.

62. Handel's *Messiah* opens with:
   a. a French overture.
   b. an Italian overture.
   c. a vigorous chorus.
   d. a da capo aria.

Answer: b
Chronological Edition: Ch. 22, p. 167
Standard Edition: Ch. 62, p. 366
Date used:

Answer: b
Chronological Edition: Ch. 22, p. 168
Standard Edition: Ch. 62, p. 367
*Shorter Edition: Ch. 20, p. 119
Date used:

Answer: b
Chronological Edition: Ch. 22, p. 168
Standard Edition: Ch. 62, p. 367
*Shorter Edition: Ch. 20, p. 119
Date used:

Answer: c
Chronological Edition: Ch. 23, p. 172
Standard Edition: Ch. 63, p. 371
*Shorter Edition: Ch. 21, p. 122
Date used:

Answer: d
Chronological Edition: Ch. 23, p. 172
Standard Edition: Ch. 63, p. 371
*Shorter Edition: Ch. 21, p. 122
Date used:

Answer: a
Chronological Edition: Ch. 23, p. 172
Standard Edition: Ch. 63, p. 371
*Shorter Edition: Ch. 21, p. 122
Date used:

Answer: d
Chronological Edition: Ch. 23, p. 172
Standard Edition: Ch. 63, p. 371
*Shorter Edition: Ch. 21, p. 122
Date used:

63. Which is NOT true of the French overture?
   a. It was developed by Lully in his operas.
   b. It opens with a fast, fugal section.
   c. Its slow section features dotted rhythms.
   d. It is generally in two sections.

64. A famous choral climax in Part II of Handel's *Messiah* is:
   a. "For unto us a Child is born".
   b. "Hallelujah Chorus".
   c. "Comfort ye, my people".
   d. "And the glory of the Lord".

65. The "Hallelujah Chorus" is the climax of which part of Handel's *Messiah*?
   a. Part I: Prophecy and birth of Christ
   b. Part II: Death and resurrection of Christ
   c. Part III: Redemption of the world through faith
   d. Part IV: Life of the world to come

66. The Baroque era witnessed the appearance of the:
   a. solo concerto.
   b. concerto grosso.
   c. both A and B
   d. neither A nor B

67. The instrumental form based upon the contrast of two dissimilar masses of sound is called:
   a. the symphony.
   b. the sonata.
   c. the suite.
   d. the concerto.

68. Who was the greatest and most prolific Italian composer of concertos?
   a. Vivaldi
   b. Scarlatti
   c. Handel
   d. Bach

69. An important instrumental form of the Baroque, based on opposition between a small group of instruments and a larger group, was:
   a. the suite.
   b. the overture.
   c. the sonata.
   d. the concerto grosso.

Answer: c
Chronological Edition: Ch. 23, p. 172
Standard Edition: Ch. 63, p. 371
*Shorter Edition: Ch. 21, p. 122
Date used:

Answer: b
Chronological Edition: Ch. 23, p. 172
Standard Edition: Ch. 63, p. 371
*Shorter Edition: Ch. 21, p. 122
Date used:

Answer: a
Chronological Edition: Ch. 23, p. 174
Standard Edition: Ch. 63, p. 373
*Shorter Edition: Ch. 21, p. 124
Date used:

Answer: b
Chronological Edition: Ch. 23, p. 174
Standard Edition: Ch. 63, p. 373
*Shorter Edition: Ch. 21, p. 124
Date used:

Answer: a
Chronological Edition: Ch. 23, p. 174
Standard Edition: Ch. 63, p. 373
*Shorter Edition: Ch. 21, p. 124
Date used:

Answer: b
Chronological Edition: Ch. 23, p. 174
Standard Edition: Ch. 63, p. 373
*Shorter Edition: Ch. 21, p. 124
Date used:

Answer: d
Chronological Edition: Ch. 23, p. 174
Standard Edition: Ch. 63, p. 373
*Shorter Edition: Ch. 21, p. 124f
Date used:

Answer: a
Chronological Edition: Ch. 23, p. 177
Standard Edition: Ch. 63, p. 376
*Shorter Edition: Ch. 21, p. 121
Date used:

70. Vivaldi was known as "the red priest" for:
    a. his political affiliations.
    b. his violent temper.
    c. the color of his hair.
    d. none of these.

71. Vivaldi lived and worked in:
    a. Florence.
    b. Venice.
    c. Rome.
    d. Bologna.

72. Which of the following is a well-known set of concertos by Vivaldi?
    a. *The Four Seasons*
    b. the *Brandenburg Concertos*
    c. the *Water Music*
    d. the *Royal Fireworks Music*

73. Which does NOT characterize Vivaldi's *Four Seasons*?
    a. Each concerto is based on a poem.
    b. They avoid ritornello form.
    c. They project pictorial images.
    d. They are structured in three-movement form.

74. The solo instrument in "Spring" from *The Four Seasons* is:
    a. violin.
    b. viola.
    c. cello.
    d. harpsichord.

75. The opening movement of "Spring" from *The Four Seasons* features _____ form.
    a. sonata–allegro
    b. ritornello
    c. minuet and trio
    d. binary

76. In the slow movement of "Spring" from *The Four Seasons*, Vivaldi evokes a dog barking through:
    a. trills and running scales.
    b. fast staccato notes
    c. a folk dance.
    d. an ostinato rhythm.

77. Who composed the *Brandenburg Concertos*?
    a. Bach
    b. Vivaldi
    c. Handel
    d. Brandenburg

Answer: c
Chronological Edition: Ch. 23, p. 177
Standard Edition: Ch. 63, p. 376
*Shorter Edition: Ch. 21, p. 121
Date used:

78. Bach's *Brandenburg Concertos* are comprised of _____ separate concertos.
   a. four
   b. five
   c. six
   d. seven

Answer: a
Chronological Edition: Ch. 23, p. 177
Standard Edition: Ch. 63, p. 376
*Shorter Edition: Ch. 21, p. 121
Date used:

79. The accompanying group in a concerto grosso is called:
   a. the ripieno.
   b. the ritornello.
   c. the concertino.
   d. the basso continuo.

Answer: c
Chronological Edition: Ch. 23, p. 177
Standard Edition: Ch. 63, p. 376
*Shorter Edition: Ch. 21, p. 121
Date used:

80. The solo group in a concerto grosso is called:
   a. the ripieno.
   b. the ritornello.
   c. the concertino.
   d. the basso continuo.

Answer: c
Chronological Edition: Ch. 23, p. 177
Standard Edition: Ch. 63, p. 376
*Shorter Edition: Ch. 21, p. 121
Date used:

81. Which instrument is NOT featured as a soloist in the *Brandenburg Concerto* No. 2?
   a. violin
   b. trumpet
   c. harpsichord
   d. flute

Answer: d
Chronological Edition: Ch. 23, p. 177
Standard Edition: Ch. 63, p. 376
Date used:

82. The opening movement of Bach's *Brandenburg Concerto* No. 2 is based on:
   a. a sonnet.
   b. an ostinato.
   c. a drone.
   d. a ritornello.

Answer: b
Chronological Edition: Ch. 24, p. 178
Standard Edition: Ch. 64, p. 377
*Shorter Edition: Ch. 22, p. 126
Date used:

83. The sonata da camera of the Baroque was:
   a. intended to be performed in church.
   b. intended to be performed at home.
   c. intended to depict a particular scene in each movement.
   d. none of the above.

Answer: c
Chronological Edition: Ch. 24, p. 178
Standard Edition: Ch. 64, p. 377
*Shorter Edition: Ch. 22, p. 126
Date used:

84. The sonata da camera was based upon:
   a. contrapuntal movements.
   b. fugal movements.
   c. dance movements.
   d. variation movements.

Answer: c
Chronological Edition: Ch. 24, p. 178
Standard Edition: Ch. 64, p. 377
*Shorter Edition: Ch. 22, p. 127
Date used:

Answer: c
Chronological Edition: Ch. 24, p. 178
Standard Edition: Ch. 64, p. 377
*Shorter Edition: Ch. 22, p. 127
Date used:

Answer: d
Chronological Edition: Ch. 24, p. 178
Standard Edition: Ch. 64, p. 377
*Shorter Edition: Ch. 22, p. 127
Date used:

Answer: a
Chronological Edition: Ch. 24, p. 178
Standard Edition: Ch. 64, p. 377
*Shorter Edition: Ch. 22, p. 127
Date used:

Answer: d
Chronological Edition: Ch. 24, p. 178
Standard Edition: Ch. 64, p. 378
*Shorter Edition: Ch. 22, p. 127
Date used:

Answer: c
Chronological Edition: Ch. 24, p. 179
Standard Edition: Ch. 64, p. 378
*Shorter Edition: Ch. 22, p. 127
Date used:

Answer: d
Chronological Edition: Ch. 24, p. 179
Standard Edition: Ch. 64, p. 378
*Shorter Edition: Ch. 22, p. 127
Date used:

85. How many players are necessary to perform a trio sonata?
    a. two
    b. three
    c. four
    d. five

86. Which of the following is a likely combination of instruments in a trio sonata?
    a. two violins and harpsichord
    b. two violins and two harpsichords
    c. two violins, cello, and harpsichord
    d. two violins and cello

87. The _____ is a Baroque instrumental form which makes use of the ground bass.
    a. concerto grosso
    b. trio sonata
    c. sonata da chiesa
    d. passacaglia

88. Which tempo pattern do the sections of an Italian overture follow?
    a. fast–slow–fast
    b. slow–fast–slow
    c. moderate–slow–fast–slow
    d. slow–fast

89. Which Baroque genre was the direct ancestor of the symphony?
    a. sonata da chiesa
    b. sonata da camera
    c. French overture
    d. Italian overture

90. All of the following are fast, lively dance types EXCEPT:
    a. gigue.
    b. bourrée.
    c. sarabande.
    d. galliard.

91. Which of the following dance types was NOT standard in a Baroque suite?
    a. allemande
    b. sarabande
    c. courante
    d. tarantella

Answer: a
Chronological Edition: Ch. 24, p. 179
Standard Edition: Ch. 64, p. 378
Date used:

92. What is the form of the individual movements in a suite?
    a. binary
    b. ternary
    c. sonata
    d. rondo

Answer: b
Chronological Edition: Ch. 24, p. 179
Standard Edition: Ch. 64, p. 378
*Shorter Edition: Ch. 22, p. 127
Date used:

93. Which does NOT characterize the suite?
    a. It contains a series of dance movements.
    b. Each movement is in a contrasting key.
    c. Each movement is a dance type derived from a different country.
    d. The movements are contrasting in tempo and characte. .

Answer: c
Chronological Edition: Ch. 24, p. 179
Standard Edition: Ch. 64, p. 378
*Shorter Edition: Ch. 22, p. 127
Date used:

94. The *Water Music* by Handel is best described as a:
    a. sonata da camera.
    b. concerto grosso.
    c. suite.
    d. passacaglia.

Answer: b
Chronological Edition: Ch. 24, p. 180
Standard Edition: Ch. 64, p. 379
Date used:

95. Handel's *Water Music* opens with a:
    a. fugue.
    b. French overture.
    c. dance.
    d. prelude.

Answer: b
Chronological Edition: Ch. 24, p. 180
Standard Edition: Ch. 64, p. 379
Date used:

96. The third movement of Handel's *Water Music* is in _____ form.
    a. French overture
    b. A–B–A
    c. minuet and trio
    d. binary

Answer: b
Chronological Edition: Ch. 25, p. 181
Standard Edition: Ch. 65, p. 381
*Shorter Edition: Ch. 22, p. 127f
Date used:

97. Which was NOT an important keyboard instrument in the Baroque?
    a. harpsichord
    b. piano
    c. organ
    d. clavichord

Answer: a
Chronological Edition: Ch. 25, p. 181
Standard Edition: Ch. 65, p. 381
*Shorter Edition: Ch. 22, p. 127f
Date used:

98. What did NOT characterize the Baroque organ?
    a. a harsh tone
    b. a pure, transparent tone
    c. capability of contrasting colors
    d. capability to let individual voices stand out

Answer: c
Chronological Edition: Ch. 25, p. 181
Standard Edition: Ch. 65, p. 381
*Shorter Edition: Ch. 22, p. 128
Date used:

99. A keyboard instrument in which the strings are plucked by quills is:
   a. the organ.
   b. the piano.
   c. the harpsichord.
   d. the clavichord.

Answer: d
Chronological Edition: Ch. 25, p. 181f
Standard Edition: Ch. 65, p. 381f
*Shorter Edition: Ch. 22, p. 128
Date used:

100. The harpsichord is different from the piano because:
   a. it usually has two keyboards, rather than one.
   b. its strings are plucked, rather than struck.
   c. it is not capable of a wide dynamic range.
   d. all of the above.

Answer: c
Chronological Edition: Ch. 25, p. 182
Standard Edition: Ch. 65, p. 382
Date used:

101. By the end of the eighteenth century, the piano supplanted the harpsichord in popularity because:
   a. it was easier to play.
   b. it had a more musical sound.
   c. it was more capable of a wide dynamic range.
   d. it was more portable.

Answer: b
Chronological Edition: Ch. 25, p. 182f
Standard Edition: Ch. 65, p. 382f
Date used:

102. Which of the following keyboard forms did NOT have a strong element of improvisation?
   a. prelude
   b. fugue
   c. toccata
   d. fantasia

Answer: a
Chronological Edition: Ch. 25, p. 183
Standard Edition: Ch. 65, p. 383
Date used:

103. A Baroque keyboard piece that is free and rhapsodic in form and marked by harmonic and fugal sections is called a:
   a. toccata.
   b. chorale prelude.
   c. gigue.
   d. fugue.

Answer: a
Chronological Edition: Ch. 25, p. 183
Standard Edition: Ch. 65, p. 383
Date used:

104. Which keyboard form derives its title from the Italian word meaning "to touch"?
   a. toccata
   b. prelude
   c. invention
   d. fugue

Answer: b
Chronological Edition: Ch. 25, p. 183
Standard Edition: Ch. 65, p. 383
Date used:

105. A short piece for keyboard in contrapuntal style is called:
   a. a prelude.
   b. an invention.
   c. a fantasia.
   d. a toccata.

Answer: a
Chronological Edition: Ch. 25, p. 184
Standard Edition: Ch. 65, p. 384
*Shorter Edition: Ch. 22, p. 129
Date used:

106. The _____ is a keyboard form based on the principle of voices imitating each other.
 a. fugue
 b. prelude
 c. invention
 d. toccata

Answer: b
Chronological Edition: Ch. 25, p. 184
Standard Edition: Ch. 65, p. 384
*Shorter Edition: Ch. 22, p. 129
Date used:

107. What is the principal element of a fugue?
 a. a beautiful melody
 b. counterpoint
 c. a chorale tune
 d. arpeggios

Answer: c
Chronological Edition: Ch. 25, p. 185
Standard Edition: Ch. 65, p. 384
*Shorter Edition: Ch. 22, p. 130
Date used:

108. In a fugue, the areas of relaxation where the subject is not heard are called:
 a. answers.
 b. countersubjects.
 c. episodes.
 d. strettos.

Answer: d
Chronological Edition: Ch. 25, p. 185
Standard Edition: Ch. 65, p. 384f
*Shorter Edition: Ch. 22, p. 130
Date used:

109. In a fugue, a section in which the theme is imitated in close succession is called:
 a. an episode.
 b. augmentation.
 c. diminution.
 d. stretto.

Answer: b
Chronological Edition: Ch. 25, p. 185
Standard Edition: Ch. 65, p. 384
*Shorter Edition: Ch. 22, p. 129
Date used:

110. After the fugue subject is stated, the second entrance of the subject is called the:
 a. episode.
 b. answer.
 c. fugato.
 d. stretto.

Answer: c
Chronological Edition: Ch. 25, p. 185
Standard Edition: Ch. 65, p. 384
*Shorter Edition: Ch. 22, p. 129
Date used:

111. The answer in a fugue is stated in the key of:
 a. the tonic.
 b. the subdominant.
 c. the dominant.
 d. none of the above.

Answer: d
Chronological Edition: Ch. 25, p. 186
Standard Edition: Ch. 65, p. 385
*Shorter Edition: Ch. 22, p. 130
Date used:

112. Bach's Prelude and Fugue in C minor is from:
 a. *The Art of the Fugue.*
 b. *The Musical Offering.*
 c. the *Brandenburg Concertos.*
 d. *The Well-Tempered Clavier.*

Answer: c
Chronological Edition: Ch. 25, p. 186
Standard Edition: Ch. 65, p. 385
*Shorter Edition: Ch. 22, p. 130
Date used:

113. How many voices, or individual lines, are there in Bach's Fugue in C minor?
 a. one
 b. two
 c. three
 d. four

Answer: b
Chronological Edition: Ch. 25, p. 186
Standard Edition: Ch. 65, p. 385
*Shorter Edition: Ch. 22, p. 130f
Date used:

Answer: c
Chronological Edition: Ch. 25, p. 188
Standard Edition: Ch. 65, p. 387
Date used:

Answer: d
Chronological Edition: Ch. 25, p. 188
Standard Edition: Ch. 65, p. 387
Date used:

Answer: c
Chronological Edition: Ch. 25, p. 188
Standard Edition: Ch. 65, p. 387
Date used:

Answer: b
Chronological Edition: Tr. III, p. 189
Standard Edition: Tr. IV, p. 388
*Shorter Edition: Tr. III, p. 132
Date used:

Answer: a
Chronological Edition: Tr. III, p. 189
Standard Edition: Tr. IV, p. 388
*Shorter Edition: Tr. III, p. 132
Date used:

Answer: a
Chronological Edition: Tr. III, p. 189
Standard Edition: Tr. IV, p. 388
*Shorter Edition: Tr. III, p. 132
Date used:

114. In which voice is the subject first heard in Bach's Fugue in C minor?
   a. the top voice, or soprano
   b. the middle voice, or alto
   c. the bottom voice, or bass
   d. none of the above

115. The Baroque composer who wrote over five hundred sonatas whose structure led to the development of sonata–allegro form was:
   a. Vivaldi.
   b. Frescobaldi.
   c. Scarlatti.
   d. Bach.

116. The instrument with which Scarlatti is most closely associated is:
   a. the organ.
   b. the piano.
   c. the clavichord.
   d. the harpsichord.

117. Which is NOT a characteristic of Scarlatti's Sonata in D major, K. 491?
   a. It is in binary form.
   b. It features brilliant runs and scale passages.
   c. It remains in the same key throughout.
   d. It is based on two themes.

118. Which is NOT true of the Rococo?
   a. It was an ornate art.
   b. It emphasized the grandiose.
   c. It aimed at enchanting the senses.
   d. The term derives from the French word for shell.

119. Who was one of the greatest painters of the Rococo?
   a. Watteau
   b. Rembrandt
   c. Rubens
   d. David

120. A great French clavecinist and Rococo composer of the mid-eighteenth century was:
   a. François Couperin.
   b. Jean Baptiste Lully.
   c. Johann Joachim Quantz.
   d. Jean Antoine Watteau.

Answer: d
Chronological Edition: Tr. III, p. 189f
Standard Edition: Tr. IV, p. 388f
Date used:

121. What types of works did Rameau write?
    a. instrumental works
    b. operas
    c. theoretical works
    d. all of the above

Answer: c
Chronological Edition: Tr. III, p. 190
Standard Edition: Tr. IV, p. 389
*Shorter Edition: Tr. III, p. 133
Date used:

122. The new pre-Classical "sensitive" style that saw the first stirrings of Romanticism was called:
    a. Rococo.
    b. Impressionism.
    c. Empfindsamkeit.
    d. Neo-Romanticism.

Answer: b
Chronological Edition: Tr. III, p. 190
Standard Edition: Tr. IV, p. 389
Date used:

123. Which eighteenth-century French composer wrote the *Treatise on Harmony*, which set forth concepts leading to modern musical theory?
    a. François Couperin
    b. Jean-Phillippe Rameau
    c. Jean Antoine Watteau
    d. Johann Christian Bach

Answer: d
Chronological Edition: Tr. III, p. 190f
Standard Edition: Tr. IV, p. 389f
Date used:

124. Which of the following did NOT write an important music treatise in the eighteenth century?
    a. C. P. E. Bach
    b. Quantz
    c. Rameau
    d. Scarlatti

Answer: d
Chronological Edition: Tr. III, p. 191
Standard Edition: Tr. IV, p. 390
Date used:

125. Which of the following was J.S. Bach's youngest son, known as the "London Bach"?
    a. Carl Philipp Emanuel
    b. Johann Christoph
    c. Wilhelm Friedemann
    d. Johann Christian

Answer: b
Chronological Edition: Tr. III, p. 191
Standard Edition: Tr. IV, p. 390
Date used:

126. Which of J.S. Bach's musical sons wrote an important theoretical treatise, the *Essay on the True Art of Playing Keyboard Instruments*?
    a. Wilhelm Friedemann Bach
    b. Carl Philipp Emanuel Bach
    c. Johann Christoph Bach
    d. Johann Christian Bach

Answer: a
Chronological Edition: Tr. III, p. 191
Standard Edition: Tr. IV, p. 390
Date used:

127. What was Quantz's principal instrument?
    a. the flute
    b. the piano
    c. the violin
    d. the oboe

Answer: d
Chronological Edition: Tr. III, p. 193
Standard Edition: Tr. IV, p. 392
Date used:

128. Which of the following eighteenth-century operas reflected the trend toward naturalness and simplicity?
    a. *The Beggar's Opera*
    b. *La serva padona*
    c. *Le devin du village*
    d. all of the above

Answer: a
Chronological Edition: Tr. III, p. 193
Standard Edition: Tr. IV, p. 392
Date used:

129. Who wrote the first opéra comique, *Le devin du village*?
    a. Rousseau
    b. Rameau
    c. Couperin
    d. Pergolesi

Answer: c
Chronological Edition: Tr. III, p. 193
Standard Edition: Tr. IV, p. 392
*Shorter Edition: Tr. III, p. 134
Date used:

130. Which of the following is noted as a reformer of eighteenth-century opera?
    a. C. P. E. Bach
    b. J. J. Quantz
    c. C. W. Gluck
    d. D. Scarlatti

Answer: d
Chronological Edition: Tr. III, p. 193f
Standard Edition: Tr. IV, p. 392f
*Shorter Edition: Tr. III, p. 134f
Date used:

131. Which of the following characterizes the operas of Gluck?
    a. choral scenes
    b. dances
    c. animated ensembles
    d. all of the above

Answer: a
Chronological Edition: Tr. III, p. 193f
Standard Edition: Tr. IV, p. 392f
*Shorter Edition: Tr. III, p. 134f
Date used:

132. Which is NOT true of Gluck's opera *Orpheus and Eurydice*?
    a. It is based on Roman history.
    b. Its librettist was Calzibigi.
    c. It was originally for a castrato singer singing Orpheus.
    d. It was a reform opera.

TRUE/FALSE QUESTIONS

Answer: F
Chronological Edition: Ch. 18, p. 128
Standard Edition: Ch. 58, p. 328
*Shorter Edition: Ch. 16, p. 96
Date used:

133. The Baroque era was an age of political freedom and democracy.

Answer: T
Chronological Edition: Ch. 18, p. 129
Standard Edition: Ch. 58, p. 329
*Shorter Edition: Ch. 16, p. 97
Date used:

134.   Amateur music-making at home was popular during the Baroque era.

Answer: T
Chronological Edition: Ch. 18, p. 130
Standard Edition: Ch. 58, p. 330
*Shorter Edition: Ch. 16, p. 97f
Date used:

135.   Religion remained a driving force behind power struggles in the Baroque era.

Answer: F
Chronological Edition: Ch. 19, p. 132
Standard Edition: Ch. 59, p. 332
*Shorter Edition: Ch. 17, p. 99
Date used:

136.   The new Baroque style of vocal music for one singer with instrumental accompaniment was known as monophony.

Answer: T
Chronological Edition: Ch. 19, p. 132
Standard Edition: Ch. 59, p. 332
*Shorter Edition: Ch. 17, p. 99
Date used:

137.   The transition from Renaissance to Baroque was characterized by the change from polyphonic to homophonic texture in music.

Answer: T
Chronological Edition: Ch. 19, p. 133
Standard Edition: Ch. 59, p. 333
*Shorter Edition: Ch. 17, p. 99
Date used:

138.   The basso continuo was performed by a bass-line instrument and a chordal instrument.

Answer: T
Chronological Edition: Ch. 19, p. 133
Standard Edition: Ch. 59, p. 333
*Shorter Edition: Ch. 17, p. 99
Date used:

139.   The Baroque era is often referred to as the period of thorough-bass.

Answer: T
Chronological Edition: Ch. 19, p. 133
Standard Edition: Ch. 59, p. 333
*Shorter Edition: Ch. 17, p. 100
Date used:

140.   One of the most significant changes in music history occurred during the Baroque era: the transition from Medieval church modes to major-minor tonality.

Answer: T
Chronological Edition: Ch. 19, p. 135
Standard Edition: Ch. 59, p. 335
*Shorter Edition: Ch. 17, p. 101
Date used:

141.   Baroque music often features a steady, vigorous beat throughout.

Answer: F
Chronological Edition: Ch. 19, p. 136
Standard Edition: Ch. 59, p. 336
*Shorter Edition: Ch. 17, p. 101
Date used:

142. Baroque melodies feature balanced, symmetrical phrases with frequent cadences.

Answer: F
Chronological Edition: Ch. 19, p. 136
Standard Edition: Ch. 59, p. 336
*Shorter Edition: Ch. 17, p. 101
Date used:

143. A characteristic of Baroque music is its constant fluctuation of dynamics.

Answer: T
Chronological Edition: Ch. 19, p. 137
Standard Edition: Ch. 59, p. 337
*Shorter Edition: Ch. 17, p. 102
Date used:

144. During the Baroque, some boy singers were castrated to preserve the high register of their voices, allowing them to sing high-pitched operatic roles.

Answer: T
Chronological Edition: Ch. 19, p. 137
Standard Edition: Ch. 59, p. 337
*Shorter Edition: Ch. 17, p. 102
Date used:

145. During the Baroque era, women began entering the ranks of professional musicians, both as composers and performers.

Answer: F
Chronological Edition: Ch. 19, p. 137
Standard Edition: Ch. 59, p. 337
*Shorter Edition: Ch. 17, p. 102
Date used:

146. Improvisation played little or no part in Baroque musical practice.

Answer: T
Chronological Edition: Ch. 19, p. 137
Standard Edition: Ch. 59, p. 337
Date used:

147. During the Baroque era, the emergence of instrumental virtuosity paralleled the design improvements introduced by the great builders of instruments in Italy.

Answer: T
Chronological Edition: Ch. 19, p. 138
Standard Edition: Ch. 59, p. 338
*Shorter Edition: Ch. 17, p. 103
Date used:

148. In Baroque instrumental music, each piece (or movement) reflected a single mood or affection.

Answer: F
Chronological Edition: Ch. 20, p. 141
Standard Edition: Ch. 60, p. 340
*Shorter Edition: Ch. 18, p. 105
Date used:

149. The subjects of early Baroque operas were generally people from "real life" and dealt with real life situations.

Answer: F
Chronological Edition: Ch. 20, p. 142
Standard Edition: Ch. 60, p. 341
Date used:

Answer: T
Chronological Edition: Ch. 20, p. 142
Standard Edition: Ch. 60, p. 341
Date used:

Answer: T
Chronological Edition: Ch. 20, p. 145
Standard Edition: Ch. 60, p. 344
*Shorter Edition: Ch. 18, p. 106
Date used:

Answer: T
Chronological Edition: Ch. 20, p. 146
Standard Edition: Ch. 60, p. 345
*Shorter Edition: Ch. 18, p. 107
Date used:

Answer: T
Chronological Edition: Ch. 20, p. 146
Standard Edition: Ch. 60, p. 345
*Shorter Edition: Ch. 18, p. 107
Date used:

Answer: T
Chronological Edition: Ch. 20, p. 146
Standard Edition: Ch. 60, p. 345
*Shorter Edition: Ch. 18, p. 107
Date used:

Answer: T
Chronological Edition: Ch. 20, p. 149
Standard Edition: Ch. 60, p. 348
*Shorter Edition: Ch. 18, p. 109
Date used:

Answer: T
Chronological Edition: Ch. 20, p. 149
Standard Edition: Ch. 60, p. 348
*Shorter Edition: Ch. 18, p. 109
Date used:

150. The plot of Monteverdi's *The Coronation of Poppea* concerns a love triangle between Nero, Poppea, and Seneca.

151. A sinfonia is a short instrumental passage that facilitates scene changes.

152. In seventeenth-century England, a popular type of aristocratic entertainment which combined vocal and instrumental music with poetry and dance was the masque.

153. The form of the bass line in Dido's lament by Purcell is a ground bass.

154. Purcell's *Dido and Aeneas* was first performed at the girls' boarding school where he taught.

155. The aria, "When I am laid in earth", is unified by a descending chromatic scale ground bass.

156. "V'adoro" from Handel's *Julius Caesar* is an example of a da capo aria.

157. It was standard performance practice to embellish the last section of a da capo aria with improvised ornamentation.

Answer: F
Chronological Edition: Ch. 21, p. 150
Standard Edition: Ch. 61, p. 349
*Shorter Edition: Ch. 19, p. 109
Date used:

Answer: T
Chronological Edition: Ch. 21, p. 150
Standard Edition: Ch. 61, p. 349
*Shorter Edition: Ch. 19, p. 110
Date used:

Answer: T
Chronological Edition: Ch. 21, p. 150
Standard Edition: Ch. 61, p. 349
*Shorter Edition: Ch. 19, p. 110
Date used:

Answer: F
Chronological Edition: Ch. 21, p. 152f
Standard Edition: Ch. 61, p. 351f
Date used:

Answer: F
Chronological Edition: Ch. 21, p. 154
Standard Edition: Ch. 61, p. 353
Date used:

Answer: T
Chronological Edition: Ch. 21, p. 154
Standard Edition: Ch. 61, p. 353
*Shorter Edition: Ch. 19, p. 111
Date used:

Answer: F
Chronological Edition: Ch. 21, p. 156f
Standard Edition: Ch. 61, p. 355f
*Shorter Edition: Ch. 19, p. 112
Date used:

Answer: T
Chronological Edition: Ch. 21, p. 157
Standard Edition: Ch. 61, p. 356
Date used:

158. A cantata must be written on a religious or sacred theme.

159. A chorale is a hymn tune associated with German Protestantism.

160. Chorale tunes were originally sung in unison to encourage congregational singing.

161. Johann Sebastian Bach lived a short, unhappy life, and had no children.

162. Bach's Mass in B minor was written entirely in 1733, while in the employ of the Duke of Weimar.

163. During his lifetime, Johann Sebastian Bach was primarily known as a great organist.

164. All movements of Bach's Cantata No. 80 make use of the chorale tune, *A Mighty Fortress Is Our God*.

165. In Baroque vocal music, roulades are groups of rapid notes that decorate the melodic line.

Answer: F
Chronological Edition: Ch. 22, p. 162
Standard Edition: Ch. 62, p. 361
*Shorter Edition: Ch. 20, p. 116
Date used:

166.   The oratorio was a dramatic, staged work with elaborate scenery and costumes.

Answer: T
Chronological Edition: Ch. 22, p. 162
Standard Edition: Ch. 62, p. 361
*Shorter Edition: Ch. 20, p. 116
Date used:

167.   The role of the chorus was especially important in the oratorio.

Answer: F
Chronological Edition: Ch. 22, p. 162
Standard Edition: Ch. 62, p. 361
Date used:

168.   Bach and Handel were well-acquainted and maintained a friendly competition throughout their careers.

Answer: F
Chronological Edition: Ch. 22, p. 164f
Standard Edition: Ch. 62, p. 363f
*Shorter Edition: Ch. 20, p. 117
Date used:

169.   Handel's career as a composer was virtually over when, at age fifty-two, he suffered a stroke from which he never recovered.

Answer: F
Chronological Edition: Ch. 22, p. 167
Standard Edition: Ch. 62, p. 366
*Shorter Edition: Ch. 20, p. 118f
Date used:

170.   Handel wrote his oratorio *Messiah* over a period of four years.

Answer: T
Chronological Edition: Ch. 22, p. 167
Standard Edition: Ch. 62, p. 366
*Shorter Edition: Ch. 20, p. 118
Date used:

171.   The libretto for Handel's oratorio *Messiah* is a compilation of verses from the Bible.

Answer: F
Chronological Edition: Ch. 22, p. 167
Standard Edition: Ch. 62, p. 366
Date used:

172.   Handel's *Messiah* opens with an Italian overture in three-part (A–B–A) form.

Answer: T
Chronological Edition: Ch. 22, p. 167
Standard Edition: Ch. 62, p. 366
Date used:

173.   The aria "Ev'ry valley shall be exalted" from Handel's *Messiah* contains examples of word painting.

Answer: T
Chronological Edition: Ch. 23, p. 171
Standard Edition: Ch. 63, p. 370
*Shorter Edition: Ch. 21, p. 121
Date used:

174. The Baroque period was the first in which instrumental music was comparable in importance to vocal music.

Answer: F
Chronological Edition: Ch. 23, p. 171
Standard Edition: Ch. 63, p. 370
*Shorter Edition: Ch. 21, p. 121
Datc uscd:

175. In modern times Baroque music is played exclusively on modern instruments.

Answer: T
Chronological Edition: Ch. 23, p. 171
Standard Edition: Ch. 63, p. 370
*Shorter Edition: Ch. 21, p. 121
Date used:

176. The art of orchestration was born as Baroque composers chose specific instruments for their color or timbre.

Answer: F
Chronological Edition: Ch. 23, p. 172
Standard Edition: Ch. 63, p. 371
*Shorter Edition: Ch. 21, p. 122
Date used:

177. Antonio Vivaldi became known as "the red priest" because of his fanatical religious beliefs.

Answer: T
Chronological Edition: Ch. 23, p. 172
Standard Edition: Ch. 63, p. 371
*Shorter Edition: Ch. 21, p. 122
Date used:

178. Vivaldi lived in Venice, where he taught music at a girls' school.

Answer: T
Chronological Edition: Ch. 23, p. 174
Standard Edition: Ch. 63, p. 373
*Shorter Edition: Ch. 21, p. 124
Date used:

179. In *The Four Seasons*, Vivaldi bases each concerto on a sonnet.

Answer: F
Chronological Edition: Ch. 23, p. 177
Standard Edition: Ch. 63, p. 376
*Shorter Edition: Ch. 21, p. 122
Date used:

180. Bach's *Brandenburg Concertos* are best described as solo concertos.

Answer: T
Chronological Edition: Ch. 23, p. 177
Standard Edition: Ch. 63, p. 376
*Shorter Edition: Ch. 21, p. 122
Date used:

181. The solo instruments in Bach's *Brandenburg Concerto* No. 2 are trumpet, flute, oboe, and violin.

Answer: T
Chronological Edition: Ch. 24, p. 178
Standard Edition: Ch. 64, p. 377
*Shorter Edition: Ch. 22, p. 126
Date used:

182. A sonata da camera was usually a suite of stylized dance movements.

Answer: F
Chronological Edition: Ch. 24, p. 178
Standard Edition: Ch. 64, p. 377
*Shorter Edition: Ch. 22, p. 126
Date used:

183. A sonata da chiesa was usually a suite of stylized dance movements.

Answer: F
Chronological Edition: Ch. 24, p. 178
Standard Edition: Ch. 64, p. 377
*Shorter Edition: Ch. 22, p. 127
Date used:

184. The trio sonata is so named because it is performed by only three instrumentalists.

Answer: F
Chronological Edition: Ch. 24, p. 178
Standard Edition: Ch. 64, p. 377
*Shorter Edition: Ch. 22, p. 127
Date used:

185. The most common instrumentation for a Baroque trio sonata was solo violin and basso continuo.

Answer: T
Chronological Edition: Ch. 24, p. 178
Standard Edition: Ch. 64, p. 377
*Shorter Edition: Ch. 22, p. 127
Date used:

186. The chaconne is a variation form based upon a repeated succession of harmonies.

Answer: F
Chronological Edition: Ch. 24, p. 178
Standard Edition: Ch. 64, p. 377
*Shorter Edition: Ch. 22, p. 127
Date used:

187. The French overture is composed in three sections.

Answer: T
Chronological Edition: Ch. 24, p. 179
Standard Edition: Ch. 64, p. 378
*Shorter Edition: Ch. 22, p. 127
Date used:

188. The standard Baroque suite consisted of a variety of international dance types.

Answer: T
Chronological Edition: Ch. 24, p. 180
Standard Edition: Ch. 64, p. 379
Date used:

189. Handel's *Water Music* was performed without continuo instruments when played outdoors.

Answer: F
Chronological Edition: Ch. 25, p. 181
Standard Edition: Ch. 65, p. 381
*Shorter Edition: Ch. 22, p. 127f
Date used:

190. The three main keyboard instruments of the Baroque were the harpsichord, organ and piano.

Answer: T
Chronological Edition: Ch. 25, p. 181
Standard Edition: Ch. 65, p. 381
*Shorter Edition: Ch. 22, p. 128
Date used:

191. The strings of a harpsichord are plucked by quills.

Answer: T
Chronological Edition: Ch. 25, p. 181f
Standard Edition: Ch. 65, p. 381f
Date used:

192. The harpsichord is incapable of crescendo and diminuendo.

Answer: T
Chronological Edition: Ch. 25, p. 182
Standard Edition: Ch. 65, p. 382
*Shorter Edition: Ch. 22, p. 128
Date used:

193. The clavichord was a popular instrument for the home.

Answer: T
Chronological Edition: Ch. 25, p. 183
Standard Edition: Ch. 65, p. 383
*Shorter Edition: Ch. 22, p. 129
Date used:

194. The prelude originated in improvisation on keyboard instruments.

Answer: F
Chronological Edition: Ch. 25, p. 183
Standard Edition: Ch. 65, p. 383
Date used:

195. The invention is a free, rhapsodic keyboard piece, featuring chords, arpeggios and scale passages.

Answer: F
Chronological Edition: Ch. 25, p. 184
Standard Edition: Ch. 65, p. 384
*Shorter Edition: Ch. 22, p. 129
Date used:

196. A fugue is a form exclusively for solo keyboard performance.

Answer: T
Chronological Edition: Ch. 25, p. 184f
Standard Edition: Ch. 65, p. 384
*Shorter Edition: Ch. 22, p. 129f
Date used:

197. A fugue is a contrapuntal composition in which a single subject is the focal point, thus unifying the work.

Answer: F
Chronological Edition: Ch. 25, p. 185
Standard Edition: Ch. 65, p. 384
*Shorter Edition: Ch. 22, p. 129f
Date used:

198. At the beginning of a fugue, the countersubject is stated alone.

Answer: T
Chronological Edition: Ch. 25, p. 185
Standard Edition: Ch. 65, p. 385
Date used:

199. An imitative passage found in a nonfugal piece of music is known as fugato.

Answer: T
Chronological Edition: Ch. 25, p. 185
Standard Edition: Ch. 65, p. 385
*Shorter Edition: Ch. 22, p. 130
Date used:

200. In a fugue, the device in which the theme is imitated in close succession is known as stretto.

Answer: F
Chronological Edition: Ch. 25, p. 186
Standard Edition: Ch. 65, p. 385
Date used:

201. The Prelude from Bach's Prelude and Fugue in C minor is a fugato.

Answer: F
Chronological Edition: Ch. 25, p. 187
Standard Edition: Ch. 65, p. 387
Date used:

202. The Scarlattian sonata is a multiple movement, ternary form.

Answer: T
Chronological Edition: Ch. 25, p. 188
Standard Edition: Ch. 65, p. 387
Date used:

203. The sonatas of Scarlatti present the seeds of sonata–allegro form.

Answer: T
Chronological Edition: Tr. III, p. 189
Standard Edition: Tr. IV, p. 388
*Shorter Edition: Tr. III, p. 132
Date used:

204. As a reaction to the grandiose gesture of the Baroque, the Rococo style was a miniature and ornate art aimed at enchantment of the senses.

Answer: F
Chronological Edition: Tr. III, p. 190
Standard Edition: Tr. IV, p. 389
*Shorter Edition: Tr. III, p. 133
Date used:

205. Empfindsamkeit was the first major classical movement that shunned emotions.

Answer: F
Chronological Edition: Tr. III, p. 191
Standard Edition: Tr. IV, p. 390
Date used:

Answer: T
Chronological Edition: Tr. III, p. 191
Standard Edition: Tr. IV, p. 390
Date used:

Answer: T
Chronological Edition: Tr. III, p. 192
Standard Edition: Tr. IV, p. 391
Date used:

Answer: T
Chronological Edition: Tr. III, p. 193
Standard Edition: Tr. IV, p. 392
*Shorter Edition: Tr. III, p. 134
Date used:

Answer: T
Chronological Edition: Tr. III, p. 194
Standard Edition: Tr. IV, p. 393
Date used:

206. Although J. S. Bach had twenty children, none of them became musicians.

207. Johann Joachim Quantz was a court composer and flute instructor to Frederick the Great.

208. The first movement of Quantz's Flute Concerto in G is based on a single theme.

209. The "War of the Buffoons" was between those who favored French court opera and the proponents of Italian comic opera.

210. In Gluck's opera, *Orpheus and Eurydice*, the lovers are united in the end.

EIGHTEENTH-CENTURY
CLASSICISM

MULTIPLE CHOICE QUESTIONS

Answer: d
Chronological Edition: Ch. 16, p. 117
Standard Edition: Ch. 36, p. 177
*Shorter Edition: Ch. 14, p. 87
Date used:

1. Tonality means that we hear a piece of music in relation to a central tone, called:
   a. the dominant.
   b. the subdominant.
   c. the scale.
   d. the tonic.

Answer: a
Chronological Edition: Ch. 16, p. 117
Standard Edition: Ch. 36, p. 177
*Shorter Edition: Ch. 14, p. 87
Date used:

2. The principle of organization whereby we hear a piece of music in relation to a central tone is called:
   a. tonality.
   b. transposition.
   c. modulation.
   d. chromaticism.

Answer: b
Chronological Edition: Ch. 16, p. 117
Standard Edition: Ch. 36, p. 177
*Shorter Edition: Ch. 14, p. 87
Date used:

3. A group of related tones with a common center, a tonic, is called:
   a. an interval.
   b. a key.
   c. an octave.
   d. a melody.

Answer: c
Chronological Edition: Ch. 16, p. 118
Standard Edition: Ch. 36, p. 178
*Shorter Edition: Ch. 14, p. 88
Date used:

4. In Western music, the octave is divided into how many equal intervals?
   a. six
   b. eight
   c. twelve
   d. fifteen

Answer: a
Chronological Edition: Ch. 16, p. 118
Standard Edition: Ch. 36, p. 178
*Shorter Edition: Ch. 14, p. 88
Date used:

5. The smallest unit of distance in our musical system is called:
   a. a half step.
   b. a whole step.
   c. an octave.
   d. a third.

Answer: a
Chronological Edition: Ch. 16, p. 118
Standard Edition: Ch. 36, p. 178
*Shorter Edition: Ch. 14, p. 88
Date used:

6. A twelve-tone scale, including all the semitones of the octave, is called:
   a. chromatic.
   b. diatonic.
   c. major.
   b. minor.

Answer: d
Chronological Edition: Ch. 16, p. 119
Standard Edition: Ch. 36, p. 179
*Shorter Edition: Ch. 14, p. 89
Date used:

Answer: b
Chronological Edition: Ch. 16, p. 120
Standard Edition: Ch. 36, p. 180
*Shorter Edition: Ch. 14, p. 89
Date used:

Answer: a
Chronological Edition: Ch. 16, p. 120
Standard Edition: Ch. 36, p. 180
*Shorter Edition: Ch. 14, p. 89f
Date used:

Answer: b
Chronological Edition: Ch. 16, p. 121
Standard Edition: Ch. 36, p. 181
*Shorter Edition: Ch. 14, p. 91
Date used:

Answer: a
Chronological Edition: Ch. 16, p. 121
Standard Edition: Ch. 36, p. 181
*Shorter Edition: Ch. 14, p. 91
Date used:

Answer: c
Chronological Edition: Ch. 17, p. 121
Standard Edition: Ch. 37, p. 181
*Shorter Edition: Ch. 15, p. 91
Date used:

Answer: a
Chronological Edition: Ch. 17, p. 122
Standard Edition: Ch. 37, p. 182
*Shorter Edition: Ch. 15, p. 91
Date used:

7. In a major scale, the greatest tension lies between what two tones?
   a. 3 and 4
   b. 4 and 5
   c. 6 and 7
   d. 7 and 8

8. In a major scale, between which intervals do the half steps occur?
   a. 2 and 3, 7 and 8
   b. 3 and 4, 7 and 8
   c. 2 and 3, 6 and 7
   d. 2 and 3, 5 and 6

9. What characterizes the minor mode?
   a. It has a lowered third degree.
   b. It always begins on the note F.
   c. It sounds the same as the major mode.
   d. It is made entirely of half steps.

10. Music based on the seven tones of a major or minor scale is called:
    a. chromatic.
    b. diatonic.
    c. modal.
    d. transposed.

11. With which era is chromatic music most frequently associated?
    a. Romantic
    b. Renaissance
    c. Classic
    d. Middle Ages

12. When a melody is transposed to another key, what remains the same?
    a. the pitch level of the melody
    b. the keynote or tonic of the melody
    c. the shape of the melodic line
    d. the number of sharps or flats

13. The process of passing from one key to another is known as:
    a. modulation.
    b. development.
    c. transposition.
    d. transformation.

Answer: a
Chronological Edition: Ch. 17, p. 123
Standard Edition: Ch. 37, p. 183
*Shorter Edition: Ch. 15, p. 92
Date used:

Answer: a
Chronological Edition: Ch. 17, p. 123
Standard Edition: Ch. 37, p. 183
*Shorter Edition: Ch. 15, p. 92
Date used:

Answer: c
Chronological Edition: Ch. 17, p. 123
Standard Edition: Ch. 37, p. 183
*Shorter Edition: Ch. 15, p. 92
Date used:

Answer: c
Chronological Edition: Ch. 17, p. 123
Standard Edition: Ch. 37, p. 183
*Shorter Edition: Ch. 15, p. 92
Date used:

Answer: d
Chronological Edition: Ch. 17, p. 123
Standard Edition: Ch. 37, p. 183
*Shorter Edition: Ch. 15, p. 92
Date used:

Answer: a
Chronological Edition: Ch. 26, p. 199
Standard Edition: Ch. 38, p. 185
*Shorter Edition: Ch. 23, p. 139
Date used:

Answer: d
Chronological Edition: Ch. 26, p. 199
Standard Edition: Ch. 38, p. 185
*Shorter Edition: Ch. 23, p. 139
Date used:

14. The triad built on the first note of the scale is called:
    a. the tonic.
    b. the dominant.
    c. the subdominant.
    d. the subtonic.

15. In harmony, a place of rest and return is:
    a. the tonic.
    b. the dominant.
    c. the subdominant.
    d. the leading tone.

16. The dominant chord is represented by which symbol?
    a. I
    b. IV
    c. V
    d. VII

17. The three most important triads used in diatonic harmony are:
    a. I-III-V
    b. I-V-VII
    c. I-IV-V
    d. I-VI-VII

18. The three triads basic to our musical system are the tonic, the dominant, and:
    a. the supertonic.
    b. the mediant.
    c. the submediant.
    d. the subdominant.

19. A theme may be fragmented by dividing it into smaller units called:
    a. motives.
    b. codas.
    c. sequences.
    d. modulations.

20. Repeating a motive at a higher or lower pitch level is called:
    a. a scale.
    b. a theme.
    c. a coda.
    d. a sequence.

Answer: c
Chronological Edition: Ch. 26, p. 199
Standard Edition: Ch. 38, p. 185
*Shorter Edition: Ch. 23, p. 139
Date used:

Answer: c
Chronological Edition: Ch. 26, p. 200
Standard Edition: Ch. 38, p. 186
*Shorter Edition: Ch. 23, p. 140
Date used:

Answer: a
Chronological Edition: Ch. 27, p. 201
Standard Edition: Ch. 39, p. 187
*Shorter Edition: Ch. 24, p. 141
Date used:

Answer: a
Chronological Edition: Ch. 27, p. 201
Standard Edition: Ch. 39, p. 187
*Shorter Edition: Ch. 24, p. 141
Date used:

Answer: c
Chronological Edition: Ch. 27, p. 201
Standard Edition: Ch. 39, p. 187
*Shorter Edition: Ch. 24, p. 141
Date used:

Answer: b
Chronological Edition: Ch. 27, p. 201
Standard Edition: Ch. 39, p. 187
*Shorter Edition: Ch. 24, p. 141
Date used:

Answer: c
Chronological Edition: Ch. 27, p. 201
Standard Edition: Ch. 39, p. 187
*Shorter Edition: Ch. 24, p. 141
Date used:

21. Which is NOT a type of thematic development?
    a. breaking up a theme into motives
    b. expanding a motive into a long melody
    c. literally repeating a melody at the same pitch level
    d. treating a motive in sequence

22. The famous four-note figure at the beginning of Beethoven's Symphony No. 5 is best described as:
    a. a key.
    b. a theme.
    c. a motive.
    d. a coda.

23. Which best describes absolute music?
    a. Music without a story or text
    b. Music without form
    c. All instrumental music
    d. The finest music from the past

24. Which movement is the most highly organized and most characteristic of the sonata cycle?
    a. first
    b. second
    c. third
    d. fourth

25. Which of the following genres does NOT usually follow the general structure of a sonata cycle?
    a. sonata
    b. symphony
    c. overture
    d. concerto

26. We can best regard sonata–allegro form as a drama between:
    a. two groups of instruments.
    b. two key areas.
    c. two forms.
    d. two motives.

27. In sonata–allegro form, a modulatory section that leads from one theme to the next is called:
    a. a codetta.
    b. development.
    c. a bridge.
    d. an introduction.

Answer: b
Chronological Edition: Ch. 27, p. 201
Standard Edition: Ch. 39, p. 187
*Shorter Edition: Ch. 24, p. 141
Date used:

28. What is the function of the bridge in sonata–allegro form?
    a. to establish the tonic
    b. to modulate to a new key
    c. to develop the themes
    d. to restate the themes

Answer: b
Chronological Edition: Ch. 27, p. 202
Standard Edition: Ch. 39, p. 188
*Shorter Edition: Ch. 24, p. 142
Date used:

29. The three main sections of sonata–allegro form are the exposition, development, and:
    a. bridge.
    b. recapitulation.
    c. coda.
    d. trio.

Answer: c
Chronological Edition: Ch. 27, p. 202
Standard Edition: Ch. 39, p. 188
*Shorter Edition: Ch. 24, p. 141
Date used:

30. In sonata–allegro form, the contrasting key is established by the statement of:
    a. the development.
    b. the bridge.
    c. the second theme.
    d. the codetta.

Answer: b
Chronological Edition: Ch. 27, p. 202
Standard Edition: Ch. 39, p. 188
*Shorter Edition: Ch. 24, p. 142
Date used:

31. In sonata–allegro form, the section that features the most tension and drama through modulation and motivic interplay is called:
    a. the exposition.
    b. the development.
    c. the recapitulation.
    d. the coda.

Answer: c
Chronological Edition: Ch. 27, p. 202
Standard Edition: Ch. 39, p. 188
*Shorter Edition: Ch. 24, p. 142
Date used:

32. The psychological climax of sonata–allegro form appears when the tonic returns at the:
    a. exposition.
    b. development.
    c. recapitulation.
    d. coda.

Answer: d
Chronological Edition: Ch. 27, p. 202
Standard Edition: Ch. 39, p. 188
*Shorter Edition: Ch. 24, p. 142
Date used:

33. The final section of a sonata–allegro movement, which rounds it off with a vigorous closing cadence, is:
    a. the exposition.
    b. the development.
    c. the recapitulation.
    d. the coda.

Answer: d
Chronological Edition: Ch. 27, p. 204
Standard Edition: Ch. 39, p. 190
*Shorter Edition: Ch. 24, p. 143
Date used:

34. Which of the following is a common characteristic of the second movement of a sonata cycle?
    a. a slow tempo
    b. theme and variations form
    c. A–B–A form
    d. all of the above

Answer: d
Chronological Edition: Ch. 27, p. 204
Standard Edition: Ch. 39, p. 190
*Shorter Edition: Ch. 24, p. 144
Date used:

Answer: b
Chronological Edition: Ch. 27, p. 205
Standard Edition: Ch. 39, p. 191
*Shorter Edition: Ch. 24, p. 144
Date used:

Answer: b
Chronological Edition: Ch. 27, p. 205
Standard Edition: Ch. 39, p. 191
*Shorter Edition: Ch. 24, p. 144
Date used:

Answer: d
Chronological Edition: Ch. 27, p. 205
Standard Edition: Ch. 39, p. 191
*Shorter Edition: Ch. 24, p. 145
Date used:

Answer: c
Chronological Edition: Ch. 27, p. 205
Standard Edition: Ch. 39, p. 191
*Shorter Edition: Ch. 24, p. 145
Date used:

Answer: b
Chronological Edition: Ch. 27, p. 206
Standard Edition: Ch. 39, p. 192
*Shorter Edition: Ch. 24, p. 145
Date used:

Answer: b
Chronological Edition: Ch. 28, p. 209
Standard Edition: Ch. 40, p. 195
*Shorter Edition: Ch. 25, p. 149
Date used:

35. In the Classical sonata cycle, the third movement was usually in:
   a. theme and variations form.
   b. sonata form.
   c. rondo form.
   d. minuet and trio form.

36. The overall form of a minuet and trio is best described as:
   a. A–B.
   b. A–B–A.
   c. A–B–A–C–A–B–A.
   d. A–B–C–D–E–F–A.

37. The second dance or the middle section of a minuet is called:
   a. minuet II.
   b. trio.
   c. da capo.
   d. scherzo.

38. How does a scherzo differ from a minuet?
   a. It is in 3/4 time.
   b. It is generally the third movement of a symphony.
   c. It has a three-part form.
   d. It is faster and sometimes humorous.

39. Which form would be most frequently found as the fourth movement of the sonata cycle?
   a. A–B–A
   b. minuet
   c. rondo
   d. scherzo

40. In the Classical sonata cycle, which movement was most commonly in a contrasting key from the other three?
   a. first
   b. second
   c. third
   d. fourth

41. How do Classic artists differ from their Romantic counterparts?
   a. They are more subjective.
   b. They emphasize clarity and beauty of form.
   c. They use art for self-expression.
   d. All of these.

Answer: d
Chronological Edition: Ch. 28, p. 210
Standard Edition: Ch. 40, p. 196
*Shorter Edition: Ch. 25, p. 150f
Date used:

Answer: d
Chronological Edition: Ch. 28, p. 210
Standard Edition: Ch. 40, p. 196
*Shorter Edition: Ch. 25, p. 150
Date used:

Answer: d
Chronological Edition: Ch. 28, p. 211
Standard Edition: Ch. 40, p. 197
*Shorter Edition: Ch. 25, p. 151
Date used:

Answer: b
Chronological Edition: Ch. 28, p. 212
Standard Edition: Ch. 40, p. 199
*Shorter Edition: Ch. 25, p. 151
Date used:

Answer: d
Chronological Edition: Ch. 28, p. 212
Standard Edition: Ch. 40, p. 199
*Shorter Edition: Ch. 25, p. 152
Date used:

Answer: a
Chronological Edition: Ch. 28, p. 214
Standard Edition: Ch. 40, p. 200
*Shorter Edition: Ch. 25, p. 152
Date used:

Answer: d
Chronological Edition: Ch. 29, p. 215
Standard Edition: Ch. 41, p. 201
*Shorter Edition: Ch. 26, p. 153
Date used:

42. What was the force that had an impact on the Classic era?
   a. the American Revolution
   b. the French Revolution
   c. the Industrial Revolution
   d. all of the above

43. Which of the following was NOT an eighteenth-century ruler?
   a. Frederick the Great of Prussia
   b. Maria Theresa of Austria
   c. Louis XV of France
   d. Elizabeth I of England

44. Interest in Greek and Roman antiquity during the eighteenth century greatly influenced:
   a. painting.
   b. architecture.
   c. literature.
   d. all of these.

45. Which American president was a leading figure during the Classical period?
   a. Abraham Lincoln
   b. Thomas Jefferson
   c. Andrew Jackson
   d. James Polk

46. The Sturm und Drang movement came about largely because of two works, written by Schiller and:
   a. Burns.
   b. Blake.
   c. Kant.
   d. Goethe.

47. Which role in musical life was socially acceptable for eighteenth-century women?
   a. performer
   b. composer
   c. church musician
   d. all of these

48. The Classical period in music ranged from approximately:
   a. 1600 to 1650.
   b. 1650 to 1700.
   c. 1700 to 1750.
   d. 1775 to 1825.

Answer: c
Chronological Edition: Ch. 29, p. 215
Standard Edition: Ch. 41, p. 201
*Shorter Edition: Ch. 26, p. 153
Date used:

Answer: b
Chronological Edition: Ch. 29, p. 216
Standard Edition: Ch. 41, p. 202
*Shorter Edition: Ch. 26, p. 153f
Date used:

Answer: b
Chronological Edition: Ch. 29, p. 216
Standard Edition: Ch. 41, p. 202
*Shorter Edition: Ch. 29, p. 162
Date used:

Answer: b
Chronological Edition: Ch. 29, p. 216
Standard Edition: Ch. 41, p. 202
*Shorter Edition: Ch. 29, p. 162
Date used:

Answer: a
Chronological Edition: Ch. 29, p. 217
Standard Edition: Ch. 41, p. 203
*Shorter Edition: Ch. 32, p. 173
Date used:

Answer: c
Chronological Edition: Ch. 29, p. 217
Standard Edition: Ch. 41, p. 203
*Shorter Edition: Ch. 29, p. 161
Date used:

Answer: a
Chronological Edition: Ch. 29, p. 218
Standard Edition: Ch. 41, p. 204
*Shorter Edition: Ch. 34, p. 182
Date used:

Answer: c
Chronological Edition: Ch. 29, p. 218
Standard Edition: Ch. 41, p. 204
*Shorter Edition: Ch. 34, p. 181
Date used:

49. Who was NOT a master of the Viennese school?
    a. Beethoven
    b. Haydn
    c. Chopin
    d. Schubert

50. What does NOT characterize the Classical style?
    a. singable, elegant melodies
    b. highly chromatic harmony
    c. strong, regular rhythms
    d. use of folk and popular elements

51. In the Classical orchestra, which group of instruments served as the ensemble's nucleus?
    a. woodwinds
    b. strings
    c. brass
    d. percussion

52. The number of players in the Classical orchestra was typically:
    a. 10–15.
    b. 30–40.
    c. 40–60.
    d. 70–90.

53. During the Classical era, the most popular solo instruments for concertos were the violin and:
    a. the piano.
    b. the flute.
    c. the harp.
    d. the viola.

54. The most important instrumental form of the Classical period was:
    a. the serenade.
    b. the string trio.
    c. the symphony.
    d. the divertimento.

55. Opera buffa is comic opera from what country?
    a. Italy
    b. France
    c. England
    d. Germany

56. Which genre was most likely to be heard in a public concert house in the eighteenth century?
    a. serenade
    b. string quartet
    c. opera
    d. divertimento

Answer: b
Chronological Edition: Ch. 30, p. 219
Standard Edition: Ch. 42, p. 205
*Shorter Edition: Ch. 27, p. 155
Date used:

Answer: d
Chronological Edition: Ch. 30, p. 219
Standard Edition: Ch. 42, p. 205
*Shorter Edition: Ch. 27, p. 155
Date used:

Answer: b
Chronological Edition: Ch. 30, p. 220
Standard Edition: Ch. 42, p. 206
*Shorter Edition: Ch. 27, p. 155
Date used:

Answer: a
Chronological Edition: Ch. 30, p. 220
Standard Edition: Ch. 42, p. 206
Date used:

Answer: c
Chronological Edition: Ch. 31, p. 222
Standard Edition: Ch. 43, p. 208
*Shorter Edition: Ch. 28, p. 158
Date used:

Answer: a
Chronological Edition: Ch. 31, p. 223f
Standard Edition: Ch. 43, p. 209f
*Shorter Edition: Ch. 28, p. 158
Date used:

Answer: c
Chronological Edition: Ch. 31, p. 225
Standard Edition: Ch. 43, p. 211
*Shorter Edition: Ch. 28, p. 158
Date used:

57. Music for a small ensemble of two to about ten players with one player to the part is called:
a. program music.
b. chamber music.
c. opera buffa.
d. pure music.

58. A string quartet consists of:
a. violin, viola, cello, and bass.
b. 3 violins and cello.
c. violin, 2 violas, and cello.
d. 2 violins, viola, and cello.

59. Which composer established the scherzo as a regular alternative to the minuet movement?
a. Mozart
b. Beethoven
c. Haydn
d. Schubert

60. In Classical string quartet literature, the longest and most complex movement is usually:
a. the first.
b. the second.
c. the third.
d. the fourth.

61. Who wrote the librettos for Mozart's *The Marriage of Figaro* and *Don Giovanni*?
a. Schikaneder
b. Metastasio
c. da Ponte
d. Mozart

62. Mozart died while writing his:
a. Requiem Mass.
b. last symphony.
c. opera, *The Magic Flute*.
d. opera, *The Marriage of Figaro*.

63. The instrument that Mozart played and that he wrote many concertos for was:
a. the cello.
b. the organ.
c. the piano.
d. the trumpet.

Answer: a
Chronological Edition: Ch. 31, p. 225
Standard Edition: Ch. 43, p. 211
Date used:

64. Mozart's compositions are often listed by their "K" numbers, which refer to:
   a. the man who first cataloged his works.
   b. the order of publication of his works.
   c. the dating of his manuscripts.
   d. the dedication he made to the Kaiser.

Answer: c
Chronological Edition: Ch. 31, p. 225
Standard Edition: Ch. 43, p. 211
*Shorter Edition: Ch. 28, p. 158f
Date used:

65. Mozart made a lasting and significant contribution to numerous genres, including:
   a. the chorale cantata.
   b. the prelude and fugue.
   c. the piano concerto.
   d. the symphonic poem.

Answer: a
Chronological Edition: Ch. 31, p. 225
Standard Edition: Ch. 43, p. 211
*Shorter Edition: Ch. 28, p. 159
Date used:

66. *Eine kleine Nachtmusik*:
   a. is German for "A Little Night Music".
   b. is an example of program music.
   c. is a symphony for full orchestra.
   d. all of these.

Answer: b
Chronological Edition: Ch. 31, p. 225
Standard Edition: Ch. 43, p. 211
*Shorter Edition: Ch. 28, p. 158
Date used:

67. Which composer wrote over twenty concertos for the piano, establishing this genre?
   a. Beethoven
   b. Mozart
   c. Haydn
   d. Schubert

Answer: b
Chronological Edition: Ch. 31, p. 225
Standard Edition: Ch.43, p. 211
*Shorter Edition: Ch. 28, p. 159
Date used:

68. Mozart's *Eine kleine Nachtmusik* is an example of:
   a. a symphony.
   b. a serenade.
   c. a sonata.
   d. a concerto.

Answer: a
Chronological Edition: Ch. 31, p. 225
Standard Edition: Ch. 43, p. 211
*Shorter Edition: Ch. 28, p. 159
Date used:

69. Which best describes the form of the first movement of Mozart's *Eine kleine Nachtmusik*?
   a. sonata–allegro
   b. theme and variations
   c. rondo
   d. minuet

Answer: b
Chronological Edition: Ch. 31, p. 226f
Standard Edition: Ch. 43, p. 211f
*Shorter Edition: Ch. 28, p. 159
Date used:

70. Which best describes the opening of the first movement of Mozart's *Eine kleine Nachtmusik*?
   a. a lilting, triple-meter dance
   b. an ascending rocket theme
   c. a lyrical, conjunct melody
   d. a slowly ascending chromatic scale

Answer: d
Chronological Edition: Ch. 32, p. 228
Standard Edition: Ch. 44, p. 214
Date used:

Answer: b
Chronological Edition: Ch. 32, p. 228
Standard Edition: Ch. 44, p. 214
Date used:

Answer: a
Chronological Edition: Ch. 32, p. 229
Standard Edition: Ch. 44, p. 215
Date used:

Answer: c
Chronological Edition: Ch. 33, p. 230
Standard Edition: Ch. 45, p. 216
*Shorter Edition: Ch. 29, p. 161
Date used:

Answer: b
Chronological Edition: Ch. 33, p. 230
Standard Edition: Ch. 45, p. 216
*Shorter Edition: Ch. 29, p. 161
Date used:

Answer: c
Chronological Edition: Ch. 33, p. 230
Standard Edition: Ch. 45, p. 216
*Shorter Edition: Ch. 29, p. 161
Date used:

Answer: a
Chronological Edition: Ch. 33, p. 230
Standard Edition: Ch. 45, p. 216
*Shorter Edition: Ch. 29, p. 162
Date used:

71. The slow movement of Haydn's String Quartet in C major, Opus 76, No. 3 is based on:
   a. a folk melody.
   b. an English popular tune.
   c. a sacred Austrian hymn.
   d. a new melody by Haydn.

72. The form of the second movement of Haydn's String Quartet , Opus 76, No. 3, is:
   a. sonata–allegro.
   b. theme and variations.
   c. minuet and trio.
   d. rondo.

73. The first movement of Beethoven's String Quartet, Opus 18, No. 1 centers around:
   a. a rhythmic motive.
   b. a lyric melody.
   c. an expansive fugue.
   d. a virtuoso violin part.

74. The Classical symphony had its roots in the:
   a. concerto.
   b. sonata.
   c. opera overture.
   d. ballet.

75. How many movements were typical of pre-Classical symphonies?
   a. two
   b. three
   c. four
   d. eight

76. The early Classical symphony was characterized by quickly ascending themes with a strong rhythmic drive. These are known as:
   a. steamroller themes.
   b. torpedo themes.
   c. rocket themes.
   d. operatic themes.

77. The first movement of a symphony is usually in:
   a. sonata–allegro form.
   b. minuet and trio form.
   c. rondo form.
   d. theme and variations form.

Answer: a
Chronological Edition: Ch. 33, p. 231
Standard Edition: Ch. 45, p. 217
*Shorter Edition: Ch. 29, p. 162
Date used:

Answer: d
Chronological Edition: Ch. 33, p. 231
Standard Edition: Ch. 45, p. 217
*Shorter Edition: Ch. 29, p. 162
Date used:

Answer: a
Chronological Edition: Ch. 33, p. 231
Standard Edition: Ch. 45, p. 217
*Shorter Edition: Ch. 29, p. 162
Date used:

Answer: c
Chronological Edition: Ch. 33, p. 231f
Standard Edition: Ch. 45, p. 217f
Date used:

Answer: c
Chronological Edition: Ch.34, p. 234
Standard Edition: Ch. 46, p. 220
*Shorter Edition: Ch. 30, p. 163
Date used:

Answer: b
Chronological Edition: Ch. 34, p. 235
Standard Edition: Ch. 46, p. 221
*Shorter Edition: Ch. 30, p. 163
Date used:

Answer: b
Chronological Edition: Ch. 34, p. 235
Standard Edition: Ch. 46, p. 221
*Shorter Edition: Ch. 30, p. 164
Date used:

78. Which composer is noted for his monothematic
sonata–allegro form?
a. Haydn
b. Mozart
c. Beethoven
d. Schubert

79. What is NOT a typical form for the second
movement of a Classical symphony?
a. sonata–allegro
b. A–B–A
c. theme and variations
d. ritornello

80. The third movement of a Classical symphony is
most frequently in:
a. minuet and trio form.
b. theme and variations form.
c. rondo form.
d. sonata–allegro form.

81. Which does NOT describe the first movement of
Mozart's Symphony No. 40 in G minor?
a. It has strong emotional content.
b. It is based on a three-note motive.
c. It remains in the same key throughout the
movement.
d. It is in sonata–allegro form.

82. Who was Haydn's principal patron?
a. Emperor Frederick the Great
b. Emperor Joseph II
c. Prince Esterházy
d. Count Razumovsky

83. Haydn enjoyed phenomenal musical success with
two trips to which country?
a. France
b. England
c. Italy
d. United States

84. Of which genre is Haydn's *Creation* representative?
a. opera
b. oratorio
c. mass
d. concerto

Answer: d
Chronological Edition: Ch. 34, p. 236
Standard Edition: Ch. 46, p. 222
*Shorter Edition: Ch. 30, p. 164
Date used:

85. What does NOT characterize Haydn's late symphonies?
    a. expansion of form
    b. varied moods
    c. rich orchestral color
    d. conservative harmonies and modulations

Answer: a
Chronological Edition: Ch. 34, p. 236
Standard Edition: Ch. 46, p. 222
*Shorter Edition: Ch. 30, p. 164
Date used:

86. Haydn was a prolific composer in all the following genres EXCEPT:
    a. ballets.
    b. string quartets.
    c. symphonies.
    d. church music.

Answer: c
Chronological Edition: Ch. 34, p. 236
Standard Edition: Ch. 46, p. 222
*Shorter Edition: Ch. 30, p. 164
Date used:

87. Which is NOT a work by Haydn?
    a. *The Creation*
    b. the *London Symphony*
    c. the *Messiah*
    d. the *Lord Nelson Mass*

Answer: c
Chronological Edition: Ch. 34, p. 237
Standard Edition: Ch. 46, p. 223
*Shorter Edition: Ch. 30, p. 165
Date used:

88. What is NOT true of Haydn's Symphony No. 104?
    a. The first movement has a slow introduction.
    b. The first movement is monothematic.
    c. The second movement is in sonata–allegro form.
    d. The finale shows folk influence.

Answer: d
Chronological Edition: Ch. 34, p. 237
Standard Edition: Ch. 46, p. 224
Date used:

89. The last movement of Haydn's Symphony No. 104 features a sustained bass-range pitch typical of some European folk instruments. This effect is called:
    a. a free variation.
    b. a counter-melody.
    c. a cadenza.
    d. a drone.

Answer: b
Chronological Edition: Ch. 34, p. 240
Standard Edition: Ch. 46, p. 226
Date used:

90. What instrument family, other than strings, is featured in the Trio section of the third movement of Haydn's Symphony No. 104?
    a. brass
    b. woodwinds
    c. percussion
    d. none of the above

Answer: d
Chronological Edition: Ch. 35, p. 241f
Standard Edition: Ch. 47, p. 227f
*Shorter Edition: Ch. 31, p. 167f
Date used:

91. Beethoven supported himself through:
    a. music lessons.
    b. publishing.
    c. public concerts.
    d. all of the above.

Answer: d
Chronological Edition: Ch. 35, p. 241f
Standard Edition: Ch. 47, p. 227f
*Shorter Edition: Ch. 31, p. 167f
Date used:

Answer: b
Chronological Edition: Ch. 35, p. 242
Standard Edition: Ch. 47, p. 228
*Shorter Edition: Ch. 31, p. 167
Date used:

Answer: c
Chronological Edition: Ch. 35, p. 243f
Standard Edition: Ch. 47, p. 228f
*Shorter Edition: Ch. 31, p. 168f
Date used:

Answer: a
Chronological Edition: Ch. 35, p. 244
Standard Edition: Ch. 47, p. 230
Date used:

Answer: b
Chronological Edition: Ch. 35, p. 244
Standard Edition: Ch. 47, p. 230
*Shorter Edition: Ch. 31, p. 168
Date used:

Answer: c
Chronological Edition: Ch. 35, p. 243f
Standard Edition: Ch. 47, p. 229f
*Shorter Edition: Ch. 31, p. 168
Date used:

Answer: b
Chronological Edition: Ch. 35, p. 244f
Standard Edition: Ch. 47, p. 230f
*Shorter Edition: Ch. 31, p. 168
Date used:

92. Beethoven's temperament could best be described as:
   a. timid and shy.
   b. humble and subservient.
   c. easy-going and carefree.
   d. explosive and independent.

93. Beethoven suffered perhaps the most traumatic of all maladies for a musician. What was it?
   a. He became blind.
   b. He became deaf.
   c. He became deaf and blind.
   d. He became paralyzed.

94. Which best describes Beethoven?
   a. A purely Classical composer, who strictly adhered to the forms established by Haydn and Mozart.
   b. A thoroughly Romantic composer who abandoned all traces of Classical form.
   c. A transitional composer, whose early works reflected many Classical elements and whose later works led the way to Romanticism.
   d. None of the above.

95. Which was Beethoven's own instrument, for which he wrote numerous concertos and sonatas?
   a. the piano
   b. the violin
   c. the cello
   d. the clarinet

96. How many symphonies did Beethoven write?
   a. 5
   b. 9
   c. 32
   d. 104

97. Which statement about Beethoven is inaccurate?
   a. He composed five piano concertos.
   b. His thirty-two piano sonatas are an indispensable part of piano literature.
   c. His principal chamber works are piano trios.
   d. He wrote only one opera.

98. In which genre was Beethoven least prolific?
   a. symphony
   b. opera
   c. sonata
   d. string quartet

Answer: d
Chronological Edition: Ch. 55, p. 245
Standard Edition: Ch.47, p. 231
*Shorter Edition: Ch. 31, p. 168
Date used:

99. Which best describes Beethoven's Symphony No. 9?
    a. Vocal soloists and chorus join the orchestra.
    b. The finale prophesies a time when "all men shall be brothers."
    c. The choral movement is based on Schiller's *Ode to Joy*.
    d. All of the above.

Answer: d
Chronological Edition: Ch. 35, p. 245
Standard Edition: Ch. 47, p. 231
*Shorter Edition: Ch. 31, p. 168
Date used:

100. Which Beethoven work is called the *Choral Symphony*?
     a. the First
     b. the Fifth
     c. the Seventh
     d. the Ninth

Answer: b
Chronological Edition: Ch. 35, p. 246
Standard Edition: Ch. 47, p. 232
*Shorter Edition: Ch. 31, p. 169
Date used:

101. What is unusual about Beethoven's Symphony No. 5?
     a. It has four movements.
     b. There is no break between the third and fourth movements.
     c. It is in a minor key.
     d. The first movement is based on two themes.

Answer: c
Chronological Edition: Ch. 35, p. 246
Standard Edition: Ch. 47, p. 232
*Shorter Edition: Ch. 31, p. 169f
Date used:

102. How many movements does Beethoven's Symphony No. 5 have?
     a. one
     b. three
     c. four
     d. five

Answer: b
Chronological Edition: Ch. 35, p. 246
Standard Edition: Ch. 47, p. 232
*Shorter Edition: Ch. 31, p. 169
Date used:

103. Which best describes the opening idea of Beethoven's Symphony No. 5?
     a. a three-note motive.
     b. a four-note motive.
     c. a rocket theme.
     d. a dance-like theme.

Answer: a
Chronological Edition: Ch. 35, p. 246
Standard Edition: Ch. 47, p. 232
*Shorter Edition: Ch. 31, p. 169f
Date used:

104. What is the form of the second movement of Beethoven's Symphony No. 5?
     a. theme and variations
     b. sonata
     c. A–B–A
     d. rondo

Answer: c
Chronological Edition: Ch. 35, p. 246
Standard Edition: Ch. 47, p. 233
*Shorter Edition: Ch. 31, p. 169
Date used:

105. Using material from an earlier movement in a symphony is called:
     a. sonata–allegro form.
     b. rondo form.
     c. cyclical form.
     d. scherzo form.

Answer: b
Chronological Edition: Ch. 36, p. 250
Standard Edition: Ch. 48, p. 236
*Shorter Edition: Ch. 32, p. 173
Date used:

106.   How many movements are in a Classical concerto?
a.   two
b.   three
c.   four
d.   six

Answer: a
Chronological Edition: Ch. 36, p. 250
Standard Edition: Ch. 48, p. 236
*Shorter Edition: Ch. 32, p. 173
Date used:

107.   The first movement of a Classical concerto features sonata–allegro form with:
a.   a double exposition.
b.   a double coda.
c.   a slow introduction.
d.   a fugal recapitulation.

Answer: c
Chronological Edition: Ch. 36, p. 250
Standard Edition: Ch. 48, p. 236
*Shorter Edition: Ch. 32, p. 173
Date used:

108.   A typical feature of a concerto is a free solo passage without orchestral accompaniment called:
a.   the introduction.
b.   the codetta.
c.   the cadenza.
d.   the development.

Answer: d
Chronological Edition: Ch. 36, p. 250
Standard Edition: Ch. 48, p. 236
*Shorter Edition: Ch. 32, p. 173
Date used:

109.   The most popular solo instruments in the Classical concerto were:
a.   the flute and clarinet.
b.   the violin and cello.
c.   the piano and cello.
d.   the violin and piano.

Answer: a
Chronological Edition: Ch. 36, p. 251
Standard Edition: Ch. 48, p. 237
*Shorter Edition: Ch. 32, p. 174
Date used:

110.   The form of the first movement of Mozart's Piano Concerto in C major, K. 467 is:
a.   sonata–allegro.
b.   rondo.
c.   minuet.
d.   theme and variations.

Answer: b
Chronological Edition: Ch. 36, p. 251
Standard Edition: Ch. 48, p. 237
*Shorter Edition: Ch. 32, p. 174
Date used:

111.   Which best describes the character of the opening theme of Mozart's Piano Concerto in C major, K. 467?
a.   a serene chant
b.   a bouncy opera buffa melody
c.   an impassioned grand opera theme
d.   a driving orchestral rocket theme

Answer: b
Chronological Edition: Ch. 36, p. 252
Standard Edition: Ch. 48, p. 238
*Shorter Edition: Ch. 32, p. 175
Date used:

112.   Which movement of Mozart's Piano Concerto, K. 467 is NOT in the tonic key of C major?
a.   the first
b.   the second
c.   the third
d.   none of the above

Answer: c
Chronological Edition: Ch. 36, p. 255
Standard Edition: Ch. 48, p. 240f
Date used:

Answer: d
Chronological Edition: Ch. 37, p. 256
Standard Edition: Ch. 49, p. 241
*Shorter Edition: Ch. 33, p. 178
Date used:

Answer: b
Chronological Edition: Ch. 37, p. 256f
Standard Edition: Ch. 49, p. 242
*Shorter Edition: Ch. 33, p. 178f
Date used:

Answer: d
Chronological Edition: Ch. 37, p. 257
Standard Edition: Ch. 49, p. 242
*Shorter Edition: Ch. 33, p. 178f
Date used:

Answer: d
Chronological Edition: Ch. 37, p. 256
Standard Edition: Ch. 49, p. 242
*Shorter Edition: Ch. 33, p. 178f
Date used:

Answer: c
Chronological Edition: Ch. 37, p. 256
Standard Edition: Ch. 49, p. 242
*Shorter Edition: Ch. 33, p. 178f
Date used:

Answer: c
Chronological Edition: Ch. 37, p. 259
Standard Edition: Ch. 49, p. 245
Date used:

113. What is unusual about Beethoven's *Emperor Concerto*?
   a. The principal cadenza is placed in the development.
   b. The last movement quotes the second.
   c. The solo piano enters immediately.
   d. It is in three movements.

114. Which is NOT a favored sonata setting in the late eighteenth century?
   a. piano alone
   b. piano and violin
   c. piano and cello
   d. piano and trumpet

115. How many movements are in Beethoven's *Pathétique Sonata*?
   a. two
   b. three
   c. four
   d. five

116. The third movement of Beethoven's *Pathétique Sonata* is in:
   a. sonata–allegro form.
   b. minuet form.
   c. scherzo form.
   d. rondo form.

117. Which does NOT characterize the slow introduction to Beethoven's *Pathétique Sonata*?
   a. a passionate intensity
   b. extreme dynamic contrasts
   c. an expressive melody
   d. a cheery major tonality

118. Which best describes the character of the opening theme of the second movement to Beethoven's *Pathétique Sonata*?
   a. cheery and light
   b. forceful and dynamic
   c. songful and expressive
   d. powerful, with extreme dynamic contrasts

119. What is unusual about the form of Mozart's Sonata in E-flat major, K. 302?
   a. It has a sonata–allegro form in the first movement.
   b. It has a rondo finale.
   c. It has only two movements.
   d. It is for violin and piano.

Answer: b
Chronological Edition: Ch. 37, p. 259
Standard Edition: Ch. 49, p. 245
Date used:

120. Which best describes the form of the second movement of Mozart's Sonata in E-flat, K. 302?
  a. a rondo pattern of A–B–A–C–A
  b. a rondo pattern of A–B–A–C–A–B–C–A.
  c. a theme and variations form.
  d. an A–B–A or ternary form.

Answer: c
Chronological Edition: Ch. 38, p. 260
Standard Edition: Ch. 50, p. 246
*Shorter Edition: Ch. 34, p. 180
Date used:

121. A musical setting of the Mass for the Dead is called:
  a. an oratorio.
  b. an opera.
  c. a requiem.
  d. a cantata.

Answer: a
Chronological Edition: Ch. 38, p. 260
Standard Edition: Ch. 50, p. 246
*Shorter Edition: Ch. 34, p. 181
Date used:

122. A dramatic composition based on a text of religious or serious character for solo voices, chorus, and orchestra is called:
  a. an oratorio.
  b. an opera.
  c. a requiem.
  d. a mass.

Answer: c
Chronological Edition: Ch. 38, p. 261
Standard Edition: Ch. 50, p. 247
Date used:

123. Which characterizes Haydn's *Lord Nelson Mass*?
  a. It was composed for voices without instruments.
  b. It was commissioned by Lord Nelson.
  c. It is notable for its heroic tone.
  d. It was written during Haydn's visit to London.

Answer: b
Chronological Edition: Ch. 38, p. 261
Standard Edition: Ch. 50, p. 247
Date used:

124. The texture of the opening section of the Credo from Haydn's *Lord Nelson Mass* is best described as:
  a. monophonic.
  b. polyphonic.
  c. homophonic.
  d. heterophonic.

Answer: b
Chronological Edition: Ch. 38, p. 261f
Standard Edition: Ch. 50, p. 247f
Date used:

125. The Credo of Haydn's *Lord Nelson Mass* is in _____ large sections.
  a. two
  b. three
  c. five
  d. six

Answer: b
Chronological Edition: Ch. 38, p. 264
Standard Edition: Ch. 50, p. 250
Date used:

126. The *Tuba mirum* from Mozart's Requiem Mass features a solo by which instrument?
  a. trumpet
  b. trombone
  c. tuba
  d. oboe

Answer: b
Chronological Edition: Ch. 38, p. 263f
Standard Edition: Ch. 50, p. 250f
Date used:

Answer: b
Chronological Edition: Ch. 39, p. 264
Standard Edition: Ch. 51, p. 250
*Shorter Edition: Ch. 34, p. 181
Date used:

Answer: a
Chronological Edition: Ch. 39, p. 264
Standard Edition: Ch. 51, p. 250
*Shorter Edition: Ch. 34, p. 181
Date used:

Answer: d
Chronological Edition: Ch. 39, p. 265
Standard Edition: Ch. 51, p. 251
*Shorter Edition: Ch. 34, p. 181
Date used:

Answer: a
Chronological Edition: Ch. 39, p. 265
Standard Edition: Ch. 51, p. 251
*Shorter Edition: Ch. 34, p. 182
Date used:

Answer: a
Chronological Edition: Ch. 39, p. 266
Standard Edition: Ch. 51, p. 252
*Shorter Edition: Ch. 34, p. 182
Date used:

Answer: b
Chronological Edition: Ch. 39, p. 265f
Standard Edition: Ch. 51, p. 252
*Shorter Edition: Ch. 34, p. 182
Date used:

127. Which is NOT true of the *Dies irae* from Mozart's Requiem Mass?
   a. It is a highly dramatic text.
   b. It is set for full chorus throughout.
   c. It is about the day of judgment.
   d. It is set in a minor key.

128. Which does NOT characterize opera seria?
   a. plots drawn from Greek antiquity
   b. a middle class appeal
   c. rigid conventions and highly formalized
   d. virtuoso display by soloists

129. During the Classic era, the prevalent form of opera that occupied itself mainly with the affairs of nobility and Greek legends was:
   a. opera seria.
   b. opera buffa.
   c. opéra comique.
   d. Singspiel.

130. How does opéra comique differ from opera seria?
   a. It was sung in the vernacular.
   b. It presented down-to-earth plots.
   c. It features ensemble, as well as solo, singing.
   d. All of the above.

131. All of the following were new opera types that sought to reflect simplicity and real human emotions EXCEPT:
   a. opera seria.
   b. opera buffa.
   c. opéra comique.
   d. Singspiel.

132. *The Marriage of Figaro* was adapted from a play by:
   a. Beaumarchais.
   b. Voltaire.
   c. Fielding.
   d. Racine.

133. Mozart's librettist for *The Marriage of Figaro* was:
   a. Count Almaviva.
   b. Lorenzo da Ponte.
   c. Pierre-Augustin Caron de Beaumarchais.
   d. Pietro Metastasio.

Answer: b
Chronological Edition: Ch. 39, p. 267
Standard Edition: Ch. 51, p. 253
*Shorter Edition: Ch. 34, p. 183
Date used:

Answer: c
Chronological Edition: Ch. 39, p. 266
Standard Edition: Ch. 51, p. 252
*Shorter Edition: Ch. 34, p. 182f
Date used:

Answer: d
Chronological Edition: Ch. 39, p. 267
Standard Edition: Ch. 51, p. 254
*Shorter Edition: Ch. 34, p. 183
Date used:

Answer: c
Chronological Edition: Ch. 39, p. 268
Standard Edition: Ch.51, p. 254
*Shorter Edition: Ch. 34, p. 183
Date used:

Answer: a
Chronological Edition: Ch. 39, p. 268
Standard Edition: Ch. 51, p. 254
*Shorter Edition: Ch. 34, p. 184
Date used:

Answer: d
Chronological Edition: Tr. IV, p. 276
Standard Edition: Tr. II, p. 262
Date used:

Answer: a
Chronological Edition: Tr. IV, p. 277
Standard Edition: Tr. II, p. 263
*Shorter Edition: Tr. IV, p. 192
Date used:

134. In T*he Marriage of Figaro*, which male role is usually sung by a woman?
 a. Basilio
 b. Cherubino
 c. Figaro
 d. the Count

135. Which description characterizes the story of *The Marriage of Figaro*?
 a. It is a tragedy.
 b. It pokes fun at the lower classes.
 c. It satirizes the upper classes.
 d. It is a sacred drama with religious overtones.

136. Which character in Mozart's *The Marriage of Figaro* is best described as a young, innocent man who is in love with love?
 a. Figaro
 b. Basilio
 c. the Count
 d. Cherubino

137. Rapid-fire, talky singing whose primary function is to advance the plot in an opera is called:
 a. bel canto singing.
 b. da capo aria.
 c. recitative.
 d. a terzetta.

138. Which three characters sing the terzetta or trio in Act I of Mozart's *The Marriage of Figaro*?
 a. the Count, Basilio, and Susanna
 b. the Count, Basilio, and Figaro
 c. the Count, the Countess, and Figaro
 d. the Count, Cherubino, and Figaro

139. Why did Schubert never finish his Symphony No. 8?
 a. He died before he could complete it.
 b. He ran out of money.
 c. He became ill.
 d. We do not know.

140. All of the following were instrumental genres favored by Classical composers EXCEPT:
 a. the symphonic poem.
 b. the symphony.
 c. the string quartet.
 d. the solo concerto.

Answer: c
Chronological Edition: Tr. IV, p. 277
Standard Edition: Tr. II, p. 263
*Shorter Edition: Tr. IV, p. 192
Date used:

141. All of the following are characteristic of music of the Classical era EXCEPT:
    a. symmetrical, phrased melodies.
    b. diatonic harmony.
    c. interest in the bizarre or macabre.
    d. interest in absolute forms.

TRUE/FALSE QUESTIONS

Answer: T
Chronological Edition: Ch. 16, p. 117
Standard Edition: Ch. 36, p. 177
*Shorter Edition: Ch. 14, p. 87
Date used:

142. A key refers to a group of related tones with a common center, a tonic, toward which they gravitate.

Answer: F
Chronological Edition: Ch. 16, p. 117
Standard Edition: Ch. 36, p. 177
*Shorter Edition: Ch. 14, p. 87
Date used:

143. Within a key, the central tone is called the semitone.

Answer: T
Chronological Edition: Ch. 16, p. 117
Standard Edition: Ch. 36, p. 177
*Shorter Edition: Ch. 14, p. 87
Date used:

144. When we listen to a composition in A major, we hear that piece in relation to the central tone A, according to the major scale built on A and the harmonies from that scale.

Answer: F
Chronological Edition: Ch. 16, p. 118
Standard Edition: Ch. 36, p. 178
*Shorter Edition: Ch. 14, p. 88
Date used:

145. When a violin string of a certain length is set in vibration, it will produce a certain pitch. Under the same conditions, a string half as long will produce a pitch one octave lower.

Answer: F
Chronological Edition: Ch. 16, p. 118
Standard Edition: Ch. 36, p. 178
*Shorter Edition: Ch. 14, p. 88
Date used:

146. In Western music, the octave is divided into seven equal parts, which make up the chromatic scale.

Answer: T
Chronological Edition: Ch. 16, p. 120
Standard Edition: Ch. 36, p. 180
*Shorter Edition: Ch. 14, p. 89
Date used:

147. A major or minor scale can begin on any of the twelve semitones of the octave.

Answer: T
Chronological Edition: Ch. 16, p. 120
Standard Edition: Ch. 36, p. 180
*Shorter Edition: Ch. 15, p. 92
Date used:

148. Tonic moving to dominant and returning to tonic becomes a basic progression of harmony and also serves as a basic principle of form.

Answer: F
Chronological Edition: Ch. 16, p. 121
Standard Edition: Ch. 36, p. 181
*Shorter Edition: Ch. 14, p. 91
Date used:

149. Chromatic music is most closely associated with the Classical era.

Answer: T
Chronological Edition: Ch. 17, p. 121
Standard Edition: Ch. 37, p. 181
*Shorter Edition: Ch. 15, p. 91
Date used:

150. The act of shifting all the tones of a musical composition a uniform distance to a different pitch level is called transposition.

Answer: T
Chronological Edition: Ch. 17, p. 122
Standard Edition: Ch. 37, p. 182
*Shorter Edition: Ch. 15, p. 91
Date used:

151. In earlier times, a composer's choice of key for a piece depended largely on the capabilities of the instruments for which it was intended.

Answer: T
Chronological Edition: Ch. 17, p. 122
Standard Edition: Ch. 37, p. 182
*Shorter Edition: Ch. 15, p. 91
Date used:

152. The process of passing from one key to another is known as modulation.

Answer: F
Chronological Edition: Ch. 17, p. 122
Standard Edition: Ch. 37, p. 182
*Shorter Edition: Ch. 15, p. 92
Date used:

153. Modulations were more frequent and abrupt in the Classic era than in the Romantic era.

Answer: T
Chronological Edition: Ch. 17, p. 123
Standard Edition: Ch. 37, p. 183
*Shorter Edition: Ch. 15, p. 92
Date used:

154. Active chords seek to be resolved to resting chords, imparting a sense of direction or goal.

Answer: T
Chronological Edition: Ch. 17, p. 123
Standard Edition: Ch. 37, p. 183
*Shorter Edition: Ch. 15, p. 92
Date used:

155. The dominant is an example of an active chord, which can cause tension in music until resolved.

Answer: F
Chronological Edition: Ch. 17, p. 124
Standard Edition: Ch. 37, p. 184
*Shorter Edition: Ch. 15, p. 92
Date used:

156. Music of the Classical era rarely modulates from the tonic key.

Answer: T
Chronological Edition: Ch. 26, p. 199
Standard Edition: Ch. 38, p. 185
*Shorter Edition: Ch. 23, p. 139
Date used:

157. The expansion and reworking of a theme within a composition is called thematic development.

Answer: F
Chronological Edition: Ch. 26, p. 199
Standard Edition: Ch. 38, p. 185
*Shorter Edition: Ch. 23, p. 139
Date used:

158. Thematic development occurs in all musical works, no matter what the size.

Answer: F
Chronological Edition: Ch. 27, p. 201
Standard Edition: Ch. 39, p. 187
*Shorter Edition: Ch. 24, p. 141
Date used:

159. The term sonata means a piece to be sounded on instruments and voices.

Answer: T
Chronological Edition: Ch. 27, p. 201
Standard Edition: Ch. 39, p. 187
*Shorter Edition: Ch. 24, p. 141
Date used:

160. The term sonata cycle is applied not only to sonatas and chamber music, but also to concertos and symphonies.

Answer: T
Chronological Edition: Ch. 27, p. 201
Standard Edition: Ch. 39, p. 187
*Shorter Edition: Ch. 24, p. 141
Date used:

161. Sonata–allegro form may be viewed as a ternary (A–B–A) design.

Answer: F
Chronological Edition: Ch. 27, p. 202
Standard Edition: Ch. 39, p. 188
*Shorter Edition: Ch. 24, p. 142
Date used:

162. The development section manipulates thematic material from the exposition, while remaining in the tonic key.

Answer: F
Chronological Edition: Ch. 27, p. 204
Standard Edition: Ch. 39, p. 190
*Shorter Edition: Ch. 24, p. 143
Date used:

163. The slow movement of a sonata cycle is most frequently the third movement.

Answer: F
Chronological Edition: Ch. 27, p. 204
Standard Edition: Ch. 39, p. 190
*Shorter Edition: Ch. 24, p. 143
Date used:

164. The only basic rule of theme and variations form is that the theme must always be easily heard.

Answer: T
Chronological Edition: Ch. 27, p. 204
Standard Edition: Ch. 39, p. 190
*Shorter Edition: Ch. 24, p. 144
Date used:

165. In the Classical sonata cycle, the third movement was typically a minuet and trio.

Answer: T
Chronological Edition: Ch. 27, p. 205
Standard Edition: Ch. 39, p. 191
*Shorter Edition: Ch. 24, p. 145
Date used:

166. In the nineteenth-century symphony, the minuet was replaced by the scherzo.

Answer: T
Chronological Edition: Ch. 28, p. 209
Standard Edition: Ch. 40, p. 195
*Shorter Edition: Ch. 25, p. 149
Date used:

167. The Classical attitude toward art is considerably more objective than the Romantic.

Answer: T
Chronological Edition: Ch. 28, p. 211
Standard Edition: Ch. 40, p. 197
*Shorter Edition: Ch. 25, p. 151
Date used:

168. The creators of the *Encyclopédie* were French philosophers who were opposed to the established order.

Answer: F
Chronological Edition: Ch. 28, p. 211
Standard Edition: Ch. 40, p. 197
*Shorter Edition: Ch. 25, p. 151
Date used:

169. Eighteenth-century thinkers idealized the Middle Ages.

Answer: T
Chronological Edition: Ch. 28, p. 211
Standard Edition: Ch. 40, p. 197
*Shorter Edition: Ch. 25, p. 151
Date used:

170. The Classical period has been called "The Age of Reason."

Answer: T
Chronological Edition: Ch. 28, p. 214
Standard Edition: Ch. 40, p. 200
*Shorter Edition: Ch. 25, p. 152
Date used:

171. The center of eighteenth-century artistic life was the palace, and the chief audience was the aristocracy.

Answer: F
Chronological Edition: Ch. 28, p. 214
Standard Edition: Ch. 40, p. 200
*Shorter Edition: Ch. 25, p. 152
Date used:

172. In the eighteenth century, composers were viewed as equals to the highest level of society.

Answer: F
Chronological Edition: Ch. 28, p. 214
Standard Edition: Ch. 40, p. 200
*Shorter Edition: Ch. 25, p. 152
Date used:

173. The audience of the eighteenth century, like that of today, was mainly interested in music from the past.

Answer: T
Chronological Edition: Ch. 29, p. 215
Standard Edition: Ch. 41, p. 201
Date used:

174. Classical composers subordinated emotional expression to accepted formal conventions.

Answer: T
Chronological Edition: Ch. 29, p. 215
Standard Edition: Ch. 41, p. 201
*Shorter Edition: Ch. 26, p. 153
Date used:

175. Romantic elements can be found in the late works of Mozart, Haydn and Beethoven.

Answer: T
Chronological Edition: Ch. 29, p. 216
Standard Edition: Ch. 41, p. 202
*Shorter Edition: Ch. 29, p. 161
Date used:

176. The Classical masters established the orchestra much as we know it today.

Answer: T
Chronological Edition: Ch. 29, p. 217
Standard Edition: Ch. 41, p. 203
*Shorter Edition: Ch. 27, p. 155
Date used:

177. Chamber music blossomed in popularity in the Classical era.

Answer: T
Chronological Edition: Ch. 29, p. 218
Standard Edition: Ch. 41, p. 204
Date used:

178. The piano grew in popularity in the eighteenth century, gradually replacing the harpsichord.

Answer: F
Chronological Edition: Ch. 29, p. 218
Standard Edition: Ch. 41, p. 204
*Shorter Edition: Ch. 34, p. 182
Date used:

179. Opera buffa was typically serious in tone, with plots dealing with historical or legendary figures.

Answer: T
Chronological Edition: Ch. 30, p. 219
Standard Edition: Ch. 42, p. 205
*Shorter Edition: Ch. 27, p. 155
Date used:

180. Chamber music is composed for a small ensemble with one player per part.

Answer: F
Chronological Edition: Ch. 30, p. 219
Standard Edition: Ch. 42, p. 205
*Shorter Edition: Ch. 27, p. 155
Date used:

181. In the Classic era, the most common type of chamber music was the trio sonata.

Answer: T
Chronological Edition: Ch. 30, p. 220
Standard Edition: Ch. 42, p. 206
*Shorter Edition: Ch. 27, p. 156
Date used:

182. The Classical string quartet literature follows the same basic formal design as the symphony and sonata.

Answer: F
Chronological Edition: Ch. 30, p. 220
Standard Edition: Ch. 42, p. 206
Date used:

183. In the Classical string quartet, the second movement is most frequently a quick, light Allegro.

Answer: T
Chronological Edition: Ch. 31, p. 221
Standard Edition: Ch. 43, p. 208
*Shorter Edition: Ch. 28, p. 157
Date used:

184. Mozart was a child prodigy, already composing by the age of five.

Answer: T
Chronological Edition: Ch. 31, p. 222
Standard Edition: Ch. 43, p. 208
*Shorter Edition: Ch. 28, p. 158
Date used:

185. Mozart was unsuccessful under the patronage system and died in poverty.

Answer: T
Chronological Edition: Ch. 31, p. 224
Standard Edition: Ch. 43, p. 210
*Shorter Edition: Ch. 28, p. 158
Date used:

186. Mozart's melodies are simple, elegant and songful.

Answer: T
Chronological Edition: Ch. 31, p. 225
Standard Edition: Ch. 43, p. 211
*Shorter Edition: Ch. 28, p. 158
Date used:

187. Mozart's late string quartets are among the finest in the genre, especially the set dedicated to Haydn.

Answer: T
Chronological Edition: Ch. 31, p. 225
Standard Edition: Ch. 43, p. 211
*Shorter Edition: Ch. 28, p. 158
Date used:

188. Mozart was a virtuoso pianist, and he wrote copiously for his favorite instrument.

Answer: F
Chronological Edition: Ch. 31, p. 225
Standard Edition: Ch. 43, p. 211
Date used:

189. Mozart's last three symphonies were performed numerous times during his lifetime and gave the composer his greatest fame.

Answer: T
Chronological Edition: Ch. 32, p. 228
Standard Edition: Ch. 44, p. 214
Date used:

190. Haydn played a central role in the evolution of the string quartet.

Answer: T
Chronological Edition: Ch. 33, p. 230
Standard Edition: Ch. 45, p. 216
*Shorter Edition: Ch. 29, p. 161
Date used:

191. The Classical symphony had its origins in the Italian opera overture.

Answer: F
Chronological Edition: Ch. 33, p. 230
Standard Edition: Ch. 45, p. 216
*Shorter Edition: Ch. 29, p. 161
Date used:

192. The establishment of a four-movement cycle for the symphony is generally credited to the London school of composers.

Answer: T
Chronological Edition: Ch. 33, p. 231
Standard Edition: Ch. 45, p. 217
*Shorter Edition: Ch. 29, p. 162
Date used:

193. The fourth movement of a Classical symphony is usually quicker and lighter than the first movement.

Answer: T
Chronological Edition: Ch. 34, p. 234
Standard Edition: Ch. 46, p. 220
*Shorter Edition: Ch. 30, p. 163
Date used:

194. The career of Joseph Haydn spanned the years from the formation of the Classical style to the beginning of Romanticism.

Answer: T
Chronological Edition: Ch. 34, p. 235
Standard Edition: Ch. 46, p. 221
*Shorter Edition: Ch. 30, p. 163f
Date used:

195. Haydn's life is an example of the patronage system working well for a composer.

Answer: T
Chronological Edition: Ch. 34, p. 236
Standard Edition: Ch. 46, p. 222
*Shorter Edition: Ch. 30, p. 164
Date used:

196. The late symphonies of Haydn call for an expanded orchestra with more wind and percussion instruments.

Answer: T
Chronological Edition: Ch. 34, p. 237
Standard Edition: Ch. 46, p. 223
*Shorter Edition: Ch. 30, p. 165
Date used:

197. Haydn's Symphony No. 104 has a slow introduction in D minor, after which it shifts to D major.

Answer: F
Chronological Edition: Ch. 34, p. 237
Standard Edition: Ch. 46, p. 223
*Shorter Edition: Ch. 30, p. 165
Date used:

198. The finale of Haydn's Symphony No. 104 presents folk-like themes derived from Spanish dance music.

Answer: F
Chronological Edition: Ch. 35, p. 241
Standard Edition: Ch. 47, p. 227
Date used:

199. Beethoven was born into a happy family that proved to be his greatest support.

Answer: T
Chronological Edition: Ch. 35, p. 241f
Standard Edition: Ch. 47, p. 227f
*Shorter Edition: Ch. 31, p. 167f
Date used:

200. Although Beethoven received support from music-loving aristocrats, he functioned primarily as a free-lance or independent composer.

Answer: F
Chronological Edition: Ch. 35, p. 242
Standard Edition: Ch. 47, p. 228
*Shorter Edition: Ch. 31, p. 167f
Date used:

201. Beethoven was unable to compose music after he became deaf.

Answer: F
Chronological Edition: Ch. 35, p. 242
Standard Edition: Ch. 47, p. 229
Date used:

202. Beethoven, like Mozart, wrote music very quickly and with great ease.

Answer: T
Chronological Edition: Ch. 35, p. 243
Standard Edition: Ch. 47, p. 229
Date used:

203. Unlike Mozart, Beethoven used sketchbooks to work out musical ideas.

Answer: T
Chronological Edition: Ch. 35, p. 243
Standard Edition: Ch. 47, p. 229
*Shorter Edition: Ch. 31, p. 167
Date used:

204. Beethoven achieved much acclaim during his lifetime and died a famous and revered composer.

Answer: T
Chronological Edition: Ch. 35, p. 243
Standard Edition: Ch. 47, p. 229
*Shorter Edition: Ch. 31, p. 167f
Date used:

Answer: T
Chronological Edition: Ch. 35, p. 244
Standard Edition: Ch. 47, p. 230
*Shorter Edition: Ch. 31, p. 168
Date used:

Answer: T
Chronological Edition: Ch. 36, p. 250
Standard Edition: Ch. 48, p. 236
*Shorter Edition: Ch. 32, p. 173
Date used:

Answer: T
Chronological Edition: Ch. 36, p. 250
Standard Edition: Ch. 48, p. 236
*Shorter Edition: Ch. 32, p. 173
Date used:

Answer: F
Chronological Edition: Ch. 36, p. 250
Standard Edition: Ch. 48, p. 236
*Shorter Edition: Ch. 32, p. 173f
Date used:

Answer: T
Chronological Edition: Ch. 36, p. 251
Standard Edition: Ch. 48, p. 236
*Shorter Edition: Ch. 32, p. 174
Date used:

Answer: T
Chronological Edition: Ch. 36, p. 251
Standard Edition: Ch. 48, p. 237
*Shorter Edition: Ch. 32, p. 174
Date used:

Answer: T
Chronological Edition: Ch. 36, p. 251
Standard Edition: Ch. 48, p. 237
*Shorter Edition: Ch. 32, p. 174
Date used:

205. Beethoven is considered by some to be the supreme architect in music.

206. Beethoven abandoned the minuet in favor of the scherzo in his symphonies.

207. The word concerto implies the opposition of two dissimilar elements, such as a soloist or solo group versus an orchestra.

208. In the first movement of a Classical concerto, there is usually a double exposition.

209. In the Classical concerto, the marking of Andante or Adagio would most likely apply to the third movement.

210. The finale of a Classical concerto is often in rondo form.

211. Mozart wrote his piano concertos primarily for his own public performances.

212. The first movement of Mozart's Piano Concerto in C major, K. 467 features theme groups rather than single themes.

Answer: F
Chronological Edition: Ch. 36, p. 255
Standard Edition: Ch. 48, p. 240
Date used:

213. In the *Emperor Concerto* by Beethoven, the piano enters after a long orchestral introduction.

Answer: T
Chronological Edition: Ch. 36, p. 255
Standard Edition: Ch. 48, p. 241
Date used:

214. Beethoven wrote out the cadenzas for his piano concertos.

Answer: F
Chronological Edition: Ch. 37, p. 256
Standard Edition: Ch. 49, p. 241
*Shorter Edition: Ch. 33, p. 178
Date used:

215. The sonata is an instrumental work in one movement for one or two solo instruments.

Answer: T
Chronological Edition: Ch. 37, p. 256
Standard Edition: Ch. 49, p. 241
*Shorter Edition: Ch. 33, p. 178
Date used:

216. Beethoven and Mozart wrote duo sonatas that treated the two instruments as nearly equal partners.

Answer: T
Chronological Edition: Ch. 37, p. 256
Standard Edition: Ch. 49, p. 241
*Shorter Edition: Ch. 33, p. 178
Date used:

217. In the Classical era, the sonata became an important genre for amateurs in the home.

Answer: T
Chronological Edition: Ch. 37, p. 256
Standard Edition: Ch. 49, p. 242
*Shorter Edition: Ch. 33, p. 178
Date used:

218. Beethoven himself gave his Piano Sonata in C minor, Op. 13 the subtitle *Pathétique*.

Answer: T
Chronological Edition: Ch. 37, p. 259
Standard Edition: Ch. 49, p. 245
Date used:

219. The second movement of Mozart's Sonata in E-flat, K. 302 is a moderately slow rondo.

Answer: F
Chronological Edition: Ch. 38, p. 260
Standard Edition: Ch. 50, p. 246
*Shorter Edition: Ch. 34, p. 180
Date used:

220. In the nineteenth century, the Mass was performed only in Church.

Answer: T
Chronological Edition: Ch. 38, p. 261
Standard Edition: Ch. 50, p. 247
Date used:

Answer: F
Chronological Edition: Ch. 38, p. 263
Standard Edition: Ch. 50, p. 249
Date used:

Answer: T
Chronological Edition: Ch. 39, p. 265
Standard Edition: Ch. 51, p. 251
*Shorter Edition: Ch. 34, p. 182
Date used:

Answer: T
Chronological Edition: Ch. 39, p. 265
Standard Edition: Ch. 51, p. 251
*Shorter Edition: Ch. 34, p. 182
Date used:

Answer: T
Chronological Edition: Ch. 39, p. 266f
Standard Edition: Ch. 51, p. 253
*Shorter Edition: Ch. 34, p. 182f
Date used:

Answer: F
Chronological Edition: Ch. 39, p. 268
Standard Edition: Ch. 51, p. 254
*Shorter Edition: Ch. 34, p. 184
Date used:

Answer: T
Chronological Edition: Ch. 39, p. 276
Standard Edition: Ch. 51, p. 263
*Shorter Edition: Ch. 34, p. 191
Date used:

Answer: F
Chronological Edition: Ch. 39, p. 276
Standard Edition: Ch. 51, p. 263
*Shorter Edition: Ch. 34, p. 191
Date used:

221. The opening of the Credo to Haydn's *Lord Nelson Mass* is in the style of a canon.

222. Mozart composed his Requiem Mass early in his career.

223. Comic opera was generally in the language of the audience, or the vernacular.

224. In the latter part of the eighteenth century, new opera types were devised that featured naturalness and simplicity.

225. *The Marriage of Figaro* uses many of the traditional devices of bedroom farce.

226. The terzetta or trio from Act I of *The Marriage of Figaro* is structured in rondo form.

227. Schubert, like Beethoven, is a transitional figure, writing in both Classical and Romantic styles.

228. In his handling of large forms, Schubert clearly shows himself as a Romantic composer.

Answer: T
Chronological Edition: Ch. 39, p. 276
Standard Edition: Ch. 51, p. 263
Date used:

229. Schubert's Symphony No. 8 is called the *Unfinished* because he only completed two movements of it.

THE NINETEENTH CENTURY

MULTIPLE CHOICE QUESTIONS

Answer: b
Chronological Edition: Ch. 40, p. 281
Standard Edition: Ch. 10, p. 58
*Shorter Edition: Ch. 35, p. 195
Date used:

1. The French Revolution signaled:
   a. the end of Classicism.
   b. the transfer of power from the aristocracy to the middle class.
   c. the beginning of the Enlightenment.
   d. the end of Romanticism.

Answer: d
Chronological Edition: Ch. 40, p. 281
Standard Edition: Ch. 10, p. 58
*Shorter Edition: Ch. 35, p. 195
Date used:

2. The democratic character of the Romantic movement is illustrated by:
   a. sympathy for the oppressed.
   b. interest in simple folk and children.
   c. faith in mankind and its destiny.
   d. all of the above.

Answer: c
Chronological Edition: Ch. 40, p. 281
Standard Edition: Ch. 10, p. 58
*Shorter Edition: Ch. 35, p. 195
Date used:

3. The nineteenth century saw the rise of a new social order shaped by:
   a. the monarchies of the major political powers.
   b. the aristocracies.
   c. the technological advances of the Industrial Revolution.
   d. the Catholic church.

Answer: d
Chronological Edition: Ch. 40, p. 282
Standard Edition: Ch. 10, p. 58
*Shorter Edition: Ch. 35, p. 195f
Date used:

4. Which is true of Romantic poets?
   a. They rebelled against conventional forms and subject matter.
   b. They leaned toward the fanciful and picturesque.
   c. They expressed with passion their new spirit of individualism.
   d. All of the above.

Answer: a
Chronological Edition: Ch. 40, p. 283
Standard Edition: Ch. 10, p. 60
*Shorter Edition: Ch. 35, p. 195f
Date used:

5. Which of the following was a Romantic painter?
   a. J.M.W. Turner
   b. Nathaniel Hawthorne
   c. Edgar Allen Poe
   d. Jean Jacques Rousseau

Answer: c
Chronological Edition: Ch. 41, p. 285
Standard Edition: Ch. 11, p. 61
*Shorter Edition: Ch. 36, p. 198
Date used:

6. Which was a new instrument of the Romantic period?
   a. trumpet
   b. flute
   c. tuba
   d. oboe

Answer: d
Chronological Edition: Ch. 41, p. 285
Standard Edition: Ch. 11, p. 61
*Shorter Edition: Ch. 36, p. 198
Date used:

Answer: d
Chronological Edition: Ch. 41, p. 285
Standard Edition: Ch. 11, p. 61
*Shorter Edition: Ch. 36, p. 198
Date used:

Answer: a
Chronological Edition: Ch. 41, p. 286
Standard Edition: Ch. 11, p. 62
*Shorter Edition: Ch. 36, p. 199
Date used:

Answer: c
Chronological Edition: Ch. 41, p. 286
Standard Edition: Ch. 11, p. 62f
*Shorter Edition: Ch. 36, p. 199
Date used:

Answer: d
Chronological Edition: Ch. 41, p. 287
Standard Edition: Ch. 11, p. 62f
*Shorter Edition: Ch. 36, p. 199f
Date used:

Answer: b
Chronological Edition: Ch. 41, p. 288
Standard Edition: Ch.116, p. 65
*Shorter Edition: Ch. 36, p. 201
Date used:

Answer: d
Chronological Edition: Ch. 41, p. 288f
Standard Edition: Ch. 11, p. 64
*Shorter Edition: Ch. 36, p. 201
Date used:

7. During the nineteenth century, concert life began to center around the _____.
   a. palace
   b. church
   c. university
   d. public concert hall

8. The concert hall came about because:
   a. people were tired of outdoor concerts.
   b. instrumental performers became more skillful.
   c. orchestras increased in efficiency.
   d. democratization brought about larger audiences.

9. What trend inspired composers to write music evoking scenes or sounds of far-off lands?
   a. exoticism
   b. nationalism
   c. chromaticism
   d. virtuosity

10. Mendelssohn's *Italian Symphony*, Bizet's *Carmen*, and Rimsky-Korsakov's *Scheherazade* are examples of:
    a. opera.
    b. nationalism.
    c. exoticism.
    d. symphonic poems.

11. Which does NOT characterize Romantic music?
    a. singable melodies
    b. expressive harmonies
    c. expanded forms
    d. reserved emotions

12. Founded during the nineteenth century, the Leipzig Conservatory became a model for music schools all over Europe and America. Its founder and director was:
    a. Franz Liszt.
    b. Felix Mendelssohn.
    c. Franz Schubert.
    d. Richard Wagner.

13. How does nineteenth-century orchestral music differ from eighteenth-century orchestral music?
    a. The symphonies are longer.
    b. Individual composers wrote fewer symphonies.
    c. Composers began writing symphonic poems as well as symphonies.
    d. All of the above.

Answer: a
Chronological Edition: Ch. 41, p. 290
Standard Edition: Ch. 11, p. 66
*Shorter Edition: Ch. 36, p. 202
Date used:

Answer: c
Chronological Edition: Ch. 41, p. 290
Standard Edition: Ch. 11, p. 66
*Shorter Edition: Ch. 36, p. 202
Date used:

Answer: b
Chronological Edition: Ch. 42, p. 291
Standard Edition: Ch. 12, p. 67
*Shorter Edition: Ch. 37, p. 203
Date used:

Answer: c
Chronological Edition: Ch. 42, p. 291
Standard Edition: Ch. 12, p. 67
*Shorter Edition: Ch. 37, p. 203
Date used:

Answer: a
Chronological Edition: Ch. 42, p. 292
Standard Edition: Ch. 12, p. 68
*Shorter Edition: Ch. 37, p. 204
Date used:

Answer: b
Chronological Edition: Ch. 42, p. 292
Standard Edition: Ch. 12, p. 68
*Shorter Edition: Ch. 37, p. 204
Date used:

Answer: c
Chronological Edition: Ch. 42, p. 292
Standard Edition: Ch. 12, p. 68
*Shorter Edition: Ch. 37, p. 204
Date used:

14. The favored chamber instrument of the nineteenth century was:
    a. the piano.
    b. the guitar.
    c. the clarinet.
    d. the harpsichord.

15. Which best describes the role of women in nineteenth-century music?
    a. None pursued careers in music.
    b. They were leaders in innovative changes of style.
    c. The piano provided them with a socially acceptable performance outlet.
    d. All of the above.

16. A song form in which the same melody is repeated with every stanza of text is called:
    a. through-composed.
    b. strophic form.
    c. Lieder.
    d. durchkomponiert.

17. A song structure that is composed from beginning to end without repetition of whole sections is called:
    a. strophic form.
    b. modified strophic form.
    c. through-composed form.
    d. theme and variation form.

18. Which is NOT an important composer of nineteenth-century Lieder?
    a. Heinrich Heine
    b. Robert Schumann
    c. Johannes Brahms
    d. Franz Schubert

19. The German term for the art song is:
    a. Gesange.
    b. Lied.
    c. durchkomponiert.
    d. chorale.

20. A solo vocal song with piano accompaniment that sets a short lyric poem is called:
    a. a sonata.
    b. a ballad.
    c. a Lied.
    d. a chant.

Answer: a
Chronological Edition: Ch. 42, p. 292
Standard Edition: Ch. 12, p. 68
*Shorter Edition: Ch. 37, p. 204
Date used:

Answer: c
Chronological Edition: Ch. 42, p. 292
Standard Edition: Ch. 12, p. 68
*Shorter Edition: Ch. 37, p. 204
Date used:

Answer: b
Chronological Edition: Ch. 43, p. 293
Standard Edition: Ch. 13, p. 69
*Shorter Edition: Ch. 38, p. 205
Date used:

Answer: a
Chronological Edition: Ch. 43, p. 295
Standard Edition: Ch. 13, p. 71
*Shorter Edition: Ch. 38, p. 206
Date used:

Answer: c
Chronological Edition: Ch. 43, p. 295
Standard Edition: Ch. 13, p. 71
*Shorter Edition: Ch. 38, p. 206
Date used:

Answer: d
Chronological Edition: Ch. 43, p. 295
Standard Edition: Ch. 13, p. 71
*Shorter Edition: Ch. 38, p. 206
Date used:

Answer: d
Chronological Edition: Ch. 43, p. 295
Standard Edition: Ch. 13, p. 71
*Shorter Edition: Ch. 38, p. 206
Date used:

Answer: d
Chronological Edition: Ch. 43, p. 296
Standard Edition: Ch. 13, p. 72
*Shorter Edition: Ch. 38, p. 206
Date used:

21. A group of Lieder unified by some narrative thread or descriptive or expressive theme is called:
    a. a song cycle.
    b. a ballad cycle.
    c. an opera.
    d. a cantata.

22. Which was NOT a typical theme of the Romantic Lied?
    a. the beauty of nature
    b. love and longing
    c. praise of the Virgin Mary
    d. the fleeting nature of human happiness

23. Franz Schubert was of _____ origin.
    a. German
    b. Austrian
    c. French
    d. Italian

24. Schubert wrote three song cycles, including:
    a. *Winterreise.*
    b. *Dichterliebe.*
    c. *Papillons.*
    d. *A German Requiem.*

25. Which composer's chamber music marks the end of Viennese Classicism?
    a. Berlioz
    b. Beethoven
    c. Schubert
    d. Mozart

26. Schubert lived a tragically short life, but was a remarkably prolific composer of:
    a. Lieder.
    b. chamber music.
    c. piano music.
    d. all of the above.

27. Schubert's song *Erlkönig* was a setting of the ballad written by:
    a. Müller
    b. Schiller
    c. Heine
    d. Goethe

28. In which form is the Lied *Erlkönig*?
    a. binary form
    b. ternary form
    c. strophic form
    d. through-composed form

Answer: d
Chronological Edition: Ch. 43, p. 296
Standard Edition: Ch. 13, p. 72
*Shorter Edition: Ch. 38, p. 206
Date used:

Answer: c
Chronological Edition: Ch. 43, p. 296
Standard Edition: Ch. 13, p. 72
*Shorter Edition: Ch. 38, p. 206f
Date used:

Answer: b
Chronological Edition: Ch. 43, p. 296
Standard Edition: Ch. 13, p. 72
*Shorter Edition: Ch. 38, p. 207
Date used:

Answer: c
Chronological Edition: Ch. 44, p. 298
Standard Edition: Ch. 14, p. 74
*Shorter Edition: Ch. 47, p. 232
Date used:

Answer: d
Chronological Edition: Ch. 44, p. 298f
Standard Edition: Ch. 14, p. 74f
*Shorter Edition: Ch. 47, p. 233
Date used:

Answer: c
Chronological Edition: Ch. 44, p. 300
Standard Edition: Ch. 14, p. 76
Date used:

Answer: a
Chronological Edition: Ch. 44, p. 300
Standard Edition: Ch. 14, p. 76
Date used:

29. Which is true of Schubert's *Erlkönig*?
    a. It is the masterpiece of his youth.
    b. It is based on the legend that whoever is touched by the King of the Elves must die.
    c. It presents four characters who are differentiated in the music.
    d. All of the above.

30. In Schubert's *Erlkönig*, the obsessive triplet rhythm of the piano accompaniment represents:
    a. the wind.
    b. the terror in the boy's mind.
    c. the galloping of the horse.
    d. all of the above.

31. Which musical devices help to portray the child's terror in *Erlkönig*?
    a. lilting melody, in major mode
    b. high range and dissonance
    c. low range and consonant harmony
    d. medium range, in minor mode

32. The composer who founded *The New Journal for Music* was:
    a. Franz Schubert.
    b. Hector Berlioz.
    c. Robert Schumann.
    d. Johannes Brahms.

33. Schumann's *Dichterliebe*:
    a. is a cycle of songs.
    b. sets poetry by Heinrich Heine.
    c. was inspired by his love for Clara Wieck.
    d. all of the above.

34. The text to Schumann's song *Ich grolle nicht* was written by:
    a. Goethe.
    b. Müller.
    c. Heine.
    d. Schiller.

35. Schumann's *Ich grolle nicht*, probably his most powerful love song, is from the song cycle:
    a. *Dichterliebe*.
    b. *Frauenliebe und Leben*.
    c. *Lieder Kreis*.
    d. *Die Schöne Mullerin*.

Answer: d
Chronological Edition: Ch. 45, p. 301
Standard Edition: Ch. 15, p. 177
*Shorter Edition: Ch. 49, p. 238
Date used:

Answer: a
Chronological Edition: Ch. 45, p. 302
Standard Edition: Ch. 15, p. 78
*Shorter Edition: Ch. 49, p. 239
Date used:

Answer: c
Chronological Edition: Ch. 45, p. 303
Standard Edition: Ch. 15, p. 79
*Shorter Edition: Ch. 49, p. 239f
Date used:

Answer: a
Chronological Edition: Ch. 45, p. 304
Standard Edition: Ch. 15, p. 79f
Date used:

Answer: b
Chronological Edition: Ch. 46, p. 305
Standard Edition: Ch. 16, p. 81
*Shorter Edition: Ch. 39, p. 209
Date used:

Answer: b
Chronological Edition: Ch. 46, p. 306
Standard Edition: Ch. 16, p. 82
*Shorter Edition: Ch. 39, p. 209
Date used:

Answer: b
Chronological Edition: Ch. 46, p. 306
Standard Edition: Ch. 16, p. 82
*Shorter Edition: Ch. 39, p. 210
Date used:

36. Which young, talented composer did Robert and Clara Schumann take into their home very near the time of Robert's tragic mental collapse?
    a. Berlioz
    b. Schubert
    c. Chopin
    d. Brahms

37. Brahms is often described as a (an) _____, because of his use of forms of the Classical masters.
    a. traditionalist
    b. Impressionist
    c. nationalist
    d. Romanticist

38. Besides Schubert and Schumann, which other nineteenth-century composer was also prolific in Lieder?
    a. Berlioz
    b. Chopin
    c. Brahms
    d. none of the above

39. Which is NOT true of Brahms's Lied, *Vergebliches Ständchen*?
    a. It is in through-composed form.
    b. It has one stanza in minor mode.
    c. It has a folklike nature.
    d. It is in triple meter.

40. The most important keyboard instrument of the Romantic period was:
    a. the harpsichord.
    b. the piano.
    c. the organ.
    d. the clavichord.

41. The short lyric piano piece was the instrumental equivalent of:
    a. the symphony.
    b. the song.
    c. the concerto.
    d. the opera.

42. Titles such as bagatelle, impromptu, and intermezzo are used for:
    a. symphonies.
    b. short, lyric piano pieces.
    c. large-scale piano pieces.
    d. Lieder.

Answer: d
Chronological Edition: Ch. 46, p. 306
Standard Edition: Ch. 16, p. 82
*Shorter Edition: Ch. 39, p. 210
Date used:

Answer: b
Chronological Edition: Ch. 47, p. 307
Standard Edition: Ch. 17, p. 83
*Shorter Edition: Ch. 40, p. 210
Date used:

Answer: c
Chronological Edition: Ch. 47, p. 307
Standard Edition: Ch. 17, p. 83
*Shorter Edition: Ch. 40, p. 211
Date used:

Answer: a
Chronological Edition: Ch. 47, p. 307
Standard Edition: Ch. 17, p. 83
*Shorter Edition: Ch. 40, p. 211
Date used:

Answer: d
Chronological Edition: Ch. 47, p. 307f
Standard Edition: Ch. 17, p. 83f
*Shorter Edition: Ch. 40, p. 211
Date used:

Answer: c
Chronological Edition: Ch. 47, p. 308
Standard Edition: Ch. 17, p. 81
*Shorter Edition: Ch. 40, p. 211
Date used:

Answer: d
Chronological Edition: Ch. 47, p. 308
Standard Edition: Ch. 17, p. 81
*Shorter Edition: Ch. 40, p. 211f
Date used:

43. Nineteenth-century composers of the short, lyric piano piece included:
   a. Brahms.
   b. Schumann.
   c. Chopin.
   d. all of the above.

44. Which composer is known as the "poet of the piano"?
   a. Schumann
   b. Chopin
   c. Berlioz
   d. Brahms

45. In which country was Chopin born?
   a. France
   b. Hungary
   c. Poland
   d. Austria

46. With which famous novelist did Chopin become romantically involved?
   a. George Sand
   b. Alexander Dumas
   c. Victor Hugo
   d. Emily Brontë

47. Chopin spent most of his productive life in

   _____.
   a. Warsaw
   b. Vienna
   c. Berlin
   d. Paris

48. The nineteenth-century composer whose entire compositional output centered around the piano was:
   a. Brahms.
   b. Liszt.
   c. Chopin.
   d. Berlioz.

49. Which was NOT a type of work written by Chopin?
   a. nocturnes
   b. polonaises
   c. ballades
   d. symphonies

Answer: c
Chronological Edition: Ch. 47, p. 308
Standard Edition: Ch. 17, p. 84
*Shorter Edition: Ch. 40, p. 308
Date used:

Answer: d
Chronological Edition: Ch. 47, p. 308
Standard Edition: Ch. 17, p. 85
Date used:

Answer: c
Chronological Edition: Ch. 47, p. 309
Standard Edition: Ch. 17, p. 85
*Shorter Edition: Ch. 40, p. 212
Date used:

Answer: b
Chronological Edition: Ch. 47, p. 309
Standard Edition: Ch. 17, p. 85
*Shorter Edition: Ch. 40, p. 212
Date used:

Answer: c
Chronological Edition: Ch. 47, p. 309
Standard Edition: Ch. 17, p. 85
*Shorter Edition: Ch. 40, p. 212
Date used:

Answer: a
Chronological Edition: Ch. 47, p. 310
Standard Edition: Ch. 17, p. 86
*Shorter Edition: Ch. 40, p. 212
Date used:

Answer: d
Chronological Edition: Ch. 48, p. 311
Standard Edition: Ch. 18, p. 88
Date used:

Answer: d
Chronological Edition: Ch. 48, p. 311f
Standard Edition: Ch. 18, p. 88f
Date used:

50. What does NOT characterize the music of Chopin?
   a. rubato
   b. virtuosity
   c. reserved emotions
   d. lyricism

51. Which of the following composers did NOT write Romantic character pieces for solo piano?
   a. Frédéric Chopin
   b. Franz Schubert
   c. Robert Schumann
   d. Hector Berlioz

52. Which of the following is a large-form work for piano?
   a. prelude
   b. etude
   c. ballade
   d. nocturne

53. The meter of Chopin's Polonaise in A flat is:
   a. duple.
   b. triple.
   c. quadruple.
   d. compound.

54. The term "tempo rubato", associated with Chopin's music, means that the performer should:
   a. play in a faster tempo.
   b. play in a slower tempo.
   c. take liberties with the tempo.
   d. play in strict time.

55. The form of Chopin's Polonaise in A flat is best described as:
   a. A–B–A
   b. A–B
   c. A–B–C
   d. A–B–A–C–A

56. In which country was Franz Liszt born?
   a. Austria
   b. France
   c. Poland
   d. Hungary

57. Liszt's career consisted of:
   a. performing on the piano.
   b. conducting.
   c. composing.
   d. all of the above.

Answer: a
Chronological Edition: Ch. 48, p. 312
Standard Edition: Ch. 18, p. 88
*Shorter Edition: Ch. 46, p. 231
Date used:

Answer: c
Chronological Edition: Ch. 48, p. 312
Standard Edition: Ch. 18, p. 88
*Shorter Edition: Ch. 46, p. 231
Date used:

Answer: c
Chronological Edition: Ch. 48, p. 313
Standard Edition: Ch. 18, p. 89
Date used:

Answer: b
Chronological Edition: Ch. 48, p. 313
Standard Edition: Ch. 18, p. 89
Date used:

Answer: a
Chronological Edition: Ch. 48, p. 314
Standard Edition: Ch. 18, p. 90
Date used:

Answer: b
Chronological Edition: Ch. 49, p. 316
Standard Edition: Ch. 19, p. 92
*Shorter Edition: Ch. 41, p. 214
Date used:

Answer: c
Chronological Edition: Ch. 49, p. 316
Standard Edition: Ch. 19, p. 92
*Shorter Edition: Ch. 41, p. 215
Date used:

58. Liszt was inspired by the virtuoso violinist:
   a. Paganini.
   b. Czerny.
   c. Spohr.
   d. Clementi.

59. Which composer is generally considered the greatest pianist and showman of the Romantic era?
   a. Berlioz
   b. Brahms
   c. Liszt
   d. Smetana

60. The compositional technique of varying a theme melodically, harmonically, rhythmically, or dynamically, and thereby changing its character, is called:
   a. modulation.
   b. tempo rubato.
   c. thematic transformation.
   d. durchkomponiert.

61. Which composer is considered the creator of the symphonic poem?
   a. Brahms
   b. Liszt
   c. Wagner
   d. Mendelssohn

62. Liszt's *Wilde Jagd* is an example of a (an) _____ for piano.
   a. étude
   b. waltz
   c. nocturne
   d. ballade

63. Clara Schumann was a virtuoso performer on:
   a. the violin.
   b. the piano.
   c. the cello.
   d. the French horn.

64. Later in her career, Clara Schumann's creative activities were supported by the devotion of which composer?
   a. Wagner
   b. Liszt
   c. Brahms
   d. Verdi

Answer: b
Chronological Edition: Ch. 49, p. 317f
Standard Edition: Ch. 19, p. 93f
*Shorter Edition: Ch. 41, p. 215f
Date used:

Answer: c
Chronological Edition: Ch. 49, p. 319
Standard Edition: Ch. 19, p. 95
Date used:

Answer: d
Chronological Edition: Ch. 50, p. 320
Standard Edition: Ch. 20, p. 96
*Shorter Edition: Ch. 42, p. 217
Date used:

Answer: b
Chronological Edition: Ch. 50, p. 321
Standard Edition: Ch. 20, p. 97
*Shorter Edition: Ch. 42, p. 217
Date used:

Answer: a
Chronological Edition: Ch. 50, p. 321
Standard Edition: Ch. 20, p. 97
*Shorter Edition: Ch. 42, p. 218
Date used:

Answer: b
Chronological Edition: Ch. 50, p. 321
Standard Edition: Ch. 20, p. 97
*Shorter Edition: Ch. 42, p. 218
Date used:

Answer: c
Chronological Edition: Ch. 50, p. 321
Standard Edition: Ch. 20, p. 97
*Shorter Edition: Ch. 42, p. 218
Date used:

65. No. 3 from *Quatre pièces fugitives* by Clara Schumann is in _____ form.
   a. A–B
   b. A–B–A
   c. A–B–A–C–A
   d. strophic

66. The names "Eusebius" and "Florestan" are associated with which of the following composers?
   a. Franz Liszt.
   b. Frédéric Chopin.
   c. Robert Schumann.
   d. Clara Schumann.

67. Which of the following compositions is least likely to be an example of program music?
   a. *1812 Overture*
   b. *Romeo and Juliet*
   c. *Harold in Italy*
   d. String Quartet in B-flat major

68. Instrumental music endowed with literary, philosophical, or pictorial associations is called:
   a. absolute music.
   b. program music.
   c. background music.
   d. pure music.

69. Music written for plays, generally consisting of an overture and a series of pieces to be performed between acts, is called:
   a. incidental music.
   b. background music.
   c. a program symphony.
   d. a symphonic poem.

70. A multi-movement work for orchestras that is programmatic is called:
   a. a symphonic poem.
   b. a program symphony.
   c. a concert overture.
   d. a sonata.

71. A piece of program music for orchestra in one movement which, through several contrasting sections, develops a poetic idea or suggests a scene or mood is called:
   a. a program symphony.
   b. an overture.
   c. a symphonic poem.
   d. incidental music.

Answer: b
Chronological Edition: Ch. 50, p. 321
Standard Edition: Ch. 20, p. 97
*Shorter Edition: Ch. 42, p. 218
Date used:

Answer: a
Chronological Edition: Ch. 50, p. 321
Standard Edition: Ch. 20, p. 97
*Shorter Edition: Ch. 42, p. 218
Date used:

Answer: a
Chronological Edition: Ch. 51, p. 322
Standard Edition: Ch. 21, p. 98
Date used:

Answer: b
Chronological Edition: Ch. 51, p. 322f
Standard Edition: Ch. 21, p. 99
Date used:

Answer: c
Chronological Edition: Ch. 51, p. 324
Standard Edition: Ch. 21, p. 100
Date used:

Answer: d
Chronological Edition: Ch. 51, p. 324f
Standard Edition: Ch. 21, p. 100f
Date used:

72. Who was the first composer to use the term symphonic poem?
   a. Berlioz
   b. Liszt
   c. Mendelssohn
   d. Tchaikovsky

73. Which of the following is NOT a type of orchestral program music?
   a. concerto
   b. symphonic poem
   c. incidental music
   d. program symphony

74. Which of the following Romantic composers was fortunate enough to be born to wealth, and who led a happy, though short, life?
   a. Felix Mendelssohn
   b. Franz Schubert
   c. Robert Schumann
   d. Johannes Brahms

75. Which gifted young composer organized a performance of Bach's *St. Matthew Passion* in 1829, an event which proved to be a turning point in the revival of Bach's music?
   a. Schubert
   b. Mendelssohn
   c. Schumann
   d. Chopin

76. *Elijah* represents the peak of Mendelssohn's achievement in the genre of:
   a. symphony.
   b. opera.
   c. oratorio.
   d. Lied.

77. Mendelssohn's *A Midsummer Night's Dream* is an example of:
   a. an opera.
   b. a program symphony.
   c. a tone poem.
   d. an overture and incidental music.

Answer: d
Chronological Edition: Ch. 51, p. 324f
Standard Edition: Ch. 21, p. 100f
Date used:

78. Which of the following is NOT one of the three main ideas in Mendelssohn's Overture to *A Midsummer Night's Dream*?
    a. fairy music played by violins in the high register
    b. a lyrical idea representing the young lovers in the play
    c. the noisy dance of the clowns
    d. the Dies irae, from the Mass for the Dead

Answer: a
Chronological Edition: Ch. 51, p. 325
Standard Edition: Ch. 21, p. 101
Date used:

79. The overture to *A Midsummer Night's Dream* is in _____ form.
    a. sonata
    b. rondo
    c. theme and variations
    d. strophic

Answer: b
Chronological Edition: Ch. 52, p. 327
Standard Edition: Ch. 22, p. 103
*Shorter Edition: Ch. 43, p. 219
Date used:

80. Which composer is considered the first great exponent of musical Romanticism in France?
    a. Schubert
    b. Berlioz
    c. Liszt
    d. Wagner

Answer: b
Chronological Edition: Ch. 52, p. 327
Standard Edition: Ch. 22, p. 103
Date used:

81. In which of the following ways did Hector Berlioz NOT earn his living?
    a. composer
    b. virtuoso pianist
    c. music critic
    d. conductor

Answer: a
Chronological Edition: Ch. 52, p. 328f
Standard Edition: Ch. 22, p. 104f
*Shorter Edition: Ch. 43, p. 220
Date used:

82. The French-born composer who is considered the creator of the modern orchestra for his daring originality and use of a larger ensemble was:
    a. Berlioz.
    b. Chopin.
    c. Mendelssohn.
    d. Brahms.

Answer: a
Chronological Edition: Ch. 52, p. 328
Standard Edition: Ch. 22, p. 104
*Shorter Edition: Ch. 43, p. 220
Date used:

83. Which of the following is NOT characteristic of the music of Berlioz?
    a. reliance on traditional forms
    b. brilliant orchestration
    c. use of programmatic implications
    d. a love for huge orchestral and choral ensembles.

Answer: c
Chronological Edition: Ch. 52, p. 329
Standard Edition: Ch. 22, p. 105
*Shorter Edition: Ch. 43, p. 220ff
Date used:

84. Berlioz's *Symphonie fantastique* is an example of:
    a. a tone poem.
    b. a symphonic poem.
    c. a program symphony.
    d. a concert overture.

Answer: d
Chronological Edition: Ch. 52, p. 329
Standard Edition: Ch. 22, p. 105
*Shorter Edition: Ch. 43, p. 221
Date used:

Answer: d
Chronological Edition: Ch. 52, p. 329
Standard Edition: Ch. 22, p. 105
*Shorter Edition: Ch. 43, p. 221
Date used:

Answer: c
Chronological Edition: Ch. 52, p. 329
Standard Edition: Ch. 22, p. 105
*Shorter Edition: Ch. 43, p. 221
Date used:

Answer: a
Chronological Edition: Ch. 52, p. 329f
Standard Edition: Ch. 22, p. 105f
*Shorter Edition: Ch. 43, p. 221
Date used:

Answer: c
Chronological Edition: Ch. 52, p. 330
Standard Edition: Ch. 22, p. 106
*Shorter Edition: Ch. 43, p. 221
Date used:

Answer: b
Chronological Edition: Ch. 53, p. 332
Standard Edition: Ch. 23, p. 108
*Shorter Edition: Ch. 54, p. 263
Date used:

85. How many movements are in Berlioz's *Symphonie fantastique*?
   a. one
   b. four
   c. three
   d. five

86. In Berlioz's *Symphonie fantastique*, the "idée fixe":
   a. symbolizes the beloved.
   b. recurs by virtue of the literary program.
   c. unifies the five movements, which are diverse in character and mood.
   d. all of the above.

87. In Berlioz's *Symphonie fantastique*, what is the "idée fixe"?
   a. a chant from the Mass for the Dead appearing in the finale
   b. a shepherd song in the third movement
   c. the basic theme of the symphony, heard in all movements
   d. a theme and variation, heard in the march movement

88. Which is NOT true of Berlioz's *Symphonie fantastique*?
   a. The program deals entirely with nature.
   b. The program was inspired by the composer's infatuation with an actress.
   c. The program presents a morbid artist in lovesick despair.
   d. The program is thought to be autobiographical.

89. The *Dies irae* is:
   a. the "idée fixe" in Berlioz's *Symphonie fantastique*.
   b. a Lied by Schubert.
   c. a chant from the Mass for the Dead.
   d. an opera by Berlioz.

90. Which Romantic composer lived well into the twentieth century?
   a. Franz Schubert
   b. Richard Strauss
   c. Johannes Brahms
   d. Hector Berlioz

Answer: b
Chronological Edition: Ch. 53, p. 332
Standard Edition: Ch. 23, p. 108
*Shorter Edition: Ch. 54, p. 263
Date used:

Answer: d
Chronological Edition: Ch. 53, p. 332
Standard Edition: Ch. 23, p. 108
Date used:

Answer: b
Chronological Edition: Ch. 53, p. 334
Standard Edition: Ch. 23, p. 110
Date used:

Answer: c
Chronological Edition: Ch. 53, p. 334
Standard Edition: Ch. 23, p. 110
Date used:

Answer: a
Chronological Edition: Ch. 54, p. 336
Standard Edition: Ch. 24, p. 112
*Shorter Edition: Ch. 44, p. 224
Date used:

Answer: a
Chronological Edition: Ch. 54, p. 336
Standard Edition: Ch. 24, p. 112
*Shorter Edition: Ch. 44, p. 225
Date used:

Answer: a
Chronological Edition: Ch. 54, p. 337
Standard Edition: Ch. 24, p. 113
*Shorter Edition: Ch. 44, p. 225
Date used:

91. Which of the following is NOT a symphonic poem by Richard Strauss?
    a. *Till Eulenspiegel's Merry Pranks*
    b. *Der Rosenkavalier*
    c. *Thus Spake Zarathustra*
    d. *Don Juan*

92. Richard Strauss's tone poems were strongly influenced by those of _____.
    a. Brahms
    b. Debussy
    c. Chopin
    d. Liszt

93. Strauss's *Don Juan* is based on a poem by:
    a. Goethe.
    b. Nicolaus Lenau.
    c. Schiller.
    d. Oscar Wilde.

94. *Don Juan* by Richard Strauss is an example of:
    a. a concert overture.
    b. a program symphony.
    c. a symphonic poem.
    d. a symphony.

95. Nationalistic composers expressed their nationalism by:
    a. employing native songs and dances of their people in their works.
    b. borrowing exotic styles from other countries.
    c. writing absolute music.
    d. all of the above.

96. A nineteenth-century Bohemian composer who is best known for his symphonic poems and his operas was:
    a. Bedřich Smetana.
    b. Carl Maria von Weber.
    c. Antonín Dvořák.
    d. Jean Sibelius.

97. *The Moldau* portrays:
    a. a river flowing through Bohemia.
    b. a castle and battle scene.
    c. a story based on Nordic legend.
    d. a people yearning to be free.

Answer: d
Chronological Edition: Ch. 54, p. 337
Standard Edition: Ch. 24, p. 113
*Shorter Edition: Ch. 44, p. 225
Date used:

Answer: c
Chronological Edition: Ch. 54, p. 339
Standard Edition: Ch. 24, p. 115
Date used:

Answer: b
Chronological Edition: Ch. 54, p. 340
Standard Edition: Ch. 24, p. 116
Date used:

Answer: b
Chronological Edition: Ch. 55, p. 341
Standard Edition: Ch. 25, p. 117
*Shorter Edition: Ch. 45, p. 228
Date used:

Answer: d
Chronological Edition: Ch. 55, p. 341f
Standard Edition: Ch. 25, p. 117f
*Shorter Edition: Ch. 45, p. 228
Date used:

Answer: b
Chronological Edition: Ch. 55, p. 342
Standard Edition: Ch. 25, p. 118
*Shorter Edition: Ch. 45, p. 229
Date used:

Answer: b
Chronological Edition: Ch. 55, p. 342
Standard Edition: Ch. 25, p. 118
*Shorter Edition: Ch. 45, p. 229
Date used:

98. What is the name of Smetana's cycle of six
     nationalistic symphonic poems, of which the best-
     known is *The Moldau*?
     a. *Finlandia*
     b. *The Bartered Bride*
     c. *Norwegian Dances*
     d. *My Country*

99. Which Czech nationalist composer wrote his well-
     known *New World* Symphony after visiting the
     United States?
     a. Bedřich Smetana
     b. Edvard Grieg
     c. Antonín Dvořák
     d. Mily Balakirev

100. Which of the following was NOT a member of the
     Russian nationalist group known as "The Mighty
     Five"?
     a. Borodin
     b. Tchaikovsky
     c. Musorgsky
     d. Rimsky-Korsakov

101. A large, multi-movement orchestral work without a
     literary program is:
     a. an overture.
     b. a symphony.
     c. a tone poem.
     d. a concert overture.

102. How many movements are in a typical symphony?
     a. one
     b. two
     c. three
     d. four

103. The first movement of a symphony is usually in
     _____ form.
     a. theme and variations
     b. sonata–allegro
     c. minuet or scherzo
     d. rondo

104. Which movement of a symphony is traditionally the
     slowest?
     a. first movement
     b. second movement
     c. third movement
     d. fourth movement

Answer: c
Chronological Edition: Ch. 55, p. 342
Standard Edition: Ch. 25, p. 118
*Shorter Edition: Ch. 45, p. 229
Date used:

Answer: c
Chronological Edition: Ch. 55, p. 342
Standard Edition: Ch. 25, p. 118
*Shorter Edition: Ch. 45, p. 229
Date used:

Answer: c
Chronological Edition: Ch. 56, p. 344
Standard Edition: Ch. 26, p. 121
*Shorter Edition: Ch. 45, p. 229
Date used:

Answer: d
Chronological Edition: Ch. 56, p. 344
Standard Edition: Ch. 26, p. 121
*Shorter Edition: Ch. 45, p. 229
Date used:

Answer: b
Chronological Edition: Ch. 56, p. 346
Standard Edition: Ch. 26, p. 123
Date used:

Answer: a
Chronological Edition: Ch. 56, p. 346
Standard Edition: Ch. 26, p. 123
Date used:

Answer: a
Chronological Edition: Ch. 57, p. 347
Standard Edition: Ch. 27, p. 124
*Shorter Edition: Ch. 46, p. 230
Date used:

105. Which form found in symphonies is most likely to be strongly rhythmic and dancelike?
   a. sonata–allegro
   b. theme and variations
   c. scherzo
   d. none of the above

106. The tempo scheme of a traditional symphony is:
   a. slow–fast–slow–fast.
   b. fast–fast–slow–fast.
   c. fast–slow–moderate–fast.
   d. slow–moderate–fast–fast.

107. What is the form of the first movement of Mendelssohn's *Italian Symphony*?
   a. A–B–A
   b. variations
   c. sonata–allegro
   d. passacaglia

108. The finale of the *Italian Symphony* is based on a popular Italian dance known as:
   a. the pavane.
   b. the galliard.
   c. the minuet.
   d. the saltarello.

109. Brahms wrote no symphonies until he was past the age of forty, in part because he was in awe of the symphonies of _____.
   a. Mozart
   b. Beethoven
   c. Schubert
   d. Berlioz

110. On which archaic form did Brahms base the fourth movement of his Symphony No. 4?
   a. passacaglia
   b. fugue
   c. canon
   d. sonata

111. A large-scale work in several movements for solo instrument(s) and orchestra is called:
   a. a concerto.
   b. a symphony.
   c. a concert overture.
   d. a suite.

Answer: c
Chronological Edition: Ch. 57, p. 347
Standard Edition: Ch. 27, p. 124
*Shorter Edition: Ch. 46, p. 230
Date used:

Answer: c
Chronological Edition: Ch. 57, p. 347
Standard Edition: Ch. 27, p. 124
*Shorter Edition: Ch. 46, p. 230
Date used:

Answer: d
Chronological Edition: Ch. 58, p. 350f
Standard Edition: Ch. 28, p. 127f
*Shorter Edition: Ch. 47, p. 233f
Date used:

Answer: c
Chronological Edition: Ch. 58, p. 352
Standard Edition: Ch. 28, p. 129
Date used:

Answer: c
Chronological Edition: Ch. 59, p. 353f
Standard Edition: Ch. 29, p. 130f
*Shorter Edition: Ch. 48, p. 236f
Date used:

112. What is the typical number of movements found in a concerto?
    a. one
    b. two
    c. three
    d. four

113. A fanciful solo passage in an improvisational style that is interpolated into a concerto movement is called:
    a. a tutti statement.
    b. a codetta.
    c. a cadenza.
    d. an exposition.

114. Which is NOT true of Schumann's Piano Concerto in A minor?
    a. The first movement is in double exposition form, and has a cadenza.
    b. The second movement is a slow, lyrical, ternary form.
    c. The third movement is a quick, sonata form in A major.
    d. The fourth movement is a fast rondo, featuring a cadenza near the end.

115. Which of the following is unusual about Tchaikovsky's Violin Concerto in D major?
    a. It is in three movements.
    b. It is highly virtuosic and difficult to play.
    c. The soloist opens the first movement with a cadenza-like introduction.
    d. The lyric qualities of the violin are exploited.

116. Which of the following statements is NOT true about Romantic choral music?
    a. Choral music flowered during the nineteenth century.
    b. Choral singing attracted many music lovers who had never learned an instrument.
    c. Only professional singers participated in nineteenth-century choruses.
    d. Schubert, Schumann, Brahms and Mendelssohn, among many others, wrote choral music.

Answer: a
Chronological Edition: Ch. 59, p. 354
Standard Edition: Ch. 29, p. 132
*Shorter Edition: Ch. 48, p. 237
Date used:

Answer: d
Chronological Edition: Ch. 59, p. 354f
Standard Edition: Ch. 29, p. 132
*Shorter Edition: Ch. 48, p. 237f
Date used:

Answer: d
Chronological Edition: Ch. 60, p. 355
Standard Edition: Ch. 30, p. 132
*Shorter Edition: Ch. 49, p. 240
Date used:

Answer: d
Chronological Edition: Ch. 60, p. 355
Standard Edition: Ch. 30, p. 133
*Shorter Edition: Ch. 49, p. 240
Date used:

Answer: b
Chronological Edition: Ch. 60, p. 356
Standard Edition: Ch. 30, p. 133
Date used:

Answer: d
Chronological Edition: Ch. 60, p. 356f
Standard Edition: Ch. 30, p. 133f
*Shorter Edition: Ch. 49, p. 240
Date used:

Answer: b
Chronological Edition: Ch. 60, p. 358
Standard Edition: Ch. 30, p. 135
Date used:

117. Which of the following choral forms was not originally intended for performance in church?
   a. partsong
   b. oratorio
   c. mass
   d. Requiem

118. Which description best characterizes a partsong?
   a. a long, solo vocal work
   b. a highly virtuosic choral work in several movements
   c. a choral and orchestral setting of a Biblical story
   d. a short, secular song for three or four voice parts

119. Which is NOT true of Brahms's *German Requiem*?
   a. Its text is drawn from the Old and New Testament.
   b. The text consoles the living, in an attempt to help them accept death.
   c. The work was written for Robert Schumann and for Brahms's own mother.
   d. The name of Christ is mentioned throughout.

120. Brahms's *German Requiem* has _____ movements.
   a. four
   b. five
   c. six
   d. seven

121. The complex polyphonic texture heard in the third movement of Brahms's *German Requiem* is:
   a. a scherzo.
   b. a fugue.
   c. a partsong.
   d. a chant.

122. The form of "How Lovely is Thy Dwelling Place", the fourth movement of Brahms's *German Requiem*, is best described as:
   a. sonata–allegro.
   b. A–B–A or ternary.
   c. A–B or binary.
   d. A–B–A–C–A or rondo.

123. *L'enfance du Christ* by Berlioz is an example of:
   a. an opera.
   b. an oratorio.
   c. a Requiem.
   d. a Mass.

Answer: b
Chronological Edition: Ch. 60, p. 358
Standard Edition: Ch. 30, p. 135
Date used:

124.   A dramatic composition based on a religious text performed by solo voices, chorus and orchestra is called:
    a.   an opera.
    b.   an oratorio.
    c.   a partsong.
    d.   a motet.

Answer: a
Chronological Edition: Ch. 20, p. 139
Standard Edition: Ch. 31, p. 136f
*Shorter Edition: Ch. 18, p. 104
Date used:

125.   Recitative is a vocal style that:
    a.   imitates the natural inflections of speech.
    b.   is spoken rather than sung.
    c.   is more lyrical than aria.
    d.   is sung in choral groups.

Answer: d
Chronological Edition: Ch. 20, p. 139
Standard Edition: Ch. 31, p. 136f
*Shorter Edition: Ch. 18, p. 104
Date used:

126.   Which of the following is NOT typical of recitative?
    a.   a disjunct, melodic style
    b.   rapid patter
    c.   question-and-answer dialogue
    d.   a conjunct, lyrical melodic line

Answer: a
Chronological Edition: Ch. 20, p. 139
Standard Edition: Ch. 31, p. 136f
*Shorter Edition: Ch. 18, p. 104
Date used:

127.   A type of recitative that moves with great freedom and has a sparse accompaniment is called:
    a.   secco.
    b.   accompagnato.
    c.   da capo.
    d.   bel canto.

Answer: a
Chronological Edition: Ch. 20, p. 139
Standard Edition: Ch. 31, p. 136
*Shorter Edition: Ch. 18, p. 104
Date used:

128.   The action of the opera occurs mainly in:
    a.   the recitatives.
    b.   the arias.
    c.   the overture.
    d.   the choruses.

Answer: c
Chronological Edition: Ch. 20, p. 139f
Standard Edition: Ch. 31, p. 137
*Shorter Edition: Ch. 18, p. 104f
Date used:

129.   Which is NOT true of an aria?
    a.   It is often in da capo (A–B–A) form.
    b.   It is usually an emotional comment on the action.
    c.   It is generally disjunct in style, with sparse accompaniment.
    d.   It can be sung out of the context of the opera, because of its audience appeal.

Answer: b
Chronological Edition: Ch. 20, p. 140
Standard Edition: Ch. 31, p. 137
*Shorter Edition: Ch. 18, p. 105
Date used:

130.   The instrumental number often found at the beginning of an opera is called:
    a.   a concerto.
    b.   an overture.
    c.   a symphony.
    d.   a sonata.

Answer: d
Chronological Edition: Ch. 20, p. 140
Standard Edition: Ch. 31, p. 137
*Shorter Edition: Ch. 18, p. 105
Date used:

Answer: a
Chronological Edition: Ch. 61, p. 360
Standard Edition: Ch. 31, p. 148
*Shorter Edition: Ch. 50, p. 242f
Date used:

Answer: a
Chronological Edition: Ch. 61, p. 360
Standard Edition: Ch. 31, p. 138
*Shorter Edition: Ch. 50, p. 242f
Date used:

Answer: d
Chronological Edition: Ch. 61, p. 360
Standard Edition: Ch. 31, p. 138
*Shorter Edition: Ch. 50, p. 243
Date used:

Answer: b
Chronological Edition: Ch. 61, p. 360
Standard Edition: Ch. 31, p. 138
*Shorter Edition: Ch. 50, p. 243
Date used:

Answer: c
Chronological Edition: Ch. 61, p. 360
Standard Edition: Ch. 31, p. 138
*Shorter Edition: Ch. 50, p. 243
Date used:

Answer: c
Chronological Edition: Ch. 61, p. 360
Standard Edition: Ch. 31, p. 138
*Shorter Edition: Ch. 50, p. 243
Date used:

131. The person who writes the text of an opera is known as:
    a. the composer.
    b. the conductor.
    c. the producer.
    d. the librettist.

132. Which of the following countries was NOT a leading opera center in the nineteenth century?
    a. England
    b. France
    c. Germany
    d. Italy

133. Opera that featured huge choruses, elaborate dance scenes, ornate costumes and scenery, and serious, historical plots is called:
    a. grand opera.
    b. Singspiel.
    c. opera buffa.
    d. opéra comique

134. Which of the following national styles is NOT a comic opera?
    a. opera buffa
    b. opéra comique
    c. Singspiel
    d. grand opera

135. Which of the following was NOT a leading composer of Italian opera?
    a. Donizetti
    b. Bizet
    c. Bellini
    d. Rossini

136. An Italian comic opera is called:
    a. opera seria.
    b. opéra comique.
    c. opera buffa.
    d. Singspiel.

137. The first spokesman for German Romantic opera was:
    a. Wagner.
    b. Schumann.
    c. Weber.
    d. Verdi.

Answer: a
Chronological Edition: Ch. 62, p. 361
Standard Edition: Ch. 32, p. 139
*Shorter Edition: Ch. 51, p. 244
Date used:

138. Which of the following was a widely loved nationalist opera composer?
   a. Verdi
   b. Chopin
   c. Brahms
   d. Liszt

Answer: d
Chronological Edition: Ch. 62, p. 363f
Standard Edition: Ch. 32, p. 141f
*Shorter Edition: Ch. 51, p. 245
Date used:

139. Which was Verdi's last opera, completed at age eighty?
   a. *Macbeth*
   b. *Rigoletto*
   c. *Aïda*
   d. *Falstaff*

Answer: c
Chronological Edition: Ch. 62, p. 364
Standard Edition: Ch. 32, p. 142
*Shorter Edition: Ch. 51, p. 245
Date used:

140. Which of the following is NOT a well-known Verdi opera?
   a. *Il trovatore*
   b. *Rigoletto*
   c. *Carmen*
   d. *Aïda*

Answer: d
Chronological Edition: Ch. 62, p. 364
Standard Edition: Ch. 32, p. 142
Date used:

141. Which Verdi opera was commissioned for performance in Cairo to mark the opening of the Suez Canal?
   a. *Falstaff*
   b. *La traviata*
   c. *Otello*
   d. *Aïda*

Answer: b
Chronological Edition: Ch. 62, p. 365
Standard Edition: Ch. 32, p. 143
*Shorter Edition: Ch. 51, p. 245
Date used:

142. The librettist for Verdi's *La traviata* was:
   a. Boito.
   b. Piave.
   c. Metastasio.
   d. Goethe.

Answer: a
Chronological Edition: Ch. 62, p. 367f
Standard Edition: Ch. 32, p. 145f
*Shorter Edition: Ch. 51, p. 245ff
Date used:

143. In which language was Verdi's *La traviata* written?
   a. Italian
   b. French
   c. English
   d. German

Answer: c
Chronological Edition: Ch. 63, p. 370
Standard Edition: Ch. 33, p. 148
*Shorter Edition: Ch. 52, p. 250
Date used:

144. Which composer has been said to be the single most important phenomenon in the artistic life of the latter half of the nineteenth century?
   a. Berlioz
   b. Schubert
   c. Wagner
   d. Schumann

Answer: c
Chronological Edition: Ch. 63, p. 371
Standard Edition: Ch. 33, p. 150
*Shorter Edition: Ch. 52, p. 251
Date used:

145. Wagner's first operatic success was a grand opera entitled:
   a. *The Flying Dutchman.*
   b. *Tristan und Isolde.*
   c. *Rienzi.*
   d. *Faust.*

Answer: a
Chronological Edition: Ch. 63, p. 372
Standard Edition: Ch. 33, p. 150
*Shorter Edition: Ch. 52, p. 252
Date used:

146. The composer who invented the "music drama" was:
   a. Wagner.
   b. Liszt.
   c. Brahms.
   d. Verdi.

Answer: d
Chronological Edition: Ch. 63, p. 372f
Standard Edition: Ch. 33, p. 150f
*Shorter Edition: Ch. 52, p. 251
Date used:

147. A special theatre was built at _____ for the presentation of Wagner's music dramas.
   a. Dresden
   b. Munich
   c. Berlin
   d. Bayreuth

Answer: a
Chronological Edition: Ch. 63, p. 372
Standard Edition: Ch. 33, p. 150
Date used:

148. Wagner was greatly influenced by the German philosopher:
   a. Schopenhauer.
   b. Kant.
   c. Nietsche.
   d. Hegel.

Answer: c
Chronological Edition: Ch. 63, p. 372
Standard Edition: Ch. 33, p. 150
*Shorter Edition: Ch. 52, p. 251
Date used:

149. Wagner's cycle of four music dramas is called:
   a. *Lohengrin.*
   b. *Tristan und Isolde.*
   c. *The Ring of the Nibelung.*
   d. *Die Meistersinger von Nürnberg.*

Answer: b
Chronological Edition: Ch. 63, p. 374
Standard Edition: Ch. 33, p. 152
*Shorter Edition: Ch. 52, p. 252
Date used:

150. The principal themes in Wagner's operas, which recur throughout a work and carry specific meanings, are called:
   a. libretti.
   b. leitmotifs.
   c. motives.
   d. fixed ideas.

Answer: d
Chronological Edition: Ch. 63, p. 374
Standard Edition: Ch. 33, p. 152
*Shorter Edition: Ch. 52, p. 252
Date used:

151. The composer whose musical language was based on chromatic harmony was:
   a. Mendelssohn.
   b. Brahms.
   c. Verdi.
   d. Wagner.

Answer: b
Chronological Edition: Ch. 63, p. 375
Standard Edition: Ch. 33, p. 153
*Shorter Edition: Ch. 52, p. 251
Date used:

Answer: c
Chronological Edition: Ch. 63, p. 375
Standard Edition: Ch. 33, p. 153
*Shorter Edition: Ch. 52, p. 252f
Date used:

Answer: b
Chronological Edition: Ch. 63, p. 374f
Standard Edition: Ch. 33, p. 153f
*Shorter Edition: Ch. 52, p. 252f
Date used:

Answer: c
Chronological Edition: Ch. 64, p. 380
Standard Edition: Ch. 34, p. 158
*Shorter Edition: Ch. 50, p. 243
Date used:

Answer: b
Chronological Edition: Ch. 64, p. 380
Standard Edition: Ch. 34, p. 158
Date used:

Answer: a
Chronological Edition: Ch. 64, p. 383
Standard Edition: Ch. 34, p. 161f
*Shorter Edition: Ch. 54, p. 261
Date used:

Answer: a
Chronological Edition: Ch. 64, p. 383
Standard Edition: Ch. 34, p. 161
Date used:

152. Which is NOT an opera from the Ring cycle?
   a. *Siegfried*
   b. *Die Meistersinger von Nürnberg*
   c. *Das Rheingold*
   d. *Götterdämmerung*

153. In the Ring cycle, who is the father of the Gods?
   a. Siegfried
   b. Loge
   c. Wotan
   d. Brünnhilde

154. Why did Wotan deprive Brünnhilde of her immortality and leave her sleeping inside a ring of fire?
   a. Because she drew the sword out of the stone.
   b. Because she, overcome with compassion, attempted to save Siegmund's life in battle.
   c. Because she fell in love with the Meistersinger from Nürnberg.
   d. Because she allowed her winged horse, Pegasus, to die in battle.

155. The French composer who wrote *Carmen* was:
   a. Berlioz.
   b. Debussy.
   c. Bizet.
   d. Chopin.

156. In which country was Georges Bizet born?
   a. Italy
   b. France
   c. Germany
   d. Switzerland

157. Which was NOT a composer of Italian opera in the post-Romantic era?
   a. Bizet
   b. Leoncavallo
   c. Puccini
   d. Mascagni

158. Which best describes Carmen's character?
   a. capricious and dangerous
   b. steadfast and loyal
   c. meek and introverted
   d. loving and warm

Answer: b
Chronological Edition: Ch. 64, p. 383
Standard Edition: Ch. 34, p. 161
Date used:

Answer: c
Chronological Edition: Ch. 64, p. 383
Standard Edition: Ch. 34, p. 162
*Shorter Edition: Ch. 54, p. 261
Date used:

Answer: d
Chronological Edition: Ch. 64, p. 384
Standard Edition: Ch. 34, p. 162
*Shorter Edition: Ch. 54, p. 261
Date used:

Answer: b
Chronological Edition: Ch. 64, p. 384
Standard Edition: Ch. 34, p. 163
Date used:

Answer: a
Chronological Edition: Ch. 64, p. 385
Standard Edition: Ch. 34, p. 163
Date used:

Answer: c
Chronological Edition: Ch. 64, p. 385f
Standard Edition: Ch. 34, p. 163f
Date used:

Answer: b
Chronological Edition: Ch. 65, p. 391
Standard Edition: Ch. 35, p. 169
Date used:

Answer: c
Chronological Edition: Ch. 65, p. 392f
Standard Edition: Ch. 35, p. 170f
*Shorter Edition: Ch. 53, p. 256
Date used:

159. The opening melody of Carmen's "Habanera" is based on:
a. an ascending chromatic scale.
b. a descending chromatic scale.
c. a disjunct, arpeggiated line.
d. a triadic outline.

160. The post-Romantic Italian opera tradition was characterized by a movement toward realism called:
a. bel canto.
b. opera seria.
c. verismo.
d. music drama.

161. Which opera is NOT by Puccini?
a. *La bohème*
b. *Tosca*
c. *Madama Butterfly*
d. *La traviata*

162. Puccini's *La bohème* is based on a novel by:
a. Dumas.
b. Murger.
c. Mérimée.
d. Wilde.

163. *La bohème* is set in:
a. Paris.
b. Seville.
c. Cairo.
d. Rome.

164. Mimi dies in *La bohème* because:
a. Rodolfo stabs her.
b. she kills herself.
c. she is ill.
d. her father, Wotan, kills her.

165. What Russian figure played a crucial role in the development of twentieth-century ballet?
a. Petipa
b. Diaghilev
c. Balakirev
d. Musorgsky

166. Who was Tchaikovsky's principal patron?
a. Anton Rubinstein
b. Vaslav Nijinsky
c. Nadezhda von Meck
d. Serge Diaghilev

Answer: a
Chronological Edition: Ch. 65, p. 394
Standard Edition: Ch. 35, p. 172
*Shorter Edition: Ch. 53, p. 256
Date used:

167. Which of the following Russian composers was famous for his ballets?
a. Tchaikovsky
b. Cui
c. Rimsky-Korsakov
d. Musorgsky

Answer: a
Chronological Edition: Ch. 65, p. 394
Standard Edition: Ch. 35, p. 172
*Shorter Edition: Ch. 53, p. 257
Date used:

168. Which of the following is NOT a ballet by Tchaikovsky?
a. *Eugene Onegin*
b. *Swan Lake*
c. *Sleeping Beauty*
d. *The Nutcracker*

Answer: d
Chronological Edition: Ch. 65, p. 394
Standard Edition: Ch. 35, p. 172
*Shorter Edition: Ch. 53, p. 257
Date used:

169. Who was the great Russian choreographer who wrote the scenario for *The Nutcracker*?
a. Diaghilev
b. Baryshnikov
c. Nijinsky
d. Petipa

TRUE/FALSE QUESTIONS

Answer: F
Chronological Edition: Ch. 40, p. 282
Standard Edition: Ch. 10, p. 58
*Shorter Edition: Ch. 35, p. 195
Date used:

170. The French Revolution did not affect the Romantic movement.

Answer: T
Chronological Edition: Ch. 40, p. 282
Standard Edition: Ch. 10, p. 58
*Shorter Edition: Ch. 35, p. 195
Date used:

171. Romantics rebelled against conventional form, leaning instead toward the fanciful and the passionate.

Answer: T
Chronological Edition: Ch. 40, p. 282
Standard Edition: Ch. 10, p. 57
*Shorter Edition: Ch. 35, p. 195
Date used:

172. One of the prime traits of Romantic arts was their emphasis on an intensely emotional expression.

Answer: T
Chronological Edition: Ch. 40, p. 283
Standard Edition: Ch. 10, p. 60
*Shorter Edition: Ch. 35, p. 196
Date used:

173. The nineteenth-century novel found its great theme in the conflict between the individual and society.

Answer: F
Chronological Edition: Ch. 41, p. 284
Standard Edition: Ch. 11, p. 61
*Shorter Edition: Ch. 36, p. 198
Date used:

174. The Industrial Revolution produced less expensive musical instruments but with no technical improvements.

Answer: F
Chronological Edition: Ch. 41, p. 285
Standard Edition: Ch. 11, p. 61
*Shorter Edition: Ch. 36, p. 198
Date used:

175. The Romantic orchestra was the same size as the Classical orchestra.

Answer: T
Chronological Edition: Ch. 41, p. 286
Standard Edition: Ch. 11, p. 61
*Shorter Edition: Ch. 36, p. 198
Date used:

176. The dynamic range of nineteenth-century orchestras was far greater than orchestras of the previous century.

Answer: F
Chronological Edition: Ch.41, p. 286
Standard Edition: Ch. 11, p. 62
*Shorter Edition: Ch. 36, p. 199
Date used:

177. Romantic music is characterized by relatively less expression than music of earlier periods.

Answer: T
Chronological Edition: Ch. 41, p. 286
Standard Edition: Ch. 11, p. 62
*Shorter Edition: Ch. 36, p. 199
Date used:

178. The desire for increased expressiveness in nineteenth-century music is communicated by the composer to the performer through new descriptive terms.

Answer: T
Chronological Edition: Ch. 41, p. 286
Standard Edition: Ch. 11, p. 62
*Shorter Edition: Ch. 36, p. 199
Date used:

179. An interest in folklore and folk music resulted from the rise of nationalism.

Answer: F
Chronological Edition: Ch. 41, p. 286
Standard Edition: Ch. 11, p. 62
*Shorter Edition: Ch. 36, p. 199
Date used:

180. Exoticism was expressed through the incorporation within a composition of folk music of one's own country.

Answer: T
Chronological Edition: Ch. 41, p. 287
Standard Edition: Ch. 11, p. 64
*Shorter Edition: Ch. 36, p. 200
Date used:

181. A Romantic symphony is generally longer than one of the Classical period.

Answer: F
Chronological Edition: Ch. 41, p. 288
Standard Edition: Ch. 11, p. 64f
*Shorter Edition: Ch. 36, p. 201
Date used:

182. Nineteenth-century musicians continued to be viewed by society as glorified servants.

Answer: T
Chronological Edition: Ch. 41, p. 290
Standard Edition: Ch. 11, p. 66
*Shorter Edition: Ch. 36, p. 202
Date used:

183. The nineteenth-century view, held principally by men, was that women lacked creativity in the arts.

Answer: T
Chronological Edition: Ch. 41, p. 290
Standard Edition: Ch. 11, p. 66
*Shorter Edition: Ch. 36, p. 202
Date used:

184. The society of the nineteenth century saw some women make careers as professional musicians.

Answer: F
Chronological Edition: Ch. 42, p. 291
Standard Edition: Ch. 12, p. 67
*Shorter Edition: Ch. 37, p. 203
Date used:

185. A song that is composed from beginning to end without repetitions of whole sections is in strophic form.

Answer: T
Chronological Edition: Ch. 42, p. 291
Standard Edition: Ch. 12, p. 67
*Shorter Edition: Ch. 37, p. 203
Date used:

186. A song in which the same melody is repeated with every stanza of the text is in strophic form.

Answer: T
Chronological Edition: Ch. 42, p. 291
Standard Edition: Ch. 12, p. 67
Date used:

187. The song form that combines features of strophic and through-composed forms is called modified strophic.

Answer: T
Chronological Edition: Ch. 42, p. 292
Standard Edition: Ch. 12, p. 68
*Shorter Edition: Ch. 37, p. 204
Date used:

188. The art song can be described as representing a union of poetry and music.

Answer: T
Chronological Edition: Ch. 42, p. 292
Standard Edition: Ch. 12, p. 68
*Shorter Edition: Ch. 37, p. 204
Date used:

189. Goethe and Heine were two of the leading nineteenth-century poets set by Lieder composers.

Answer: T
Chronological Edition: Ch. 42, p. 292
Standard Edition: Ch. 12, p. 68
*Shorter Edition: Ch. 37, p. 204
Date used:

190. The rise of the piano as a household instrument influenced the popularity of the Lied.

Answer: F
Chronological Edition: Ch. 43, p. 294f
Standard Edition: Ch. 13, p. 70f
*Shorter Edition: Ch. 38, p. 205f
Date used:

191. Schubert was a thoroughly Romantic composer whose music abandoned the forms and stylistic principles of Classicism.

Answer: T
Chronological Edition: Ch. 43, p. 295
Standard Edition: Ch. 13, p. 71
*Shorter Edition: Ch. 38, p. 205f
Date used:

192. Franz Schubert composed over 600 Lieder.

Answer: T
Chronological Edition: Ch. 43, p. 295
Standard Edition: Ch. 13, p. 71
*Shorter Edition: Ch. 38, p. 205f
Date used:

193. Schubert's prolific output includes works of every major genre.

Answer: F
Chronological Edition: Ch. 43, p. 295
Standard Edition: Ch. 13, p. 71
*Shorter Edition: Ch. 38, p. 206
Date used:

194. The poem *Erlkönig* was written by Heinrich Heine.

Answer: T
Chronological Edition: Ch. 43, p. 296
Standard Edition: Ch. 13, p. 72
*Shorter Edition: Ch. 38, p. 206
Date used:

195. The form of Schubert's Lied, *Erlkönig*, is through-composed.

Answer: T
Chronological Edition: Ch. 44, p. 298
Standard Edition: Ch. 14, p. 74
*Shorter Edition: Ch. 47, p. 232
Date used:

196. Robert Schumann was married to the gifted pianist and composer Clara Wieck.

Answer: F
Chronological Edition: Ch. 44, p. 298f
Standard Edition: Ch. 14, p. 74f
*Shorter Edition: Ch. 47, p. 232f
Date used:

197. Schumann was a carefree spirit with a happy disposition who lived a long, productive life as a composer.

Answer: T
Chronological Edition: Ch. 44, p. 299
Standard Edition: Ch. 14, p. 75
Date used:

198.   A favorite theme of Schumann's Lieder was love seen from a woman's perspective.

Answer: F
Chronclogical Edition: Ch. 44, p. 300
Standard Edition: Ch. 14, p. 76
Date used:

199.   The form of *Ich grolle nicht* is strophic throughout.

Answer: T
Chronological Edition: Ch. 45, p. 301
Standard Edition: Ch. 15, p. 78
*Shorter Edition: Ch. 49, p. 238f
Date used:

200.   Brahms's purity of Classical style and mastery of musical architecture brought him closer to the spirit of Beethoven than any of his contemporaries.

Answer: T
Chronological Edition: Ch. 45, p. 302
Standard Edition: Ch. 15, p. 78
*Shorter Edition: Ch. 49, p. 238
Date used:

201.   The true love of Brahms's life was Clara Schumann.

Answer: T
Chronological Edition: Ch. 45, p. 302f
Standard Edition: Ch. 15, p. 78f
*Shorter Edition: Ch. 49, p. 238
Date used:

202.   Brahms wrote in virtually all genres of music except opera.

Answer: T
Chronological Edition: Ch. 46, p. 305
Standard Edition: Ch. 16, p. 81
*Shorter Edition: Ch. 39, p. 209
Date used:

203.   The rise in popularity of the piano was an important factor in shaping the musical culture of the Romantic era.

Answer: T
Chronological Edition: Ch. 46, p. 305
Standard Edition: Ch. 16, p. 81
*Shorter Edition: Ch. 39, p. 209
Date used:

204.   The piano underwent crucial technical improvements during the nineteenth century.

Answer: F
Chronological Edition: Ch. 47, p. 308
Standard Edition: Ch. 17, p. 84
*Shorter Edition: Ch. 40, p. 211
Date used:

205.   Chopin wrote in all genres of music, including opera and symphony.

The Nineteenth Century   259

Answer: T
Chronological Edition: Ch. 47, p. 309
Standard Edition: Ch. 17, p. 85
Date used:

Answer: F
Chronological Edition: Ch. 47, p. 311
Standard Edition: Ch. 17, p. 87
Date used:

Answer: T
Chronological Edition: Ch. 48, p. 312
Standard Edition: Ch. 18, p. 88
*Shorter Edition: Ch. 46, p. 231
Date used:

Answer: T
Chronological Edition: Ch. 48, p. 312
Standard Edition: Ch. 18, p. 88
*Shorter Edition: Ch. 46, p. 231
Date used:

Answer: T
Chronological Edition: Ch. 48, p. 312f
Standard Edition: Ch. 18, p. 88f
Date used:

Answer: T
Chronological Edition: Ch. 48, p. 314
Standard Edition: Ch. 18, p. 90
Date used:

Answer: T
Chronological Edition: Ch. 49, p. 316
Standard Edition: Ch. 19, p. 92
*Shorter Edition: Ch. 41, p. 214
Date used:

Answer: T
Chronological Edition: Ch. 49, p. 316f
Standard Edition: Ch. 19, p. 92f
*Shorter Edition: Ch. 41, p. 214f
Date used:

206. An étude is a short but highly technical study piece for piano.

207. The melody in Chopin's Prelude in E minor moves in disjunct motion through a wide range.

208. Although a very popular showman, Franz Liszt was a virtuoso pianist-composer and an innovator of modern piano technique.

209. Liszt became aware of the possibilities of virtuoso solo playing through the influence of the sensational violinist Paganini.

210. Franz Liszt described the style of his music, along with that of Wagner and Berlioz, as the "music of the future".

211. Liszt's *Wilde Jagd* is an étude that evokes the image of the hunt.

212. Clara Schumann was not generally acknowledged as a composer during her lifetime.

213. Pianist Clara Schumann gave the first performances of her husband Robert's important works, and also became known as a leading interpreter of the music of Brahms and Chopin.

Answer: F
Chronological Edition: Ch. 49, p. 317
Standard Edition: Ch. 19, p. 93
*Shorter Edition: Ch. 41, p. 215
Date used:

Answer: T
Chronological Edition: Ch. 49, p. 318
Standard Edition: Ch. 19, p. 94
Date used:

Answer: F
Chronological Edition: Ch. 49, p. 319
Standard Edition: Ch. 19, p. 95
Date used:

Answer: F
Chronological Edition: Ch. 50, p. 320
Standard Edition: Ch. 20, p. 96
*Shorter Edition: Ch. 42, p. 217
Date used:

Answer: F
Chronological Edition: Ch. 50, p. 320
Standard Edition: Ch. 20, p. 96
*Shorter Edition: Ch. 42, p. 217
Date used:

Answer: T
Chronological Edition: Ch. 51, p. 323
Standard Edition: Ch. 21, p. 99
Date used:

Answer: F
Chronological Edition: Ch. 51, p. 324
Standard Edition: Ch. 21, p. 100
Date used:

Answer: T
Chronological Edition: Ch. 51, p. 325
Standard Edition: Ch. 21, p. 101
Date used:

214.   Clara Schumann's *Quatre pièces fugitives* is a set of three short piano pieces written for Brahms.

215.   *Carnaval* is a series of piano miniatures unified by a central idea, and is thus the pianistic counterpart of the song cycle.

216.   "Eusebius" represents the vigorous, passionate side of Robert Schumann's personality.

217.   Music endowed with literary or pictorial associations is called pure music.

218.   Brahms's Symphony No. 2 in D Major is a good example of a program symphony.

219.   Although he composed in the Romantic style, Mendelssohn was dedicated to preserving the tradition of Classical forms.

220.   Mendelssohn wrote *A Midsummer Night's Dream* as incidental music to Shakespeare's comedy, *The Merchant of Venice*.

221.   The nocturne is a later movement from Mendelssohn's incidental music for *A Midsummer Night's Dream*.

Answer: T
Chronological Edition: Ch. 52, p. 328
Standard Edition: Ch. 22, p. 104
*Shorter Edition: Ch. 43, p. 220
Date used:

222. Berlioz was one of the boldest musical innovators of the nineteenth century.

Answer: T
Chronological Edition: Ch. 52, p. 329
Standard Edition: Ch. 22, p. 105
*Shorter Edition: Ch. 43, p. 221
Date used:

223. In his *Symphonie fantastique*, Berlioz used a recurrent theme that symbolizes the beloved, which he called the "idée fixe".

Answer: F
Chronological Edition: Ch. 52, p. 329
Standard Edition: Ch. 22, p. 105
*Shorter Edition: Ch. 43, p. 221
Date used:

224. In Berlioz's *Symphonie fantastique*, the "idée fixe" melody appears only at the very end of the fourth movement, "March to the Scaffold".

Answer: T
Chronological Edition: Ch. 53, p. 332
Standard Edition: Ch. 23, p. 108
*Shorter Edition: Ch. 54, p. 263
Date used:

225. Although he lived well into the twentieth century, Richard Strauss's tone poems belong to the Romantic tradition.

Answer: T
Chronological Edition: Ch. 53, p. 334
Standard Edition: Ch. 23, p. 110
Date used:

226. Strauss's *Don Juan* is a symphonic poem about a favorite literary character.

Answer: T
Chronological Edition: Ch. 54, p. 335
Standard Edition: Ch. 24, p. 111
*Shorter Edition: Ch. 44, p. 223f
Date used:

227. Expressions of nationalism were more prevalent in Romantic music than in works of the Classical period.

Answer: T
Chronological Edition: Ch. 54, p. 335
Standard Edition: Ch. 24, p. 111
*Shorter Edition: Ch. 44, p. 223f
Date used:

228. Nationalism found natural expression in music, among other arts.

Answer: T
Chronological Edition: Ch. 54, p. 335
Standard Edition: Ch. 24, p. 111
*Shorter Edition: Ch. 44, p. 224
Date used:

229. The growth of nationalism became a decisive force within the Romantic movement.

Answer: F
Chronological Edition: Ch. 54, p. 339f
Standard Edition: Ch. 24, p. 116
Date used:

Answer: T
Chronological Edition: Ch. 55, p. 341
Standard Edition: Ch. 25, p. 117
*Shorter Edition: Ch. 45, p. 228
Date used:

Answer: F
Chronological Edition: Ch. 55, p. 341
Standard Edition: Ch. 25, p. 117
*Shorter Edition: Ch. 45 p. 228
Date used:

Answer: F
Chronological Edition: Ch. 55, p. 341
Standard Edition: Ch. 25, p. 117f
*Shorter Edition: Ch. 45 p. 228
Date used:

Answer: F
Chronological Edition: Ch. 56, p. 342f
Standard Edition: Ch. 26, p. 119f
*Shorter Edition: Ch. 45 p. 229
Date used:

Answer: T
Chronological Edition: Ch. 56, p. 346
Standard Edition: Ch. 26, p. 123
Date used:

Answer: T
Chronological Edition: Ch. 57, p. 347
Standard Edition: Ch. 27, p. 124
*Shorter Edition: Ch. 46, p. 230
Date used:

Answer: T
Chronological Edition: Ch. 57, p. 347
Standard Edition: Ch. 27, p. 124
*Shorter Edition: Ch. 46, p. 230
Date used:

230. Antonín Dvořák was a Finnish nationalist composer, who wrote the much-loved symphonic poem, *Finlandia*.

231. In absolute music, musical ideas are organized without the aid of external images provided by a program.

232. The symphony was a new genre in the Romantic era.

233. Nineteenth-century symphonic composers were more prolific than their forebears because their works grew steadily shorter.

234. Mendelssohn's *Italian Symphony* incorporated Italian folk dances into all its movements.

235. The finale of Brahms's Symphony No. 4 is a passacaglia, an archaic form borrowed from the Baroque period.

236. Within a concerto, the two-fold statement of themes by the orchestra and the soloist is called a double exposition.

237. A unique feature of the concerto is the cadenza, a fanciful solo passage performed in the manner of an improvisation.

Answer: T
Chronological Edition: Ch. 57, p. 348
Standard Edition: Ch. 27, p. 125
*Shorter Edition: Ch. 46, p. 231
Date used:

238. Technical brilliance became a significant element of the concerto style in the nineteenth century.

Answer: T
Chronological Edition: Ch. 58, p. 349f
Standard Edition: Ch. 28, p. 126
*Shorter Edition: Ch. 46, p. 233
Date used:

239. Schumann's Piano Concerto in A minor generally fits the traditional concerto scheme.

Answer: T
Chronological Edition: Ch. 58, p. 351
Standard Edition: Ch. 28, p. 128
Date used:

240. Tchaikovsky's Violin Concerto in D major was so technically difficult that the original dedicatee refused to play it.

Answer: T
Chronological Edition: Ch. 59, p. 353
Standard Edition: Ch. 29, p. 130
*Shorter Edition: Ch. 48, p. 236
Date used:

241. Singing in a chorus generally requires less skill than playing in an orchestra.

Answer: T
Chronological Edition: Ch. 59, p. 353
Standard Edition: Ch. 29, p. 130
*Shorter Edition: Ch. 48, p. 236
Date used:

242. Choral music offered the public an outlet for their creative energies.

Answer: T
Chronological Edition: Ch. 59, p. 354
Standard Edition: Ch. 29, p. 131
Date used:

243. A mass is a musical setting of the most solemn service of the Roman Catholic Church.

Answer: T
Chronological Edition: Ch. 60, p. 355
Standard Edition: Ch. 30, p. 133
*Shorter Edition: Ch. 49, p. 240
Date used:

244. The overall structure of Brahms's *German Requiem* is that of an arch, with the fourth movement as the center.

Answer: T
Chronological Edition: Ch. 60, p. 358
Standard Edition: Ch. 30, p. 135
Date used:

245. The "Farewell of the Shepherds", from *L'enfance du Christ*, is a chorus in strophic form.

Answer: T
Chronological Edition: Ch. 61, p. 360
Standard Edition: Ch. 31, p. 136
*Shorter Edition: Ch. 50, p. 241f
Date used:

246. Viewing opera often requires suspending logic and reality in order to appreciate its drama and music.

Answer: T
Chronological Edition: Ch. 61, p. 139
Standard Edition: Ch. 31, p. 136
*Shorter Edition: Ch. 18, p. 104
Date used:

247. A drama that is sung and combines soloists, ensembles, chorus and orchestra is called an opera.

Answer: T
Chronological Edition: Ch. 61, p. 140
Standard Edition: Ch. 31, p. 137
*Shorter Edition: Ch. 18, p. 105
Date used:

248. The text of an opera is called the libretto.

Answer: F
Chronological Edition: Ch. 61, p. 360
Standard Edition: Ch. 31, p. 138
*Shorter Edition: Ch. 50, p. 243
Date used:

249. A Singspiel was an instrument invented by Richard Wagner for his extended orchestrations.

Answer: T
Chronological Edition: Ch. 61, p. 361
Standard Edition: Ch. 31, p. 139
*Shorter Edition: Ch. 50, p. 243
Date used:

250. The master of the Italian bel canto style was Giuseppe Verdi.

Answer: T
Chronological Edition: Ch. 62, p. 362
Standard Edition: Ch. 32, p. 140
*Shorter Edition: Ch. 51, p. 244f
Date used:

251. Verdi's operas stirred a revolutionary spirit within the Italian people.

Answer: F
Chronological Edition: Ch. 62, p. 365
Standard Edition: Ch. 32, p. 143
*Shorter Edition: Ch. 51, p. 245
Date used:

252. Verdi's *La traviata* is based on a play by Honoré de Balzac.

Answer: T
Chronological Edition: Ch. 62, p. 365
Standard Edition: Ch. 32, p. 143
*Shorter Edition: Ch. 51, p. 246
Date used:

253. In Verdi's *La traviata*, the heroine dies at the close.

Answer: T
Chronological Edition: Ch. 62, p. 366
Standard Edition: Ch. 32, p. 144
*Shorter Edition: Ch. 51, p. 246
Date used:

254. A climax is reached in the finale to Act II of Verdi's *La traviata* with the ensemble number.

Answer: T
Chronological Edition: Ch. 63, p. 371
Standard Edition: Ch. 33, p. 149
Date used:

255. Unlike Verdi, Wagner wrote all of his own libretti.

Answer: T
Chronological Edition: Ch. 63, p. 371
Standard Edition: Ch. 33, p. 149
*Shorter Edition: Ch. 52, p. 251
Date used:

256. Wagner's operas employ the supernatural as an element of drama, and glorify the German land and people.

Answer: T
Chronological Edition: Ch. 63, p. 373
Standard Edition: Ch. 33, p. 151
*Shorter Edition: Ch. 52, p. 251
Date used:

257. Wagner eventually married Cosima, the daughter of his good friend, Franz Liszt.

Answer: T
Chronological Edition: Ch. 63, p. 373
Standard Edition: Ch. 33, p. 151f
*Shorter Edition: Ch. 52, p. 252
Date used:

258. Unlike the divisions of aria and recitative in Italian opera, Wagner strived for a continuous flow of melody.

Answer: F
Chronological Edition: Ch. 63, p. 373
Standard Edition: Ch. 33, p. 152
*Shorter Edition: Ch. 52, p. 252
Date used:

259. Wagner did not wish to change the prevailing form of opera in the nineteenth century.

Answer: T
Chronological Edition: Ch. 63, p. 374
Standard Edition: Ch. 33, p. 152
*Shorter Edition: Ch. 52, p. 252
Date used:

260. Wagner pushed the major-minor tonality to extreme limits with his style of chromatic harmony.

Answer: F
Chronological Edition: Ch. 63, p. 373f
Standard Edition: Ch. 33, p. 152
*Shorter Edition: Ch. 52, p. 252
Date used:

261. The focal point of Wagnerian music drama is the voice.

Answer: T
Chronological Edition: Ch. 63, p. 374
Standard Edition: Ch. 33, p. 152
*Shorter Edition: Ch. 52, p. 252
Date used:

262. Wagner's recurring themes that represent specific characters, emotions, or ideas are called leitmotifs.

Answer: T
Chronological Edition: Ch. 64, p. 380
Standard Edition: Ch. 34, p. 158
Date used:

263. The story of *Carmen* is more realistic than most operas of its time.

Answer: T
Chronological Edition: Ch. 64, p. 381
Standard Edition: Ch. 34, p. 159
Date used:

264. The opera *Carmen* is set in Seville, Spain.

Answer: F
Chronological Edition: Ch. 64, p. 383
Standard Edition: Ch. 34, p. 161
Date used:

265. The form of Carmen's "Habanera" is through-composed.

Answer: F
Chronological Edition: Ch. 64, p. 385
Standard Edition: Ch. 34, p. 163
Date used:

266. *La bohème* is known for its fantasy-like treatment of life.

Answer: T
Chronological Edition: Ch. 64, p. 385
Standard Edition: Ch. 34, p. 163
Date used:

267. Puccini's *La bohème* features both recitatives and arias.

Answer: F
Chronological Edition: Ch. 65, p. 391
Standard Edition: Ch. 35, p. 169
Date used:

268. The "pas de deux" is a western-style two-step dance.

Answer: T
Chronological Edition: Ch. 65, p. 393f
Standard Edition: Ch. 35, p. 172
*Shorter Edition: Ch. 53, p. 257
Date used:

269. Tchaikovsky was known for his symphonies and operas as well as ballets.

Answer: T
Chronological Edition: Ch. 65, p. 394
Standard Edition: Ch. 35, p. 172
*Shorter Edition: Ch. 53, p. 257
Date used:

Answer: F
Chronological Edition: Ch. 65, p. 394
Standard Edition: Ch. 35, p. 172f
*Shorter Edition: Ch. 53, p. 257f
Date used:

270. *The Nutcracker* is based on a story by E. T. A. Hoffmann.

271. *The Nutcracker* is a real-life story set at Christmastime.

THE TWENTIETH CENTURY

MULTIPLE CHOICE QUESTIONS

Answer: b
Chronological Edition: Tr. V, p. 399
Standard Edition: Tr. V, p. 397
*Shorter Edition: Tr. V, p. 261
Date used:

1. What name is given to the twentieth-century composers who continued the Romantic tradition?
   a. Impressionist
   b. post-Romantic
   c. Minimalist
   d. Expressionist

Answer: c
Chronological Edition: Tr. V, p. 399
Standard Edition: Tr. V, p. 397
*Shorter Edition: Tr. V, p. 261
Date used:

2. The movement that, along with post-Romanticism, ushered in the twentieth century was known as:
   a. Classicism.
   b. Modernism.
   c. Impressionism.
   d. Traditionalism.

Answer: c
Chronological Edition: Tr. V, p. 399
Standard Edition: Tr. V, p. 397
*Shorter Edition: Tr. V, p. 261f
Date used:

3. With which of the following movements is Gustav Mahler most closely associated?
   a. Classical
   b. Romantic
   c. post-Romantic
   d. Impressionist

Answer: b
Chronological Edition: Tr. V, p. 399f
Standard Edition: Tr. V, p. 397f
*Shorter Edition: Tr. V, p. 261f
Date used:

4. _____ was a dynamic composer and conductor who served as director of both the Vienna Opera and New York Philharmonic in his lifetime.
   a. Claude Debussy
   b. Gustav Mahler
   c. Maurice Ravel
   d. Edvard Grieg

Answer: a
Chronological Edition: Tr. V, p. 401
Standard Edition: Tr. V, p. 399
Date used:

5. Which of the following was NOT written by Gustav Mahler?
   a. *Clair de lune*
   b. *Songs of a Wayfarer*
   c. *The Youth's Magic Horn*
   d. *The Song of the Earth*

Answer: c
Chronological Edition: Tr. V, p. 401
Standard Edition: Tr. V, p. 399
Date used:

6. The *Songs on the Death of Children* by Mahler:
   a. is a cycle for voice and orchestra.
   b. is set to poems of Rückert.
   c. is autobiographical.
   d. all of the above.

Answer: d
Chronological Edition: Tr. V, p. 402
Standard Edition: Tr. V, p. 400
Date used:

Answer: b
Chronological Edition: Tr. V, p. 402
Standard Edition: Tr. V, p. 400
Date used:

Answer: c
Chronological Edition: Tr. V, p. 402
Standard Edition: Tr. V, p. 400
Date used:

Answer: d
Chronological Edition: Ch. 66, p. 403
Standard Edition: Ch. 66, p. 401
*Shorter Edition: Ch. 54, p. 264
Date used:

Answer: d
Chronological Edition: Ch. 66, p. 403
Standard Edition: Ch. 66, p. 401
*Shorter Edition: Ch. 54, p. 264f
Date used:

Answer: c
Chronological Edition: Ch. 66, p. 403
Standard Edition: Ch. 66, p. 401
*Shorter Edition: Ch. 54, p. 264f
Date used:

Answer: a
Chronological Edition: Ch. 66, p. 403
Standard Edition: Ch. 66, p. 401
*Shorter Edition: Ch. 54, p. 264
Date used:

7. What is unusual about Mahler's Symphony No. 4?
    a. It has four movements.
    b. It has a scherzo movement.
    c. Its slow movement uses theme and variation form.
    d. Its last movement is for solo voice with orchestra.

8. What is the basis for the text of the last movement of Mahler's Symphony No. 4?
    a. a Symbolist poem by Merimée
    b. a folk poem from the *Youth's Magic Horn*
    c. a novel by Honoré de Balzac
    d. a nursery rhyme from Mother Goose

9. Which best describes the sense of the text that Mahler set in his Fourth Symphony?
    a. a legend about a mythological creature
    b. a description of a pagan ritual
    c. a child's view of Heaven
    d. a nationalistic war story

10. The leader of the Impressionist painters is considered to have been:
    a. Auguste Renoir.
    b. Edgar Degas.
    c. Edouard Manet.
    d. Claude Monet.

11. Which of the following painters was NOT associated with the Impressionist school?
    a. Manet
    b. Degas
    c. Renoir
    d. Goya

12. Which of the following best describes the works of the Impressionist painters?
    a. They adhered firmly to academic traditions.
    b. The hero of their painting was man.
    c. They attempted to capture the freshness of first impressions.
    d. They preferred to do their painting indoors.

13. Impressionism was a style cultivated principally in:
    a. Paris.
    b. London.
    c. Berlin.
    d. Rome.

Answer: c
Chronological Edition: Ch. 66, p. 403
Standard Edition: Ch. 66, p. 401
*Shorter Edition: Ch. 54, p. 264
Date used:

Answer: b
Chronological Edition: Ch. 66, p. 404
Standard Edition: Ch. 66, p. 402
*Shorter Edition: Ch. 54, p. 265
Date used:

Answer: a
Chronological Edition: Ch. 66, p. 404
Standard Edition: Ch. 66, p. 402
*Shorter Edition: Ch. 54, p. 265
Date used:

Answer: d
Chronological Edition: Ch. 66, p. 404
Standard Edition: Ch. 66, p. 402
*Shorter Edition: Ch. 54, p. 265
Date used:

Answer: a
Chronological Edition: Ch. 66, p. 405
Standard Edition: Ch. 66, p. 403
*Shorter Edition: Ch. 54, p. 266
Date used:

Answer: b
Chronological Edition: Ch. 66, p. 406
Standard Edition: Ch. 66, p. 404
*Shorter Edition: Ch. 54, p. 267
Date used:

Answer: d
Chronological Edition: Ch. 66, p. 407
Standard Edition: Ch. 66, p. 405
*Shorter Edition: Ch. 54, p. 267
Date used:

14. Which best describes the effect achieved by Impressionist painting?
   a. bold, brilliant colors
   b. drab, dark colors
   c. luminous, shimmering colors
   d. consistent use of a single color

15. The post-Romantic movement in poetry that revolted against traditional modes of expression was called:
   a. Impressionism.
   b. Symbolism.
   c. Modernism.
   d. neo-Romanticism.

16. Baudelaire, Mallarmé and Verlaine were all:
   a. Symbolist poets.
   b. Impressionist painters.
   c. Impressionist composers.
   d. none of the above.

17. The Symbolist poets were strongly influenced by the works of:
   a. George Sand.
   b. Emily Brontë.
   c. Robert Frost.
   d. Edgar Allan Poe.

18. Impressionism in music is best exemplified by the works of:
   a. Claude Debussy.
   b. Gustav Mahler.
   c. Hector Berlioz.
   d. Frédéric Chopin.

19. The whole-tone scale used by Debussy derives from:
   a. the post-Romantic music of Mahler.
   b. non-Western music.
   c. Medieval church music.
   d. the Classical-Romantic tradition.

20. Which of the following was NOT characteristic of Impressionist music?
   a. whole-tone scales
   b. parallel chords
   c. ninth chords
   d. accents on the first beat of each measure

Answer: b
Chronological Edition: Ch. 66, p. 407
Standard Edition: Ch. 66, p. 405
*Shorter Edition: Ch. 54, p. 267
Date used:

Answer: b
Chronological Edition: Ch. 66, p. 408
Standard Edition: Ch. 66, p. 406
*Shorter Edition: Ch. 54, p. 268
Date used:

Answer: c
Chronological Edition: Ch. 66, p. 410
Standard Edition: Ch. 66, p. 408
*Shorter Edition: Ch. 54, p. 268
Date used:

Answer: d
Chronological Edition: Ch. 66, p. 407
Standard Edition: Ch. 66, p. 405
Date used:

Answer: c
Chronological Edition: Ch. 66, p. 408
Standard Edition: Ch. 66, p. 406
*Shorter Edition: Ch. 54, p. 266
Date used:

Answer: c
Chronological Edition: Ch. 66, p. 411
Standard Edition: Ch. 66, p. 409
*Shorter Edition: Ch. 54, p. 270
Date used:

Answer: c
Chronological Edition: Ch. 66, p. 412
Standard Edition: Ch. 66, p. 410
*Shorter Edition: Ch. 54, p. 270
Date used:

21. The _____ is a pattern built entirely without half-step intervals.
    a. chromatic scale
    b. whole-tone scale
    c. major scale
    d. minor scale

22. What nationality was Claude Debussy?
    a. German
    b. French
    c. Italian
    d. Austrian

23. Debussy's opera *Pelléas et Mélisande* is based on a Symbolist drama by:
    a. Giraud.
    b. Ibsen.
    c. Maeterlinck.
    d. Mallarmé.

24. Debussy's opera *Pelléas et Mélisande* came to be known as "the land of the ninths" because:
    a. there are nine scenes in each act.
    b. there are nine acts.
    c. there are nine main characters.
    d. ninth chords play a prominent role in the harmony.

25. The Impressionist painters' interest in color is paralleled by the Impressionist composers' interest in:
    a. rhythm.
    b. melody.
    c. timbre.
    d. texture.

26. Which of the following is NOT a piece by Debussy?
    a. *Clair de lune*
    b. *La mer*
    c. *Pavane pour une infante défunte*
    d. *Prelude to "The Afternoon of a Faun"*

27. What is unusual about the opening of Debussy's *Prelude to "The Afternoon of a Faun"*?
    a. It opens with solo bassoon in the high register.
    b. It opens with a drum roll and fanfare.
    c. It opens with a flute solo in the velvety lower register.
    d. It opens with unison strings.

Answer: d
Chronological Edition: Ch. 66, p. 412
Standard Edition: Ch. 66, p. 410
*Shorter Edition: Ch. 54, p. 270
Date used:

Answer: b
Chronological Edition: Ch. 66, p. 412f
Standard Edition: Ch. 66, p. 410f
*Shorter Edition: Ch. 54, p. 270f
Date used:

Answer: a
Chronological Edition: Ch. 66, p. 412f
Standard Edition: Ch. 66, p. 410f
*Shorter Edition: Ch. 54, p. 270f
Date used:

Answer: a
Chronological Edition: Ch. 67, p. 412
Standard Edition: Ch. 67, p. 414
Date used:

Answer: d
Chronological Edition: Ch. 67, p. 415
Standard Edition: Ch. 67, p. 413
Date used:

Answer: b
Chronological Edition: Ch. 67, p. 415f
Standard Edition: Ch. 67, p. 414
Date used:

Answer: c
Chronological Edition: Ch. 67, p. 416
Standard Edition: Ch. 67, p. 415
Date used:

28. The program of Debussy's *Prelude to "The Afternoon of a Faun"* evokes:
   a. a nationalistic folk dance.
   b. a river flowing through France.
   c. a child's view of Heaven.
   d. a pagan landscape of a mythological creature.

29. The overall form of Debussy's *Prelude to "The Afternoon of a Faun"* is best described as:
   a. binary.
   b. ternary.
   c. sonata–allegro.
   d. rondo.

30. Which instrument is NOT prominently heard in the opening of Debussy's *Prelude to "The Afternoon of a Faun"*?
   a. trombone
   b. harp
   c. flute
   d. oboe

31. In his youth, Ravel was part of a group of avant-garde painters, poets, and musicians known as:
   a. the Apaches.
   b. Les Six.
   c. Les Club.
   d. the Mighty Five.

32. Which is NOT true of Ravel's music?
   a. He was drawn to Classical forms.
   b. His rhythms are incisive and driving.
   c. He was attracted to exotic subjects and to Medieval scales.
   d. His harmonies are highly consonant with little sense of key or tonality.

33. Which of the following was NOT a piece by Ravel?
   a. *Bolero*
   b. *Pelléas et Mélisande*
   c. *Daphnis et Chloé*
   d. *Le tombeau de Couperin*

34. Ravel's *Le tombeau de Couperin* is a set of dance pieces originally composed for:
   a. violin.
   b. oboe.
   c. piano.
   d. cello.

Answer: c
Chronological Edition: Ch. 67, p. 416
Standard Edition: Ch. 67, p. 414
Date used:

35. Ravel's *Le tombeau de Couperin* was written as a tribute to François Couperin. Couperin was:
   a. a close friend of Ravel's.
   b. a Romantic poet.
   c. a Baroque harpsichord composer.
   d. a Classical opera composer.

Answer: b
Chronological Edition: Ch. 68, p. 418
Standard Edition: Ch. 68, p. 417
*Shorter Edition: Ch. 55, p. 273
Date uscd:

36. Which early twentieth-century style dealt with the realm of the unconscious, distorted images, and the inner self?
   a. neo-Classicism
   b. Expressionism
   c. Impressionism
   d. post-Romanticism

Answer: d
Chronological Edition: Ch. 68, p. 418
Standard Edition: Ch. 68, p. 419
*Shorter Edition: Ch. 55, p. 273
Date used:

37. In which country did the Expressionist movement originate?
   a. England
   b. United States
   c. Italy
   d. Germany

Answer: d
Chronological Edition: Ch. 68, p. 418
Standard Edition: Ch. 68, p. 419
*Shorter Edition: Ch. 55, p. 273f
Date used:

38. The primitive impulses of Expressionism are expressed through all of the following EXCEPT:
   a. the paintings of Paul Klee.
   b. the music of Arnold Schoenberg.
   c. the writings of Franz Kafka.
   d. the poetry of Stéphane Mallarmé.

Answer: d
Chronological Edition: Ch. 68, p. 418f
Standard Edition: Ch. 68, p. 417f
*Shorter Edition: Ch. 55, p. 274
Date used:

39. Which of the following was NOT associated with Expressionism?
   a. Kandinsky
   b. Klee
   c. Schoenberg
   d. Debussy

Answer: a
Chronological Edition: Ch. 68, p. 419f
Standard Edition: Ch. 68, p. 418f
*Shorter Edition: Ch. 55, p. 274
Date used:

40. The early twentieth-century style that sought to revive certain principles of earlier music was:
   a. New Classicism.
   b. post-Romanticism.
   c. Impressionism.
   d. Expressionism.

Answer: a
Chronological Edition: Ch. 68, p. 420
Standard Edition: Ch. 68, p. 419
*Shorter Edition: Ch. 55, p. 275
Date used:

41. Which of the following genres was NOT favored by the new Classicists of the early twentieth century?
   a. the symphonic poem
   b. the symphony
   c. the opera
   d. the concerto

Answer: c
Chronological Edition: Ch. 68, p. 420
Standard Edition: Ch. 68, p. 419
*Shorter Edition: Ch. 55, p. 274
Date used:

Answer: b
Chronological Edition: Ch. 69, p. 421
Standard Edition: Ch. 69, p. 420
*Shorter Edition: Ch. 56, p. 275
Date used:

Answer: b
Chronological Edition: Ch. 69, p. 422
Standard Edition: Ch. 69, p. 421
*Shorter Edition: Ch. 56, p. 276
Date used:

Answer: c
Chronological Edition: Ch. 69, p. 422
Standard Edition: Ch. 69, p. 421
*Shorter Edition: Ch. 56, p. 276
Date used:

Answer: c
Chronological Edition: Ch. 69, p. 423
Standard Edition: Ch. 69, p. 422
*Shorter Edition: Ch. 56, p. 276
Date used:

Answer: b
Chronological Edition: Ch. 69, p. 423
Standard Edition: Ch. 69, p. 422
*Shorter Edition: Ch. 56, p. 276
Date used:

Answer: c
Chronological Edition: Ch. 69, p. 423f
Standard Edition: Ch. 69, p. 422f
*Shorter Edition: Ch. 56, p. 276f
Date used:

42. Which of the following composers would NOT have been emulated during the neoclassical era?
   a. Vivaldi
   b. Bach
   c. Beethoven
   d. Handel

43. The use of several rhythmic patterns simultaneously is known as:
   a. compound meter.
   b. polyrhythms.
   c. syncopation.
   d. serialism.

44. A triad with an additional third piled on top is called:
   a. a quadrad.
   b. a seventh chord.
   c. a ninth chord.
   d. a skyscraper chord.

45. The system that bases chord construction on the interval of the fourth is known as:
   a. tertial harmony.
   b. polyharmony.
   c. quartal harmony.
   d. serialism.

46. The concept of total abandonment of a key within a piece of music is known as:
   a. polytonality.
   b. dissonance.
   c. atonality.
   d. chromaticism.

47. Which composer invented the twelve-tone method?
   a. Berg
   b. Schoenberg
   c. Webern
   d. Bartók

48. Which is NOT a term for the early twentieth-century unification principle developed by Schoenberg to replace tonality?
   a. serial music
   b. twelve-tone music
   c. polytonal music
   d. dodecaphonic music

Answer: b
Chronological Edition: Ch. 69, p. 424
Standard Edition: Ch. 69, p. 423
*Shorter Edition: Ch. 56, p. 277
Date used:

Answer: c
Chronological Edition: Ch. 69, p. 424
Standard Edition: Ch. 69, p. 423
*Shorter Edition: Ch. 56, p. 277
Datc used:

Answer: d
Chronological Edition: Ch. 69, p. 425
Standard Edition: Ch. 69, p. 424
*Shorter Edition: Ch. 56, p. 277f
Date used:

Answer: a
Chronological Edition: Ch. 69, p. 425
Standard Edition: Ch. 69, p. 424
*Shorter Edition: Ch. 56, p. 278
Date used:

Answer: a
Chronological Edition: Ch. 69, p. 425
Standard Edition: Ch. 69, p. 424
*Shorter Edition: Ch. 56, p. 278
Date used:

Answer: d
Chronological Edition: Ch. 70, p. 426f
Standard Edition: Ch. 70, p. 425f
*Shorter Edition: Ch. 57, p. 280f
Date used:

49. All of the following are alternative forms of a tone row EXCEPT:
   a. transposition.
   b. chromaticism.
   c. inversion.
   d. retrograde.

50. The technique whereby the pitches of a tone row are given in reverse order is called:
   a. inversion.
   b. transposition.
   c. retrograde.
   d. retrograde inversion.

51. The early twentieth-century orchestra exhibited all of the following characteristics EXCEPT:
   a. it was a smaller group with a leaner sound.
   b. it featured the use of instruments in extreme ranges.
   c. it featured the use of darker-sounding instruments.
   d. the strings continued to serve as the nucleus of the group.

52. The early twentieth century saw the ultimate expansion of traditional forms in the gigantic symphonies of:
   a. Mahler and Strauss.
   b. Stravinsky.
   c. Debussy and Ravel.
   d. Schoenberg.

53. The goal of the new Classicism, that strove for purity of line and proportion, was known as:
   a. formalism.
   b. serialism.
   c. atonality.
   d. expressionism.

54. Which of the following was a Russian-born composer who wrote in post-Impressionist, neoclassical and serial styles, among others?
   a. Bartók.
   b. Schoenberg
   c. Prokofiev.
   d. Stravinsky.

Answer: c
Chronological Edition: Ch. 70, p. 426
Standard Edition: Ch. 70, p. 426
*Shorter Edition: Ch. 57, p. 279
Date used:

Answer: a
Chronological Edition: Ch. 70, p. 427
Standard Edition: Ch. 70, p. 427
*Shorter Edition: Ch. 57, p. 280
Date used:

Answer: c
Chronological Edition: Ch. 70, p. 428
Standard Edition: Ch. 70, p. 427
*Shorter Edition: Ch. 57, p. 280
Date used:
Percent correct:

Answer: c
Chronological Edition: Ch. 70, p. 428
Standard Edition: Ch. 70, p. 429
*Shorter Edition: Ch. 57, p. 280f
Date used:

Answer: b
Chronological Edition: Ch. 70, p. 428
Standard Edition: Ch. 70, p. 429
*Shorter Edition: Ch. 57, p. 280f
Date used:

Answer: b
Chronological Edition: Ch. 71, p. 432
Standard Edition: Ch. 71, p. 432
*Shorter Edition: Ch. 58, p. 283f
Date used:

Answer: d
Chronological Edition: Ch. 71, p. 432
Standard Edition: Ch. 71, p. 431
*Shorter Edition: Ch. 58, p. 283
Date used:

55. Who was the impresario of the Paris-based Russian ballet who commissioned Stravinsky to write ballets?
a. Nijinsky
b. Fokine
c. Diaghilev
d. Balanchine

56. Which of the following is NOT a ballet by Stravinsky?
a. *Daphnis et Chloé*
b. *The Firebird*
c. *Petrushka*
d. *The Rite of Spring*

57. Which of the following Stravinsky works is from his neoclassical period?
a. *The Rite of Spring*
b. *Agon*
c. *Symphony of Psalms*
d. *The Firebird*

58. The opening of Stravinsky's *The Rite of Spring* features:
a. a folk dance theme, heard in the trumpet.
b. pounding, dissonant chords with irregular accents.
c. an eerie bassoon melody, played in its uppermost range.
d. a blues-type melody, presented in the violins.

59. Stravinsky's *The Rite of Spring* is representative of:
a. serialism.
b. primitivism.
c. Impressionism.
d. Expressionism.

60. Which of the following early twentieth-century composers moved to the United States and taught composition in a southern California university?
a. Stravinsky
b. Schoenberg
c. Berg
d. Bartók

61. Alban Berg and Anton Webern were disciples of:
a. Stravinsky.
b. Debussy.
c. Mahler.
d. Schoenberg.

Answer: a
Chronological Edition: Ch. 71, p. 432f
Standard Edition: Ch. 71, p. 432f
*Shorter Edition: Ch. 58, p. 285
Date used:

Answer: b
Chronological Edition: Ch. 71, p. 433
Standard Edition: Ch. 71, p. 432
*Shorter Edition: Ch. 58, p. 285
Date used:

Answer: c
Chronological Edition: Ch. 71, p. 433
Standard Edition: Ch. 71, p. 432
*Shorter Edition: Ch. 58, p. 285
Date used:

Answer: a
Chronological Edition: Ch. 71, p. 433f
Standard Edition: Ch. 71, p. 433
*Shorter Edition: Ch. 58, p. 285
Date used:

Answer: b
Chronological Edition: Ch. 71, p. 434
Standard Edition: Ch. 71, p. 434
*Shorter Edition: Ch. 58, p. 286
Date used:

Answer: c
Chronological Edition: Ch. 71, p. 434
Standard Edition: Ch. 71, p. 434
*Shorter Edition: Ch. 58, p. 285f
Date used:

Answer: d
Chronological Edition: Ch. 71, p. 434
Standard Edition: Ch. 71, p. 434
Date used:

62. The Viennese composer who, after writing in both post-Romantic and atonal styles, invented the twelve-tone method was:
   a. Schoenberg.
   b. Webern.
   c. Berg.
   d. Stravinsky.

63. With which period in Schoenberg's career is *Pierrot lunaire* associated?
   a. the post-Romantic phase
   b. the atonal-Expressionist phase
   c. the twelve-tone or serial phase
   d. the American phase

64. Schoenberg created a new style in which vocal melodies were spoken rather than sung with exact pitches and rhythms. This was known as:
   a. Singspiel.
   b. recitative.
   c. Sprechstimme.
   d. Klangfarbenmelodie.

65. *Pierrot lunaire* is based on a cycle of poems written by:
   a. Giraud.
   b. Verlaine.
   c. Mallarmé.
   d. Rimbaud.

66. How many songs are in *Pierrot lunaire*?
   a. twelve
   b. twenty-one
   c. twenty-four
   d. thirty-two

67. What accompanies the voice in *Pierrot lunaire*?
   a. an orchestra
   b. a piano
   c. a chamber group
   d. a choir

68. Schoenberg experimented with the idea of tone-color melody, or shifting each note of a melody to a different instrument. He called this:
   a. Sprechstimme.
   b. polymelody.
   c. Singspiel.
   d. Klangfarbenmelodie.

Answer: b
Chronological Edition: Ch. 71, p. 434
Standard Edition: Ch. 71, p. 434
Date used:

Answer: c
Chronological Edition: Ch. 71, p. 434
Standard Edition: Ch. 71, p. 434
Date used:

Answer: a
Chronological Edition: Ch. 72, p. 437f
Standard Edition: Ch. 72, p. 437f
*Shorter Edition: Ch. 58, p. 287
Date used:

Answer: a
Chronological Edition: Ch. 72, p. 438
Standard Edition: Ch. 72, p. 438
Date used:

Answer: d
Chronological Edition: Ch. 72, p. 439
Standard Edition: Ch. 72, p. 438
Date used:

Answer: c
Chronological Edition: Ch. 72, p. 439
Standard Edition: Ch. 72, p. 438
*Shorter Edition: Ch. 58, p. 287
Date used:

Answer: c
Chronological Edition: Ch. 72, p. 439
Standard Edition: Ch. 72, p. 439
*Shorter Edition: Ch. 58, p. 287
Date used:

69. Klangfarbenmelodie refers to:
   a. a form of the tone row.
   b. a style that gives each note of a melody to a different instrument.
   c. a style in which a vocal is spoken rather than sung on exact pitches.
   d. a French poetic form of thirteen lines.

70. Which is NOT true of Schoenberg's *Pierrot lunaire*?
   a. It uses the vocal style of Sprechstimme.
   b. It employs Klangfarbenmelodie or tone color melody.
   c. It is concerned with pagan rituals.
   d. It expresses mood changes from guilt and depression to playfulness.

71. Which composer was a disciple of Schoenberg and is best known for his operas *Wozzeck* and *Lulu*?
   a. Berg
   b. Webern
   c. Stravinsky
   d. Bartók

72. Which of the following is NOT a work by Alban Berg?
   a. *A Survivor from Warsaw*
   b. *Wozzeck*
   c. *Lulu*
   d. the *Lyric Suite*

73. Berg spent the last years of his life trying to complete:
   a. the *Lyric Suite*.
   b. his Violin Concerto.
   c. his opera, *Wozzeck*.
   d. his opera, *Lulu*.

74. Berg's opera, *Wozzeck* is based on a play by:
   a. Wedekind.
   b. Strindberg.
   c. Büchner.
   d. Ibsen.

75. Berg's opera *Wozzeck* is best described as an example of:
   a. Impressionism.
   b. post-Romanticism.
   c. Expressionism.
   d. New Classicism.

Answer: b
Chronological Edition: Ch. 72, p. 439
Standard Edition: Ch. 72, p. 439
Date used:

Answer: a
Chronological Edition: Ch. 72, p. 440
Standard Edition: Ch. 72, p. 440
Date used:

Answer: b
Chronological Edition: Ch. 73, p. 445
Standard Edition: Ch. 73, p. 445
*Shorter Edition: Ch. 58, p. 287
Date used:

Answer: d
Chronological Edition: Ch. 73, p. 445
Standard Edition: Ch. 73, p. 445
*Shorter Edition: Ch. 58, p. 287
Date used:

Answer: a
Chronological Edition: Ch. 73, p. 445f
Standard Edition: Ch. 73, p. 445f
*Shorter Edition: Ch. 58, p. 287
Date used:

Answer: c
Chronological Edition: Ch. 73, p. 445
Standard Edition: Ch. 73, p. 445
*Shorter Edition: Ch. 58, p. 287
Date used:

Answer: b
Chronological Edition: Ch. 73, p. 446
Standard Edition: Ch. 73, p. 446
Date used:

76. Berg's opera, *Wozzeck*, centers on:
    a. a clown's obsession with the moon.
    b. a soldier's obsession with unhappy love.
    c. a steadfast expression of religious faith.
    d. a battle in Medieval Russia.

77. The final heart-breaking scene of Berg's *Wozzeck* concludes with:
    a. the son of Marie and Wozzeck, alone.
    b. the death of Marie.
    c. the death of Wozzeck.
    d. more experiments performed on Wozzeck.

78. Which was the more radical of Schoenberg's famous students?
    a. Stravinsky
    b. Webern
    c. Copland
    d. Berg

79. Which was NOT a composer of the modern Viennese school?
    a. Webern
    b. Schoenberg
    c. Berg
    d. Wagner

80. Which of the following does NOT characterize the music of Webern?
    a. emotional qualities
    b. brevity
    c. complex serialism
    d. unusual combination of instruments

81. Which disciple of Schoenberg is credited with extending serial techniques to include timbre and rhythm?
    a. Prokofiev
    b. Berg
    c. Webern
    d. Strauss

82. To which technique in painting can Klangfarbenmelodie be likened?
    a. primitivism
    b. pointillism
    c. abstract expressionism
    d. minimalism

Answer: d
Chronological Edition: Ch. 73, p. 446
Standard Edition: Ch. 73, p. 446
Date used:

Answer: d
Chronological Edition: Ch. 73, p. 447
Standard Edition: Ch. 73, p. 447
Date used:

Answer: b
Chronological Edition: Ch. 73, p. 448
Standard Edition: Ch. 73, p. 448
Date used:

Answer: d
Chronological Edition: Ch. 74, p. 449
Standard Edition: Ch. 74, p. 449
Date used:

Answer: c
Chronological Edition: Ch. 74, p. 449
Standard Edition: Ch. 74, p. 449
Date used:

Answer: b
Chronological Edition: Ch. 74, p. 450
Standard Edition: Ch. 74, p. 450
*Shorter Edition: Ch. 59, p. 292
Date used:

Answer: c
Chronological Edition: Ch. 74, p. 450
Standard Edition: Ch. 74, p. 450
*Shorter Edition: Ch. 59, p. 292
Date used:

83. The form of the second movement of Webern's Symphony, Opus 21 is:
    a. sonata–allegro.
    b. canon.
    c. rondo.
    d. theme and variations.

84. Which of the following influences can be found in the music of Messiaen?
    a. bird songs
    b. religious feelings
    c. Gregorian chant
    d. all of these

85. Which is NOT true of Messiaen's *Vingt regards sur l'enfant Jesus*?
    a. It is a series of miniatures for solo piano.
    b. It explores new possibilities of orchestral sonorities.
    c. It reflects the composer's religious faith.
    d. It has several unifying themes that recur throughout.

86. Which of the following twentieth-century French composers was NOT a follower of Erik Satie?
    a. Milhaud
    b. Poulenc
    c. Honegger
    d. Ravel

87. The French composer who developed polytonality and wrote a ballet entitled *The Creation of the World* was:
    a. Poulenc.
    b. Honegger.
    c. Milhaud.
    d. Debussy.

88. Which of the following was NOT a member of the twentieth-century Russian school?
    a. Rachmaninoff
    b. Delius
    c. Prokofiev
    d. Shostakovich

89. Which of the following English composers is viewed as one of the foremost opera composers of today?
    a. Delius
    b. Elgar
    c. Britten
    d. Vaughan Williams

Answer: a
Chronological Edition: Ch. 74, p. 450
Standard Edition: Ch. 74, p. 450
*Shorter Edition: Ch. 59, p. 292
Date used:

Answer: c
Chronological Edition: Ch. 74, p. 450
Standard Edition: Ch. 74, p. 450
*Shorter Edition: Ch. 59, p. 292
Date used:

Answer: c
Chronological Edition: Ch. 74, p. 450f
Standard Edition: Ch. 74, p. 450f
*Shorter Edition: Ch. 59, p. 293
Date used:

Answer: a
Chronological Edition: Ch. 74, p. 451
Standard Edition: Ch. 74, p. 451
*Shorter Edition: Ch. 59, p. 293
Date used:

Answer: b
Chronological Edition: Ch. 74, p. 451
Standard Edition: Ch. 74, p. 451
Date used:

Answer: b
Chronological Edition: Ch. 74, p. 452
Standard Edition: Ch. 74, p. 453
Date used:

Answer: d
Chronological Edition: Ch. 74, p. 452
Standard Edition: Ch. 74, p. 452
Date used:

90. Who composed the opera *Peter Grimes*?
    a. Britten
    b. Orff
    c. Williams
    d. Elgar

91. The cantata *Carmina Burana* was written by:
    a. Kurt Weill.
    b. Béla Bartók.
    c. Carl Orff.
    d. Erik Satie.

92. Which of the following composers represents the twentieth-century Czech school?
    a. Bartók
    b. Bloch
    c. Janáček
    d. Kodály

93. One of the few composers of Jewish background who consciously identified himself with his heritage was:
    a. Bloch.
    b. Messiaen.
    c. Stravinsky.
    d. Scriabin.

94. Which of the following was NOT a significant influence on Vaughan Williams's compositional style?
    a. an interest in native folksong and dance
    b. an interest in twelve-tone or serial movement
    c. an interest in Elizabethan madrigals
    d. an interest in older formal structures

95. Vaughan Williams's work, *Fantasia on a Theme by Thomas Tallis*, pays tribute to a great composer of:
    a. Medieval England.
    b. Renaissance England.
    c. seventeenth-century England.
    d. none of the above.

96. On which Shakespearean play is Vaughan Williams's opera, *Sir John in Love*, based?
    a. *The Merchant of Venice*
    b. *The Tempest*
    c. *Twelfth Night*
    d. *The Merry Wives of Windsor*

Answer: d
Chronological Edition: Ch. 74, p. 455
Standard Edition: Ch. 74, p. 455
Date used:

Answer: b
Chronological Edition: Ch. 74, p. 455f
Standard Edition: Ch. 74, p. 455f
Date used:

Answer: a
Chronological Edition: Ch. 74, p. 458
Standard Edition: Ch. 74, p. 458
*Shorter Edition: Ch. 59, p. 288f
Date used:

Answer: a
Chronological Edition: Ch. 74, p. 458
Standard Edition: Ch. 74, p. 458
*Shorter Edition: Ch. 59, p. 289
Date used:

Answer: c
Chronological Edition: Ch. 74, p. 458f
Standard Edition: Ch. 74, p. 458f
*Shorter Edition: Ch. 59, p. 288f
Date used:

Answer: d
Chronological Edition: Ch. 74, p. 460
Standard Edition: Ch. 74, p. 460
*Shorter Edition: Ch. 59, p. 289
Date used:

Answer: b
Chronological Edition: Ch. 74, p. 461
Standard Edition: Ch. 74, p. 462
*Shorter Edition: Ch. 59, p. 290
Date used:

97. What element was NOT identified by Prokofiev as basic to his style?
   a. Classical roots
   b. lyricism
   c. innovation
   d. counterpoint

98. Which is NOT true of Prokofiev's *Alexander Nevsky*?
   a. It was originally written as a film score.
   b. It deals with the tension mounting in pre-World War II Europe.
   c. It is nationalistic in its subject matter.
   d. It was arranged by the composer as a cantata for chorus, orchestra, and soloist.

99. The Hungarian composer who combined native folk music characteristics with main currents of European music was:
   a. Bartók.
   b. Bloch.
   c. Sibelius.
   d. Albéniz.

100. Béla Bartók traveled around Hungary collecting peasant songs with the composer:
   a. Kodály.
   b. Janáček.
   c. Sibelius.
   d. Satie.

101. The model for Bartók's melodies can be found in:
   a. Wagnerian operas.
   b. the works of Beethoven.
   c. Hungarian folk songs.
   d. Elizabethan dances.

102. Which is NOT a characteristic of Bartók's music?
   a. polytonality
   b. primitive rhythms
   c. traditional forms
   d. major-minor tonality

103. One of Bartók's most popular works is his *Music for Strings, Percussion and* _____.
   a. Cello
   b. Celesta
   c. Clavichord
   d. Clarinet

Answer: d
Chronological Edition: Ch. 74, p. 462
Standard Edition: Ch. 74, p. 462
*Shorter Edition: Ch. 59, p. 290f
Date used:

Answer: c
Chronological Edition: Ch. 75, p. 463
Standard Edition: Ch. 75, p. 463
*Shorter Edition: Ch. 60, p. 294
Date used:

Answer: b
Chronological Edition: Ch. 75, p. 464
Standard Edition: Ch. 75, p. 464
*Shorter Edition: Ch. 60, p. 294
Date used:

Answer: b
Chronological Edition: Ch. 75, p. 464
Standard Edition: Ch. 75, p. 464
*Shorter Edition: Ch. 60, p. 294
Date used:

Answer: d
Chronological Edition: Ch. 75, p. 464
Standard Edition: Ch. 75, p. 465
*Shorter Edition: Ch. 60, p. 294
Date used:

Answer: b
Chronological Edition: Ch. 75, p. 465
Standard Edition: Ch. 75, p. 465
*Shorter Edition: Ch. 60, p. 294
Date used:

Answer: c
Chronological Edition: Ch. 75, p. 465
Standard Edition: Ch. 75, p. 465
*Shorter Edition: Ch. 60, p. 294
Date used:

104. The fourth movement of Bartók's *Music for Strings, Percussion and Celesta* is best described as:
a. a fugue.
b. a sonata form.
c. a nocturne.
d. a rondo.

105. Early American music was dominated by the music of what country?
a. France
b. Germany
c. England
d. Spain

106. Which nineteenth-century American composer is best remembered for his popular songs?
a. William Billings
b. Stephen Foster
c. Charles Griffes
d. Charles Ives

107. Which early American composer is known for his hymns, anthems, and fuging tunes?
a. Stephen Foster
b. William Billings
c. Louis Gottschalk
d. Charles Griffes

108. Music and musicians from what country dominated the American concert hall in the mid-nineteenth century?
a. England
b. France
c. Italy
d. Germany

109. A nineteenth-century American composer who incorporated features of the Afro-American musical idiom into his music was:
a. Stephen Foster.
b. Louis Gottschalk.
c. Charles Griffes.
d. Charles Ives.

110. A nineteenth-century American composer who was influenced by the French Impressionists was:
a. Stephen Foster.
b. Louis Gottschalk.
c. Charles Griffes.
d. William Billings.

Answer: c
Chronological Edition: Ch. 75, p. 466
Standard Edition: Ch. 75, p. 466
Date used:

111. While composing in his spare time, Charles Ives made his living as:
    a. a church organist.
    b. a conductor.
    c. an insurance executive.
    d. a college professor.

Answer: c
Chronological Edition: Ch. 75, p. 466f
Standard Edition: Ch. 75, p. 466f
Date used:

112. Which of the following statements about Charles Ives is INCORRECT?
    a. He was born in New England.
    b. He was the head of a large insurance company.
    c. His music was very popular.
    d. He rarely heard his music performed.

Answer: d
Chronological Edition: Ch. 75, p. 466f
Standard Edition: Ch. 75, p. 466f
*Shorter Edition: Ch. 60, p. 294f
Date used:

113. The first major prophet of American art music was:
    a. Stephen Foster.
    b. Louis Gottschalk.
    c. Charles Griffes.
    d. Charles Ives.

Answer: b
Chronological Edition: Ch. 75, p. 467
Standard Edition: Ch. 75, p. 467
Date used:

114. For which work was Ives given a Pulitzer Prize?
    a. *Concord Sonata*
    b. Symphony No. 3
    c. *Three Places in New England*
    d. Symphony No. 2

Answer: d
Chronological Edition: Ch. 75, p. 467f
Standard Edition: Ch. 75, p. 467f
*Shorter Edition: Ch. 60, p. 295
Date used:

115. What does NOT characterize the music of Ives?
    a. polyrhythms
    b. dissonant cluster chords
    c. use of American tunes
    d. consistent use of traditional forms

Answer: c
Chronological Edition: Ch. 75, p. 469
Standard Edition: Ch. 75, p. 469
Date used:

116. How many movements does Ives's Symphony No. 2 have?
    a. three
    b. four
    c. five
    d. six

Answer: d
Chronological Edition: Ch. 75, p. 469
Standard Edition: Ch. 75, p. 469
Date used:

117. Which is NOT an American tune quoted in Ives's Symphony No. 2?
    a. *Camptown Races*
    b. *Columbia, the Gem of the Ocean*
    c. *Long, Long Ago*
    d. *The Stars and Stripes Forever*

Answer: b
Chronological Edition: Ch. 75, p. 471
Standard Edition: Ch. 75, p. 471
*Shorter Edition: Ch. 60, p. 296
Date used:

118. With whom did Copland study composition?
    a. Charles Ives
    b. Nadia Boulanger
    c. Arnold Schoenberg
    d. Charles Griffes

Answer: a
Chronological Edition: Ch. 75, p. 471f
Standard Edition: Ch. 75, p. 471f
*Shorter Edition: Ch. 60, p. 296f
Date used:

Answer: b
Chronological Edition: Ch. 75, p. 472
Standard Edition: Ch. 75, p. 472
*Shorter Edition: Ch. 60, p. 296f
Date used:

Answer: b
Chronological Edition: Ch. 75, p. 472
Standard Edition: Ch. 75, p. 472
*Shorter Edition: Ch. 60, p. 297
Date used:

Answer: d
Chronological Edition: Ch. 75, p. 473
Standard Edition: Ch. 75, p. 473
*Shorter Edition: Ch. 60, p. 297
Date used:

Answer: a
Chronological Edition: Ch. 76, p. 474
Standard Edition: Ch. 76, p. 474
*Shorter Edition: Ch. 61, p. 299
Date used:

Answer: b
Chronological Edition: Ch. 76, p. 474
Standard Edition: Ch. 76, p. 474
*Shorter Edition: Ch. 61, p. 299
Date used:

Answer: c
Chronological Edition: Ch. 76, p. 475
Standard Edition: Ch. 76, p. 475
*Shorter Edition: Ch. 61, p. 299
Date used:

119. Which of the following is NOT a ballet by Copland?
   a. *Treemonisha*
   b. *Rodeo*
   c. *Appalachian Spring*
   d. *Billy the Kid*

120. Which American composer wrote ballets on American themes, such as *Billy the Kid* and *Rodeo*?
   a. Leonard Bernstein
   b. Aaron Copland
   c. Charles Ives
   d. George Gershwin

121. What famous choreographer gave Copland the inspiration for *Rodeo*?
   a. Serge Diaghilev
   b. Agnes de Mille
   c. Nadia Boulanger
   d. Nijinsky

122. The last dance episode from Copland's ballet *Rodeo* is:
   a. "Buckaroo Holiday."
   b. "Corral Nocturne."
   c. "Saturday Night Waltz."
   d. "Hoe-Down."

123. Who is the popular late nineteenth/early twentieth-century American composer of marches?
   a. Sousa
   b. Joplin
   c. Strauss
   d. Armstrong

124. What American composer is known as the "King of Ragtime"?
   a. Sousa
   b. Joplin
   c. Strauss
   d. Armstrong

125. What is the principal musical characteristic of ragtime?
   a. imitation
   b. improvisation
   c. syncopation
   d. use of American tunes

Answer: c
Chronological Edition: Ch. 76, p. 475
Standard Edition: Ch. 76, p. 475
Date used:

Answer: b
Chronological Edition: Ch. 76, p. 475
Standard Edition: Ch. 76, p. 475
Date used:

Answer: a
Chronological Edition: Ch. 76, p. 476
Standard Edition: Ch. 76, p. 476
Date used:

Answer: d
Chronological Edition: Ch. 76, p. 476
Standard Edition: Ch. 76, p. 476
*Shorter Edition: Ch. 61, p. 299
Date used:

Answer: b
Chronological Edition: Ch. 76, p. 477
Standard Edition: Ch. 76, p. 477
*Shorter Edition: Ch. 61, p. 300
Date used:

Answer: a
Chronological Edition: Ch. 76, p. 477
Standard Edition: Ch. 76, p. 477
*Shorter Edition: Ch. 61, p. 299f
Date used:

Answer: c
Chronological Edition: Ch. 76, p. 477
Standard Edition: Ch. 76, p. 477
*Shorter Edition: Ch. 61, p. 300
Date used:

126. Joplin's piano rags gained popularity when they were used in the soundtrack for the famous 1973 film, _____.
    a. *The Entertainer*
    b. *Paper Moon*
    c. *The Sting*
    d. A *Touch of Class*

127. What does NOT characterize the rags of Joplin?
    a. classical forms
    b. irregular phrasing
    c. catchy tunes
    d. clear key structure

128. Which is NOT true of Joplin's opera, *Treemonisha*?
    a. It was an immediate success in the theater.
    b. It was awarded the Pulitzer Prize.
    c. It is a story about black Americans.
    d. It incorporated elements of ragtime.

129. Which composer tried to merge ragtime with classical styles?
    a. Joplin
    b. Stravinsky
    c. Debussy
    d. all of them

130. Which best describes the form of a blues text?
    a. A–B–A
    b. A–A–B
    c. A–B–C
    d. none of these

131. Which does NOT characterize blues?
    a. It is a form of African folk music.
    b. It has a three-line text stanza, the first two of which are identical.
    c. The harmonic progression is usually twelve or sixteen measures long.
    d. It uses a "blue" note, a slight drop of pitch on certain pitches.

132. What American city could be considered the birthplace of jazz?
    a. New York
    b. Chicago
    c. New Orleans
    d. Los Angeles

Answer: c
Chronological Edition: Ch. 76, p. 477f
Standard Edition: Ch. 76, p. 477f
*Shorter Edition: Ch. 61, p. 300f
Date used:

Answer: d
Chronological Edition: Ch. 76, p. 477
Standard Edition: Ch. 76, p. 477
*Shorter Edition: Ch. 61, p. 300
Date used:

Answer: c
Chronological Edition: Ch. 76, p. 477
Standard Edition: Ch. 76, p. 477
*Shorter Edition: Ch. 61, p. 300
Date used:

Answer: c
Chronological Edition: Ch. 76, p. 477
Standard Edition: Ch. 76, p. 477
*Shorter Edition: Ch. 61, p. 300
Date used:

Answer: a
Chronological Edition: Ch. 76, p. 478
Standard Edition: Ch. 76, p. 478
*Shorter Edition: Ch. 61, p. 300
Date used:

Answer: b
Chronological Edition: Ch. 76, p. 478
Standard Edition: Ch. 76, p. 478
*Shorter Edition: Ch. 61, p. 300
Date used:

Answer: c
Chronological Edition: Ch. 76, p. 478
Standard Edition: Ch. 76, p. 478
*Shorter Edition: Ch. 61, p. 301
Date used:

Answer: b
Chronological Edition: Ch. 76, p. 478f
Standard Edition: Ch. 76, p. 478f
*Shorter Edition: Ch. 61, p. 301
Date used:

133. In New Orleans jazz, which instrument usually played the melody?
    a. trombone
    b. clarinet
    c. cornet
    d. piano

134. What is a bent or "blue" note?
    a. a note that is not heard
    b. a note that is sustained
    c. a note in which the pitch rises slightly
    d. a note in which the pitch drops slightly

135. Which is NOT true of New Orleans jazz?
    a. It combines elements of ragtime and blues.
    b. Improvisation is a basic element.
    c. There were no set forms or progressions.
    d. Its texture was largely polyphonic, each instrument having its own part.

136. Bessie Smith was a noted:
    a. ragtime composer.
    b. jazz pianist.
    c. blues singer.
    d. big-band leader.

137. Which instrument did Louis Armstrong play?
    a. trumpet
    b. trombone
    c. clarinet
    d. piano

138. Louis Armstrong was also known as:
    a. "Jelly Roll."
    b. "Satchmo."
    c. "King."
    d. "Hot Lips."

139. A jazz style of singing that sets nonsense syllables to an improvised vocal line is known as:
    a. Singspiel.
    b. Sprechstimme.
    c. scat singing.
    d. holler.

140. Which was NOT an innovation introduced to jazz by Louis Armstrong?
    a. stop-time choruses
    b. three-line blues texts
    c. solo choruses
    d. double time choruses

Answer: a
Chronological Edition: Ch. 76, p. 479
Standard Edition: Ch. 76, p. 479
*Shorter Edition: Ch. 61, p. 301
Date used:

Answer: a
Chronological Edition: Ch. 76, p. 479
Standard Edition: Ch. 76, p. 479
*Shorter Edition: Ch. 61, p. 302
Date used:

Answer: d
Chronological Edition: Ch. 76, p. 479
Standard Edition: Ch. 76, p. 479
*Shorter Edition: Ch. 61, p. 302
Date used:

Answer: b
Chronological Edition: Ch. 76, p. 479
Standard Edition: Ch. 76, p. 479
*Shorter Edition: Ch. 61, p. 302
Date used:

Answer: d
Chronological Edition: Ch. 76, p. 481
Standard Edition: Ch. 76, p. 481
*Shorter Edition: Ch. 61, p. 302
Date used:

Answer: c
Chronological Edition: Ch. 76, p. 481
Standard Edition: Ch. 76, p. 481
*Shorter Edition: Ch. 61, p. 302
Date used:

Answer: c
Chronological Edition: Ch. 76, p. 481
Standard Edition: Ch. 76, p. 481
*Shorter Edition: Ch. 61, p. 302
Date used:

Answer: b
Chronological Edition: Ch. 76, p. 481
Standard Edition: Ch. 76, p. 481
*Shorter Edition: Ch. 61, p. 304
Date used:

141. Armstrong's *West End Blues* is based on:
    a. a twelve-bar blues form.
    b. a sixteen-bar blues form.
    c. a thirty-two bar song form.
    d. a free form.

142. What kind of jazz is "Duke" Ellington known for?
    a. big band
    b. New Orleans
    c. bebop
    d. third stream

143. Which American jazz composer was also a pianist and a master of orchestration for big bands?
    a. Louis Armstrong
    b. Earl "Fatha" Hines
    c. "Jelly Roll" Morton
    d. "Duke" Ellington

144. Which is NOT true of Ellington's *Ko-Ko*?
    a. It is a twelve-bar blues.
    b. It is in a major key.
    c. It was inspired by African drum ceremonies.
    d. It was written for big band.

145. What was the trademark of bebop?
    a. a twelve-bar progression
    b. use of minor keys
    c. dissonant counterpoint
    d. a two-note phrase

146. Who was NOT a contributor to the 1940's style known as bebop?
    a. Dizzie Gillespie
    b. Charlie Parker
    c. Louis Armstrong
    d. Thelonius Monk

147. A combination of jazz and classical idioms is called:
    a. bebop.
    b. cool jazz.
    c. third stream.
    d. musique concrète

148. Who was the creator of the Modern Jazz Quartet?
    a. Duke Ellington
    b. John Lewis
    c. Louis Armstrong
    d. Dizzie Gillespie

Answer: c
Chronological Edition: Ch. 76, p. 481
Standard Edition: Ch. 76, p. 481
*Shorter Edition: Ch. 61, p. 304
Date used:

Answer: d
Chronological Edition: Ch. 76, p. 481
Standard Edition: Ch. 76, p. 481
*Shorter Edition: Ch. 61, p. 304
Date used:

Answer: b
Chronological Edition: Ch. 76, p. 481
Standard Edition: Ch. 76, p. 481
*Shorter Edition: Ch. 61, p. 304
Date used:

Answer: d
Chronological Edition: Ch. 76, p. 482
Standard Edition: Ch. 76, p. 482
*Shorter Edition: Ch. 61, p. 304
Date used:

Answer: c
Chronological Edition: Ch. 76, p. 482
Standard Edition: Ch. 76, p. 482
*Shorter Edition: Ch. 61, p. 304
Date used:

Answer: b
Chronological Edition: Ch. 76, p. 482
Standard Edition: Ch. 76, p. 482
*Shorter Edition: Ch. 61, p. 304
Date used:

Answer: a
Chronological Edition: Ch. 76, p. 483
Standard Edition: Ch. 76, p. 483
*Shorter Edition: Ch. 61, p. 304
Date used:

149. The instrumentation of the Modern Jazz Quartet is:
a. piano, clarinet, trumpet, drums.
b. piano, trombone, string bass, drums.
c. piano, vibraphone, string bass, drums.
d. piano, saxophone, trumpet, drums.

150. John Lewis's piece, *Sketch*, is best described as:
a. ragtime.
b. blues.
c. big-band jazz.
d. third stream jazz.

151. Lewis's work, *Sketch*, combines the Modern Jazz Quartet with:
a. an orchestra.
b. a string quartet.
c. a big band.
d. a solo vocalist.

152. Which composer did not employ jazz elements in his works?
a. Stravinsky
b. Weill
c. Milhaud
d. Webern

153. What is considered to be America's unique contribution to world theater?
a. the operetta
b. the pantomime
c. the musical
d. the ballad opera

154. Which of the following was NOT a composer of American musicals?
a. Sigmund Romberg
b. Jacques Offenbach
c. Victor Herbert
d. Jerome Kern

155. What American folk opera by George Gershwin was far ahead of its time?
a. *Porgy and Bess*
b. *My Fair Lady*
c. *Show Boat*
d. *Guys and Dolls*

Answer: d
Chronological Edition: Ch. 76, p. 483
Standard Edition: Ch. 76, p. 483
Date used:

156. Which of the following musicals was NOT based on an already existing book or play?
a. *My Fair Lady*
b. *Show Boat*
c. *Kiss Me, Kate*
d. *Sunday in the Park with George*

Answer: a
Chronological Edition: Ch. 76, p. 483
Standard Edition: Ch. 76, p. 483
Date used:

157. Which of the following musicals was NOT a collaboration of Rodgers and Hammerstein?
a. *Phantom of the Opera*
b. *Oklahoma*
c. *Carousel*
d. *South Pacific*

Answer: c
Chronological Edition: Ch. 76, p. 483
Standard Edition: Ch. 76, p. 483
*Shorter Edition: Ch. 61, p. 305
Date used:

158. Which of the following is an example of a rock musical?
a. *Sweeney Todd*
b. *Evita*
c. *Hair*
d. *Sunday in the Park with George*

Answer: a
Chronological Edition: Ch. 76, p. 483
Standard Edition: Ch. 76, p. 483
*Shorter Edition: Ch. 61, p. 305
Date used:

159. Which of the following is an established, living American composer of musicals?
a. Stephen Sondheim
b. Andrew Lloyd Webber
c. Jerome Kern
d. Richard Rodgers

Answer: b
Chronological Edition: Ch. 76, p. 483
Standard Edition: Ch. 76, p. 483
*Shorter Edition: Ch. 61, p. 305
Date used:

160. Which of the following is NOT a musical by the British composer Andrew Lloyd Webber?
a. *Evita*
b. *Les Misérables*
c. *Cats*
d. *The Phantom of the Opera*

Answer: c
Chronological Edition: Ch. 76, p. 485
Standard Edition: Ch. 76, p. 485
*Shorter Edition: Ch. 61, p. 305
Date used:

161. Who wrote the book and lyrics for *West Side Story*?
a. Leonard Bernstein
b. Oscar Hammerstein
c. Stephen Sondheim
d. Andrew Lloyd Webber

Answer: d
Chronological Edition: Ch. 76, p. 485
Standard Edition: Ch. 76, p. 485
*Shorter Edition: Ch. 61, p. 305
Date used:

162. *West Side Story* is a modern-day musical setting of Shakespeare's _____.
a. *Twelfth Night*
b. *The Merchant of Venice*
c. *Macbeth*
d. *Romeo and Juliet*

Answer: c
Chronological Edition: Ch. 76, p. 485
Standard Edition: Ch. 76, p. 485
*Shorter Edition: Ch. 61, p. 306
Date used:

163. Bernstein's *West Side Story* updates the feud of the Capulets and the Montagues to that between:
    a. Tony and Maria.
    b. the Jets and the police.
    c. the Jets and the Sharks.
    d. the blacks and the Puerto Ricans.

Answer: c
Chronological Edition: Ch. 76, p. 485
Standard Edition: Ch. 76, p. 485
*Shorter Edition: Ch. 61, p. 306f
Date used:

164. Which is NOT true of Bernstein's *West Side Story*?
    a. It incorporates jazz and Latin American rhythms.
    b. It has a number of elaborate dance segments.
    c. It has a happy ending.
    d. It has memorable songs that recur in the musical.

Answer: c
Chronological Edition: Ch. 77, p. 488
Standard Edition: Ch. 77, p. 488
Date used:

165. The pre-World War I Italian movement that aspired to the "art of Noises," foreshadowing the development of electronic music, was:
    a. Dadaism.
    b. Serialism.
    c. Futurism.
    d. Surrealism.

Answer: a
Chronological Edition: Ch. 77, p. 489
Standard Edition: Ch. 77, p. 489
*Shorter Edition: Ch. 62, p. 310
Date used:

166. Which artistic trend, represented by the painter Salvador Dali, exploited the world of dreams?
    a. Surrealism
    b. Cubism
    c. Dadaism
    d. Futurism

Answer: c
Chronological Edition: Ch. 77, p. 490f
Standard Edition: Ch. 77, p. 490f
*Shorter Edition: Ch. 62, p. 311
Date used:

167. Andy Warhol's style of art is best described as:
    a. Cubism.
    b. Abstract Expressionism.
    c. Pop Art.
    d. Surrealism.

Answer: b
Chronological Edition: Ch. 77, p. 491
Standard Edition: Ch. 77, p. 491
Date used:

168. Early attempts at indeterminacy in music are credited to:
    a. Milton Babbitt.
    b. John Cage.
    c. Ruth Crawford.
    d. Pierre Boulez.

Answer: c
Chronological Edition: Ch. 77, p. 492
Standard Edition: Ch. 77, p. 492
Date used:

169. With which avant-garde choreographer did composer John Cage collaborate?
    a. George Balanchine
    b. Martha Graham
    c. Merce Cunningham
    d. Bob Fosse

Answer: b
Chronological Edition: Ch. 77, p. 493
Standard Edition: Ch. 77, p. 493
*Shorter Edition: Ch. 62, p. 312
Date used:

Answer: c
Chronological Edition: Ch. 77, p. 494
Standard Edition: Ch. 77, p. 494
*Shorter Edition: Ch. 62, p. 312f
Date used:

Answer: d
Chronological Edition: Ch. 77, p. 494f
Standard Edition: Ch. 77, p. 494f
*Shorter Edition: Ch. 62, p. 313f
Date used:

Answer: a
Chronological Edition: Ch. 77, p. 494
Standard Edition: Ch. 77, p. 494
*Shorter Edition: Ch. 62, p. 313f
Date used:

Answer: b
Chronological Edition: Ch. 77, p. 495
Standard Edition: Ch. 77, p. 495
*Shorter Edition: Ch. 62, p. 314
Date used:

Answer: b
Chronological Edition: Ch. 77, p. 495
Standard Edition: Ch. 77, p. 495
*Shorter Edition: Ch. 62, p. 315
Date used:

Answer: b
Chronological Edition: Ch. 77, p. 495f
Standard Edition: Ch. 77, p. 495f
*Shorter Edition: Ch. 62, p. 315f
Date used:

170. The recent artistic trend in cinema toward experiment and abstraction is called:
a. Pop Art.
b. New Wave.
c. Theater of the Absurd.
d. Futurism.

171. In the 1950's, serial form in music:
a. was extinct.
b. was diluted.
c. was applied to other elements.
d. continued as before.

172. Which best describes a piece of aleatoric music?
a. It is strictly organized.
b. It is based on the twelve-tone method.
c. It is computer-generated.
d. It is recreated fresh each time it is performed.

173. A compositional style in which some details are left to chance or the performer's choice is known as:
a. aleatoric music.
b. total serialism.
c. closed form.
d. collage.

174. A technique, used by Lucas Foss, in which composers incorporate music from the past in their compositions is called:
a. open form.
b. collage.
c. total serialism.
d. microtonal.

175. A dominant contemporary figure in French music and a former music director of the New York Philharmonic is:
a. John Cage.
b. Pierre Boulez.
c. Jacques Ibert.
d. Milton Babbitt.

176. Which is NOT a major European composer of avant-garde music?
a. Boulez
b. Babbitt
c. Berio
d. Penderecki

Answer: a
Chronological Edition: Ch. 77, p. 496
Standard Edition: Ch. 77, p. 496
*Shorter Edition: Ch. 62, p. 315
Date used:

177. The foremost composer of late twentieth-century Poland is:
a. Penderecki.
b. Berio.
c. Shostakovich.
d. Xenakis.

Answer: c
Chronological Edition: Ch. 77, p. 496f
Standard Edition: Ch. 77, p. 496f
*Shorter Edition: Ch. 63, p. 319
Date used:

178. Intervals smaller than semitones are called:
a. blue notes.
b. diminished tones.
c. microtones.
d. aleatoric.

Answer: b
Chronological Edition: Ch. 77, p. 498
Standard Edition: Ch. 77, p. 498
*Shorter Edition: Ch. 62, p. 317
Date used:

179. Which woman composer was an active member of *Les Six*, studied at the Paris Conservatory, and became a leader in the modern movement in France?
a. Nadia Boulanger
b. Germaine Tailleferre
c. Ruth Crawford
d. Ellen Taafe Zwilich

Answer: a
Chronological Edition: Ch. 77, p. 498
Standard Edition: Ch. 77, p. 498
*Shorter Edition: Ch. 62, p. 317
Date used:

180. Which of the following women was a noted French composition teacher whose pupils included Copland, Musgrave, Carter and Glass?
a. Nadia Boulanger
b. Germaine Tailleferre
c. Ruth Crawford
d. Ellen Taafe Zwilich

Answer: a
Chronological Edition: Ch. 77, p. 498
Standard Edition: Ch. 77, p. 498
Date used:

181. Which twentieth-century woman composer became interested in folksongs through the music of her stepson, Pete Seeger?
a. Ruth Crawford
b. Louise Talma
c. Miriam Gideon
d. Joan Tower

Answer: d
Chronological Edition: Ch. 77, p. 498
Standard Edition: Ch. 77, p. 498
*Shorter Edition: Ch. 62, p. 317
Date used:

182. Which of the following women, the first recipient of a Guggenheim fellowship to study composition in Europe, made her reputation among the avant-garde composers of the 1920's?
a. Ellen Taafe Zwilich
b. Louise Talma
c. Nadia Boulanger
d. Ruth Crawford

Answer: c
Chronological Edition: Ch. 77, p. 498
Standard Edition: Ch. 77, p. 498
*Shorter Edition: Ch. 62, p. 317
Date used:

Answer: c
Chronological Edition: Ch. 78, p. 501
Standard Edition: Ch. 78, p. 501
*Shorter Edition: Ch. 63, p. 319
Date used:

Answer: c
Chronological Edition: Ch. 78, p. 501
Standard Edition: Ch. 78, p. 501
*Shorter Edition: Ch. 63, p. 319
Date used:

Answer: a
Chronological Edition: Ch. 78, p. 501
Standard Edition: Ch. 78, p. 501
*Shorter Edition: Ch. 63, p. 319
Date used:

Answer: b
Chronological Edition: Ch. 78, p. 501
Standard Edition: Ch. 78, p. 501
*Shorter Edition: Ch. 63, p. 319
Date used:

Answer: c
Chronological Edition: Ch. 78, p. 501
Standard Edition: Ch. 78, p. 501
*Shorter Edition: Ch. 63, p. 319
Date used:

Answer: d
Chronological Edition: Ch. 78, p. 501f
Standard Edition: Ch. 78, p. 501f
*Shorter Edition: Ch. 63, p. 318f
Date used:

183. The first woman composer to be awarded a Pulitzer Prize was:
    a. Joan Tower.
    b. Louise Talma.
    c. Ellen Taafe Zwilich.
    d. Ruth Crawford.

184. Music that exists in oral tradition is:
    a. always sung.
    b. spoken rather than sung.
    c. transmitted orally from one generation to another and never written down.
    d. written down, but rarely performed.

185. How is the music of most cultures transmitted?
    a. written notation
    b. improvisation
    c. oral tradition
    d. recordings

186. A three-note scale pattern, found in some South African cultures, is called:
    a. tritonic.
    b. pentatonic.
    c. heptatonic.
    d. microtonal.

187. A five-note scale used in some African and Far Eastern music is called:
    a. tritonic.
    b. pentatonic.
    c. heptatonic.
    d. microtonal.

188. A seven-note scale fashioned from a different combination of intervals than major and minor scales is called:
    a. tritonic.
    b. pentatonic.
    c. heptatonic.
    d. microtonal.

189. How does non-Western music differ from Western music?
    a. Much of it lacks a sophisticated harmonic system.
    b. Rhythm is generally more complex.
    c. Melodies are based on scales other than just major and minor.
    d. All of these.

Answer: a
Chronological Edition: Ch. 78, p. 502f
Standard Edition: Ch. 78, p. 502f
*Shorter Edition: Ch. 63, p. 321
Date used:

190. The accompaniment of one or several repeated notes for harmonic support is called:
   a. drone.
   b. tala.
   c. microtones.
   d. pentatonic.

Answer: a
Chronological Edition: Ch. 78, p. 503
Standard Edition: Ch. 78, p. 503
*Shorter Edition: Ch. 63, p. 321
Date used:

191. Another name for call-and-response type of singing is called:
   a. responsorial.
   b. ostinato.
   c. antecedent-consequent.
   d. antiphonal.

Answer: a
Chronological Edition: Ch. 78, p. 503
Standard Edition: Ch. 78, p. 503
*Shorter Edition: Ch. 63, p. 321
Date used:

192. Instruments that produce sound by using air as the primary vibrating means are called:
   a. aerophones.
   b. chordophones.
   c. idiophones.
   d. membranophones.

Answer: b
Chronological Edition: Ch. 78, p. 503
Standard Edition: Ch. 78, p. 503
*Shorter Edition: Ch. 63, p. 321
Date used:

193. Instruments that produce sound from a vibrating string stretched between two points are called:
   a. aerophones.
   b. chordophones.
   c. idiophones.
   d. membranophones.

Answer: c
Chronological Edition: Ch. 78, p. 503
Standard Edition: Ch. 78, p. 503
*Shorter Edition: Ch. 63, p. 321
Date used:

194. Instruments that produce sound from the substance of the instrument itself are called:
   a. aerophones.
   b. chordophones.
   c. idiophones.
   d. membranophones.

Answer: d
Chronological Edition: Ch. 78, p. 503
Standard Edition: Ch. 78, p. 503
*Shorter Edition: Ch. 63, p. 321
Date used:

195. Instruments sounded from tightly stretched membranes are called:
   a. aerophones.
   b. chordophones.
   c. idiophones.
   d. membranophones.

Answer: b
Chronological Edition: Ch. 78, p. 504f
Standard Edition: Ch. 78, p. 504f
*Shorter Edition: Ch. 63, p. 321
Date used:

196. Of the following, which American composer was NOT greatly affected by the philosophy of the Far East?
   a. Cage
   b. Copland
   c. Cowell
   d. Partch

Answer: b
Chronological Edition: Ch. 78, p. 505
Standard Edition: Ch. 78, p. 505
Date used:

197. Which innovative composer evolved a scale of forty-three microtones to the octave and built instruments to play with this tuning?
   a. Aaron Copland
   b. Harry Partch
   c. Henry Cowell
   d. John Cage

Answer: a
Chronological Edition: Ch. 78, p. 505
Standard Edition: Ch. 78, p. 505
Date used:

198. The Japanese koto is a member of the _____ family of instruments.
   a. string
   b. brass
   c. woodwind
   d. percussion

Answer: c
Chronological Edition: Ch. 78, p. 504f
Standard Edition: Ch. 78, p. 504f
Date used:

199. Which composer combined Asian instruments with traditional Western ensembles and experimented with exotic scales?
   a. Aaron Copland
   b. Harry Partch
   c. Henry Cowell
   d. John Cage

Answer: a
Chronological Edition: Ch. 78, p. 505
Standard Edition: Ch. 78, p. 505
Date used:

200. With what tuning system did Harry Partch experiment?
   a. microtonal
   b. modal
   c. pentatonic
   d. whole tone

Answer: b
Chronological Edition: Ch. 78, p. 505
Standard Edition: Ch. 78, p. 505
*Shorter Edition: Ch. 63, p. 322f
Date used:

201. Who invented the prepared piano?
   a. Partch
   b. Cage
   c. Cowell
   d. Boulez

Answer: b
Chronological Edition: Ch. 78, p. 506
Standard Edition: Ch. 78, p. 506
*Shorter Edition: Ch. 63, p. 322f
Date used:

202. Which musical concept is NOT associated with John Cage?
   a. noise as music
   b. serial music
   c. chance music
   d. gamelan type ensembles

Answer: c
Chronological Edition: Ch. 78, p. 506
Standard Edition: Ch. 78, p. 506
*Shorter Edition: Ch. 63, p. 323
Date used:

203. Cage's work, *Sonatas and Interludes* evokes the sounds of:
   a. the bagpipe of Eastern Europe.
   b. the Japanese koto.
   c. the Javanese gamelan.
   d. the sitar of India.

Answer: a
Chronological Edition: Ch. 78, p. 506
Standard Edition: Ch. 78, p. 506
Date used:

Answer: a
Chronological Edition: Ch. 79, p. 508
Standard Edition: Ch. 79, p. 508
Date used:

Answer: c
Chronological Edition: Ch. 79, p. 508
Standard Edition: Ch. 79, p. 508
*Shorter Edition: Ch. 64, p. 324
Date used:

Answer: d
Chronological Edition: Ch. 79, p. 509
Standard Edition: Ch. 79, p. 509
*Shorter Edition: Ch. 64, p. 324
Date used:

Answer: b
Chronological Edition: Ch. 79, p. 509
Standard Edition: Ch. 79, p. 509
Date used:

Answer: c
Chronological Edition: Ch. 79, p. 509f
Standard Edition: Ch. 79, p. 509f
Date used:

Answer: d
Chronological Edition: Ch. 79, p. 510
Standard Edition: Ch. 79, p. 510
*Shorter Edition: Ch. 64, p. 324
Date used:

204. Which is NOT true of Cage's *Sonatas and Interludes*?
    a. They are for a traditional piano.
    b. They were inspired by the sound of the Javanese gamelan.
    c. They call for insertion of objects between the piano's string.
    d. They are a set of sixteen sonatas with four interludes interspersed.

205. A twentieth-century American composer who uses "metrical modulation," and composed Pulitzer Prize-winning string quartets is:
    a. Elliot Carter.
    b. György Ligeti.
    c. John Cage.
    d. George Crumb.

206. Carter's Eight Etudes and a Fantasy is written for:
    a. solo piano.
    b. voice and synthesizer.
    c. four woodwind instruments.
    d. string quartet.

207. The works of György Ligeti gained international fame when they were included in the soundtrack of the film:
    a. *Star Wars*.
    b. *Star Trek*.
    c. *2010*.
    d. *2001: A Space Odyssey*.

208. Micropolyphony is associated with the music of:
    a. Elliott Carter.
    b. György Ligeti.
    c. John Cage.
    d. Henry Cowell.

209. Which of the following is an example of micropolyphony?
    a. Carter: Eight Etudes and a Fantasy
    b. Crumb: *Ancient Voices of Children*
    c. Ligeti: *Atmosphères*
    d. Picker: *Old and Lost Rivers*

210. From what country does Lutosławski come?
    a. United States
    b. Germany
    c. Hungary
    d. Poland

Answer: d
Chronological Edition: Ch. 79, p. 510
Standard Edition: Ch. 79, p. 510
Date used:

211. What style has characterized the music of Lutosławski?
    a. serial
    b. traditional
    c. chance
    d. all of the above

Answer: c
Chronological Edition: Ch. 79, p. 510
Standard Edition: Ch. 79, p. 510
*Shorter Edition: Ch. 64, p. 324
Date used:

212. Lutosławski writes music in which pitches for all parts are written out, but the rhythms are improvised within given rules. He calls this technique:
    a. micropolyphony.
    b. metric modulation.
    c. aleatoric counterpoint.
    d. futuristic polyrhythms.

Answer: b
Chronological Edition: Ch. 79, p. 512
Standard Edition: Ch. 79, p. 512
*Shorter Edition: Ch. 64, p. 324f
Date used:

213. The music of George Crumb includes many settings of the poetry of:
    a. Robert Frost.
    b. Federico García Lorca.
    c. Rod McKuen.
    d. Emily Dickinson.

Answer: d
Chronological Edition: Ch. 79, p. 512
Standard Edition: Ch. 79, p. 512
*Shorter Edition: Ch. 64, p. 325
Date used:

214. What is unusual about Crumb's song cycle, *Ancient Voices of Children*?
    a. It uses electronic instruments.
    b. It simulates the human voice electronically.
    c. It is aleatoric in form.
    d. It employs non-traditional instruments and vocal techniques.

Answer: c
Chronological Edition: Ch. 80, p. 514
Standard Edition: Ch. 80, p. 514
*Shorter Edition: Ch. 64, p. 326
Date used:

215. Music made up of natural sounds that are recorded and then altered is called:
    a. overtones.
    b. synthetic music.
    c. musique concrète.
    d. electronically generated music.

Answer: b
Chronological Edition: Ch. 80, p. 515
Standard Edition: Ch. 80, p. 515
*Shorter Edition: Ch. 64, p. 326
Date used:

216. The first electronic synthesizer was:
    a. the Columbia-Princeton synthesizer.
    b. the RCA Electronic Music synthesizer.
    c. the Cologne studio synthesizer.
    d. the Moog synthesizer.

Answer: c
Chronological Edition: Ch. 80, p. 515
Standard Edition: Ch. 80, p. 515
*Shorter Edition: Ch. 64, p. 326f
Date used:

217. Which was NOT one of the stages in the development of electronic music?
    a. the use of magnetic tape recording
    b. the development of synthesizers
    c. the invention of micropolyphony
    d. the use of computers as sound generators

Answer: d
Chronological Edition: Ch. 80, p. 516
Standard Edition: Ch. 80, p. 516
*Shorter Edition: Ch. 64, p. 326
Date used:

Answer: b
Chronological Edition: Ch. 80, p. 516
Standard Edition: Ch. 80, p. 516
*Shorter Edition: Ch. 64, p. 328
Date used:

Answer: a
Chronological Edition: Ch. 80, p. 517
Standard Edition: Ch. 80, p. 517
*Shorter Edition: Ch. 64, p. 328
Date used:

Answer: d
Chronological Edition: Ch. 80, p. 517
Standard Edition: Ch. 80, p. 517
Date used:

Answer: b
Chronological Edition: Ch. 80, p. 518
Standard Edition: Ch. 80, p. 518
*Shorter Edition: Ch. 64, p. 327
Date used:

Answer: c
Chronological Edition: Ch. 80, p. 518
Standard Edition: Ch. 80, p. 518
Date used:

Answer: c
Chronological Edition: Ch. 80, p. 520
Standard Edition: Ch. 80, p. 520
Date used:

218. Electronically generated music can be heard today:
    a. in movie soundtracks.
    b. in TV commercials.
    c. in rock bands.
    d. all of the above.

219. What composer has extensively explored the combination of electronic sounds with live music?
    a. Crumb
    b. Davidovsky
    c. Stockhausen
    d. Varèse

220. When was most of Varèse's music written?
    a. 1920's–30's
    b. 1950's
    c. 1960's
    d. after 1970

221. On which family of instruments does much of Varèse's music focus?
    a. strings
    b. brass
    c. woodwinds
    d. percussion

222. Varèse composed *Poème électronique* for:
    a. the United Nations.
    b. a World's Fair.
    c. a wealthy patron.
    d. private performance.

223. Which is NOT true of Varèse's *Poème électronique*?
    a. It was written in collaboration with the French architect Le Corbusier.
    b. It was first performed in a pavilion at the Brussels World Fair.
    c. It was written for traditional instruments as well as electronic sounds.
    d. It was accompanied by projections of images.

224. At what university does Milton Babbitt teach?
    a. Yale
    b. Harvard
    c. Princeton
    d. Columbia

Answer: a
Chronological Edition: Ch. 80, p. 520
Standard Edition: Ch. 80, p. 520
Date used:

225. With what compositional system is Babbitt most closely associated?
a. serial
b. aleatory
c. electronic
d. traditional

Answer: a
Chronological Edition: Ch. 80, p. 521
Standard Edition: Ch. 80, p. 521
Date used:

226. Which is NOT true of Babbitt's *Phonemena*?
a. It sets a text by the Spanish poet Federico Garcia Lorca.
b. It is for soprano voice and electronic tape.
c. It is highly technical, requiring great vocal virtuosity.
d. Its vocal style is disjunct, with a wide range.

Answer: a
Chronological Edition: Ch. 81, p. 522
Standard Edition: Ch. 81, p. 522
*Shorter Edition: Ch. 65, p. 329f
Date used:

227. Who is NOT associated with the New Romanticism?
a. Babbitt
b. Barber
c. Rorem
d. Tredici

Answer: b
Chronological Edition: Ch. 81, p. 522
Standard Edition: Ch. 81, p. 522
*Shorter Edition: Ch. 65, p. 329
Date used:

228. Of which nationality is Thea Musgrave, the composer of *Mary, Queen of Scots*?
a. English
b. Scottish
c. American
d. French

Answer: b
Chronological Edition: Ch. 81, p. 522
Standard Edition: Ch. 81, p. 522
*Shorter Edition: Ch. 65, p. 329
Date used:

229. Musgrave's *Mary, Queen of Scots* is representative of the _____ movement.
a. Expressionist
b. New Romantic
c. Minimalist
d. Electronic

Answer: d
Chronological Edition: Ch. 81, p. 527
Standard Edition: Ch. 81, p. 527
Date used:

230. Tobias Picker began his career writing _____ music.
a. aleatoric
b. minimalist
c. electronic
d. serial

Answer: b
Chronological Edition: Ch. 81, p. 527
Standard Edition: Ch. 81, p. 527
Date used:

231. Picker's *Old and Lost Rivers* deals with:
a. a scene in Scotland.
b. a location in southern Texas.
c. a boat trip down the Mississippi River.
d. an exploration of the Nile Delta.

Answer: b
Chronological Edition: Ch. 81, p. 528
Standard Edition: Ch. 81, p. 528
*Shorter Edition: Ch. 65, p. 330
Date used:

232. Music that features the repetition, with little variation, of melodic, rhythmic, and harmonic patterns, is known as:
a. musique concrète.
b. minimalist music.
c. New Romantic music.
d. serial music.

Answer: d
Chronological Edition: Ch. 81, p. 528f
Standard Edition: Ch. 81, p. 528f
*Shorter Edition: Ch. 65, p. 330
Date used:

233. Which of the following composers is NOT a minimalist?
a. Steve Reich
b. Philip Glass
c. John Adams
d. Thea Musgrave

Answer: b
Chronological Edition: Ch. 81, p. 529
Standard Edition: Ch. 81, p. 529
*Shorter Edition: Ch. 65, p. 330
Date used:

234. Who wrote the opera *Nixon in China*?
a. Riley
b. Adams
c. Reich
d. Glass

Answer: c
Chronological Edition: Ch. 81, p. 530
Standard Edition: Ch. 81, p. 530
*Shorter Edition: Ch. 65, p. 330
Date used:

235. Adam's *Short Ride in a Fast Machine* exemplifies the current compositional trend of:
a. New Romanticism.
b. New Classicism.
c. Minimalism.
d. musique concrète.

TRUE/FALSE QUESTIONS

Answer: T
Chronological Edition: Ch. 66, p. 400
Standard Edition: Ch. 66, p. 398
Date used:

236. Mahler converted from Judaism to Catholicism because of strong anti-Semitic feelings in the Austrian empire.

Answer: T
Chronological Edition: Ch. 66, p. 401
Standard Edition: Ch. 66, p. 399
*Shorter Edition: Ch. 54, p. 262
Date used:

237. Mahler wrote nine symphonies that were completed and left his Tenth Symphony unfinished at his death.

Answer: T
Chronological Edition: Ch. 66, p. 401
Standard Edition: Ch. 66, p. 399
*Shorter Edition: Ch. 54, p. 263
Date used:

238. Mahler, like his predecessors Schubert and Schumann, cultivated the song cycle.

Answer: F
Chronological Edition: Ch. 66, p. 402
Standard Edition: Ch. 66, p. 400
Date used:

239.   Mahler's Fourth Symphony uses no forms or structural procedures from earlier eras.

Answer: T
Chronological Edition: Ch. 66, p. 403
Standard Edition: Ch. 66, p. 401
*Shorter Edition: Ch. 54, p. 264
Date used:

240.   Impressionism takes its name from a painting by Claude Monet.

Answer: T
Chronological Edition: Ch. 66, p. 403
Standard Edition: Ch. 66, p. 401
*Shorter Edition: Ch. 54, p. 264
Date used:

241.   The Impressionist artist abandoned the grandiose subjects of Romanticism.

Answer: T
Chronological Edition: Ch. 66, p. 405
Standard Edition: Ch. 66, p. 403
*Shorter Edition: Ch. 54, p. 266
Date used:

242.   The Impressionists turned to the open intervals and church modes of Medieval music for inspiration.

Answer: F
Chronological Edition: Ch. 66, p. 405
Standard Edition: Ch. 66, p. 403
*Shorter Edition: Ch. 54, p. 266
Date used:

243.   Debussy's music reflects a strong adherence to traditional forms and scales of Western music.

Answer: F
Chronological Edition: Ch. 66, p. 406
Standard Edition: Ch. 66, p. 404
*Shorter Edition: Ch. 54, p. 266f
Date used:

244.   Impressionist composers felt, even more strongly than their predecessors, the need to resolve all chords back to the tonic.

Answer: F
Chronological Edition: Ch. 66, p. 407
Standard Edition: Ch. 66, p. 405
*Shorter Edition: Ch. 54, p. 266f
Date used:

245.   Impressionist composers avoided parallel motion of chords since it was prohibited in the Classical system of harmony.

Answer: T
Chronological Edition: Ch. 66, p. 408f
Standard Edition: Ch. 66, p. 406f
*Shorter Edition: Ch. 54, p. 268
Date used:

246.   Like Berlioz, Debussy won the coveted Prix de Rome during his compositional studies at the Paris Conservatory.

Answer: T
Chronological Edition: Ch. 66, p. 411
Standard Edition: Ch. 66, p. 409
Date used:

247. Debussy was important in establishing the French art song.

Answer: F
Chronological Edition: Ch. 66, p. 412
Standard Edition: Ch. 66, p. 410
*Shorter Edition: Ch. 54, p. 270
Date used:

248. Debussy's *Prelude to "The Afternoon of a Faun"* was inspired by a poem by Maurice Maeterlinck.

Answer: T
Chronological Edition: Ch. 67, p. 414
Standard Edition: Ch. 67, p. 412
Date used:

249. Ravel's art reflects the twin goals of Impressionism and neo-Classicism.

Answer: T
Chronological Edition: Ch. 67, p. 415
Standard Edition: Ch. 67, p. 413
*Shorter Edition: Ch. 54, p. 272
Date used:

250. Ravel, like Debussy, was drawn to both images that attracted Impressionist painters and to exotic subjects as well.

Answer: F
Chronological Edition: Ch. 67, p. 416
Standard Edition: Ch. 67, p. 414
Date used:

251. A "tombeau" was a Romantic form of homage, commemorating the death of someone.

Answer: T
Chronological Edition: Ch. 67, p. 416
Standard Edition: Ch. 67, p. 415
Date used:

252. The Rigaudon from Ravel's *Le tombeau de Couperin* is only loosely based on the original court dance form.

Answer: T
Chronological Edition: Ch. 68, p. 417
Standard Edition: Ch. 68, p. 416
*Shorter Edition: Ch. 55, p. 273
Date used:

253. The early twentieth century was impelled by the desire to throw off the oppressive style of the nineteenth century, and to capture the spontaneity of primitive life.

Answer: T
Chronological Edition: Ch. 68, p. 418
Standard Edition: Ch. 68, p. 417
*Shorter Edition: Ch. 55, p. 273
Date used:

254. Expressionism in music took its impulse from painters whose canvases delved into the realm of the unconscious.

Answer: F
Chronological Edition: Ch. 68, p. 418f
Standard Edition: Ch. 68, p. 417f
*Shorter Edition: Ch. 55, p. 273
Date used:

255.   Expressionism was the German equivalent of French Impressionism, and had the same goals and artistic qualities.

Answer: T
Chronological Edition: Ch. 68, p. 419f
Standard Edition: Ch. 68, p. 418f
*Shorter Edition: Ch. 55, p. 275
Date used:

256.   Neoclassical composers preferred absolute music and forms to program music.

Answer: T
Chronological Edition: Ch. 69, p. 421
Standard Edition: Ch. 69, p. 420
*Shorter Edition: Ch. 56, p. 276
Date used:

257.   Early twentieth-century composers preferred freer rhythms, including those drawn from popular styles such as ragtime and jazz.

Answer: F
Chronological Edition: Ch. 69, p. 422
Standard Edition: Ch. 69, p. 421
*Shorter Edition: Ch. 56, p. 275
Date used:

258.   Twentieth-century composers conceived melody vocally, attempting to make the instruments "sing".

Answer: T
Chronological Edition: Ch. 69, p. 422f
Standard Edition: Ch. 69, p. 421f
*Shorter Edition: Ch. 56, p. 276
Date used:

259.   The expanded tonality of the early twentieth century broke down the distinction between diatonic and chromatic and between major and minor.

Answer: T
Chronological Edition: Ch. 69, p. 422
Standard Edition: Ch. 69, p. 421
*Shorter Edition: Ch. 56, p. 276
Date used:

260.   The so-called "skyscraper" chords used by early twentieth-century composers produced highly dissonant harmonies.

Answer: T
Chronological Edition: Ch. 69, p. 423
Standard Edition: Ch. 69, p. 422
*Shorter Edition: Ch. 56, p. 276
Date used:

261.   Atonal music moves from one level of dissonance to another without areas of relaxation.

Answer: F
Chronological Edition: Ch. 69, p. 423
Standard Edition: Ch. 69, p. 422
*Shorter Edition: Ch. 56, p. 276
Date used:

262.   The concept of atonality is usually associated with the music of Debussy and his followers.

Answer: T
Chronological Edition: Ch. 69, p. 423f
Standard Edition: Ch. 69, p. 422f
*Shorter Edition: Ch. 56, p. 277
Date used:

Answer: T
Chronological Edition: Ch. 69, p. 424
Standard Edition: Ch. 69, p. 423
*Shorter Edition: Ch. 56, p. 277
Date used:

Answer: T
Chronological Edition: Ch. 69, p. 424
Standard Edition: Ch. 69, p. 423
*Shorter Edition: Ch. 56, p. 277
Date used:

Answer: T
Chronological Edition: Ch. 69, p. 424f
Standard Edition: Ch. 69, p. 423f
*Shorter Edition: Ch. 56, p. 277
Date used:

Answer: F
Chronological Edition: Ch. 70, p. 426
Standard Edition: Ch. 70, p. 426
*Shorter Edition: Ch. 57, p. 279
Date used:

Answer: T
Chronological Edition: Ch. 70, p. 426f
Standard Edition: Ch. 70, p. 425f
*Shorter Edition: Ch. 57, p. 279
Date used:

Answer: T
Chronological Edition: Ch. 70, p. 427
Standard Edition: Ch. 70, p. 428
*Shorter Edition: Ch. 57, p. 279
Date used:

Answer: F
Chronological Edition: Ch. 70, p. 428
Standard Edition: Ch. 70, p. 428
*Shorter Edition: Ch. 57, p. 280
Date used:

263. Serial music treats all twelve chromatic tones equally.

264. Twentieth-century composers emancipated dissonance by freeing it from the obligation to resolve to consonance.

265. A tone row is an established series of pitches from which a composer builds themes, harmonies and counterpoints.

266. Early twentieth-century music emphasized a linear texture of dissonant counterpoint.

267. Stravinsky's ballets all achieved immediate popularity with their audiences.

268. The Russian composer Igor Stravinsky lived for many years in France and eventually became an American citizen.

269. Stravinsky's ballet *The Rite of Spring* had a revolutionary impact on music of the twentieth century.

270. Stravinsky's ballet *The Rite of Spring* evokes scenes of post-World War I Russia.

Answer: F
Chronological Edition: Ch. 70, p. 428
Standard Edition: Ch. 70, p. 429
*Shorter Edition: Ch. 57, p. 280f
Date used:

Answer: T
Chronological Edition: Ch. 71, p. 433
Standard Edition: Ch. 71, p. 432
*Shorter Edition: Ch. 58, p. 284
Date used:

Answer: T
Chronological Edition: Ch. 71, p. 433
Standard Edition: Ch. 71, p. 433
*Shorter Edition: Ch. 58, p. 285
Date used:

Answer: T
Chronological Edition: Ch. 71, p. 434
Standard Edition: Ch. 71, p. 434
Date used:

Answer: F
Chronological Edition: Ch. 71, p. 434
Standard Edition: Ch. 71, p. 433
*Shorter Edition: Ch. 58, p. 285f
Date used:

Answer: T
Chronological Edition: Ch. 71, p. 434
Standard Edition: Ch. 71, p. 434
*Shorter Edition: Ch. 58, p. 285f
Date used:

Answer: F
Chronological Edition: Ch. 72, p. 439
Standard Edition: Ch. 72, p. 439
Date used:

Answer: T
Chronological Edition: Ch. 72, p. 439f
Standard Edition: Ch. 72, p. 439f
Date used:

271. Stravinsky's *The Rite of Spring* is written for a small, lean orchestra with no percussion section.

272. Like Stravinsky, Schoenberg became an American citizen and spent a major portion of his creative life in the United States.

273. Schoenberg developed the new vocal style of Sprechstimme in an attempt to bring together the spoken word and music.

274. Each of the poems set in Schoenberg's *Pierrot lunaire* is in rondeau form.

275. Schoenberg's *Pierrot lunaire* is a series of miniatures for voice and orchestra.

276. In Schoenberg's *Pierrot lunaire*, the principal character is obsessed with the moon.

277. In Berg's opera, Wozzeck drowns because he was following moonbeams into the lake.

278. Berg's *Wozzeck* reflects the ideals of Expressionism through its focus on the macabre and the world of dreams.

Answer: F
Chronological Edition: Ch. 73, p. 444
Standard Edition: Ch. 73, p. 444
Date used:

Answer: F
Chronological Edition: Ch. 73, p. 445
Standard Edition: Ch. 73, p. 445
Date used:

Answer: T
Chronological Edition: Ch. 73, p. 446
Standard Edition: Ch. 73, p. 446
Date used:

Answer: T
Chronological Edition: Ch. 73, p. 446
Standard Edition: Ch. 73, p. 446
Date used:

Answer: T
Chronological Edition: Ch. 73, p. 447f
Standard Edition: Ch. 73, p. 447f
Date used:

Answer: T
Chronological Edition: Ch. 74, p. 450
Standard Edition: Ch. 74, p. 450
*Shorter Edition: Ch. 59, p. 292
Date used:

Answer: F
Chronological Edition: Ch. 74, p. 452
Standard Edition: Ch. 74, p. 452
Date used:

Answer: T
Chronological Edition: Ch. 74, p. 453
Standard Edition: Ch. 74, p. 453
Date used:

279. Under the Nazi regime, Webern's music was fostered and promoted.

280. As two leading serial composers, the music of Berg and Webern sound very similar.

281. Webern's Symphony, Opus 21 abounds in contrapuntal procedures.

282. Webern's Symphony, Opus 21 combines serial technique with traditional forms.

283. Messiaen's compositions reflect his interest in non-Western music and instruments.

284. Rachmaninoff, Prokofiev, and Shostakovich were all prominent composers in the twentieth-century Russian school.

285. Vaughan Williams believed in art for art's sake.

286. Vaughan Williams's *Fantasia on "Greensleeves"* is in A–B–A, or ternary form.

Answer: T
Chronological Edition: Ch. 74, p. 453
Standard Edition: Ch. 74, p. 453
Date used:

287. Vaughan Williams's *Fantasia on "Greensleeves"* makes use of two English folk songs.

Answer: T
Chronological Edition: Ch. 74, p. 455
Standard Edition: Ch. 74, p. 455
Date used:

288. Prokofiev's *Alexander Nevsky* was originally written as film music.

Answer: F
Chronological Edition: Ch. 74, p. 455
Standard Edition: Ch. 74, p. 455
Date used:

289. Prokofiev wrote *War and Peace* as a soundtrack to accompany the film based on Tolstoy's book.

Answer: T
Chronological Edition: Ch. 74, p. 454
Standard Edition: Ch. 74, p. 454
Date used:

290. Prokofiev's music was banned by the Communist party in 1948, who accused him of following non-Soviet trends in the arts.

Answer: T
Chronological Edition: Ch. 74, p. 455
Standard Edition: Ch. 74, p. 455
Date used:

291. Prokofiev's music can be viewed as having neoclassical elements.

Answer: T
Chronological Edition: Ch. 74, p. 460
Standard Edition: Ch. 74, p. 460
*Shorter Edition: Ch. 59, p. 289
Date used:

292. Bartók found authentic Hungarian folk music to be based on ancient modes, unfamiliar scales, and nonsymmetrical rhythms.

Answer: T
Chronological Edition: Ch. 74, p. 461
Standard Edition: Ch. 74, p. 461
*Shorter Edition: Ch. 59, p. 290
Date used:

293. Bartók wrote six string quartets that rank among the finest achievements of twentieth-century chamber music.

Answer: F
Chronological Edition: Ch. 74, p. 461
Standard Edition: Ch. 74, p. 461
*Shorter Edition: Ch. 59, p. 289
Date used:

294. Bartók generally avoided Classical structures.

Answer: T
Chronological Edition: Ch. 74, p. 461
Standard Edition: Ch. 74, p. 461
Date used:

Answer: T
Chronological Edition: Ch. 74, p. 462
Standard Edition: Ch. 74, p. 462
*Shorter Edition: Ch. 59, p. 290f
Date used:

Answer: T
Chronological Edition: Ch. 75, p. 463
Standard Edition: Ch. 75, p. 463
*Shorter Edition: Ch. 60, p. 294
Date used:

Answer: F
Chronological Edition: Ch. 75, p. 464
Standard Edition: Ch. 75, p. 464
Date used:

Answer: T
Chronological Edition: Ch. 75, p. 464
Standard Edition: Ch. 75, p. 465
*Shorter Edition: Ch. 60, p. 294
Date used:

Answer: F
Chronological Edition: Ch. 75, p. 466f
Standard Edition: Ch. 75, p. 466f
*Shorter Edition: Ch. 60, p. 294f
Date used:

Answer: T
Chronological Edition: Ch. 75, p. 467f
Standard Edition: Ch. 75, p. 467f
*Shorter Edition: Ch. 60, p. 294f
Date used:

Answer: T
Chronological Edition: Ch. 75, p. 469
Standard Edition: Ch. 75, p. 469
*Shorter Edition: Ch. 60, p. 295
Date used:

295. Bartók's *Music for Strings, Percussion, and Celesta* calls for a specific arrangement of the players on the stage.

296. The themes of the fourth movement of Bartók's *Music for Strings, Percussion, and Celesta* resemble folk songs in their rhythms and modal structure.

297. The *Bay Psalm Book* was the first music book printed in the colonies of North America.

298. America's first permanent symphony orchestra was the Boston Symphony.

299. European music and musicians dominated American concert life in the nineteenth century.

300. The music of Charles Ives was very popular and performed frequently during his lifetime.

301. Charles Ives's music reflects his roots in New England through the use of popular songs and American historical themes.

302. Ives's Symphony No. 2 was first performed in public many years after it was written.

Answer: T
Chronological Edition: Ch. 75, p. 471
Standard Edition: Ch. 75, p. 471
*Shorter Edition: Ch. 60, p. 296
Date used:

303. During his career, Copland employed both jazz and Neoclassic elements.

Answer: T
Chronological Edition: Ch. 75, p. 472
Standard Edition: Ch. 75, p. 472
*Shorter Edition: Ch. 60, p. 297
Date used:

304. Copland's ballet *Rodeo* incorporates American square dance tunes.

Answer: T
Chronological Edition: Ch. 76, p. 474
Standard Edition: Ch. 76, p. 474
*Shorter Edition: Ch. 61, p. 299
Date used:

305. John Philip Sousa was a great American composer of marches.

Answer: T
Chronological Edition: Ch. 76, p. 475
Standard Edition: Ch. 76, p. 475
*Shorter Edition: Ch. 61, p. 299
Date used:

306. Ragtime was named for its ragged, highly syncopated rhythms and melodies.

Answer: F
Chronological Edition: Ch. 76, p. 475
Standard Edition: Ch. 76, p. 475
Date used:

307. Joplin wrote only for the piano.

Answer: F
Chronological Edition: Ch. 76, p. 475
Standard Edition: Ch. 76, p. 475
Date used:

308. During his lifetime, Scott Joplin won the Pulitzer Prize for his opera, *Treemonisha*.

Answer: T
Chronological Edition: Ch. 76, p. 476
Standard Edition: Ch. 76, p. 476
Date used:

309. Joplin's opera *Treemonisha* incorporates elements of ragtime and other dance styles.

Answer: T
Chronological Edition: Ch. 76, p. 477
Standard Edition: Ch. 76, p. 477
*Shorter Edition: Ch. 61, p. 299
Date used:

310. Jazz is an art form created mainly by black Americans in the early twentieth century as they blended elements from African music with traditions of the west.

Answer: T
Chronological Edition: Ch. 76, p. 477
Standard Edition: Ch. 76, p. 477
*Shorter Edition: Ch. 61, p. 300
Date used:

311. New Orleans jazz depended upon simultaneous improvisations by the players, which created a polyphonic texture.

Answer: T
Chronological Edition: Ch. 76, p. 478
Standard Edition: Ch. 76, p. 478
*Shorter Edition: Ch. 61, p. 301
Date used:

312. Louis Armstrong was an important force in the development of early jazz styles.

Answer: T
Chronological Edition: Ch. 76, p. 478
Standard Edition: Ch. 76, p. 478
*Shorter Edition: Ch. 61, p. 301
Date used:

313. Ella Fitzgerald was known for her virtuosic level of scat singing.

Answer: F
Chronological Edition: Ch. 76, p. 479f
Standard Edition: Ch. 76, p. 479f
*Shorter Edition: Ch. 61, p. 302
Date used:

314. The big band depended much more on improvisation than New Orleans jazz.

Answer: T
Chronological Edition: Ch. 76, p. 479f
Standard Edition: Ch. 76, p. 479f
*Shorter Edition: Ch. 61, p. 302
Date used:

315. Each occurrence of a twelve-bar blues progression in a piece is called a chorus.

Answer: T
Chronological Edition: Ch. 76, p. 481
Standard Edition: Ch. 76, p. 481
*Shorter Edition: Ch. 61, p. 302
Date used:

316. Bebop and cool jazz styles represented a rebellion against the limitations of big-band jazz.

Answer: F
Chronological Edition: Ch. 76, p. 481
Standard Edition: Ch. 76, p. 481
*Shorter Edition: Ch. 61, p. 302
Date used:

317. Gunther Schuller coined the term "third stream" to describe a combination of blues and jazz styles.

Answer: F
Chronological Edition: Ch. 76, p. 482
Standard Edition: Ch. 76, p. 482
Date used:

318. The vibraphone is a member of the brass family.

Answer: T
Chronological Edition: Ch. 76, p. 482
Standard Edition: Ch. 76, p. 482
*Shorter Edition: Ch. 61, p. 302
Date used:

319. Many prominent European composers have been influenced by American jazz.

Answer: T
Chronological Edition: Ch. 76, p. 482
Standard Edition: Ch. 76, p. 482
*Shorter Edition: Ch. 61, p. 304
Date used:

320. The American musical theater developed out of the European comic opera or operetta tradition.

Answer: T
Chronological Edition: Ch. 76, p. 483
Standard Edition: Ch. 76, p. 483
Date used:

321. The use of pre-existing literary sources such as books and plays for the plots of musical helped the new genre to gain maturity and permanence.

Answer: F
Chronological Edition: Ch. 76, p. 483
Standard Edition: Ch. 76, p. 483
*Shorter Edition: Ch. 61, p. 305
Date used:

322. The musical has remained exclusively an American art form, not attempted by composers of other countries.

Answer: T
Chronological Edition: Ch. 76, p. 484
Standard Edition: Ch. 76, p. 484
*Shorter Edition: Ch. 61, p. 305
Date used:

323. Leonard Bernstein was the first American-born musician to be appointed conductor of the New York Philharmonic.

Answer: T
Chronological Edition: Ch. 76, p. 484
Standard Edition: Ch. 76, p. 484
*Shorter Edition: Ch. 61, p. 305f
Date used:

324. Leonard Bernstein has written both popular and art music.

Answer: F
Chronological Edition: Ch. 76, p. 485
Standard Edition: Ch. 76, p. 485
*Shorter Edition: Ch. 61, p. 306
Date used:

325. Bernstein's *West Side Story* deals with rival youth gangs in Los Angeles.

Answer: T
Chronological Edition: Ch. 77, p. 487
Standard Edition: Ch. 77, p. 487
*Shorter Edition: Ch. 62, p. 309
Date used:

326. The artistic trend that rejected art as something beautiful and to be admired, reducing it to the absurd was Dadaism.

Answer: F
Chronological Edition: Ch. 77, p. 492
Standard Edition: Ch. 77, p. 492
*Shorter Edition: Ch. 62, p. 311
Date used:

Answer: F
Chronological Edition: Ch. 77, p. 494
Standard Edition: Ch. 77, p. 494
*Shorter Edition: Ch. 62, p. 312
Date used:

Answer: T
Chronological Edition: Ch. 77, p. 494
Standard Edition: Ch. 77, p. 494
*Shorter Edition: Ch. 62, p. 312f
Date used:

Answer: T
Chronological Edition: Ch. 77, p. 494
Standard Edition: Ch. 77, p. 494
*Shorter Edition: Ch. 62, p. 313f
Date used:

Answer: T
Chronological Edition: Ch. 77, p. 495
Standard Edition: Ch. 77, p. 495
*Shorter Edition: Ch. 62, p. 314f
Date used:

Answer: T
Chronological Edition: Ch. 77, p. 495
Standard Edition: Ch. 77, p. 495
*Shorter Edition: Ch. 62, p. 313
Date used:

Answer: T
Chronological Edition: Ch. 77, p. 496
Standard Edition: Ch. 77, p. 496
*Shorter Edition: Ch. 62, p. 313
Date used:

Answer: T
Chronological Edition: Ch. 77, p. 497
Standard Edition: Ch. 77, p. 497
*Shorter Edition: Ch. 62, p. 316f
Date used:

327. The Theater of the Absurd was a famous playhouse in the Soho district of New York City.

328. Total serialism in music allowed the composer complete freedom from forms and procedures.

329. Total serialism is an extremely complex ultrarational music that organized every aspect of the music.

330. Aleatoric music leaves some details to chance or performer choice.

331. Since World War II, the United States has been the birthplace of many significant new developments in art music.

332. One type of aleatoric music is open form.

333. The concept of a predetermined form is alien to the spirit of new music.

334. Women have played a considerably more prominent role in the contemporary music scene than they did in earlier times.

Answer: T
Chronological Edition: Ch. 78, p. 499
Standard Edition: Ch. 78, p. 499
*Shorter Edition: Ch. 63, p. 316
Date used:

335. Unlike Europe, the continents of Asia and Africa do not constitute single cultural units.

Answer: T
Chronological Edition: Ch. 78, p. 500
Standard Edition: Ch. 78, p. 500
*Shorter Edition: Ch. 63, p. 318
Date used:

336. Music serves some roles which are common to all societies.

Answer: T
Chronological Edition: Ch. 78, p. 500
Standard Edition: Ch. 78, p. 500
*Shorter Edition: Ch. 63, p. 318
Date used:

337. The musics of Eastern and Western cultures are steadily drawing closer together.

Answer: T
Chronological Edition: Ch. 78, p. 501
Standard Edition: Ch. 78, p. 501
*Shorter Edition: Ch. 63, p. 319
Date used:

338. Music transmitted by example or imitation and performed from memory is said to exist in oral tradition.

Answer: T
Chronological Edition: Ch. 78, p. 501f
Standard Edition: Ch. 78, p. 501f
*Shorter Edition: Ch. 63, p. 319
Date used:

339. Some music of non-Western cultures uses microtonal intervals or inflections.

Answer: T
Chronological Edition: Ch. 78, p. 502
Standard Edition: Ch. 78, p. 502
*Shorter Edition: Ch. 63, p. 320
Date used:

340. Music from southern India depends on a fixed time cycle known as a tala.

Answer: T
Chronological Edition: Ch. 78, p. 503
Standard Edition: Ch. 78, p. 503
*Shorter Edition: Ch. 63, p. 320
Date used:

341. Simple harmonies and polyphonic textures are typical of some non-Western cultures.

Answer: T
Chronological Edition: Ch. 78, p. 503
Standard Edition: Ch. 78, p. 503
*Shorter Edition: Ch. 63, p. 321
Date used:

342. Specialists devised an alternate method of instrument classification based on how they generate sound. This was developed because some instruments do not neatly fit into the Western instrument families of strings, brass, woodwinds, and percussion.

Answer: F
Chronological Edition: Ch. 78, p. 503
Standard Edition: Ch. 78, p. 503
*Shorter Edition: Ch. 63, p. 320
Date used:

343. Western instruments cannot be classified according to the scientific categories of aerophones, chordophones, idiophones, and membranophones.

Answer: F
Chronological Edition: Ch. 78, p. 505
Standard Edition: Ch. 78, p. 505
*Shorter Edition: Ch. 63, p. 322f
Date used:

344. John Cage's "prepared piano" was one that was carefully tuned prior to each performance.

Answer: T
Chronological Edition: Ch. 78, p. 506
Standard Edition: Ch. 78, p. 506
*Shorter Edition: Ch. 63, p. 323
Date used:

345. Cage's *Sonatas and Interludes* are for prepared piano.

Answer: T
Chronological Edition: Ch. 78, p. 507
Standard Edition: Ch. 78, p. 507
*Shorter Edition: Ch. 63, p. 323
Date used:

346. Non-Western sounds also influenced American jazz and rock music.

Answer: T
Chronological Edition: Ch. 79, p. 507
Standard Edition: Ch. 79, p. 507
*Shorter Edition: Ch. 64, p. 323
Date used:

347. Contemporary music has grown increasingly more technically demanding, requiring a high degree of virtuosity on the part of performers.

Answer: T
Chronological Edition: Ch. 79, p. 508
Standard Edition: Ch. 79, p. 508
Date used:

348. Carter's Eight Etudes and a Fantasy grew out of his activity as a teacher.

Answer: F
Chronological Edition: Ch. 79, p. 509
Standard Edition: Ch. 79, p. 509
Date used:

349. A *perpetuum mobile*, such as the eighth etude from Carter's Eight Etudes and a Fantasy, is based on rapidly shifting tempos.

Answer: T
Chronological Edition: Ch. 79, p. 509
Standard Edition: Ch. 79, p. 509
Date used:

350. Ligeti's compositional style of interweaving many lines of music into a complex polyphonic fabric is called micropolyphony.

Answer: T
Chronological Edition: Ch. 79, p. 510
Standard Edition: Ch. 79, p. 510
Date used:

Answer: T
Chronological Edition: Ch. 79, p. 512
Standard Edition: Ch. 79, p. 512
*Shorter Edition: Ch. 64, p. 325
Date used:

Answer: T
Chronological Edition: Ch. 79, p. 513
Standard Edition: Ch. 79, p. 513
*Shorter Edition: Ch. 64, p. 325
Date used:

Answer: T
Chronological Edition: Ch. 80, p. 514
Standard Edition: Ch. 80, p. 514
*Shorter Edition: Ch. 64, p. 326
Date used:

Answer: T
Chronological Edition: Ch. 80, p. 514f
Standard Edition: Ch. 80, p. 514f
*Shorter Edition: Ch. 64, p. 326
Date used:

Answer: T
Chronological Edition: Ch. 80, p. 516
Standard Edition: Ch. 80, p. 516
*Shorter Edition: Ch. 64, p. 326
Date used:

Answer: F
Chronological Edition: Ch. 80, p. 516
Standard Edition: Ch. 80, p. 516
*Shorter Edition: Ch. 64, p. 326
Date used:

Answer: T
Chronological Edition: Ch. 80, p. 518
Standard Edition: Ch. 80, p. 518
*Shorter Edition: Ch. 64, p. 327
Date used:

351. Lutosławski's *Venetian Games* contains aleatoric sections.

352. Vocalise is a wordless melody sung on phonetic sounds.

353. Crumb's song cycle, *Ancient Voices of Children*, explores the sounds of some non-Western percussion instruments.

354. One of the most important musical developments of the 1950's and 1960's was the emergence of electronic music.

355. Synthesizers are devices that combine sound generators and sound modifiers in one package with a unified control system.

356. Electronic music and synthesizers have greatly influenced the commercial world of music.

357. Computer sound-generation is the least flexible of all electronic media.

358. Varèse's *Poème électronique* is produced entirely by electronic means.

Answer: T
Chronological Edition: Ch. 80, p. 518
Standard Edition: Ch. 80, p. 518
Date used:

Answer: T
Chronological Edition: Ch. 80, p. 521
Standard Edition: Ch. 80, p. 521
Date used:

Answer: T
Chronological Edition: Ch. 80, p. 521
Standard Edition: Ch. 80, p. 521
Date used:

Answer: T
Chronological Edition: Ch. 81, p. 521
Standard Edition: Ch. 81, p. 521
*Shorter Edition: Ch. 65, p. 328
Date used:

Answer: F
Chronological Edition: Ch. 81, p. 521
Standard Edition: Ch. 81, p. 521
*Shorter Edition: Ch. 65, p. 328
Date used:

Answer: T
Chronological Edition: Ch. 81, p. 522
Standard Edition: Ch. 81, p. 522
*Shorter Edition: Ch. 65, p. 328
Date used:

Answer: T
Chronological Edition: Ch. 81, p. 522
Standard Edition: Ch. 81, p. 522
*Shorter Edition: Ch. 65, p. 329
Date used:

Answer: F
Chronological Edition: Ch. 81, p. 528
Standard Edition: Ch. 81, p. 528
*Shorter Edition: Ch. 65, p. 330
Date used:

359. Varèse's *Poème électronique* combined sounds of the human voice, electronically manipulated, with synthetic sounds and percussion.

360. Babbitt's *Phonemena* was written expressly for the virtuoso singer Bethany Beardslee.

361. The text of Babbitt's *Phonemena* is built entirely from phonemes, the smallest units of speech.

362. The New Romanticism evolved from the feeling that the abstract, atonal music of the twentieth century had created a gap between composers and their audience.

363. Recent music has continued its avoidance of emotional appeal.

364. Composers adhering to the New Romanticism have combined the general language of Romantic music with other new trends.

365. Musgrave's opera, *Mary, Queen of Scots*, could be viewed as a nationalistic work.

366. The salient feature of minimalism is contrast.

Answer: **T**
Chronological Edition: Ch. 81, p. 530
Standard Edition: Ch. 81, p. 530
*Shorter Edition: Ch. 65, p. 331f
Date used:

367.   Adam's work, *Short Ride in a Fast Machine*, features an insistent ostinato.

ESSAY QUESTIONS

THE MATERIALS OF MUSIC

Chronological Edition: Ch. 1, p. 7f
Standard Edition: Ch. 1, p. 7f
*Shorter Edition: Ch. 1, p. 7ff
Date used:

1. Discuss the basic criteria for describing a melody.

Chronological Edition: Ch. 2, p. 10f
Standard Edition: Ch. 2, p. 10f
*Shorter Edition: Ch. 2, p. 10ff
Date used:

2. Define rhythm, beat, and meter, and describe the way they work together in music.

Chronological Edition: Ch. 3, p. 14f
Standard Edition: Ch. 3, p. 14f
*Shorter Edition: Ch. 3, p. 13ff
Date used:

3. Describe the relationship between melody and harmony in music.

Chronological Edition: Ch. 5, p. 23f
Standard Edition: Ch. 5, p. 23f
*Shorter Edition: Ch. 5, p. 21ff
Date used:

4. Describe the basic elements of musical form.

Chronological Edition: Ch. 6, p. 26f
Standard Edition: Ch. 6, p. 26f
*Shorter Edition: Ch. 6, p. 24ff
Date used:

5. Describe how tempo and dynamics affect our response to music. Cite examples to support your response.

Chronological Edition: Ch. 7, p. 30f
Standard Edition: Ch. 7, p. 30f
*Shorter Edition: Ch. 7, p. 29ff
Date used:

6. Choose four musical instruments, one representing each of the four families of instruments, and describe their physical appearance and how they produce sound.

Chronological Edition: Ch. 9, p. 43f
Standard Edition: Ch. 9, p. 43f
*Shorter Edition: Ch. 9, p. 40ff
Date used:

7. Describe the principal types of musical ensembles (vocal and instrumental) and how they differ from each other.

Chronological Edition: Ch. 9, p. 48f
Standard Edition: Ch. 9, p. 48f
Date used:

8. Describe the role of conductors, mentioning the elements of music for which they are responsible.

Chronological Edition: Tr. I, p. 52f
Standard Edition: Tr. I, p. 52f
*Shorter Edition: Tr. I, p. 46ff
Date used:

9. What defines the style of a work of art? How are different musical styles achieved and how do we categorize them?

MEDIEVAL AND RENAISSANCE MUSIC

Chronological Edition: Ch. 11, p. 60f
Standard Edition: Ch. 53, p. 270f
*Shorter Edition: Ch. 10, p. 51ff
Date used:

10. Describe the influence of the Roman Catholic Church on music in the Middle Ages.

Chronological Edition: Ch. 11, p. 60f
Standard Edition: Ch. 53, p. 270f
*Shorter Edition: Ch. 11, p. 53ff
Date used:

11. Describe the specific elements that make early music sound archaic to modern listeners.

Chronological Edition: Ch. 11, p. 63f
Standard Edition: Ch. 53, p. 273f
*Shorter Edition: Ch. 11, p. 56ff
Date used:

12. Describe the development of polyphony and the contributions of the Notre Dame School composers.

Chronological Edition: Ch. 12, p. 69f
Standard Edition: Ch. 54, p. 279f
*Shorter Edition: Ch. 11, p. 57ff
Date used:

13. What roles did secular music play in Medieval life?

Chronological Edition: Ch. 12, p. 69f
Standard Edition: Ch. 54, p. 279f
*Shorter Edition: Ch. 11, p. 57ff
Date used:

14. What role did chivalry play in Medieval court life and how was this reflected in secular music?

Chronological Edition: Ch. 13, p. 82f
Standard Edition: Ch. 55, p. 293f
*Shorter Edition: Ch. 12, p. 64ff
Date used:

15. Describe the ways in which Renaissance thought differed from that of the Middle Ages.

Chronological Edition: Ch. 13, p. 85f
Standard Edition: Ch. 55, p. 295f
*Shorter Edition: Ch. 12, p. 67ff
Date used:

16. Describe the various ways that early musicians could make a living.

Chronological Edition: Ch. 14, p. 87f
Standard Edition: Ch. 56, p. 297f
*Shorter Edition: Ch. 12, p. 68ff
Date used:

17. Describe the major types of Renaissance sacred music. Give an example of each.

Chronological Edition: Ch. 15, p. 98f
Standard Edition: Ch. 57, p. 308f
*Shorter Edition: Ch. 12, p. 75ff
Date used:

18. Describe the major types of Renaissance secular music. Give an example of each.

Chronological Edition: Ch. 15, p. 98f
Standard Edition: Ch. 57, p. 308f
*Shorter Edition: Ch. 12, p. 76ff
Date used:

19. How did Renaissance composers achieve a union of words and music?

Chronological Edition: Ch. 16, p. 117f
Standard Edition: Ch. 36, p. 177f
*Shorter Edition: Ch. 14, p. 87ff
Date used:

20. We describe our perception of Western harmony in terms of tonality. What does this mean?

Chronological Edition: Ch. 16, p. 117f
Standard Edition: Ch. 36, p. 177f
*Shorter Edition: Ch. 14, p. 89ff
Date used:

21. What makes major and minor scales sound different? Describe the character of each.

THE BAROQUE ERA

Chronological Edition: Ch. 19, p. 132f
Standard Edition: Ch. 59, p. 332f
*Shorter Edition: Ch. 17, p. 98ff
Date used:

22. Discuss the main currents of early Baroque musical style.

Chronological Edition: Ch. 19, p. 138f
Standard Edition: Ch. 59, p. 338f
*Shorter Edition: Ch. 17, p. 102ff
Date used:

23. What is the "doctrine of the affections" and how did it influence Baroque music?

Chronological Edition: Ch. 20, p. 139f
Standard Edition: Ch. 60, p. 339f
*Shorter Edition: Ch. 18, p. 104ff
Date used:

24. Describe the various components of opera, commenting on the function of each to the drama.

Chronological Edition: Ch. 20, p. 139f
Standard Edition: Ch. 60, p. 339f
*Shorter Edition: Ch. 18, p. 105ff
Date used:

25. Discuss Monteverdi's contributions to the development of opera.

Chronological Edition: Ch. 21, p. 150f
Standard Edition: Ch. 61, p. 349f
*Shorter Edition: Ch. 19, p. 109ff
Date used:

26. Define the chorale and discuss Bach's use of it in the cantata.

Chronological Edition: Ch. 22, p. 162f
Standard Edition: Ch. 62, p. 361f
*Shorter Edition: Ch. 20, p. 116ff
Date used:

27. Compare the genres of opera and oratorio, using examples of each to support your response.

Chronological Edition: Ch. 22, p. 162f
Standard Edition: Ch. 62, p. 361f
*Shorter Edition: Ch. 20, p. 116ff
Date used:

28. Compare the lives and output of Bach and Handel. Who was the more international composer and why? For what audiences did each compose?

Chronological Edition: Ch. 23, p. 171f
Standard Edition: Ch. 63, p. 370f
*Shorter Edition: Ch. 21, p. 121ff
Date used:

29. Describe the new instrumental forms of the Baroque era.

Chronological Edition: Ch. 23, p. 171f
Standard Edition: Ch. 63, p. 370f
*Shorter Edition: Ch. 21, p. 121ff
Date used:

30. Describe the concerto in the Baroque era. Cite representative examples.

Chronological Edition: Ch. 25, p. 184f
Standard Edition: Ch. 65, p. 384f
*Shorter Edition: Ch. 22, p. 121ff
Date used:

31. Discuss the fugue, its structure, and its polyphonic devices.

Chronological Edition: Tr. III, p. 195f
Standard Edition: Tr. IV, p. 394f
*Shorter Edition: Tr. III, p. 135f
Date used:

32. Compare general style characteristics of the Baroque and Classical periods.

EIGHTEENTH-CENTURY CLASSICISM

Chronological Edition: Ch. 28, p. 209f
Standard Edition: Ch. 40, p. 195f
*Shorter Edition: Ch. 25, p. 149ff
Date used:

33. What are the primary characteristics of Classicism? How are they reflected in eighteenth-century music?

Chronological Edition: Ch. 28, p. 214f
Standard Edition: Ch. 40, p. 200f
*Shorter Edition: Ch. 25, p. 152ff
Date used:

34. Describe the patronage system, its advantages and disadvantages to the composer, and how it affected the careers of Haydn, Mozart, and Beethoven.

Chronological Edition: Ch. 29, p. 217f
Standard Edition: Ch. 41, p. 203f
*Shorter Edition: Ch. 27, p. 155ff
Date used:

35. Describe the principal forms of chamber music in the Classical era.

Chronological Edition: Ch. 31, p. 221
Standard Edition: Ch. 43, p. 207f
*Shorter Edition: Ch. 28, p. 157ff
Date used:

36. Describe the creative life and music of Mozart. Mention important works in your answer.

Chronological Edition: Ch. 34, p. 234f
Standard Edition: Ch. 46, p. 220f
*Shorter Edition: Ch. 30, p. 163ff
Date used:

37. Describe the creative life and music of Haydn. Mention important works in your answer.

Chronological Edition: Ch. 34, p. 234f
Standard Edition: Ch. 46, p. 220f
*Shorter Edition: Ch. 30, p. 163ff
Date used:

38. What were Haydn's contributions to the development of the symphony?

Chronological Edition: Ch. 35, p. 241f
Standard Edition: Ch. 47, p. 228f
*Shorter Edition: Ch. 31, p. 167ff
Date used:

39. Describe the creative life and music of Beethoven. Mention important works in your answer.

Chronological Edition: Ch. 35, p. 241f
Standard Edition: Ch. 47, p. 228f
*Shorter Edition: Ch. 31, p. 167ff
Date used:

40. What are the Romantic qualities found in the music of Beethoven? Why is he still considered to be a Classical composer?

Chronological Edition: Ch. 35, p. 243f
Standard Edition: Ch. 47, p. 230f
*Shorter Edition: Ch. 31, p. 167ff
Date used:

41. What innovations did Beethoven contribute to the symphony?

Chronological Edition: Ch. 36, p. 250f
Standard Edition: Ch. 48, p. 236f
*Shorter Edition: Ch. 32, p. 173ff
Date used:

42. Describe the typical form of a Classical concerto. Which solo instruments were favored and which composers contributed to the genre?

Chronological Edition: Ch. 39, p. 264f
Standard Edition: Ch. 51, p. 250f
*Shorter Edition: Ch. 34, p. 181ff
Date used:

43. Discuss opera buffa, using Mozart's *The Marriage of Figaro* as an example.

THE NINETEENTH CENTURY

Chronological Edition: Ch. 40, p. 281f
Standard Edition: Ch. 10, p. 57f
*Shorter Edition: Ch. 35, p. 195ff
Date used:

44. Compare the Classical and Romantic approaches to the arts.

Chronological Edition: Ch. 40, p. 281f
Standard Edition: Ch. 10, p. 57f
*Shorter Edition: Ch. 35, p. 195ff
Date used:

45. What were the principal ideals underlying Romanticism? How are they reflected in music, art, and literature?

Chronological Edition: Ch. 40, p. 281f
Standard Edition: Ch. 10, p. 57f
*Shorter Edition: Ch. 35, p. 195ff
Date used:

46. Describe the sociological, political, and economic conditions that had an impact on the beginnings of the Romantic movement in music.

Chronological Edition: Ch. 41, p. 288f
Standard Edition: Ch. 11, p. 65f
*Shorter Edition: Ch. 36, p. 200ff
Date used:

47. Discuss the rise of the virtuoso performer in the nineteenth century. How did this phenomenon affect music?

Chronological Edition: Ch. 41, p. 289f
Standard Edition: Ch. 11, p. 66f
*Shorter Edition: Ch. 36, p. 202ff
Date used:

48. Describe the roles that women played in music in the nineteenth century. Which were socially acceptable? Cite examples of successful women musicians from this era.

Chronological Edition: Ch. 42, p. 291f
Standard Edition: Ch. 12, p. 67f
*Shorter Edition: Ch. 37, p. 203ff
Date used:

49. Compare the texts, forms, and overall character of the Romantic Lied with popular songs of today.

Chronological Edition: Ch. 46, p. 305f
Standard Edition: Ch. 35, p. 81f
*Shorter Edition: Ch. 39, p. 209ff
Date used:

50. Describe the role of the piano in nineteenth-century life. What new types of works were developed to support this role?

Chronological Edition: Ch. 47, p. 307f
Standard Edition: Ch. 16, p. 83f
*Shorter Edition: Ch. 40, p. 210ff
Date used:

51. Describe why Chopin has been called the "poet of the piano".

Chronological Edition: Ch. 50, p. 320f
Standard Edition: Ch. 20, p. 96f
*Shorter Edition: Ch. 42, p. 217ff
Date used:

52. Describe the difference between program and absolute music, citing examples of each.

Chronological Edition: Ch. 52, p. 327f
Standard Edition: Ch. 22, p. 103f
*Shorter Edition: Ch. 43, p. 220ff
Date used:

53. What is "Romantic" about the program and music of Berlioz's *Symphonie fantastique*?

Chronological Edition: Ch. 54, p. 335f
Standard Edition: Ch. 24, p. 111f
*Shorter Edition: Ch. 44, p. 223ff
Date used:

54. How was nationalism reflected in nineteenth-century music? Cite several examples in your response.

Chronological Edition: Ch. 55, p. 341f
Standard Edition: Ch. 25, p. 117f
*Shorter Edition: Ch. 45, p. 228ff
Date used:

55. Discuss the Romantic symphony, citing several examples in your response.

Chronological Edition: Ch. 59, p. 353f
Standard Edition: Ch. 29, p. 130f
*Shorter Edition: Ch. 48, p. 236ff
Date used:

56. Describe the rise of choral music in the nineteenth century, citing the various genres with examples of each.

Chronological Edition: Ch. 61, p. 359f
Standard Edition: Ch. 31, p. 136f
*Shorter Edition: Ch. 50, p. 241ff
Date used:

57. What are the principal characteristics of nineteenth-century Italian opera? Name the major composers and several representative works.

Chronological Edition: Ch. 63, p. 370f
Standard Edition: Ch. 33, p. 148f
*Shorter Edition: Ch. 52, p. 250ff
Date used:

58. Describe Wagner's innovations in opera and his desire to unite music and drama.

THE TWENTIETH CENTURY

Chronological Edition: Tr. V, p. 399f
Standard Edition: Tr. V, p. 397f
*Shorter Edition: Tr. V, p. 261ff
Date used:

59. Discuss Mahler as a post-Romantic composer. Give consideration to his use of song in the symphony.

Chronological Edition: Ch. 66, p. 403f
Standard Edition: Ch. 66, p. 401f
*Shorter Edition: Ch. 54, p. 266ff
Date used:

60. Describe the musical characteristics of Impressionism. Which of these are heard in Debussy's *Prelude to "The Afternoon of a Faun"*?

Chronological Edition: Ch. 68, p. 417f
Standard Edition: Ch. 68, p. 416f
*Shorter Edition: Ch. 54, p. 266ff
Date used:

61. What effects did non-Western music have on Impressionist and early twentieth-century composers? Cite examples.

Chronological Edition: Ch. 69, p. 422f
Standard Edition: Ch. 69, p. 421f
*Shorter Edition: Ch. 56, p. 275ff
Date used:

62. What is serialism in music, who was responsible for it, and what developments led to this procedure?

Chronological Edition: Ch. 70, p. 426f
Standard Edition: Ch. 70, p. 425f
*Shorter Edition: Ch. 57, p. 279ff
Date used:

63. Discuss the creative life and music of Stravinsky, citing specific examples.

Chronological Edition: Ch. 72, p. 437f
Standard Edition: Ch. 72, p. 437f
Date used:

64. Discuss Berg's opera *Wozzeck* as an example of Expressionism in music.

Chronological Edition: Ch. 74, p. 466f
Standard Edition: Ch. 74, p. 466f
*Shorter Edition: Ch. 59, p. 288ff
Date used:

65. Describe twentieth-century musical nationalism, citing European and American examples.

Chronological Edition: Ch. 75, p. 466f
Standard Edition: Ch. 75, p. 466f
Date used:

66. Charles Ives has been described as one of the most original spirits of his time. Discuss his life and music within this context.

Chronological Edition: Ch. 76, p. 477f
Standard Edition: Ch. 76, p. 477f
*Shorter Edition: Ch. 61, p. 299ff
Date used:

67. Describe the structure of the blues, its texts and its music.

Chronological Edition: Ch. 76, p. 477f
Standard Edition: Ch. 76, p. 477f
*Shorter Edition: Ch. 61, p. 301ff
Date used:

68. Discuss the contributions of Louis Armstrong and Duke Ellington to jazz.

Chronological Edition: Ch. 76, p. 481f
Standard Edition: Ch. 76, p. 481f
*Shorter Edition: Ch. 61, p. 302ff
Date used:

69. Discuss the influence of jazz on art music. Include third stream jazz in your response.

Chronological Edition: Ch. 77, p. 488f
Standard Edition: Ch. 77, p. 488f
*Shorter Edition: Ch. 62, p. 309ff
Date used:

70. Discuss some of the twentieth-century trends in the arts that have influenced music.

Chronological Edition: Ch. 78, p. 499f
Standard Edition: Ch. 78, p. 499f
*Shorter Edition: Ch. 63, p. 316ff
Date used:

71. In what ways have non-Western music and philosophy influenced Western art music? Mention specific examples.

Chronological Edition: Ch. 80, p. 514f
Standard Edition: Ch. 80, p. 514f
*Shorter Edition: Ch. 64, p. 326ff
Date used:

72. Discuss the development of electronic music.

Chronological Edition: Ch. 81, p. 521f
Standard Edition: Ch. 81, p. 521f
*Shorter Edition: Ch. 65, p. 328ff
Date used:

73. Discuss the contemporary trends of minimalism and the New Romanticism in music, citing examples.

LISTENING QUESTIONS

MULTIPLE CHOICE QUESTIONS

Answer:
Chronological Edition: Ch. 1, p. 7f
Standard Edition: Ch. 1, p. 7f
*Shorter Edition: Ch. 1, p. 7f
Date used:

1. Which best describes the melodic line of this excerpt?
   a. disjunct
   b. conjunct
   c. dissonant
   d. consonant

Answer:
Chronological Edition: Ch. 1, p. 7f
Standard Edition: Ch. 1, p. 7f
*Shorter Edition: Ch. 1, p. 7f
Date used:

2. Which best describes the melodic range of this excerpt?
   a. narrow
   b. medium
   c. wide
   d. symmetrical

Answer:
Chronological Edition: Ch. 1, p. 7f
Standard Edition: Ch. 1, p. 7f
*Shorter Edition: Ch. 1, p. 7f
Date used:

3. The melodic line of this excerpt is best described as disjunct.

Answer:
Chronological Edition: Ch. 1, p. 7f
Standard Edition: Ch. 1, p. 7f
*Shorter Edition: Ch. 1, p. 7f
Date used:

4. The melodic phrase structure of this excerpt is best described as symmetrical.

Answer:
Chronological Edition: Ch. 2, p. 10f
Standard Edition: Ch. 2, p. 10f
*Shorter Edition: Ch. 2, p. 10f
Date used:

5. Which best describes the meter of this excerpt?
   a. duple
   b. triple
   c. changing
   d. nonmetric

Answer:
Chronological Edition: Ch. 2, p. 10f
Standard Edition: Ch. 2, p. 10f
*Shorter Edition: Ch. 2, p. 10f
Date used:

6. This excerpt illustrates triple meter.

Answer:
Chronological Edition: Ch. 2, p. 10f
Standard Edition: Ch. 2, p. 10f
*Shorter Edition: Ch. 2, p. 10f
Date used:

7. The rhythm of this excerpt is syncopated.

Answer:
Chronological Edition: Ch. 3, p. 14f
Standard Edition: Ch. 3, p. 14f
*Shorter Edition: Ch. 3, p. 14f
Date used:

Answer:
Chronological Edition: Ch. 3, p. 14f
Standard Edition: Ch. 3, p. 14f
*Shorter Edition: Ch. 3, p. 14f
Date used:

Answer:
Chronological Edition: Ch. 4, p. 18f
Standard Edition: Ch. 4, p. 18f
*Shorter Edition: Ch. 4, p. 17f
Date used:

Answer:
Chronological Edition: Ch. 4, p. 18f
Standard Edition: Ch. 4, p. 18f
*Shorter Edition: Ch. 4, p. 17f
Date used:

Answer:
Chronological Edition: Ch. 5, p. 22f
Standard Edition: Ch. 5, p. 22f
*Shorter Edition: Ch. 5, p. 21f
Date used:

Answer:
Chronological Edition: Ch. 5, p. 22f
Standard Edition: Ch. 5, p. 22f
*Shorter Edition: Ch. 5, p. 21f
Date used:

Answer:
Chronological Edition: Ch. 5, p. 22f
Standard Edition: Ch. 5, p. 22f
*Shorter Edition: Ch. 5, p. 21f
Date used:

Answer:
Chronological Edition: Ch. 5, p. 22f
Standard Edition: Ch. 5, p. 22f
*Shorter Edition: Ch. 5, p. 21f
Date used:

8. Which best describes the harmonic character of this excerpt?
    a. conjunct
    b. disjunct
    c. consonant
    d. dissonant

9. The harmony of this excerpt is best described as consonant.

10. Which best describes the texture of this excerpt?
    a. monophonic
    b. homophonic
    c. polyphonic
    d. heterophonic

11. The texture of this excerpt is best described as polyphonic.

12. Which best describes the form of this excerpt?
    a. A–B
    b. A–B–A
    c. A–B–A–C–A
    d. A–A–A–A–A

13. Which best describes the form of this excerpt?
    a.
    b.
    c.
    d.

14. Which best describes the form of this excerpt?
    a.
    b.
    c.
    d.

15. Which best describes the form of this excerpt?
    a.
    b.
    c.
    d.

Answer:
Chronological Edition: Ch. 5, p. 22f
Standard Edition: Ch. 5, p. 22f
*Shorter Edition: Ch. 5, p. 21f
Date used:

Answer:
Chronological Edition: Ch. 5, p. 22f
Standard Edition: Ch. 5, p. 22f
*Shorter Edition: Ch. 5, p. 21f
Date used:

Answer:
Chronological Edition: Ch. 5, p. 22f
Standard Edition: Ch. 5, p. 22f
*Shorter Edition: Ch. 5, p. 21f
Date used:

Answer:
Chronological Edition: Ch. 5, p. 22f
Standard Edition: Ch. 5, p. 22f
*Shorter Edition: Ch. 5, p. 21f
Date used:

Answer:
Chronological Edition: Ch. 6, p. 26f
Standard Edition: Ch. 6, p. 26f
*Shorter Edition: Ch. 6, p. 24f
Date used:

Answer:
Chronological Edition: Ch. 6, p. 26f
Standard Edition: Ch. 6, p. 26f
*Shorter Edition: Ch. 6, p. 24f
Date used:

Answer:
Chronological Edition: Ch. 6, p. 26f
Standard Edition: Ch. 6, p. 26f
*Shorter Edition: Ch. 6, p. 24f
Date used:

Answer:
Chronological Edition: Ch. 6, p. 26f
Standard Edition: Ch. 6, p. 26f
*Shorter Edition: Ch. 6, p. 24f
Date used:

16. Which best describes the form of this excerpt?
    a.
    b.
    c.
    d.

17. Which best describes the form of this excerpt?
    a.
    b.
    c.
    d.

18. The form of this excerpt is best described as binary.

19. This excerpt demonstrates the formal principle of repetition.

20. Which is the most likely tempo marking for this excerpt?
    a.
    b.
    c.
    d.

21. Which is the most likely tempo marking for this excerpt?
    a.
    b.
    c.
    d.

22. Which is the most likely tempo marking for this excerpt?
    a.
    b.
    c.
    d.

23. The tempo marking for this excerpt is likely to be Allegro.

Answer:
Chronological Edition: Ch. 6, p. 26f
Standard Edition: Ch. 6, p. 26f
*Shorter Edition: Ch. 6, p. 25f
Date used:

Answer:
Chronological Edition: Ch. 6, p. 26f
Standard Edition: Ch. 6, p. 26f
*Shorter Edition: Ch. 6, p. 25f
Date used:

Answer:
Chronological Edition: Ch. 6, p. 26f
Standard Edition: Ch. 6, p. 26f
*Shorter Edition: Ch. 6, p. 25f
Date used:

Answer:
Chronological Edition: Ch. 7, p. 30f
Standard Edition: Ch. 7, p. 30f
*Shorter Edition: Ch. 7, p. 29f
Date used:

Answer:
Chronological Edition: Ch. 7, p. 30f
Standard Edition: Ch. 7, p. 30f
*Shorter Edition: Ch. 7, p. 29f
Date used:

Answer:
Chronological Edition: Ch. 7, p. 30f
Standard Edition: Ch. 7, p. 30f
*Shorter Edition: Ch. 7, p. 29f
Date used:

Answer:
Chronological Edition: Ch. 7, p. 30f
Standard Edition: Ch. 7, p. 30f
*Shorter Edition: Ch. 7, p. 29f
Date used:

24. Which is the most likely dynamic marking for this excerpt?
a.
b.
c.
d.

25. Which is the most likely dynamic marking for this excerpt?
a.
b.
c.
d.

26. The dynamic marking for this excerpt is likely to be piano.

27. Which best describes the voice range heard in this excerpt?
a. soprano
b. alto
c. tenor
d. bass

28. Which family of instruments is heard in this excerpt?
a. strings
b. woodwinds
c. brass
d. percussion

29. The solo instrument heard in this excerpt represents the _____ family.
a. string
b. woodwind
c. brass
d. percussion

30. Identify the solo instrument heard in this excerpt.
a.
b.
c.
d.

Answer:
Chronological Edition: Ch. 7, p. 30f
Standard Edition: Ch. 7, p. 30f
*Shorter Edition: Ch. 7, p. 29f
Date used:

Answer:
Chronological Edition: Ch. 7, p. 30f
Standard Edition: Ch. 7, p. 30f
*Shorter Edition: Ch. 7, p. 29f
Date used:

Answer:
Chronological Edition: Ch. 7, p. 30f
Standard Edition: Ch. 7, p. 30f
*Shorter Edition: Ch. 7, p. 29f
Date used:

Answer:
Chronological Edition: Ch. 7, p. 30f
Standard Edition: Ch. 7, p. 30f
*Shorter Edition: Ch. 7, p. 29f
Date used:

Answer:
Chronological Edition: Ch. 7, p. 30f
Standard Edition: Ch. 7, p. 30f
*Shorter Edition: Ch. 7, p. 29f
Date used:

Answer:
Chronological Edition: Ch. 7, p. 30f
Standard Edition: Ch. 7, p. 30f
*Shorter Edition: Ch. 7, p. 29f
Date used:

Answer:
Chronological Edition: Ch. 7, p. 30f
Standard Edition: Ch. 7, p. 30f
*Shorter Edition: Ch. 7, p. 29f
Date used:

Answer:
Chronological Edition: Ch. 7, p. 30f
Standard Edition: Ch. 7, p. 30f
*Shorter Edition: Ch. 7, p. 29f
Date used:

31. Identify the solo instrument heard in this excerpt.
   a.
   b.
   c.
   d.

32. Identify the solo instrument heard in this excerpt.
   a.
   b.
   c.
   d.

33. Identify the solo instrument heard in this excerpt.
   a.
   b.
   c.
   d.

34. Identify the solo instrument heard in this excerpt.
   a.
   b.
   c.
   d.

35. Identify the solo instrument heard in this excerpt.
   a.
   b.
   c.
   d.

36. Identify the solo instrument heard in this excerpt.
   a.
   b.
   c.
   d.

37. Identify the solo instrument heard in this excerpt.
   a.
   b.
   c.
   d.

38. Identify the solo instrument heard in this excerpt.
   a.
   b.
   c.
   d.

Answer:
Chronological Edition: Ch. 7, p. 30f
Standard Edition: Ch. 7, p. 30f
*Shorter Edition: Ch. 7, p. 29f
Date used:

Answer:
Chronological Edition: Tr. I, p. 53
Standard Edition: Tr. I, p. 53
*Shorter Edition: Tr. I, p. 47
Date used:

Answer:
Chronological Edition: Tr. I, p. 53
Standard Edition: Tr. I, p. 53
*Shorter Edition: Tr. I, p. 47
Date used:

Answer:
Chronological Edition: Tr. I, p. 53
Standard Edition: Tr. I, p. 53
*Shorter Edition: Tr. I, p. 47
Date used:

Answer:
Chronological Edition: Tr. I, p. 53
Standard Edition: Tr. I, p. 53
*Shorter Edition: Tr. I, p. 47
Date used:

Answer:
Chronological Edition: Tr. I, p. 53
Standard Edition: Tr. I, p. 53
*Shorter Edition: Tr. I, p. 47
Date used:

Answer:
Chronological Edition: Tr. I, p. 53
Standard Edition: Tr. I, p. 53
*Shorter Edition: Tr. I, p. 47
Date used:

Answer:
Chronological Edition: Tr. I, p. 53
Standard Edition: Tr. I, p. 53
*Shorter Edition: Tr. I, p. 47
Date used:

39. Identify the solo instrument heard in this excerpt.
   a.
   b.
   c.
   d.

40. In which style period was this work most likely written?
   a.
   b.
   c.
   d.

41. In which style period was this work most likely written?
   a.
   b.
   c.
   d.

42. In which style period was this work most likely written?
   a.
   b.
   c.
   d.

43. In which style period was this work most likely written?
   a.
   b.
   c.
   d.

44. In which style period was this work most likely written?
   a.
   b.
   c.
   d.

45. Identify the following excerpt.
   a.
   b.
   c.
   d.

46. Identify the following excerpt.
   a.
   b.
   c.
   d.

Answer:
Chronological Edition: Tr. I, p. 53
Standard Edition: Tr. I, p. 53
*Shorter Edition: Tr. I, p. 47
Date used:

Answer:
Chronological Edition: Tr. I, p. 53
Standard Edition: Tr. I, p. 53
*Shorter Edition: Tr. I, p. 47
Datc used:

Answer:
Chronological Edition: Tr. I, p. 53
Standard Edition: Tr. I, p. 53
*Shorter Edition: Tr. I, p. 47
Date used:

Answer:
Chronological Edition: Tr. I, p. 53
Standard Edition: Tr. I, p. 53
*Shorter Edition: Tr. I, p. 47
Date used:

Answer:
Chronological Edition: Tr. I, p. 53
Standard Edition: Tr. I, p. 53
*Shorter Edition: Tr. I, p. 47
Date used:

Answer:
Chronological Edition: Tr. I, p. 53
Standard Edition: Tr. I, p. 53
*Shorter Edition: Tr. I, p. 47
Date used:

Answer:
Chronological Edition: Tr. I, p. 53
Standard Edition: Tr. I, p. 53
*Shorter Edition: Tr. I, p. 47
Date used:

Answer:
Chronological Edition: Tr. I, p. 53
Standard Edition: Tr. I, p. 53
*Shorter Edition: Tr. I, p. 47
Date used:

47. Identify the following excerpt.
    a.
    b.
    c.
    d.

48. Identify the following excerpt.
    a.
    b.
    c.
    d.

49. Identify the following excerpt.
    a.
    b.
    c.
    d.

50. Identify the following excerpt.
    a.
    b.
    c.
    d.

51. Identify the following excerpt.
    a.
    b.
    c.
    d.

52. Identify the following excerpt.
    a.
    b.
    c.
    d.

53. Identify the following excerpt.
    a.
    b.
    c.
    d.

54. Identify the following excerpt.

Answer:
Chronological Edition: Tr. I, p. 53
Standard Edition: Tr. I, p. 53
*Shorter Edition: Tr. I, p. 47
Date used:

55.   Identify the following excerpt.

Answer:
Chronological Edition: Tr. I, p. 53
Standard Edition: Tr. I, p. 53
*Shorter Edition: Tr. I, p. 47
Date used:

56.   Identify the following excerpt.

Answer:
Chronological Edition: Tr. I, p. 53
Standard Edition: Tr. I, p. 53
*Shorter Edition: Tr. I, p. 47
Date used:

57.   Identify the following excerpt.

Answer:
Chronological Edition: Tr. I, p. 53
Standard Edition: Tr. I, p. 53
*Shorter Edition: Tr. I, p. 47
Date used:

58.   Identify the following excerpt.